Charles Haliday, John P. Prendergast

**The Scandinavian Kingdom of Dublin**

Charles Haliday, John P. Prendergast

**The Scandinavian Kingdom of Dublin**

ISBN/EAN: 9783337171377

Printed in Europe, USA, Canada, Australia, Japan

Cover: Foto ©ninafisch / pixelio.de

More available books at **www.hansebooks.com**

# THE SCANDINAVIAN KINGDOM

## OF

# DUBLIN

BY

CHARLES HALIDAY

LATE OF THE CITY OF DUBLIN, MERCHANT

EDITED
WITH SOME NOTICE OF THE AUTHOR'S LIFE
BY
JOHN P. PRENDERGAST.
BARRISTER-AT-LAW.

Second Edition.

DUBLIN
M. H. GILL & SON, 50 UPPER SACKVILLE STREET
LONDON
SIMPKIN, MARSHALL, AND CO.

MDCCCLXXXIV.

# CONTENTS.

|  | Page |
|---|---|
| Some notice of the Life of Charles Haliday, | iii |

### Book I.
| | |
|---|---|
| The Scandinavians of Dublin, | 1 |

### Book II.
| | |
|---|---|
| The Scandinavians of Dublin, and their relations with neighbouring Kingdoms, | 82 |

### Book III.
| | |
|---|---|
| The Scandinavian Antiquities of Dublin, | 143 |

### Appendix.
| | |
|---|---|
| I. On the Ancient Name of Dublin, | 202 |
| II. Observations explanatory of Sir Bernard de Gomme's Map of the City and Harbour of Dublin, made A.D. 1673, | 228 |
| TABLE OF CHAPTERS, | 253 |
| INDEX, | 259 |

LIST OF PLATES WITH INSTRUCTIONS TO BINDER.

1. Rocque's Map, A.D. 1756, showing the Piles, to face p. cxiii.
2. Map of the Down Survey, A.D. 1654, with the Long Stone of the Steyne, to face p. 151.
3. Woodcut of the Thingmount of Dublin, to face p. 163.
4. Sir Bernard de Gomme's Map of City and Harbour, A.D. 1673, to face p. 229.
5. Captain Greenvill Collins's Map of 1685, to face p. 235.
6. Ground Plan of Chichester House, 1723, to face p. 239.
7. Captain Perry's Map of the Harbour, &c., &c., A.D. 1728, to face p. 249.

ERRATA.

Page 149, line 2.—Omit 'part of the Steyne,'
Page 229, in footnote.—For '23rd December, 1655,' read 23rd December, 1665.

# SOME NOTICE

### OF THE

# LIFE OF CHARLES HALIDAY.

MERCHANTS are not much given to the making of books. <small>Few merchants authors.</small>
They seldom leave behind them any of their own compos-
ing, save their cash books and their ledgers. There can
scarcely be named a merchant in the ranks of literary
writers, except Rogers, author of the "Pleasures of Memory"
and other poems, rather satirically described by Byron as
"the bard, the beau, the banker."

But a banker is not a merchant, and often gives no more
to the bank than his money and his name, and employs
his time and his leisure as he likes.

Whence comes this disinclination to literary labour? It
is not so much perhaps that the merchant's mind is too
absorbed in business to leave him leisure as that it would
detract from his character to be suspected of literary pursuits.

Poetry was at one time held to be as derogatory to a lawyer.
Sir Richard Cox had a strong bent to poetry (says Walter
Harris). He wrote some lines on the death, in 1696, of
Lord Chancellor Porter, Sir Richard being at that time a
Judge of the Common Pleas. But his verses being trans-
mitted to his friend and patron, Sir Robert Southwell, Sir
Robert wrote in reply that poetry was not the way to pre-
ferment, but a weed in a judge's garden.

Poetry is classed among the liberal arts. If there be
illiberal ones perhaps they may be those having the direct
pursuit of wealth for their aim.

Soldiers, artists, lawyers, all pursue wealth, but glory is associated in their cases with gain, and they sometimes prefer their glory to their gain; but with merchants their sole aim is wealth, wealth is their glory, and the pursuit of it renders all other pursuits tasteless. That it is not want of leisure may be known from this that lawyers, physicians, prime ministers, and others as fully absorbed by their professions as merchants are, yet find time to essay their pens. Rabelais said of the monks of his day that they considered it a monstrous thing to see a learned monk. A literary merchant is nearly as great a monster.

The poet Crabbe, who has described a merchant as "an eating, drinking, buying, bargaining man," notes the distaste of merchants for literary pursuits, which they consider as inimical to a mercantile career. He makes one of them warn his young charge, who has shown an inclination to the Muses, against indulging a taste for poetry and letters. "He, when informed," says this youth—

> "how men of taste could write
> Looked on his ledger with supreme delight.
> Then would he laugh, and with insulting joy
> Tell me aloud 'That's poetry, my boy!
> These are your golden numbers, them repeat,
> The more you have the more you'll find them sweet.'"

*Haliday's taste for literature.* It is therefore the more singular and honourable to the merchants of Dublin to find amongst them one like the author of these essays who, while he gave himself up to the earnest and assiduous pursuit of a merchant's business, yet found time for the study of literature.

Not that he was known to be addicted to literary pursuits. It was in secret that he indulged this taste. He probably felt that such a habit would be prejudicial to his character as a merchant if divulged. An old and leading physician of Dublin calling on a younger one found him whiling away his leisure with his violin while waiting for practice. He expressed his horror, and to the excuses of his less experienced brother replied "Well, if you must and will do it, do it as if it was a sin."

Charles Haliday was known amongst his brother mer- *Sent to London to learn business.* chants as an active energetic man of business. Being destined by his father for the life of a merchant in London, he was sent thither about the year 1809 or 1810 to acquire a knowledge of business. This of course did not hinder him from entering into society and enjoying the pleasures of youth. Being lively, handsome, and accomplished, he was introduced into much good society, and made acquaintance with many of higher rank than himself. Meeting some of these gay acquaintances in the streets when sent of messages, and in his office dress he felt ashamed, he told me, of his inferior employments, and would seek to shun the notice of his gayer companions.

Feeling that he was in an inconsistent position he determined at once to give up gay society and thus escape from being any longer liable to such feelings. Among the gay houses he frequented was that of Delacour's, a wealthy house in the city connected with Cork, but having a residence in the fashionable part of the town. The next invitation he received after taking this resolution he declined, and Mr. Delacour inquiring of him the reason he told him of his determination. Mr. Delacour looked at him with surprise, but with approval, for he said "You'll do, my boy! If you ever have need of me come to me, and I undertake to help you."

After spending some time at other commercial houses, he *Does not neglect study.* was entered as a clerk at Lubbock's Bank, in order to complete his mercantile education. Here, as elsewhere, there is no doubt but that he assiduously applied himself to the business he was engaged upon. But this did not hinder him from pursuing his literary studies.

He had chambers at Gray's Inn, not then confined exclusively to lawyers, and there, as he told me, he read very hard during such hours as were not given to business. His love of study and his desire for accomplishments commenced with his earliest years,—indeed, seems to have been born with him and to have never quitted him during his life. He never offered at the shrine of luxury that greatest of all sacrifices, the sacrifice of time. He deemed nothing nobler than a life of toil; nothing more derogatory than one of luxury and self-indulgence. Before he left Ireland for London he had learned to draw, to ride, and to play the violin.

A manuscript volume of pieces of original poetry, as well as poetical translations by his pen from the French dated from Gray's Inn, from Homerton, and elsewhere in 1812, show how actively he indulged his literary taste during his stay in London.

*Literary friends in London.*

And if a man's character is shown, as is said, by his companions, Mr. Haliday's early inclination to letters will appear from the men he associated with. He was in the habit of dining, he said, during the time he was a clerk at Lubbock's at a tavern in the city, and there made the acquaintanceship of Lamb, author of "Essays by Elia," and of the Brothers Horace and James Smith, joint authors of "Rejected Addresses," all of them employed in the city in houses of trade, and accustomed to dine at the same house.

It was such companionship and a reputation for literary acquirements probably that got him introduced to Horne Tooke, a man no less celebrated for his literary tastes as exhibited in his "Diversions of Purley," than for his political notoriety, having run the risk of his life in a trial for high treason for his opinions only,—opinions that might at this day be expressed with impunity and without question.[1]

[1] The following curious anecdote is from a work of General Arthur O'Connor's. "In my youth," says O'Connor, "I passed a day with Horne Tooke at his house at Wimbledon. The French law of succession was the subject of discussion. In the midst of it Tooke drew a long knife from his pocket, opened the blade, and presenting it towards me with a furious look, 'This,' said he, 'is the argument I employ with men who take the side of the question that you do.' I took an early moment to quit the room, and was followed by Sir

Haliday, who, in later life at any rate, held opinions very different from those of Horne Tooke, being asked what kind of looking man he was, said jocularly, "As ill-looking a thief as you ever saw in your life."

In April, 1812, he had commenced business in London as a commission agent for J. N. D'Esterre,[1] of 11, Bachelor's-walk, Dublin, then engaged in the provision trade, and for one or two others, when an event occurred that changed the course of his life by bringing him back to settle in Ireland. That event was the death of his eldest brother, William Haliday, who died in the month of October, 1812.

*Commences business in Dublin.*

William had married the daughter and only child of Mr. Alder, a merchant engaged in the bark trade.

Mr. Alder intended that William Haliday should either become his partner, or should succeed him in his business.

Francis Burdett who was so shocked with this action of Tooke's, that he expressed his sorrow and astonishment so superior a man should in his own house break off a discussion in so brutal a manner."—"Monopoly the Cause of all Evil," by Arthur Condorcet O'Connor, General of Division, Vol. 1, p. 276 (Paris and London; Firmin Didot), 3 Volumes, Imperial 8vo, 1848. Haliday Library, Royal Irish Academy.

[1] This was the D'Esterre that fell in a duel with O'Connell, fought the 30th January, 1815, at Bishopscourt Demesne, then the seat of Lord Ponsonby, now of the Earl of Clonmell, fifteen miles from Dublin, on the road to Cork. D'Esterre had been in the navy and saved his life by his courage. The mutineers of the Nore endeavoured to force him to join them, and on his refusal placed a rope round his neck to string him up. They asked him again before hanging him to join them, but he cried out, "No! Haul away and be d—d. God save the king!" In admiration of his undaunted courage they spared him. Morgan O'Connell tells the following anecdote concerning the duel. His father and Major MacNamara, his second, driving back to town after the duel, were met by a detachment of cavalry, and the officer coming to the carriage said, "Gentlemen, have you heard anything of a duel that was to take place in this neighbourhood?" "It is over," said MacNamara. "And what was the result?" "Mr. D'Esterre has fallen." The officer thereupon bowed, and turning to his men cried, "Right about face." The guard had been sent to protect D'Esterre from the fury of the mob if O'Connell had been killed.

But William having died just six months after his marriage without issue, Mr. Alder offered, if Charles Haliday would come over, to give him up the business. He acceded to this proposal, and bidding adieu to his literary friends in London, he returned to Dublin in the year 1813, and soon afterwards commenced business as a merchant principally in the bark trade. He took up his residence at a very good house formerly occupied by his father on Arran-quay, at one time a fashionable quarter and inhabited by persons of rank.[1]

*Carries on business and study together.* He was thus launched into a life of business, and became fully engaged in commerce, that career most inimical to letters; yet with characteristic energy he determined to carry on trade and study together. With this view it was his habit, he told me, to go to bed at eight o'clock in the evening and to be wakened up at half-past eleven, when his family were going to bed. He would then rise and study till five, and then returning to bed would sleep till half-past eight, and commence business at the usual hour.

*The consequences.* One night as he went to lock the hall-door according to his custom before sitting down to study, he was surprised and alarmed at seeing a robber in the hall. Grasping the large key to defend himself, he called loudly for his family, and on their coming pointed to the robber. They saw none. It was an illusion of the overtaxed brain. On his next visit to London he waited on Sir Astley Cooper, the eminent surgeon, and on telling him the occurrence Sir Astley said, " You must either go there," pointing downwards, to indicate the grave, " or there," pointing to a madhouse, " or give up your night studies."

---

[1] Edmund Burke's father at one time lived on Arran-quay, next door to Haliday's, and a little further off stood in former times Agar House, the town abode of Viscount Clifden's ancestors. Henry Viscount Clifden, who died in 1836, has often told old Tom Whelan, the bailiff of the estate, how he slept in the garrets of Agar House, and saw the rats about his bed.

He was accordingly obliged to moderate his ardour, but he still was enabled to give some of his leisure to his favourite pursuits.

During the years 1813, 1814, and 1815 his poetical effusions were not unfrequent as appears by his manuscript collection. But they grew fewer and fewer as business called his thoughts to less graceful occupations. And in 1818 he would seem to have bade a final farewell to the Muses. *His farewell to the Muses.*

To Mrs. Hetherington, who had asked him in her " poetical epistle " for a drawing for her screen, he wrote in reply dated " Arran-quay, 25th of October, 1818 :"—

> " My portefeuille of all bereft,
> And not one drawing was there left,
> When commerce changed my mode of life
> From one of peace to one of strife ;
> Changed all the labour to the pen,
> And drove me to the haunts of men ;
> And little time have I, I trow,
> For poetry or painting now,
> My brushes all are turned to quills,
> And nothing can I draw but bills."

About the year 1834, being desirous of a more agreeable abode than his house at Arran-quay, he moved out to Monkstown, and took a lease of a pretty villa called " Fairy Land," adjacent to the beautiful plot of ground which he afterwards purchased. Here he passed a pleasant life intermingling society and business. He drew, he played the violin, he rode to hounds. He also saw company, but the society he cultivated was that of a few intellectual and social men rather than an interchange of costly banquets. Amongst the intellectual few were Dr. Robert James Graves, that most distinguished physician afterwards of European reputation, and Maziere Brady, eventually Lord Chancellor of Ireland. *Life at " Fairy Land."*

Dr. Graves was joint editor with Daniel Haliday, M.D., (a younger brother of Mr. Haliday's), of a medical journal, Daniel Haliday living in Paris and communicating French medical intelligence. Dr. Graves was an independent thinker, and a lively and instructive companion. The improvement he introduced into the practice of medicine gained him great fame abroad as well as at home. The "Clinical Lectures," by Graves and Stokes, is quite a handbook abroad, and has been frequently reprinted there. Dr. Trousseau, of Paris, said to an Irish gentleman who consulted him—"I always have the Clinical Lectures of Graves and Stokes in my hand," and showed him it on his table. A lady from this country a few years since consulted Nelaton, the eminent French surgeon. He asked her where she came from, and on her answering from Ireland, said: "Then I will take no fee. We owe too much to your countryman, Dr. Graves, ever to be able to repay his services."

Dr. Graves reversed the treatment of fever. He used to say, "I would wish no other epitaph than this—'He fed fever.'" "If I have had more success than others," he said in his published Clinical Lectures, "in the treatment of fever, I think it is owing to the advice of a country physician of great shrewdness who advised me never to let my patients die of starvation."

*Change of habits.*

Maziere Brady was also a pleasant companion. At length Mr. Haliday became dissatisfied with his progress. In other words he was not making enough. So he determined to give himself up wholly to business until he had acquired such an amount of capital as he had fixed upon in his own mind as enough for his security. After this he would no longer make the acquisition of wealth his sole object. It is easier to form such a resolution than to keep it; for it is hard to set bounds to the desire of getting. Men go on adding to their capital, afraid to use it and enjoy it. The more they get, they more they desire to get. For strange as it may seem, it is not want but wealth that for the most part produces avarice.

When one of Gargantua's companions had his head cut off in a fight, and it was afterwards sewed on again, he said, that among other strange mutations which he observed in the shades below—such as Alexander the Great turned into an old breeches-patcher, Pope Alexander a ratcatcher, &c., he found the misers and usurers spending all their time there in hunting for brass pins and rusty nails in the street gutters. And how many a gay good fellow, on getting an unexpected accession of fortune, turns Shylock-like and grows penurious—

> "While in the silent growth of cent. per cent.,
> In dirt and darkness hundreds stink content."

But Charles Haliday could set bounds to this desire, and stop when he had reached the appointed limit, and then use and enjoy his wealth and spend his leisure in other aims besides the mere acquisition of more.

It must be observed, however, that Mr. Haliday had no children to provide for, and therefore was not under the same obligation as men who have families dependent on them.

"I now gave up," he said to me, "dinners and drawing, fiddling and hunting, and lived upon one-third of my income, and less." Though he was more engrossed with business after taking this resolution, yet he did not abandon all reading, for it was at this very period that he made schemes for improving his mind by study.

From a journal he kept of his reading for the years from 1836 to 1839, some notion may be formed of his desire to improve his mind. On a blank page at the beginning of this book appears the following:—"Fairy Land, Kingstown, 1836. I have but little time to read, but I must not therefore neglect to read. Before eight o'clock in the morning or after ten at night I may read a few pages, and (with the help of God), I will do so. If I mark the date when I read each book it may stimulate me by keeping before me a register of time lost or employed."

In another—" Much may be done in those little shreds

*Journals of his reading.*

and patches of time which every day produces and which most men throw away, but which nevertheless will make at the end of it no small deduction from the life of man."

The following extracts are copied from these journals or registers of his study :—

### 1836.

July.—Read Spence's Britain Independent of Commerce, 1808. Mill's Commerce defended. Spence's reply to Mill, entitled, Agriculture, the Source of Wealth, 1808. Bentham's Defence of Usury.

August.—Edinburgh and Quarterly Reviews. Reid on the Powers of the Human Mind.

September.—Lyell's Geology. Ricardo's Political Economy.

November.—Third Report of the Commission of Inquiry into the State of the Poor in Ireland. Burns on the Poor of Scotland. Page on the English Poor Laws. Report of Commissioners of Inquiry into the State of the English Poor. Poor Laws in Ireland, by J. Richman. C. Poulet Scrope. Plan of a Poor Law for Ireland. Appeal on behalf of the Poor, by H. M'Cormac, M.D. Plan for relief of the unemployed Poor by the same. Poor Laws in Ireland, by Sir John Walsh, 1830.

December.—Appendix to Third Report of Commissioners for Inquiry into state of the Poor in Ireland, so far as relates to the Charitable Institutions of Dublin. Report of Commissioners of Inquiry into state of Joint Stock Banks. Harris on Lightning Conductors to Ships. Quarterly Review, CVI. Poor Laws, p. 473. Heiderman, by Cooper, pp. 400. Some of Cæsar's Commentaries. Part of Dupin's Ecclesiastical History. Part of Mosheim's Ecclesiastical History.

### 1837.

January.—Read Grattan's Miscellaneous Works; London, 1822, pp. 388.

P. 75.—In the petition to His Majesty we find the simile. "So in the great works of Nature and in the rivers that bring fertility along with them, we find irregularity and deluge. Shall we therefore pronounce the Shannon a nuisance?"

P. 120.—This is with a little variation repeated in the "Answer to Lord Clare." "In great moral operations as well as in the great operations of Nature there is always a degree of waste and overflow. So it is with the sea. Shall we therefore pronounce the ocean a nuisance?"

P. 76.—In the petition to His Majesty we find. "We say if we consider that the people so exiled, so impoverished, so plundered, so persecuted, so enslaved, so disfranchised, did at last spontaneously associate, unite, arm, array, defend, illustrate, and free their country, overawe bigotry, silence riot, and produce out of their own head, armed cap-a-pie, like Wisdom issuing from the head of the Thunderer, Commerce and Constitution. What shall we say of such a people?"

P. 121.—Again in the "Answer to Lord Clare" we find. "That such a people and such a parliament should spontaneously unite, arm, array, defend, illustrate and free their country, overawe bigotry, suppress riot, prevent invasion and produce as the offspring of their own head armed cap-a-pie, like the Goddess of Wisdom issuing from the head of the Thunderer, Commerce and Constitution, what shall we say of such a people and such a Parliament?"

The similarity of expression in these two papers may be attributed to the fact that the petition was not published, or if published was very little known. These extracts show however that Grattan treasured up similes and laboured his compositions. The petition was written about 1798. The "Answer to Lord Clare" in April, 1800, and it will be perceived that the simile in the latter is more carefully worded than that of the former. (C.H.)

Sunday, 12th February. Life of Colonel Gardiner by Dr. Doddridge.

In these memoirs are collected the acts of a man who is held up for imitation as an eminent Christian (and by a Minister of Christ), and yet this man appears to have had no repugnance whatsoever to engage in offensive wars—nor does his biographer appear to condemn them. Colonel Gardiner was engaged in the wars of Marlborough—and to those who are acquainted with the history of the times, the lawfulness, the necessity of these wars must be very doubtful. Yet was Colonel Gardiner an active agent throughout the campaign of Flanders and Germany, and evidently anxious for promotion in his trade of blood, at a moment when Doddridge represents him as always rising two hours before the fixed time for marching that he might read that Gospel which preached peace towards men. The 37th Article of the Church of England says " it is lawful for Christian men at the commandment of the Magistrate to wear weapons and serve in the wars;" but this must be understood to mean defensive and necessary wars."

This sacrifice of his tastes met its due reward. In ten or twelve years he felt at ease. He had acquired that amount of capital which he had marked out in his own mind as essential, and having done this he had the force of character to adhere to the rest of his resolution and to cease thenceforth from making the pursuit of wealth his sole purpose.

In this he exhibited more strength of mind than in his

first sacrifice. For there could be no greater proof of self-control, nothing being more difficult or less common than voluntarily to stop in the midst of a successful career.

*Builds a villa at Monkstown.* Being now more at ease, he resolved to purchase himself a villa. He was anxious he told me to get some freehold land not subject to any rent; but after a long search, finding none to be had, he fixed himself about the year 1843 in the beautiful spot where he so long resided. This was Monkstown Park, previously the residence of Lord Ranelagh. Exactly opposite, divided from it only by the road, is the ancient castle of the Cheeverses, built probably in the time of King Henry VI. to defend this southern boundary of the English Pale. At Cromwell's Conquest he gave it to General Ludlow, while Walter Cheevers and his household were transplanted to Connaught. The ground of Monkstown Park, within a narrow circuit, presents a very varied surface. A gentle swell of the land between it and the sea shuts off the keener eastern air, and the general slope of the ground is towards the south and west, with a delightfully warm and sheltered aspect. It is well timbered, and at a short distance to the south are the Dublin mountains. Lord Ranelagh's mansion stood almost upon the roadside, near the present entrance gate.

But Mr. Haliday pulled down the old residence, and built himself a beautiful villa on another and a better site.

In erecting this mansion he took the following course:—Having fixed on the number and size of the rooms it was to consist of, he chose for its character or general outward design an oblong square in the Italian style, and then gave the whole to an architect to criticise and correct.

*His method of choosing the site.* Having thus determined the size of it, he marked out the exact dimensions on the spot he had selected for its site by ropes and pegs, easy to be shifted, and by visiting the spot at the various seasons of the year, and at different times of the day, and shifting the ropes and pegs, he tried the different aspects, and ascertained which was most suitable for the different apartments by actual experiment. He thus raised an unusually elegant and comfortable mansion. In admiration of its beauty, I sometimes repeated to him, in jest, as we walked up from the garden to dinner, the saying of Edward Vaughan of Golden Grove, near Roscrea, in the county of Tipperary, as if such were his secret thoughts: " Oh Golden Grove, Golden Grove! if I might only keep you, I would give up my chances of Heaven!"

Of this new mansion, the library, to use Cicero's expression, might be considered the soul. But beyond the library he had a hole of a study, small enough to please the late Lord Palmerston. That great and popular minister was found by Dr. Granville in a little room of Cambridge House, Piccadilly, up to his knees in manuscript papers, foreign and domestic (for he said he never had time to read print). Dr. Granville said to him, he wondered that he would not choose a larger study. But Lord Palmerston laughed, and said he wondered how a man could collect his thoughts in a larger space. Mr. Haliday's study was a long and narrow slice as it were, lighted by one window from the east. There he sat on a low stool at the farthest distance from the window, and the light to humour his eyes, with a rug over his knees in cold weather. Immediately about him were those books of Scandinavian history and antiquities, purchased for him abroad, at Copenhagen and elsewhere. *Small size of his study.*

In the larger library was the great collection of pamphlet and other literature relating to Ireland, which it had been the labour and pleasure of his life to bring together, before he became immersed just at the close of it in the study of the Scandinavian antiquities of Dublin. *His library.*

In his earlier studies concerning the history of the port of Dublin, he applied to the Corporation for the use of their Assembly Rolls and other ancient records and had them. Hard as these were to decipher, through age and the mediæval character of the writing, he yet laboured at them industriously in the early morning hours, until it was time for him to join in business in town. To aid him he often had to use a large magnifying glass. One day he discovered to his astonishment and regret, that he was totally blind of one eye, a calamity produced by his intense labour over these ancient rolls, and by the use, probably, of the large lens. He never knew when the loss of his eye occurred, and it was thus a comparatively small misfortune; but it kept him ever after in terrible fear of losing the other.

<small>Loses the sight of one eye through study.</small>

This proves the wisdom of President Jefferson, of the United States of America, who called upon his son to observe "How much pain have evils cost us that never happened!" For it may be truly said, that when Mr. Haliday died, his fingers held the pen, as he was engaged on a pamphlet concerning the sanitary condition of Kingstown when he retired from his study to his bed and died in a few hours.

It was this defect of his eyes, that made the dark corner of his study suitable to his sight.

<small>His book collections.</small>

He had one of the largest and best private collections of historical works on Ireland, if not the best in the kingdom. I have not ascertained, at what time he began to collect the works on Irish history; but one would imagine, it must have been at a comparatively early period, for it would take years to bring together such a body of pamphlets and broadsides as he was possessed of, being things only obtainable occasionally and by long watching.

Every auctioneer of books, of course, sent him his catalogue of sale; but besides this, he had most of the waste-paper sellers of Cook-street and elsewhere, to bring him any old books, papers, or broadsides, that came to them. With these they would wait on him at his residence Arran-quay, or at the Bank of Ireland, or the Ballast Board.

<small>The Secret Service Money Book.</small>

At auctions it was his custom always to buy through a commissioned agent, as the price would be raised against him if he appeared in person, but of course he inspected the books previously. In his collection, was the celebrated

Secret Service Money Book, in manuscript, with the payments made for secret information in 1798, amongst other payments, sums paid to the informer for tracking Lord Edward Fitzgerald to the house where he was captured. It is of course full of interest, and Richard R. Madden, M.D., has made great use of it in his "Lives of the United Irishmen."

Haliday purchased the book at an auction of Joseph Scully's, bookseller, 24, Upper Ormond-quay, near the Four Courts.

He told me that on going to inspect this, and the other articles for sale there, he met his old rival, Doctor Murphy, Roman Catholic Bishop of Cork, a great book collector, engaged in the same pursuit.

Besides the Secret Service Money Book, there was for sale on this occasion depositions and papers concerning Father Sheehy's case, hanged for supposed complicity with a Whiteboy murder in 1766. So Haliday said to Dr. Murphy, "I know you would like to have both these rarities, and so should I. But if we were each to have only one of them I should wish to have the Secret Service Money Book, and you the Sheehy papers. Let us agree then not to bid against one another. Do you get yours, and let me get mine." And so it was arranged. *How got by Haliday.*

From Dr. Madden, author of the "Lives of the United Irishmen," who has made so much use of this book in his endeavour to identify the betrayer of Lord Edward Fitzgerald, I learned this further history of the Secret Service Money Book.

About forty-five years ago, when he was engaged upon the "Lives of the United Irishmen," the late James Hardiman, author of the "History of the Town of Galway" and other works, came to him, and told him that he knew where this book was to be had, and at Dr. Madden's earnest request he brought it to him to look at. Dr. Madden having copied from it such items as he wanted, he *Its history.*

handed it back to Hardiman, who returned it to the person he borrowed it from.

Dr. Madden said that this book was kept in the Record Tower of Dublin Castle, and that a carpenter employed there purloined it with a mass of other papers. The whole was sold to a grocer in Capel-street. From him it was that Hardiman borrowed it.

*O'Connell and the Secret Service Money Book.*

Before Dr. Madden published his work he became anxious lest he might be called in question for citing this book; and he asked the opinion of a barrister of his acquaintance, but he was unable to advise. So Dr. Madden betook himself to Daniel O'Connell. O'Connell asked to see the book, and Dr. Madden brought it to him. O'Connell read and read for near twenty minutes absorbed in the iniquity it disclosed. At length, coming to a particular item, he struck the table, and said involuntarily, " My God !" He would not tell Dr. Madden what it was, but he watched the spot, and found that it was the name of a Priest of the county of Cork, shown to have been in receipt of money for giving secret information to the Government in 1798.

Dr. Madden put the question to him, " May I venture to publish what I have copied ? " " Did you steal the book ?" said O'Connell. " No." " Then publish." When Dr. Madden's " Lives of the United Irishmen " came out, he presented a copy to O'Connell, but he returned it. He had a horror, said Dr. Madden, of their proceedings.

The Secret Service Money Book was finally sold to Scully, a seller of old books, on Ormond-quay, for ten pounds, and was bought from him by C. Haliday, under the circumstances already detailed for twenty pounds.

*Extent of Haliday's collection.*

This most interesting record is preserved among the Haliday collection in the Royal Irish Academy. The extent of Mr. Haliday's collections may be judged from this, that the pamphlets relating principally to Ireland numbered 29,000. There were 21,997 in 2,211 (two thousand two hundred and eleven) volumes octavo uniformly bound in one series, and about 700 pamphlets in quarto, of very early date unbound. There were besides all the best works concerning Ireland, and broadsides, ballads and a mass of rare and curious materials for the student of Irish history, ancient and modern. This library passed with the rest of Mr. Haliday's property by his will, to his wife, and was by her presented shortly after his death to the Royal Irish Academy, in the belief that she was thus fulfilling a wish she had sometimes heard Mr. Haliday casually express that his collections might be kept together in some public library.

But book collectors are too often collectors only. I remember calling on old Dr. Willis, of Ormond-quay and Rathmines, a great collector, to see his collection of ancient maps, and talking of Haliday and his having had a project of writing some account of the Scandinavian Antiquities of Dublin he ridiculed the idea of his writing anything, adding, "Collectors are never writers or readers." Collectors seldom readers.

The Rev. Reginald Heber was a great collector. His Library at Hodnet sold for £53,000. "Mr. Heber," said Porson to him with his usual caustic humour, "You have collected a great many books. Pray, when do you mean to begin to read them?" But Heber was well acquainted with the contents of his library. And so was Haliday. His books were purchased for use, not show. He was "Not like our modern dealers minding only the margin's breadth and binding." Nor could it be said of him and of his library as of Pope's ostentatious Peer:

> "His study! with what authors is it stored?
> In books not authors curious is my lord:
> To all their dated backs he turns you round:
> These Aldus printed, those Du Seuil has bound.
> Lo! some are vellum, and the rest as good:
> For all his Lordship knows but they are wood."

And they were not only for his own use, but for the use of others—for there was no one freer to lend his books. Just as the learned Rabelais wrote in the front of all his books, Francisci Rabelæsi καὶ τῶν αυτον φιλῶν, so there might have been inscribed over Mr. Haliday's library door, "The Books of Charles Haliday and his friends."

<small>Haliday's Sunday dinner.</small>
Now that he is gone it gratifies me to think that I had an opportunity to pay him this well-deserved compliment publicly, in his lifetime. It will be found in the preface to the Cromwellian Settlement of Ireland, first published in 1865. But, however, he may have been secretly pleased with this testimony to his liberality, he was not so when he found his abode described there as "his Lucullan Villa" declaring it was too bad to use such terms of a place where he never gave me anything but a leg of mutton. For such was invariably his Sunday dinner, as he used to let all his servants but one go out until dinner time, this one being kept to watch the roast, and it was only this joint he said which any one could attend to. This humanity to his servants was exhibited in other ways.

<small>His Saturday entertainments.</small>
Saturday being a favourite banqueting day among merchants as the eve of a day of rest from their labours, he gave way to their humour; but whenever he had a dinner party on this day he locked the dining-room door when his guests were gone at night, leaving the wine, the dessert, the silver plate and the glass and the whole table just as it was, till Monday morning, not to break in upon his servants' Sunday rest.

He used to say there were two reasons assigned for the Sabbath in different places in Scripture. One being that given in the twelve Commandments, in the 20th chapter of Exodus, that is to say because God rested on that day, the other in the 23rd chapter, "that thine ox and thine ass may rest, and the son of thy handmaid," and that this last was the one he preferred to keep in view.

But I pacified him by pointing out to him that it was not his table I referred to so much as his library, having taken care to specify that Plutarch in describing the elegance of Lucullus's Villa praised him for the libraries he had collected, and that they were open to all. The Greeks added Plutarch repaired at pleasure to the galleries and porticoes as to the retreat of the Muses. So that his house was in fact an asylum and senate-house to all the Greeks that visited Rome.

And this too was true as regarded Haliday. For there was no one engaged upon any subject that could be illustrated from his collection but he received him, discussed it intelligently, and lent what was applicable from his collection.

He was Lucullus-like also in his reception of foreigners of merit, considering it as a kind of public duty to show them the hospitality of his house.

My intimacy with Charles Haliday began about the year 1850, the time when at the request of his colleagues in the commission for preserving and improving the port of Dublin, he undertook to collect materials for a history of the harbour, principally with a view to trace the progress of improvement in the navigable channel of the Liffey, and to preserve some record of the plans proposed, and of the effect of works executed for deepening the river, and rendering the port commodious for shipping.[1] I had known him for many years, as he was tenant to Viscount Clifden for his house on Arran-quay, and my father, my grandfather, and I had been during seventy years agents in succession of that family for their properties in the city and county of Dublin, and counties of Meath and Kildare. But, to say the truth, I had at first no liking for Haliday, because of his haughty mien and distant manners. The Agar Ellises, Viscounts Clifden, derived through Sir John and Sir William Ellis, a valuable leasehold interest from the Corporation of Dublin along Arran-quay, Ellis's-quay, Pembroke-quay, and thence westward to the Phœnix Park. The leases were some of them

*Beginning of intimacy with Haliday.*

---

[1] See the opening passage of his essay on "The Ancient Name of Dublin," Translations of the Royal Irish Academy, volume xxii., Polite Literature.'' Read June 12, 1855.

as early as 1662, and had maps of parts of the Liffey as forming the boundary of the demised premises.

One morning Mr. Haliday waited on me in my study at 17, Hume-street, to ask me if I would show him one of the Corporation leases made to Sir William Ellis, as it probably had the map attached, whilst that appended to the other part of the lease in the Corporation muniments was lost. He explained to me that it was for historical and antiquarian purposes only.

I was rather surprised to find him engaged in such pursuits, as I had only known him as a merchant seated among his clerks and ledgers.

<small>His spirit of independence.</small>

But as I was not too well inclined to him I said I would mention his desire to Lord Clifden and inform him of his lordship's pleasure. He started back with as much disdain, and to as great a distance, as the great lady of Paris, at the shameful proposals of Panurge, an utter stranger, made to her in plain terms without preface or preamble at their first meeting.

He scorned to be obliged to any nobleman. He showed similar feelings on another occasion.

In 1865 the fine library at Charlemont House containing the collections of early English and Italian books made by the first earl being placed under my care by his grandson, the present earl, Mr. Haliday appointed a time to come to see it.

But he would scarce look at anything, and was uneasy until he could get out of the place. He evidently feared that Lord Charlemont might come in, and that it might be thought he sought his acquaintance. For, though well fitted to grace and enjoy the highest society, he studiously associated himself with the class he belonged to. Unless as a matter of public duty he never appeared at the Castle of Dublin. It was only as accompanying a deputation he was seen there. He was proud, but to those who would complain of it, one might say, when we remember his humanity, his charity, his love of learning, his zeal for the service of his country and city, Be proud in the same way.

Fortunately our first interview was a little prolonged, and he learned with equal surprise that I, whom he had looked upon as a mere working barrister, was also fond of historical and antiquarian studies.

In the following year I remember calling on him one Sunday afternoon at Monkstown Park, being the first time I had ever visited him there, and his hoping I would stay to partake of his four o'clock Sunday dinner, "I never invite anyone," said he, "to such a dinner, but if you will only come when you can uninvited you will generally find me too glad to stay you here."

From that time forward till his death I very generally dined with him on Sunday, none else being ever there, and came thus to know something of the general tenor of his pursuits, but unfortunately too little of his life. I never thought of asking him where he was at school, or when he began to study Irish History, or when he began collecting books and pamphlets, as I never thought of its falling to my lot to publish some notice of his life and labours. Our conversation was generally of the topics of the hour. He preferred anecdotes and repartee to more serious subjects having a great fund of such lore to draw upon. For with Bacon he deemed gaiety and liveliness suitable to meal times, just as Lycurgus set up an image of the God of Laughter in each dinner hall at Sparta. *His table talk.*

Mr. Haliday being now fitted with a public aim for his reading and researches, instead of studying as previously for self improvement or for materials for conversation (for vain is the reading and useless the study that in due time is not brought to some useful end) he set to work with that energy and earnestness which he exhibited in everything he did. He was now up every morning, winter as well as summer, by five o'clock, working without a fire as many early rising students are in the habit of doing. They know *His early morning studies.*

that one's study is thus always ready, and that it is easy to put on warm coats and rugs,[1] and that besides this a man does not sit with his feet in the draught of cold air drawn along the floor by the heat of the fire, and indeed there was no fireplace in Mr. Haliday's study.

This practice of early rising he continued to his latest day, thus living not merely a double length of life but enjoying in those early hours a freedom from visitors and a quiet not to be had during the rest of the day. The head too is then free from the fumes of meat and wine. It was these advantages probably that gave rise to the saying of the Greeks Φιλῇ ταις Μουσαις ηως, Morning is friendly to the Muses, so finely paraphrased by Pope—

> "On morning's wings how active springs the mind
> That leaves the load of yesterday behind;
> How easy every labour it pursues
> How coming to the poet every Muse."

His own library furnished him with every printed work relating to Ireland and Dublin in particular.

He would not however rely on an author's statements, but would verify them by referring to the original sources, saying that an author writing of things done a hundred years before his own time, even though his name were Spencer, Davys, or Ware, was no better than he was as to personal knowledge.

*His commonplace books.* It is only by his commonplace books of which there are six quarto volumes began on undertaking the history of the Port of Dublin, that a true notion of his activity of research can be obtained. These are most clearly written, in a systematic manner, with correct references. They form a vast repertory of information relating to the Port of Dublin and to the antiquities of the city. By these it

---

[1] There is an old French proverb,
Tenez chaud les pieds et teste
Au demeurant vivez en beste:
Thus paraphrased—
The head and feet keep warm
The rest will take no harm.
See Randle Cotgrave's French and English Dictionary, A.D., 1610.

appears that having ransacked all printed sources of knowledge he next applied to the Corporation of Dublin for access to their ancient records, the Corporation of Dublin being the sole owners and managers of the port and river in early times. He now eagerly embarked in the study of the ancient muniments of the Corporation of Dublin consisting of the Assembly Rolls, the Chain Book, and the White Book of the City. How zealously he noted all that was to be found in these curious records may be seen from the four volumes in quarto in his handwriting now in the Royal Irish Academy containing all that is to be found in the Assembly Rolls concerning the River and Harbour of Dublin, besides many other matters he observed in them either curious or instructive.

Mr. Haliday naturally found it hard not merely to master the mediæval characters and contractions used by the scribes of early times, but also to decipher some of the earlier Corporation Rolls as they were much defaced by age, and still more by the marks of nut galls made use of for reviving the faded writing by (I believe) the Record Commissioners of 1810 in their examination of them.

In the ancient records of the Court of Exchequer too there was also a vast amount of materials to be found illustrative of the history of the port of Dublin. These being in the care of James Frederic Ferguson, with whom I had some short time before formed a close friendship, I had the pleasure of making him known to Mr. Haliday.

*James Frederic Ferguson.*

A curious accident led to my acquaintanceship with Mr. Ferguson. When leaving the Four Courts one afternoon, early in the year 1850, by the western quadrangle, I observed two labourers carrying each a load on his shoulder of what seemed to be Cumberland flagstones, but a further inspection showed them parchments covered with dust. They were Bills and Answers of the Equity side of the Court of Exchequer. They told me they were removing them from the Exchequer Offices then kept in the buildings on the extreme west of the Four Courts building and nearest the Quay, and were taking them to the Benchers' Buildings in the rere of the Four Courts.

<small>History of James Frederic Ferguson.</small>

Following these guides and mounting a temporary wooden staircase I found myself in the presence of a solitary figure, sole master of a suite of empty rooms, engaged in sorting vast masses of parchments, books, and papers. These and a couple of chairs their only furniture. He seemed about fifty, and was of good stature. His hair very dark, his complexion sallow, with full dark lustrous eyes. His mien was mild, modest and retiring, and rather marked with melancholy. This was James Frederic Ferguson. He was then engaged under the authority of the Lords of the Treasury in sorting and cataloguing the Exchequer Records preparatory to the division to be made of them between the Chancery and Exchequer on the abolition of the Equity Jurisdiction of the Court of Exchequer. He was born at Charleston in South Carolina in 1806, where his father, a native of France but of Scottish descent, was a professor in the College. This gentleman's grandfather left Scotland because of his joining the Pretender in 1745 and settled in Sweden. In 1814 young Ferguson came from Charleston to England and remained in London until 1821 when he came to Ireland, with Mr. Samuel Cooke, of Sunderland, in the county of Durham, formerly a banker, then employed about the recovering of certain advowsons supposed to belong to the heir of the Lords Barnewall of Turvey, Viscounts Kingsland.

<small>Samuel Cooke of Sunderland, and the Kingsland advowsons.</small>

The heir to this ancient title was Mathew Barnewall who, from being a butcher's basket-boy at Castle Market, and afterwards a waiter at a tavern in Dawson-street, recovered the title as told in Sir Bernard Burke's "Vicissitudes of Families." Length of time had barred all claim to the lands, but as no lapse of time then barred the claims of the Church, this low-born peer found speculators in London to risk £10,000 on his visionary rights, and in 1817 to employ Mr. Cooke at a salary of £800 a year to establish them in Ireland. The evidence to support them lay, if anywhere, in the ancient records of the Common Pleas and the Exchequer, and Mr. Cooke knowing little of anything but of shooting and fishing, in 1821 brought over young Ferguson, a connexion of his by marriage, to do this work.

From the opening of the office doors in the morning till their shutting, Ferguson was at work on the Kingsland claims. After the failure of this business (for there was only recovered the poor living of Garristown near the Naul, in the county of Dublin), he became assistant to William Lynch, sub-commissioner of the Records, author of Feudal Dignities in Ireland, and afterwards Record Agent for Peerage Claims in London, and was invaluable to him for his zeal and for his knowledge of Irish records.

Mr. Ferguson, who was gifted with intellectual qualities of a high order and had a refined literary taste, was a contributor to the historical literature of his country, although generally unknown, for with characteristic unobtrusiveness his name was generally withheld from the public. In him every archæological inquirer found a ready friend and earnest, self-denying assistant. *Ferguson's gratuitous aid to inquirers.*

The only inquiries he had a distaste for were genealogical ones, and yet he would labour gratuitously over his records with such inquirers as if he liked it and were paid for it. Often have I seen him closing the door after one of them, gently raise his hands as if he was glad "to be shutt of him," saying mildly, "How I hate a pedigree hunter."

The records placed under his charge were his only care and object; they were to him instead of companions, family, and friends, and to them and those who esteemed them and valued them as he did, he devoted his entire life. One instance that I was myself conversant of will give some notion of his love of records. In the month of April, 1853, Mr. R. L. Pearsall, then resident at the Château de Wartenau on the southern or Swiss side of the Lake of Constance *His journey to the Castle of Meersburg in Germany.*

communicated to his friend the Rev. H. F. Ellacombe, rector of Clyst St. George, Topsham, Devonshire, that a German gentleman living in the Duchy of Baden, on the north side of the same lake, the ancient Suabia, had in his possession some ancient rolls of the King's Bench of Ireland, of the reign of Edward III. On receiving this information from Mr. Ellacombe, Mr. Ferguson at once wrote to the Lord Chief Justice of the Queen's Bench, and to the Lords of the Treasury, and as both turned a deaf ear to his suggestions, Mr. Ferguson, small as were his means, travelled at his own cost to Mr. Pearsall at the Lake of Constance, and accompanied him to the possessor of the records.

This was Joseph von Lassberg, a German antiquary, dwelling in the old moated Suabian Castle of Meersburgh,[1] who had in 1851 purchased these records of a Jew at Frankfort. The old gentleman's cupidity was at once roused, by the fact of an officer of the Courts (employed by the Government as he supposed) travelling from Ireland thither to purchase them; and he asked such an inordinate price, so much beyond Ferguson's small means, that Ferguson was in despair, and with characteristic devotion as he could not get them, he actually sat up all night making abstracts of them.

*Recovers some ancient Queen's Bench Rolls.* But in the morning von Lassberg finding that Ferguson had not the price, took all the money he had, which was sixty pounds sterling, and poor Ferguson returned with his

---

[1] "The town and castle of Meersburg crowns a white cliff on the northern shore of the Boden See. The place first belonged to King Dagobert (A.D. 628) then to Charles Martel; finally (A.D. 1629) to the Bishops of Constance. In 1836 it was purchased by Joseph von Lassberg, an antiquary and poet. His library contained 12,000 printed books, his manuscripts were 273. He was tall, handsome, with a long flowing white beard. He died in 1855. In 1877, a Tyrolese nobleman of similar tastes, purchased the castle for a store of ancient armour, which he had collected and kept at Munich."—The Shores and Cities of the Boden See in 1879-80. By Samuel James Capper, M.P. Delarue, London, 8vo, 1881.

*dear* records without regret or repining. After his death, which occurred on the 26th November, 1855, they were sold, and were purchased at the auction of his small effects for the government—

> " For still the great had kindness in reserve,
> They helped to bury whom they helped to starve."

Mr. Ferguson's large dark eyes (inherited, probably, from his grandmother, Anne Marguerite Delaporte, daughter of the French consul at Stockholm) were most powerful, and he had, apparently, the art (without the aid of jesting Rabelais' miraculous spectacles) of reading the effaced writing of ancient rolls. But Ferguson himself, attributed his strength of sight to night watching on board of Mr. Cooke's fishing boats in the bay of Dublin. For this gentleman, who dwelt, while in Ireland, at Sandymount, where his household consisted of the poor, low-born Lord Kingsland (lest, perhaps, he should get into other hands) and James Ferguson, had a lease of the Poolbeg salmon fishing at the mouth of the Liffey. Cooke had, besides salmon nets for the mouth of the Liffey, also great nets to stretch across the broad but shallow bight (or bay) running up towards Ringsend, between Sandymount and the Pigeonhouse Fort, and my friend and fellow barrister, William Monk Gibbon, LL.D., of Sandymount, remembers when he was a boy to have frequently seen him with a large number of soldiers of the fort, employed in laying and drawing this great net. *[His strength of sight.]*

Mr. Ferguson's learning and modesty, made him most acceptable to Mr. Haliday.

He took a pleasure in getting him to copy for him from the ancient records under his care, and he kept him almost constantly employed for the few short years of their acquaintanceship; for it only commenced about 1852. *[Makes extracts from the Rolls for Haliday.]*

Mr. Haliday got liberty from the Corporation to employ Ferguson on the earlier City Assembly Rolls; of the later he made abstracts by his own hand. And he kept him continually at work in making copies of entries relating to the port and harbour of Dublin, to be found on the rolls of the Court of Exchequer.

<small>List of Ferguson's copies for Haliday.</small>

Among his other talents, Mr. Ferguson was a consumate master of clerkship, writing in a fine legible hand, with great rapidity and accuracy, as will be at once seen by the great amount of his writing in the Haliday collection in the Royal Irish Academy. The following works to be seen there are of his penmanship—

A.D. 1260–1261.—Complete transcript of the Roll of the 45th year of King Henry the 3rd. Folio.

A.D. 1200–1224. — Extracts from the Charter, Close, and Patent Rolls of England, relating to the trade of Ireland, to St. Mary's Abbey, and to the port of Dublin. Folio.

A.D. 1303–1308.—Abstracts, and some translations in full of Entries on the Memoranda Rolls relating to the collection of the customs at various ports in Ireland by the Friscobaldi and other Florentine merchants, to whom they had been mortgaged by the King as security for loans made to him, 31st to 35th King Edward 1st. Folio.

A.D. 1272–1325.—Calendar of the Memoranda Rolls of Edward 1st and Edward 2nd. Folio.

A.D. 1319.—Extracts from the Memoranda Rolls of Edward 2nd of this year, concerning the King's Mills near Dublin, concerning the Abbey of St. Mary's there, the Florentine merchants, shipping, and trade. Folio.

A.D. 1326–1379.—Translations of Miscellaneous Entries from the Memoranda Rolls from 3rd to 50th year of Edward 3rd. Folio.

A.D. 1383–1643.—Extracts from the Memoranda Rolls, concerning the customs, trade, and port of Dublin. Folio.

A.D. 1554–1555.—Memoranda Roll of 1st and 2nd Philip and Mary. Extracts mostly concerning the nunnery of St. Mary le Hogges. Folio.

A.D. 1613–1633.—Extracts from the Communia Rolls of the Exchequer, of entries relating to the trade and port of Dublin. Folio.

A.D. 1295–1613.—Extracts from the Judgment Rolls. Folio.

Copy of the By-Laws of Dublin. Folio.

A.D. 1320–1685.—Municipal Records of the city of Dublin. Extracts relating to ships, the trade, and the port and harbour of Dublin.

Translation of the Register of St. Thomas' Abbey, Dublin, commonly called Coppinger's' Register being made by Thomas Coppinger. Folio.[1]

A.D. 1468-1552.—Assembly Rolls of Corporation of Dublin. Quarto.

A.D. 1468-1509.—Memoranda and Freeman Rolls of the Corporation of Dublin. Quarto.

It will be seen from the journals of Haliday's reading that while his earlier studies were for the most part general and miscellaneous he still kept himself fully informed of all that was published from time to time on trade, banking, and commerce.

He was also deeply interested in all social subjects, such as the relief of the poor and their general well-being, and was a large but anonymous contributor to the public journals. He wrote letters and articles on trade, banking, the poor, the public markets, the taxes, and whatever else concerned the public interest, but he abstained from politics, though of pronounced Conservative opinions of an enlarged kind, and with a spirited national feeling of his own. He left a large scrap book of these contributions which remains an interesting monument to show how constantly his thoughts and his pen were employed unobserved for the public interest. *Haliday's writings in the daily press.*

On the cover inside appears the following note in his handwriting:—

"I have collected in this volume some of the trifles which I have written and published, that I may be reminded of past exertions and stimulated to new ones for the public good."

---

[1] On parchment in fine bold engrossing hand on the title page is the following :—" Copia vera quarandam evidentiarum monasterii Sancti Thomæ Martyris juxta Dublinum extractarum per me, Willielmum Coppinger, suæ nationis capitaneum, Anno Domini, 1526.

Another portion of this register, made by Coppinger, with similar notice, A.D. 1526, is preserved in the Rawlinson MSS. (No. 499), Bodleian Library, Oxford. It is bound and stamped with Sir James Ware's coat of arms.

The first contains private grants, the other volume grants of different kings, and other public concessions.

<small>Pamphlets by C. Haliday:</small>

But besides these fugitive pieces, he published some pamphlets.

<small>On Temperance.</small>

His first publication of this kind, which was anonymous, was an Inquiry into the influence of the excessive use of Spirituous Liquors in producing Crime, Disease, and Poverty in Ireland.[1] It appeared in 1830. In a presentation copy of it to Mr. James Haughton, there is the following note in Mr. Haliday's writing:—

"This, I believe, was the first publication of the temperance movement in Ireland."

<small>On the Mendicity Society.</small>

He was an active member of the Society for the Suppression of Mendicity in Dublin, commonly called the Mendicity Society.

This Society, at a time when there was no legal relief for the poor, and the streets of Dublin were crowded with beggars, took a lease of Moira House, on Usher's-quay, and opened it to receive all poor who should come there of their own accord or with a ticket given by anyone whom they had solicited alms from, and they were there provided with wholesome food for the day, on condition of stonebreaking for men and boys, and other suitable work for women.

Archbishop Whately pronounced it the best system of relief that he knew. Here Mr. Haliday gave his personal attendance. And when the cholera morbus made its first terrible visitation to Dublin in the year 1832, and seized its most hopeless victims amongst the poorest, it naturally committed awful ravages amongst the needy frequenters of the Mendicity Society at Moira House; yet Mr. Haliday never flinched or deserted his post, but was present at his usual hours, and helped those seized to carriages to convey them to the hospitals, while his family and friends were filled with fear for him, and indeed for themselves.

The experience he acquired at this institution caused

---

[1] 8vo, Dublin, pp. 127, Milliken, 1830.

him to write a pamphlet in 1838 on the necessity of some law of settlement to be introduced into the Poor Relief measure then before Parliament.[1]

"When the society first commenced its measure for suppressing mendicity, in 1818," said Mr. Haliday, "they found in the streets of Dublin 5,000 beggars. In the course of investigation it became evident that no system of relief dependent on voluntary contributions could create a reasonable hope of success without some plan or modification of the system of settlement." The association, therefore, declared that no one should be considered an object for relief who could not prove a residence within the city or its precincts for six months. In the first year the number of destitute persons registered exceeded 5,500. Of these, 2,251 were sent to their homes or friends in England, Scotland, and the country parts of Ireland; and about 2,400 were rejected for the want of six months' residence. As a further means to suppress mendicancy, they appointed street inspectors, and with the aid of the police, they in one year had upwards of 4,300 beggars apprehended and brought before the magistrates. To these exertions was owing the diminution of vagrancy and pauperism then apparent in Dublin.

*On a Law of Settlement.*

From these facts Mr. Haliday contended for a law of settlement in the Poor Relief Act, and published his reasons in an anonymous pamphlet with the title in the foot note. In a short preface to it, dated Dublin, February 20th, 1838, he styles himself "A Member of the Mendicity Association."

On the face of the pamphlet there is the following observation in Mr. Haliday's handwriting:—" A letter from the Duke of Wellington shows that this pamphlet produced the clause of Electoral Division rating."

The next topic of a kindred nature which engaged his

---

[1] Necessity of Combining a Law of Settlement with Local Assessment in the proposed Bill for the Relief of the Poor of Ireland, pp. 26, 8vo. Dublin, Milliken and Son, 1838.

pen, after treating of this measure, the compulsory relief of the poor of Ireland, was a consideration of the miserable habitations of so many of those that dwelt outside of the poorhouses.

<small>On Sanitary Legislation for Towns.</small>

The Census Commissioners of 1841, reported that nearly one-half of the families of the rural population, and somewhat more than a third of the families of the civic population, were living in accommodation equivalent to a cabin consisting of a single room. A Commission of Inquiry was shortly afterwards issued into the state of the tenure and occupation of land and of means of improving the relations of landlord and tenant, and Mr. Haliday pleaded for a similar inquiry into the sanitary condition of the labouring classes in towns, of whom, according to the Census, one-third were so miserably lodged.

He gave instances, and contended that there was need of some new law for the regulation of house property in towns and for the protection of the health, comfort, and rights of the poorer classes, some modification perhaps of the medical police system of German cities, and the Conseil de Salubrité of Paris. Such an authority, he added, as would compel the builders of houses to secure a supply of pure water for their tenants, to build sewers, and to provide all essentials to decency and cleanliness, before any of the houses could be let in tenements. This body being made the guardians of the public rights, could prevent individuals, however powerful from depriving the labouring classes of the advantages which open spaces, public walks and pathways, and access to rivers and the sea afford.[1] He was thus early an advocate of sanitary legislation, which had not then commenced, but has latterly been so productive of improvement.

---

[1] He entitled this pamphlet, which was anonymous—"A letter to the Commissioners of Landlord and Tenant Inquiry, on the state of the Law in respect of the Building and Occupation of Houses in Towns in Ireland." 8vo., Dublin, Grant and Bolton, 1844.

In the course of his inquiries respecting the cleanliness and health of the poor, he elicited the remarkable fact—that within the previous five or six years (he was writing in 1844), the poor of Kingstown and Dunleary, although residing on the sea shore, had been deprived of the means of preserving health and promoting cleanliness which sea bathing afforded.

Before the Kingstown railway was carried across the harbour, the strand was open to the public, and under the high cliffs which extended from Salthill to the west pier there were small bays or inlets completely sheltered and secluded, where the women and children of the town and surrounding country freely bathed. But as it was deemed necessary for the extension of the railway that it should pass between these cliffs and the sea, the cliffs were levelled and formed into a railway embankment across the strand, and the poor were excluded from the benefit of those prescriptive rights which they had previously enjoyed unquestioned. Noblemen and gentlemen, whose seaward boundaries this railway traversed, protected their own rights, and for them the Dublin and Kingstown Railway Company were compelled to erect splendid baths and other costly works. Commodious baths were also erected for those who paid for using them; but for those who were unable to pay—for the poor of Kingstown and the surrounding country—no accommodation whatever had been provided in lieu of that of which they were deprived.[1] For three whole years he laboured to obtain for the poor the restoration of their rights, by private addresses to the railway directors and others, but failing in his efforts, he had recourse to the press. This publication, issued in 1847, is entitled, "An Appeal to His Excellency the Lord Lieutenant on behalf of the Labouring Classes," and in this he sets

*On the taking by the Railway of the bathing place of the Kingstown poor.*

[1] *Ibid*, pp. 7, 8.
It was anonymous and intended only for private circulation. There is no publisher's name. It was printed by P. D. Hardy and Son, Dublin. 8vo., pp. 54.

forth fully the steps by which the railway company had contrived to deprive the public of their access to the shore.

On the title page of Mr. Haliday's copy is a note in his own hand (written the very year of his death):—"This Appeal procured for the Labouring Classes at Kingstown a free bathing place for women, now in course of erection at Salthill, and one for men at the West pier." The last effort of his pen was still pleading for the poor. It was a letter to the Commissioners for the Improvement of Kingstown, urging them to improve the dwellings of the poor of that town.

*On the state of the Kingstown poor.*

He had personally visited many of the worst parts of it, and found the cottages in want of sewerage and accommodations necessary to cleanliness, health and decency. He showed the Commissioners that they could make main drains, and could compel the owners to make house drains into these from the cottages, and even might obtain public money for building cottages. The inspections were made at various hours of the day and in the evening, and being carried on in the face of a new visitation of cholera, his family believed that he fell by disease caught in the discharge of his self-imposed public duty. While correcting the proof sheets of this publication, he was seized with illness, and carried from his study to his bed, and died in a few hours.[1]

But these publications of Mr. Haliday's, though they indicate his public spirit and humanity, were only the products of the spare moments of his life.

*Public offices filled by C. Haliday.*

His occupation as a merchant absorbed his day. He had his counting house and his clerks to attend to. He frequented

---

[1] The editing of this last work of Mr. Haliday's was undertaken and executed by Dr. Thomas M. Madden. It is entitled, "A Statistical Inquiry into the Sanitary Condition of Kingstown, by the late Charles Haliday, esq., M.R.I.A. Edited, with some preliminary observations on the connexion between the sanitary defects of Kingstown and the recent Epidemic Cholera, by Dr. Thomas More Madden, M.R.I.A. 8vo., Dublin, pp. 33. John E. Fowler, 1867.

the Corn Exchange; he was a Director of the Bank of Ireland, he was Honorary Secretary of the Chamber of Commerce, and a Member of the Ballast Board. In each employment he exhibited that energy and intelligence that were the characteristics of his life.

Often have I seen him at his counting-house, at Arran-quay, seated on a high stool amongst his clerks, carefully going over the large ledgers and other books, to see that they were duly and regularly posted up.

At ten o'clock he would be found in the Directors' room of the Bank of Ireland, attending to the business of that great establishment.

He gave great attention also to the business of the Chamber of Commerce, and on retiring from the office of Honorary Secretary of that Chamber, after a service of seventeen years, he was presented by that society with a testimonial in recognition of the great benefits he had rendered it.  Honorary Secretary of Chamber of Commerce.

He signalized his accession to the office by his energetic investigation into the right of the owner of the Skerries Lighthouse, off the coast of Anglesea, to levy tolls amounting to three thousand a year off the shipping frequenting the port of Dublin. It appeared that a charter or patent was granted by Queen Anne, authorising one William Trench to build a lighthouse on Skerries Rock, near Holyhead,[1] and to levy specified dues on all vessels passing by or near the rock; but as the patent was in many respects defective and never had (and probably never was intended to have) effect in Ireland, an attempt was made to do by an English statute what could not be done by an English patent, and the English Act of the third year of George II., cap. 36, enacted

---

[1] It was at this rock, and not at Skerries near Balbriggan, that on the 15th of December, 1619, the Viscount Thurles, father of the great Duke of Ormonde was wrecked on his voyage to Ireland, and drowned in company with the son of Lord Dunboyne. See Calendar of State Papers of King James I. (Ireland) 1615-1625. p. 270. Carte's Life of Ormonde. p. 1.

*The Skerries Light dues.*

that the dues granted by the patent should continue in force for ever, and that other dues should be paid by vessels trading to or from particular ports in Ireland. Under that Act, the then proprietor of the Lighthouse, Mr. Jones, was levying about £16,000 per annum, of which £3,000 per annum, part of the gross amount, was levied on the trade of Dublin, and was enforced from vessels that did not pass by, or near, or in sight of Skerries, whether loaded or in ballast, or sailing on any of the voyages mentioned in the Act; and in all cases fourfold as heavy, and in some eight times as heavy, as the sums charged by the Irish Lighthouse Board for any lighthouse on the coast of Ireland.

As these tolls were collected for the owner of the Skerries Lighthouse by the Collector of Customs at Dublin, who received a commission on the dues and would give no clearance unless they were paid, there was no escape, and resistance seemed hopeless. Masters of vessels from time to time made opposition, but the labour and expense always paralysed exertion, and after a brief period of struggle the extra tax was submitted to. Ship owners frequenting the Irish Channel also applied to the Trinity House Corporation of London; but the Trinity Brethren declined to interfere, on the ground that the Skerries Lighthouse was private property. The Chamber of Commerce however, in the year 1839, obtained the opinion of the Irish Law Officers, that no tolls whatever could be legally levied in Ireland by the proprietor of the Skerries Lighthouse, because at the establishment of the Legislative Independence of Ireland, in 1782, it was conceded that English Statutes did not bind Ireland, and therefore that the statute of third George II. was of no force, being an Act made in England, and thus the only warrant for these tolls failed. This opinion being transmitted to the Lords of the Treasury, they directed that the Collector of Customs should no longer assist in collecting the Skerries Lighthouse tolls.

But as the Trinity Board were, in the year 1841, about to

purchase the interest of the owner of the Skerries Lighthouse, and would then be able under another statute to fix Lighthouse tolls with the assent of the Privy Council, the Chamber of Commerce and the Directors of the Steamboat Companies combined and brought an action in the Queen's Bench, in the name of Mr. Boyce, a ship owner, against Mr. Jones, the Skerries Lighthouse owner, and obtained a verdict that the tolls were illegal. This verdict and judgment were obtained in the month of January, 1842, and since then all ships sailing to or from Dublin to the southward, all Irish coasting vessels, and all vessels in ballast are freed from this charge.[1] This contest began in the year 1836, and continued for six years, conducted principally by Mr. Haliday, until success finally crowned the efforts of the Chamber of Commerce.

So highly were Mr. Haliday's services appreciated by the Steamboat Companies that they presented him with a very costly and handsome piece of plate, with the following inscription:— *Recognition of his services about the Skerries Light dues.*

"Presented by the Directors of the City of Dublin, the British and Irish, and the Glasgow Steam Packet Companies, to Charles Haliday, esq., Honorary Secretary to Chamber of Commerce, in testimony of his eminent services and of the untiring zeal and ability successfully exerted by him in effecting the abolition of the unjust impost for many years levied under the name of the "Skerries Light Dues," operating injuriously and vexatiously on the coasting trade of Ireland, but most particularly on that of this Port.

"Dublin, 17th March, 1842."

Encouraged by their success in the case of the Skerries Lighthouse tolls, the Chamber of Commerce, in the year 1845, determined to resist the dues exacted by the Commissioners of the Ramsgate Harbour of Refuge on vessels merely passing that harbour on their voyages to any port in Ireland. This charge (which was two pence per ton) was enforced at the Custom Houses in Ireland, and clearances were refused to ships until the amount was paid. It

---

[1] These particulars have been obtained from the yearly Reports of the Chamber of Commerce, drawn up by Mr. Haliday.

was levied under a local Act of 32nd George III. cap. 97, and so little public was it, that though all the trade of Ireland was taxed under it, not a copy of the Act was to be found in any collection of the statutes, nor was any copy of it to be found (said the Report of the Chamber of Commerce) in the Law Library of the Four Courts, or of the Inns of Court. On a case submitted to the Law Officers of the Crown in Ireland, they gave their opinion that the exaction was illegal on the same grounds as that of the Skerries Lighthouse dues, namely as being claimed to be levied in Ireland under an English statute made in 1792, at a time when these statutes did not bind Ireland; and having submitted this opinion to the Ramsgate Harbour Commissioners, the Chambers were in hopes that they would desist; but they persisted and submitted a case on their own behalf to the Attorney- and Solicitor-General of England. The case was framed that the answers might mislead; for one of the queries was, " Whether the Commissioners might appoint collectors in Ireland ?" and the answer was that they might; and so they might (says the Chamber of Commerce in their report) appoint collectors in any part of Europe. But a very different question was whether these collectors or others could go on board vessels to distrain or detain them for these dues. Another of their queries was, " Whether they could sue in the Irish Law Courts for tolls due to them ?" It was answered that they might; so (say the Chamber of Commerce) could any one else, provided they could prove a debt legally due.

The Chamber then applied to the Attorney-General of England, and having obtained his opinion, that these dues were illegal, they forwarded the case and opinion to the Ramsgate Harbour Commissioners. These Commissioners then yielded; and by the letter of their Secretary, dated 31st March, 1846, informed the Chamber of Commerce that they had given orders to their collectors at the several ports in Ireland in future not to demand dues from vessels trading to and from Ireland, and not touching at any British ports nor passing through or being detained in the Downs. Thus was the Chamber of Commerce enabled to relieve the trade of Dublin and of Ireland from another of those exactions to which it had been long subjected, "exactions which, though separately they might not be of a large amount (continues the Report), were in the aggregate a heavy burden on the foreign trade of Ireland, and particularly objectionable in this instance, as the Legislature unquestionably did not intend that this tax should be levied in Ireland for the maintenance of an English harbour."

In these Reports will be found Mr. Haliday's careful statement of the point, forcibly put, and supported by convincing evidence, showing a great amount of labour and an equal amount of intelligence. When he retired from the office of Honorary Secretary to the Chamber, he received a handsome present of silver plate, with the following inscription: *Testimonials of his conduct as Secretary of Chamber of Commerce.*

The Merchants of Dublin to Charles Haliday, Esq.

In testimony of their high sense of his eminent public services during the seventeen years in which he filled the office of Honorary Secretary to the Chamber of Commerce.

| | |
|---|---|
| Sir T. O'Brien, Bart, Lord Mayor. | Wm. Murphy. |
| Arthur Guinness. | James Murphy. |
| Edward Atkinson. | George M'Bride. |
| J. C. Bacon. | John M'Donnell. |
| John Martin. | Sir Edward M'Donnell. |
| Alex. Boyle. | Denis Moylan. |
| Thomas Bewley. | Valentine O'Brien O'Connor. |
| Joseph Boyce. | Wm. H. Pim. |
| Peter Brophy. | John Power. |
| Robert Callwell. | Sir James Power. |
| Francis Codd. | Patrick Reid. |
| Thomas Crosthwaite. | George Roe. |
| Leland Crosthwaite. | Philip Meadows Taylor. |
| Sir John Ennis, Bart. | Thomas Wilson. |
| John English. | Francis E. Codd. |
| John Darcy. | T. L. Kelly. |
| James Fagan. | J. B. Kennedy. |
| James Ferrier. | Jonathan Pim. |
| James Foxall. | Alex. Parker. |
| Benjm. Lee Guinness. | George Pim. |
| Sir John Kingston James, Bart. | H. Thompson. |
| Thomas Hutton. | William Digges LaTouche. |

*Losses of Merchants by Custom House fire in 1833.*

So sensible indeed were the mercantile community of Dublin of his intelligence, that in public inquiries they were willing and anxious that he should be one of their spokesmen. He was thus selected to solicit the claims of the merchants of Dublin to compensation from the Treasury for the goods lost by the great fire in 1833, when a great part of the Custom House stores were burnt down. The stores had been let by the Government, but as the lessee was incapable of paying damages it was a matter of the utmost moment to establish the liability of the Government. The lawyer selected to advocate the case of the merchants, was O'Connell, and Mr. Haliday and another were to be present to supply him with information at the hearing of the cause.

*O'Connell's dexterity.*

In after years Mr. Haliday would give with much zest an instance of O'Connell's dexterity. Having forgotten the line he ought to have taken about one branch of the case, he used an argument destructive of the cause. Haliday was overwhelmed, but could not interrupt, when fortunately the tribunal adjourned for a few minutes, and O'Connell was then informed of his mistake. On returning, he at once with the utmost coolness began "When we left off, I was engaged in showing what might be said by my adversaries ; but "——and then he answered his own argument and undid the effect.

*Currency inquiry in 1857.*

In 1857 and 1858 there was a Committee of the House of Commons appointed to inquire concerning the operation of the Bank Acts of Scotland and Ireland of 1845, and the causes of the late commercial distress, and to investigate how far it had been affected by the laws for regulating the issue of bank notes payable on demand. In view of this inquiry, the directors of the Bank of Ireland elected Mr. Haliday to the office of Governor of the Bank, that he might appear before the Committee of Inquiry with more dignity and authority. He underwent a long examination, and acquitted himself with great credit, the committee being evidently much impressed with the extent and accuracy of his knowledge, not merely of the concerns of the Bank, but of currency and trade. I may here mention that he told me on one occasion that the object of Sir Robert Peel's Bank Act (in his opinion) making gold the common currency, was that the Government, in case of a foreign war, might find it in the country, and keep it for Government use by an Act rendering paper notes a good tender, instead of having to buy it abroad at heavy cost.

But, whilst Mr. Haliday paid such close attention to his own affairs and to all those public institutions he was connected with, there was one which interested him beyond all others and that was the Ballast Board, afterwards named the Corporation for Preserving and Improving the Port of Dublin. The history of this Corporation will be found set forth in detail in Charles Haliday's Essay, entitled, Observations Explanatory of Sir Bernard de Gomme's Map, showing the state of the Harbour and River at Dublin in the year 1673. Ballast Board

Mr. Haliday became a member of this Board in the year 1833, and for thirty years and upwards, that is to say till the time of his death in 1866, he constantly attended the meetings of the Board and interested himself in all that concerned it.

He made himself familiar with the many Acts of Parliament regulating its proceedings, and as he was certainly one of the best instructed members of the Board, his advice was much sought for and regarded. In the year 1848, with the consent of the Board, he undertook the defence of their jurisdiction over the lighthouses of Ireland, against the report made by Captain Washington, R.N., one of the Tidal Harbour Commissioners, which recommended that the management of the Irish lighthouses and their funds should be transferred to a central board to be established in London. Captain Washington in his report to the Harbour Department of the Admiralty, dated 10th of November, 1847, charged the Ballast Board with two omissions ; one, that they had failed to improve attacked by Tidal Harbour Commissioners.

the quays and piers and similar works within harbours; the other, the neglect to provide Lights on the south coast of Ireland. The defence of the Board was made by Mr. Haliday in a pamphlet in the form of a letter, as from Henry Vereker, Secretary of the Ballast Board, to Sir William Somerville, Bart., then Secretary of State for Ireland.[1]

*His pamphlet in defence.*

To Captain Washington's first complaint there was this ready answer, that the Board were not authorized to expend lighthouse funds on constructing harbour works; the powers of the Board being confined to erecting and maintaining lighthouses, beacons, and buoys.

As to the second, the want of lights on the south and south-west coast of Ireland, Mr. Haliday showed that since 1810, when the Irish Lighthouse Board was transferred to the Ballast Board, sixty lighthouses and lightships had been established, and twelve more were in progress, and all this without increasing the light dues levied, without any grant of public money; whilst the Board had at the same time made a reduction of twenty per cent. on the light dues, which even previously were lower than those of either England or Scotland, and further had commenced an accumulation (then amounting to £100,000) which if permitted to increase and act as a sinking fund, would not only be sufficient to erect all the lighthouses required in future, but would yield £4,000 a year, and ultimately relieve all vessels from any charge of maintaining the lighthouses on the coasts and harbours of Ireland.

Mr. Haliday in this pamphlet also complained much of the inaccuracy of a printed map appended to Captain Washington's report, lithographed and coloured for the

---

[1] Letter to the Right Honorable Sir William Somerville, Bart. M.P., from the Corporation for Preserving and Improving the Port of Dublin, with Observations on the Report of Captain Washington, R.N., to the Harbour Department of the Admiralty on the State of the Harbours and Lighthouses on the south and south-west of Ireland. 8vo. Dublin pp. 37. P. D. Hardy and Sons, 1849.

purpose of exhibiting the "region of darkness," as Mr. Haliday ironically calls it, through the want of lighthouses on the south-west coast. And he answered it admirably by a similar map, but correctly coloured, showing every lighthouse and the range of its light, and how fully they served their purpose.

"Honest Tom Steele," O'Connell's Head Pacificator, a learned man in spite of his strange political opinions and conduct, educated at Cambridge, a member also, as he subscribes himself, of the Chamber of Commerce, bore testimony to the ability displayed in this pamphlet, in a letter to the public press, dated 6th January, 1847. "The letter of Mr. Vereker," says Mr. Steele, "is in my opinion a most triumphant refutation, written with exquisite good taste and good temper, of the report of the Commission on the state of the port of Dublin and the lighthouse system of Ireland. I do not envy (he continues) Captain Washington, 'Examining Officer of the Commission,' the bitter castigation he has quietly received in the politest terms from the Secretary of the Ballast Board. This Captain Washington may be a 'General Washington' of examining officers, but it would do him no harm if he could infuse into himself a little of the generous candour of Sir James Dombrain, R.N., or of Captain Beechy, R.N." These were both public officers who had borne testimony to the great merits of the Ballast Board.

It was this peculiar interest about the port of Dublin shown by Mr. Haliday, added to the extensive knowledge he had acquired, concerning all that related to it in its then state, that pointed him out to his brother members of the Ballast Board as the fittest person to write the history of the port. They desired to show what changes had been affected under the direction of the Board in the bed of the river and in the harbour, by deepening and straightening the bed of the Liffey and by lowering the bar. In this view it was necessary to know the early state of the river and harbour, and they considered that there was no one who

*Engages to write a history of the port of Dublin.*

could investigate it with the energy and sagacity of Mr. Haliday.

They accordingly requested him, about the year 1850, to undertake the task. He joyfully acceded to their request. When his brother directors of the Ballast Board engaged him to undertake a history of the port, they probably thought that his previous study of the various Parliamentary enactments and inquiries, added to the information to be supplied by their own records or servants, would render this a not very laborious undertaking to one of his energetic habits. If such was their impression they little foresaw to what extensive inquiries and searches into antiquity the subject would lead him. The first notice the public had of the extent of his studies was his Essay on "The Ancient Name of Dublin," read at the Royal Irish Academy in 1854, and printed in the appendix to the present volume. And his mode of treating this small branch of his subject gives a good idea of the method he employed throughout his study concerning the port and harbour of Dublin.

The port of Dublin extended inland to the first bridge. This was in ancient times at Church-street, just above the present Four Courts, and the first Custom house was near it, at the foot of Winetavern-street leading up Christ Church Cathedral hill.

<small>Bridge of the Ostmen.</small> In the published histories of Ireland he found it almost invariably stated that the first bridge at Dublin was built by King John, and his Charter of the 3rd of July, 1215, was cited in proof of that statement; and as William of Worcester states that in the same year King John built the first bridge at Bristol (having shortly before sent to France for Isenbert the architect to construct the first stone bridge at London) his desire for bridge-building had led to the building of the bridge at Dublin, the chief seat of his lordship of Ireland, and the seat of his Bristol colony. But Mr. Haliday, not content to rely on printed authorities went to the Tower of London to examine the original rolls, and to the Corporation

of Dublin for their muniments, and on referring to these, as well as to the register of Thomas Court Abbey in his own possession, he clearly showed that King John not merely granted to his citizens of Dublin liberty to build a bridge over the Liffey wherever they would, but that they might take down the other bridge formerly made if they found it to their advantage to do so. It was thus evident that there was a bridge at Dublin, prior to the Charter of 1215. By other evidence he showed that this bridge was standing in A.D. 1177, and even at an earlier date. Examining the earliest grants he found this old bridge described in them as the Bridge of the Ostmen, and gave grounds for presuming that it was built by them.

It might perhaps be thought he had done enough in tracing the erection of this bridge to the Ostmen or Scandinavian occupants of Dublin. But as long as there was any possibility of further evidence Mr. Haliday was not content to rest. He wished for its earlier history. He had therefore recourse to the native Irish records, and established for it a much higher antiquity.

In these he found evidence that the name given by the Irish to this bridge at Dublin was Droichet Dubhgall.

Thus in the nearly contemporary history of the battle of Clontarf fought in A.D. 1014, where the Irish were victorious, after a great slaughter of the flying Danes, it is stated that only nine of them escaped, and it is added, that the household of Seigne O'Kelly followed these and slew them at the head of the bridge of Ath-Cliath, that is Dubhgall's Bridge," Dubhgall being probably as Mr. Haliday says, the name given by the Irish to the Danish founder of the bridge.

<small>Droichet Dubhgall.</small>

Dubhgall (literally "black stranger"), was a name, says Mr. Haliday, the Irish frequently gave to their Danish invaders. It was thus they called one of the Danish chieftains slain in the battle of Clontarf. This is the earliest direct reference to be found concerning this Droichet Dubhgall or Dublin bridge. But between the settling of the Danes at Dublin and A.D. 1014 (the date of the battle of Clontarf), there is an interval of about one hundred and fifty years. And Mr. Haliday shows the great probability that the Danes must in this interval have erected a regular bridge at Dublin, for they had subjugated England and held frequent intercourse with it. Godfred II., king of Dublin in A.D. 922, was also king of Northumberland. They must therefore have been familiar with the bridges there. For although (says Mr. Haliday) it may be doubtful if the Romans ever erected a stone bridge in Britain, it is certain they erected many of wood, the material most commonly used until the close of the twelfth century when St. Benedict founded his order of Pontifices, or stone bridge builders.

<small>Bally-ath-Cliath, or the Hurdleford.</small> Having thus assigned to the Danes the erecting of this old bridge he proceeds to prove that before ever the Danes had a bridge here, the Irish had a fixed passage over the Liffey at the very same place. The ancient name of Dublin was Bally-ath-Cliath, pronounced Bally-a-clay, the town of the Hurdleford.

Mr. Haliday exposes the mistakes of Stanihurst, Camden, and others who thought that this meant that Dublin was built upon hurdles, by reason of the soft, boggy site requiring hurdles for the foundation of the houses. And then shows the probability that the Hurdleford referred to was a means of passing the Liffey at this spot. Dublin in his opinion was never a city or place of note until the time of the Danes. And this may account for the fact that between the close of the tenth century and the commencement of the fifth century there are no notices of a bridge here. But for the probability that there was one, he relies upon the various proofs in the "Annals of the Four Masters," that bridges over small rivers in Ireland were common, and that a king of Ulster was celebrated for bridge-building in A.D. 739. Even without these direct proofs of their knowledge of bridges they must have known of them through their travel abroad, as it was within this period that the Irish were noted as missionaries of religion throughout Europe, then full of Roman structures. And as from Ireland ecclesiastics travelled to teach, so to it European scholars came to learn. "We may therefore rest assured," he concludes, "that whatever of art or science was then known elsewhere was not unknown in Ireland."[1]

[1] Proofs of these travels and knowledge are found in the work of Dicuil (Recherches Géographiques et Critiques sur le livre, "De mensura orbis terræ," composé en Irlande au commencement du neuvième siecle, par Dicuil, suivies du texte restitué, par A. Letronne. Paris. 8vo. 1814"). Dicuil completed his work as he specifically tells us in A.D. 825. For likening himself after this labour to the ox who had been in the plough, but had rest at night, he says:

"Post octingentos viginti quinque peraetos,
Summi annos Domini . . .
Nocte bobus requies largitur fine laboris,"

in other words, "After the year of our Lord 825 had been completed, the ox at night was allowed to rest from his labours." From Dicuil one obtains a better notion than from other works of the learning and study pursued in the Monasteries of Ireland in the ninth century when the peace that this island alone in all Europe enjoyed, having escaped both Roman conquest and the irruption of the barbarians, was interrupted by the descents of the Northern sea-rovers on our shores. Dicuil had studied Priscian and "after composing," as he says, "a treatise on the ten grammatical arts . . . . determined to follow it with a book on the measure of the [Roman] world, as measured by the Commissioners employed by the Emperor Theodosius for that purpose."

He deplores, however, the errors of the manuscript, and says, "I shall correct the text where faulty as best I can, and where I cannot I shall leave vacant spaces." He illustrates his work by extracts concerning the countries treated of, from Pliny, Solinus, Pomponius, Mela, Orosius, Isidore of Seville, and Priscian, from which we may see the libraries of these monasteries were well furnished with manuscripts. But he gives in addition the more curious information derived in conversation from Irish monks who had travelled to Egypt and Palestine, to Iceland and the Faroe Islands.

Thus Dicuil, when treating of the Nile, and the account given of it by the ancients, adds the following curious information:—

"Although we nowhere find it stated," he says, "in the books of any author that part of the Nile flows into the Red Sea, yet Brother Fidelis, in my presence, told my master, Abbot Suiblhne (and it is

*d*

Thus they had the power to erect a structure for crossing the Liffey if there was any road requiring it at this point. And that there was such a road is curiously proved.

*The five Slighes.*

" In our oldest manuscripts it is stated," says Mr. Haliday, "that in the first century Ireland was intersected by five great roads, leading from the different provinces, or petty kingdoms, to the seat of supreme royalty at Tara."

to him, under God, I owe it if I have made any progress in learning), that some clerks and laymen from Ireland, going to Jerusalem to worship there, sailed to the Nile, and embarking on that river they came, after a long voyage, to the seven granaries of S. Joseph" (being the name in the middle ages of the Pyramids of Gizeh and Sakkara). "From a distance they looked like mountains. The same brother," continues Dicuil, "who gave this account to Fidelis measured one side of one of the granaries from angle to angle, and found it to measure 400 feet.

"Then, embarking on the Nile, they sailed to the entrance of the Red Sea. It is but a short distance across from that port to the eastern shore to where Moses passed. The same monk who measured the granary wished to go by sea to the port where Moses entered with his people that he might see the tracks of Pharaoh's chariot wheels, but the sailors refused."

At a later part of his work he announces a discovery he had made confirming the truth of these travellers' story. "'To-day," says Dicuil, "I have found stated in the 'Cosmography,' compiled when Julius Cæsar and Anthony were Consuls, that part of the Nile issues

into the Red Sea at the city of Clysma and the Camp of Moses."

Monsieur Letronne enlarges on the value of this work of Dicuil's, to prove that the canal made 500 years before the Christian era by some of the Pharaohs, between Babylon (Old Cairo) and Clysma (Suez), had not only been cleared by Hadrian after it had silted up since its reopening by Ptolemy Philadelphus 300 years before, but that it was again opened and had been sailed down by Brother Fidelis. It had been doubted if Hadrian cleared it, but Lucian (says Letronne) speaks of a young man who had gone by water from Alexandria to Clysma, and Lucian was contemporary with Hadrian, and had held an important office in Egypt.

This canal was actively used in the fifth century, and was open at the commencement of the sixth, but then silted up. Gregory, of Tours A.D. 590, says Letronne, who had, no doubt, met pilgrims from Egypt and the Holy Land, speaks of a place where the Nile discharges into the Red Sea. In A.D. 640 the Arabs conquered Egypt, and a famine occurring in Arabia, Amrou, who commanded in Egypt cleared out the canal, and in six months, in order to send grain to Arabia, says

During the Ordnance Survey of Ireland the remains of Tara were laid down according to accurate measurement on a map. While the Royal Engineers were employed in the field, Dr. Petrie and Dr. O'Donovan, who were then attached to the Survey, made a careful search in all ancient manuscripts for such evidence as might tend to identify or illustrate the existing vestiges of Tara.

The result proved that descriptions previously regarded as mere bardic fictions were perfectly accurate.

In the early manuscripts referred to by Mr. Haliday concerning the five great roads, leading from different provinces, or petty kingdoms, to the seat of supreme royalty at Tara, the 'Slighe' or road called 'the Sligh Cualann,' was the one traced with the greatest apparent certainty by the Ordnance Survey. It led by way of Ratoath and Dublin, into Cualann, a district extending from Dalkey southwards and westwards, part of which, including Powerscourt, is designated in Anglo-Norman records as Fercullen, or the territory of the men of Cualann. This road must have crossed the Liffey and that it did so near Dublin is confirmed by the fact that the passage across the river there

*Sligh Cualann.*

an Arabian author, vessels sailed from the Nile to the Red Sea. But in A.D. 767 a revolt occurred at Mecca and Medina, and it was closed again to hinder the rebels from getting supplies from Egypt. There is no evidence that it was ever opened again, and Monsieur Letronne shows how possible it was for these Irish monks to have travelled down it between A.D. 762 and 765.

But Fidelis was not the only travelled Irish ecclesiastic. It was a common thing for pilgrims from the latter end of the fourth century, says Letronne, to visit Jerusalem, and to take Egypt in their way, to

see the solitary hermits in the Thebaid and the "granaries of Joseph," and the tracks of Pharaoh's chariots in the Red Sea. In their travels, therefore, as Mr. Haliday suggests, they must have seen temples and bridges, and the masterpieces of Roman architects.

Thus the Irish had the knowledge and power to erect a structure for crossing the Liffey if there was any road requiring it at this point, and that there was such a road is curiously proved both by record, and the still existing remains of this road.

is frequently termed Ath-Cliath-Cualann. To carry this roadway across the Liffey unless by a bridge or structure of some kind raised above ordinary highwater mark was impossible, and such a structure formed of timber or hurdles, the only material then used for that purpose was doubtless that which in the figurative language of the time was termed an Ath-Cliath or ford of hurdles.

Mr. Haliday having thus traced the history of Dublin bridge through all the English and Irish sources it now struck him that perhaps something might be learned of it from the Scandinavian records.

The bridge had been built by the Ostmen. He had found a reference to it in the old Irish manuscript called the "Wars of the Gaëdhill and the Gaill" (or the Danes and the Irish), in connexion with the battle of Clontarf, furnished him by his friend the Rev. Dr. Todd, who was then engaged in editing this manuscript. Much more might be contained in the Scandinavian records. He sent therefore to London, Paris, and Copenhagen, and purchased every Scandinavian historical work that he could hear of as likely to throw light on the subject of his study.

*Dublin as the capital of the Ostmen.*

The history of the Ostmen or Scandinavians in Ireland had hitherto been studied through Irish sources.

The ravages of the Danes were carefully recorded in the Irish Annals. But no one almost had thought of having recourse to Scandinavian sources.

By means of these a new world was opened to his view. Dublin, the chief object of his studies, assumed a new importance. It was always known to have been founded by a Scandinavian king, and to have been the chief place of Scandinavian power in Ireland. But why Dublin, with its little river Liffey issuing into the Bay through a waste of land, should have been preferred by the Scandinavians as their capital, to Cork, Waterford, or Limerick, all Scandinavian cities, with noble harbours, does not at first view appear. But when their settlements in

Scotland and England are kept in view, Dublin will be seen to have held a very central and convenient position for the Scandinavians.

About the time when Dublin was founded by Aulaf the White, in A.D. 852, the Scandinavians held not only Sutherlandshire and Caithness on the mainland, but also all the northern and western islands of Scotland ; as well as Man.

In England they held all north of the Humber.

For a maritime people like the Scandinavians, Dublin was thus central and accessible.

It therefore naturally became a place of great importance during the sway of the Scandinavians.

But besides the natural importance of Dublin in Scandinavian history, it so happens that all early Scandinavian history is derived from Iceland, and Iceland being largely colonized from Dublin, it received in these histories its due share of notice, as will be found in Mr. Haliday's references to Scandinavian literature.

It was in the year 874 that Iceland began to be colonized by the Norsemen, and they have recorded that they found on landing there that it had been previously inhabited by Irish Christians, called Papæ, who had left behind them "Irish books, bells, and crosiers." Dicuil, in his work already cited, when treating of Thule (Iceland), says, that at midsummer there is scarcely any night there and at the winter solstice scarcely any day; and in proof of this statement adds :— *[margin: Iceland first inhabited by Irish hermits.]*

"It is now thirty years since I was told by some Irish ecclesiastics who had dwelt in that island from the 1st of February to the 1st of August, that the sun scarcely sets there in summer, but always leaves, even at midnight, light enough for one to do any ordinary business, such as to pick lice, for instance, from one's shirt, and this as well as in full daylight" (*pediculos de camisiâ abstrahere tanquam in presentiâ solis*).

These ecclesiastics who gave this account to Dicuil were probably visitors to anchorites already settled in Iceland, for a retreat to deserts in search of religious solitude and as an escape from the world, after the manner of the monks of the Thebaïd, seems to have been a common custom in the early ages in Ireland.

It was thus they made hermitages in the rocky islet of Seelig Michil (Skelig rock) lying in the Atlantic some miles off the coast of Kerry, in the isle of Inishmurry off the coast of Sligo, in the island of Cape Clear off the coast of Cork, and many others. They also sought for desert retreats on the mainland.

Hence the names so common in Irish topography of Desert-Martin, Desert-Creat, Desert-Serges, &c.

*Irish hermits in the Faroe and Shetland isles.*

Thus, too, Cormac, pupil of Adamnan, in the 7th century, sailed three several times, once for fourteen summer days and nights in search of some such desert retreat in the Northern Ocean. And when Dicuil comes to treat of islands in the British Ocean he says:—"There are islands in this ocean distant two long days and nights voyage from the northern islands of Britain;" (the latter, the Shetland and Orkney Isles); adding—"A faithworthy ecclesiastic told me that he reached one of them in a two-benched (perhaps in a four-oared) boat in two summer days and one night." These were plainly the Faroe Isles, lying half-way between the Orkneys and Iceland. He further adds—"some of these islands are very small and separated from one another by narrow friths. Within one hundred years they were inhabited by hermits who had sailed thither from Ireland (*ex nostra Scotia*). But they are now deserted, because of the Norwegian pirates, and are swarming with sheep and sea-fowl." It is probable therefore that it was by similar religious hermits that Iceland was once inhabited, and afterwards deserted for the same reason as were the Faroe Islands.

Having regard, then, to the religious ideas of that remote age, there was an object to be obtained by Irish ecclesiastics in seeking an abode in Iceland; but what, it may be asked, could induce Norwegians to settle in that inhospitable region, at the utmost verge of the world, even though the volcano of Hecla had not yet burst forth, and forests and grass then grew where the land is now covered with lava or ashes.[1]

It was in search of liberty. It was the same motive in one sense, as that which took the Pilgrim Fathers to America. But it was not religious liberty they sought, but their ancient liberties, destroyed or infringed by Harold Fair Hair of Norway, who seems to have been led by the example of Charlemagne to desire to make himself sole King of Norway, and to reduce the other chiefs to the state of vassals. This they resented and resisted, till Harold obtained a complete victory over them at the battle of Hafursfiord, A.D., 872. *Early Scandinavian exodus to the Orkneys*

They then in disgust (or many of them) left Norway and sought free abodes.

But long before the year 872 the Scandinavians had colonies and settlements in the Orkneys and Shetland Isles, and in the Hebrides.

In 795 they had from these regions begun their depredations in Ireland, and continued them with intermissions for near one hundred years. So that the fugitives from Norway, on account of Harold Harfagre's despotism, were only an addition (and a late one) to the bands of these sea rovers.

Amongst those who left their native country disliking the new order of things, were probably the two first settlers in Iceland named Ingolf and Leif who settled there in A.D. 874.

The island had been seen and visited a few years before. The first who discovered Iceland was Gardar, a Swede. He *Scandinavians reach Iceland.*

---

[1] It burst forth on 24th of June, A.D. 1000, celebrated for the reception of Christianity by Iceland, and was thought by some to signify Thor's anger at being deposed. "Burnt Nial," or the Story of Life in Iceland at the end of the Tenth Century, from the Icelandic Nial's Saga, preface, p. xci., and n. *Ibid.* By George Webb Dasent, D.C.L. Demy 8vo; 2 vols.; Edinburgh, 1861.

sailed round it and found it to be an island. This was in A.D. 864. Returning to Norway, he praised the island, which from him was called Gardar's Island. "At that time the land between the mountains and the shores was a wood."[1]

The next who went to look for Gardar's Isle was Floki. In the ship with him was a Norwegian from the Hebrides. He brought with him three ravens. The first being let go came back to the ship, also the second, but the third flew from the prow without returning, and Floki and his company following in the same direction they found the land.

The spring was a late one, and Floki going up a high mountain and seeing the sea to the northward all covered with ice he named the island "Iceland," the name which it has since retained.[2]

*Scandinavians settle in Iceland.* The next to look for Iceland were two friends, sworn brothers, named Ingolf and Leif, and they resolved to sell their lands in Norway and seek the land discovered by Raven Floki, "or Floki of the ravens." Getting to sea, they reached Iceland; and returning to Norway the following summer Ingolf sold his lands in order to settle in Iceland; but Leif took to sea-roving and piracy, and landing in Ireland and entering a great dark subterranean dwelling could see nothing till he caught sight of the glitter of a sword. It was in the hand of a man who had fled thither from Leif, through terror. Leif killed the man and took and carried off the sword and many precious things. Hence Leif got the name of Hjörleif, or "Leif of the Sword," for the sword was one of extraordinary value. During this summer Leif took much other booty in the western parts, and there he also took ten Irishmen as servants or slaves, the chief of them being named Dufthack.

[1] Hist. Olavi Tryggvii filii, Pars Prior, cap. 114, Vol. I. "Scripta Historica Islandorum," translated from the original into Latin, under the care of the Royal Society of Northern Antiquaries, by Sweinbiörn Egilsson. XII. volumes; 12mo; Copenhagen, 1822.

[2] *Ibid*, cap. 115.

Then Hjörleif returned to Norway, and there met Ingolf, and the following spring they set sail thence for Iceland, Hjörleif with his captives, and Ingolf with his stock.[1]

We here see already, at the very first peopling of Iceland, that it had a mixture of Irish as well as Scandinavians, though the first Irish were captives who had been made serfs. But soon there came thither from Ireland many of more distinguished rank of both nations. After King Aulaf's death, Queen Auda, his widow, retired thither.[2]

After his decease (says also Dr. Gudbrand Vigfusson) and the death of their son, Thorstein, slain in what appears to have been a rising of the Irish against their conquerors, she left Ireland taking with her one grandson and six granddaughters, marrying one after another on her journey.

She was followed by a large company of kinsfolk, friends, and dependants, Norse and Irish. After staying sometime at the Faroe Islands on her way she went to Iceland.[3] Her brothers, Biorn Austman and Helgi Beola,

*Mixture of Irish and Scandinavians in Iceland.*

---

[1] *Ibid*, cap. 116. Ingolf and Leif were the two first settlers. In the same chapter it is said that their settlement took place seven years after they first went in search of Iceland, in the thirteenth year of the reign of Harold Fairhair, and two years after the battle of Harfursfiord, four years after the killing of Edmund, Saint and King of England, and in the year of our Lord 874. The cause of Hjörleif's being murdered by his Irish servants was this:—The first spring, he ordered these men to draw his plough, though he had an ox, and this they were to do while he and his family were setting up a house. On Dufthack's advice, he and his Irish comrades killed the ox, and sent word to Hjörleif that a bear had killed it. Hjörleif and his men went here and there through the wood looking for the bear, and were all easily killed while dispersed. The Irishmen then carried off the wives and goods of those they had murdered to some small islands to the south. Ingolf afterwards finding all out, surprised them at supper, and slew all of them, except those that were killed by falling down precipices trying to escape. Hence these islands are called the Westmen's Islands.

[2] *Ibid*, Book II., chapter III.

[3] Sturlunga Saga, including the Islendinga Saga of Law-man. Sturla Thordson with prolegomena, pp. xix, xx. Edited by Dr. Gudbrand Vigfusson. Clarendon Press, Oxford, 1878.

with her brother-in-law, Helgi Magri, had previously settled there, says Mr. Haliday,

Nearly all the grandchildren of Aulaf and Auda also settled in Iceland and established large families there. Olaf Feilan, son of Thorstein the Red, married Asdisa Barcysku, daughter of Konal. Their son, Thordas Geller, became one of the most distinguished of the Icelanders; and their daughter Thora having married Thorstein, became the mother of Thorgrim, whose son was Snorri, the celebrated lag-man and priest.[1] Thorskabitr son of Thorolf Mostrars-kegg (the priest and founder of the first Pagan temple in the colony). From this mighty kindred of Queen Auda (continues Dr. Vigfusson) sprang the most distinguished Icelandic families,[2] and he attributes to the connexion of Iceland with Ireland an Irish influence over the character of their literature.

<small>Irish influence on Icelandic literature.</small> The Icelandic bards and saga makers, or professional oral chroniclers, were men who had dwelt for at least one generation among a Keltic population, and had felt the influence which an old and strongly marked civilization invariably exercises upon those brought under it. To this intercourse with the Irish he attributes the fine artistic spirit manifested in their sagas. And he remarks that it is precisely with the west of the island, the classic land of Icelandic letters, that the greatest proportion of these bards and chroniclers is found. Irish names were borne, he says, by some of the foremost characters of the heroic age in Iceland, especially the poets, of whom it was also remarked that most of them were dark men.[3]

Now, whatever may have been the influence of Ireland upon the literature of Iceland, this literature is perhaps the most wonderful in Europe. For is it not marvellous that in this remote island without the aid of writing, the history of the Scandinavian nations should have been preserved?

---

[1] Book II., chapter III., p. 193.     [3] *Ibid*, p.
[2] Sturlunga Saga. *Ibid*.

It was not until the twelfth century that they made use of written characters and surprised the world with the beauty and accuracy of their sagas.

Critics of the most competent taste have praised their beauty; their truth and accuracy is confirmed by contemporary chronicles of Ireland, England, and Wales. *Songs and Sagas of Iceland.*

Before the introduction of writing into their original country, or into the island of their adoption, the settlers carried with them thither the songs or rhymes which contained the history of their country. For at first, in the days before writing, everything was necessarily in rhyme, as there was no other way of recording the smallest history, memory without such aid being too treacherous.

Such was the literature of the rhapsodists of ancient Greece, and thus were recorded the genealogies of the gods, and even precepts of morality by Hesiod, and thus was preserved the history of the early Greeks by Homer. After their settlement in Iceland the Norsemen, their sons and descendants, brought thither fresh news of the old country, acquired in their yearly voyages to Norway as traders or otherwise.[1] These they put into sagas or tales; or the scalds, the professional oral chroniclers, recited them at banquets and public meetings, interspersing in their recitals fragments of ancient verse to adorn and enliven them, a practice they probably learned in Ireland. For it will be seen how regularly this was the Irish practice by turning to the Annals of the Four Masters, or to the Wars of the Gaedhil with the Gaill.

But having learned so much from their intercourse with the Irish, it may seem strange that they did not adopt the practice of writing, which had been in use in Ireland from the introduction there of the Roman alphabet by Saint Patrick (A.D. 450). For that there was no use of writing in Iceland, or even of an alphabet, is an admitted fact by all

---

[1] See Series Dynastarum et Regum Daniæ, &c., per Thormodum Torfœum, Liber I., cap. 6. De historiarum Islandicarm fundamentis ac authoritate, pp. 49-61; 4to, Havniæ, 1702.

historians. A few Runes for inscriptions on monumental stones, or on the margin of shields, or for epitaphs, is all that can be alleged by the most zealous contenders for early letters, and Torfœus shows that Adam of Bremen, and Saxo Grammaticus had nothing to rely on but the Icelandic sagas,[1] and that they are found to be mistaken whenever they go beyond them.

He ridicules, as false and impudent, Saxo's allegations that he got some of his materials from Runes on rocks, for Torfœus says, that they can scarce be read and that they supply no knowledge, and quotes Bartholinus (De antiquitatibus Danicis) as being of the same opinion.[2]

Ari, the historian (the Herodotus or father of Scandinavian history), was born A.D. 1067, and died A.D. 1148. He sprang from Queen Auda and Auláf, the White King of the Ostmen of Dublin, from whom he was eighth in descent. He was the first who wrote in the Norse tongue histories relating to his own times and the ancient history of the Scandinavians. All preceding histories were sagas or oral recitations. And the date of Ari's writing was about A.D. 1110, and not later than A.D. 1120.[3]

The first step taken others soon followed in Ari's steps. Saga after saga was reduced to writing, and before the year 1200 it is reckoned that all the pieces of that composition which relate to the history of the Icelanders (and of Scandinavia) previous to the introduction of Christianity, had passed from the oral to the written shape.[4]

*Introduction of writing into Iceland.* With the change of faith and conversion of the Icelanders to Christianity, continues Sir George Webb Dasent, came writing, and the materials for writing about the year 1000. With the Roman alphabet too came not only a readier means of recording thoughts, but also a class of men who were wont thus to express them. "The Norseman's Life" he

---

[1] Chap. vii., De vetustissimarum rerum Danicarum Scriptorum auctoritate et fundamentis.
[2] *Ibid.*, cap. 7.
[3] Sturlunga Saga, pp. xxviii.
[4] Burnt Nial, preface, pp. x–xii.

adds, called upon him for acts rather than words. Even when acting as priest his memory was only burdened with a few solemn forms of words taken in the temples, and some short prayers and toasts recited and uttered at sacrifices and feasts. But the Christian monk was by the very nature of his services and by the solitude of his cell thrown into fellowship with letters.[1]

It thus appears clearly that whilst the Norsemen of Iceland were familiar with writing, from their habitation in Ireland and constant intercourse with it, they yet made no use of it from the date of their settlement in A.D. 874 till the year 1000, the date of the introduction of Christianity, and with it of writing.

And for one hundred years after its introduction writing was confined to ecclesiastics, the earliest fragments of MSS. that have survived being portions of ecclesiastical legends which the clergy had composed in the Icelandic language for the edification of their flocks.[2]

This contempt of writing and of the use of scribes by a people so interested as the Icelanders evidently were in the history of Iceland and Norway, as is proved by their sagas, can only be accounted for by the life of daring and warfare, of piracy and conquest, at sea and on land, begun at the age of eleven and twelve and continued to old age. These early centuries were an age of brute force. Whilst the Norsemen fought and plundered at sea, the rest of the northern hordes passed a similar life on land, overwhelming the wealthier but weaker inhabitants of the ancient Roman world.

*Early contempt of letters in Europe.*

In that age of darkness and violence letters and learning were held in scorn by the strong, and thought fit pursuits only for priests and monks. The highest warriors and chiefs could not write, and appended only their marks or seals to their charters and treaties. Clerk is only cleric (or

---

[1] *Ibid.*       [2] Burnt Nial, *ibid.*

ecclesiastic), and to be able to read even was a proof of belonging to the clergy, as proved by the practice of our law courts, where a culprit saved himself from being hanged upon a first conviction by reading a verse of a psalm, and thus gaining his "benefit of clergy." The Norseman whose life was passed in storms of wind on the ocean, and in the storms of battle on land, who gloried in blood, wounds, and death, must have had a particular contempt for this priest-like, clerk-like occupation. He must have viewed the Irish monks and their monastic occupations of reading, writing, and praying with such feelings as the Irish warriors must have regarded the preaching of Saint Patrick in their unconverted state, when one of his converts, King Leogaire, notwithstanding his professed adoption of the saint's principles of peace and forgiveness, insisted on being buried sword in hand in his rath at Tara with his face to the east as in defiance of his foes of Leinster.[1]

[1] Life of George Petrie, LL.D., by Whitley Stokes, M.D., p. 97, 8vo; Dublin, 1868.

The following paraphrase of a Fenian tale well expresses such sentiments. It represents Oisin contending with St. Patrick, and lamenting the Fenians slain.

OISIN.

. . . .
If lived the son of Mornè fleet,
Who ne'er for treasure burned;
Or Diune's son to woman sweet,
Who ne'er from the battle turned,
But fearless with his single glaive
A hundred foemen dared to brave.

. . . .
More sweet one breath of their's would be
Than all thy clerks sad psalmody.

PATRICK.
Thy chiefs renowned extol no more,
Oh, Son of Kings! nor number oer;
But low on bended knees record
The power and glory of "the Lord."
And beat the breast and shed the tear,
And still his holy name revere;
Almighty, by whose potent breath,
The vanquished Fenians sleep in death.

OISIN.

Alas for Oisin! dire the tale,
No music in thy voice I hear;
Not for thy wrathful God I wail,
But for my Fenians dear.
Thy God! a rueful God I trow,
Whose love is earned in want and woe!
Since came thy dull psalm-singing crew,
How rapid away all our pastimes flew,
And all that charms the soul!
Where now are the royal gifts of gold
The flowing robe with its satin fold,
And the heart-delighting bowl?
Where now the feast and revel high,
And the jocund dance and sweet minstrelsy—
And the steed loud neighing in the morn
And well armed guards of coast and bay?

Yet though the Norsemen of Iceland thus scorned to apply themselves to make written chronicle, they gave themselves up, as we have seen, to the composing of verse and sagas, and to the singing and reciting of the history of their native and adopted countries at their public feasts and Althings. And thus is preserved a history more ancient and perfect than in most other countries of Europe, except only in Ireland, and there the record was in writing.

And this peculiarity and similarity arose probably from the remarkable fact that in these two islands of Ireland and Iceland only, lying at the western verge of the world, peace prevailed.

Iceland being thus the fountain of northern history, (for nowhere else, says Laing, was the profession of scald and sagaman (or poet and chronicler) heard of, not even in Norway), and as from thence was derived all the intellectual labour required in the north of Europe,[1] it is no wonder that there are constant references to Ireland in the sagas. For the intercourse with Ireland and its Scandinavian inhabitants was continuously maintained.

*Iceland the source of all Scandinavian History.*

But the sagas, whilst they give the public and more im-

But now we have clerks with their holy qualms,
And books and bells and eternal psalms,
And fasting, that waster gaunt and grim,
That strips of all beauty both body and limb.
PATRICK.
Oh! cease the strain, no longer dare
Thy Fion or his chiefs compare
With him who reigns in matchless might—
The King of Kings enthroned in light!
. . . . . .

'Tis he who calls fair fields to birth,
And bids each blooming branch expand.
. . .
OISIN.
To weeds and grass his princely eye,
My sire ne'er fondly turned,
But he raised his country's glory high
When the strife of warriors burned.
To shine in games of strength and skill,
To breast the torrent from the hill,
To lead the van of the bannered host—
These were his deeds and these his boast.[2]

[1] The Heims Kringla, a Chronicle of the kings of Norway, translated from the Icelandic of Snorro Sturleson, by Samuel Laing, Vol. I., p. 17, London, 3 vols., 8vo, 1844.

[2] The Chase: a Fenian tale. "Irish Penny Journal," Vol. I., No. 13 (September 26th, 1840), p. 102.

portant events occurring in their intercourse with the Irish such as the invasion and battles, the intermarriages between the Scandinavian kings and chiefs with the Irish, they omit those details of social life which add such charm to the accounts in the sagas of life in Iceland and Norway.

*An Irish sheep dog, (A.D 990).* It is not often they give such graphic accounts as that of King Aulaf Tryggvesson and the Irish sheep dog. In one of his plunderings in Ireland (A.D. 990, being then twenty years of age) he had collected a great herd of cows, sheep, and goats, and was driving them to his ships when a poor Irishman rushed to Aulaf and begged of him to give him up his cows and sheep to drive home. "How can I do it," said Aulaf, "since neither you nor anyone else could separate them from such a great herd?" "Only let me send my dog in," replied the poor man, "and he will find them out!" "If your dog can do it you may send him in, but mind that he does not delay us long."

On a sign from his master in rushed the dog, searched through the herd and before half an hour had his master's cattle out. Aulaf, astonished at the extraordinary sagacity of the dog, asked for it, and the poor man immediately gave it, whereupon Aulaf gave the poor man a heavy ring of gold, and what was of greater value his friendship, and so they parted friends.[1]

*Magnus of Norway adopts the Irish dress.* Magnus Barefoot, king of Norway, had been much in Ireland, and got his name from going barefoot, and wearing, with many of his courtiers, short cloaks as well as shirts, the custom of western lands (Ireland and the Erse or Irish of the Scottish Islands).[2] He seems to have been particularly fond of Ireland. In A.D. 1102, sailing from the Orkneys, he took a great part of the city of Dublin and of the Dyfflinarskiri by the aid of his ally, Miarkartan, king of

---

[1] Historia Olavi Tryggvii filii, cap. 13, p. 234, Scripta Historica Islandorum, &c., Vol. X.; 12mo. Havniæ, 1841.

[2] Historia Magni Nudipedis, Vol. VII., cap. 32, *ibid.*

Connaught. He passed the winter of that year in Connaught with Miarkartan, and agreed upon a marriage between his son Sigurd and Biadinyua, Miarkartan's daughter, Sigurd being then nine years of age and she five.

The following summer he and Miarkartan reduced a great part of Ulster. Miarkartan had returned to Connaught, and King Magnus's fleet stood at anchor off the northern coast to carry him to Norway when a force of Irish barred the way. Eyvind, one of his commanders, advised him to break through, but Magnus saw no reason for not retiring to safer ground. And then (says the Saga) Magnus burst forth in the following verses :—

"Why should we hurry home?
For my heart is at Dublin;
And this autumn I will not visit
The matrons of Drontheim.[1]

I am happy that a young woman
Does not forbid my addresses,
For there is an Irish girl
That I love better than myself."

We are left to conjecture, as far at least as the Sagas are concerned, about their building a bridge at their city of "Dyfflin," or Ath-Cliagh, as the Irish called it, and Mr. Haliday had heavy labour to seek for the proofs. Yet, there would seem to be no great difficulty in believing that the Scandinavians were the founders, if, as was no doubt the fact, it was made of timber. "We know from the Grágas" (says Sir G. Webb Dasent) " that the bridges in Iceland were commonly of timber."[2] In like manner we are left to discover from other sources than the Sagas whether " the fortress of the foreigners at Ath-Cliath," so constantly referred to in the Irish annals, was a castle of stone and lime or a structure of earth or wood. But, we know from Giraldus Cambrensis, that the English advanced with banners displayed against " the walls " of Waterford, and that M'Murrough led his allies to " the walls " of

*Danish Castles in Ireland.*

---

[1] " Matronas Nidarosienses," ibid.: "'Nidarosia' hodiernum emporium Norvegiæ Throndhjem dictum . . . ab Olavo rege Norvegiæ Tryggvii filio, principio condita est . . . ad ostium amnis Nidæ (*Nidar ôs*) sita. Regesta Geographica." *Ibid*, vol. xii.

[2] " Burnt Nial or Life in Iceland," &c., preface, p. cxxix.

Dublin, and that it was Milo de Cogan who rushed to "the walls" to the assault, and took the city.¹ Reginald's tower at Waterford, still standing, stood there at the time of the English invasion. And castles, built by the earliest invaders, under Turgesius, were to be seen in Giraldus's day, empty and neglected by the Irish, who, he adds, despised stone walls, and made woods their strongholds, and bogs their trenches.²

If the Ostmen have left few such monuments in England they have left there strong evidence of their conquests by the many names of places to be found with Danish terminations. The contrast between the effects of their rule in England and Ireland in this respect is striking.

*Danish names of places in England.*  Considering their long residence in Ireland it is surprising how few names of places underwent a change such as took place in the north and east of England, and in the Hebrides. In the latter country the examination of 12,700 names of places showed that they were nearly all Norse names; and that any Gaelic names were bestowed after the Gaelic language was reintroduced, subsequent to the cession of the Hebrides to Scotland in 1266.³

---

¹ "Conquest of Ireland," chapters xvi., xvii. The Norman "Geste" of the Conquest also says (p. 129):—
" Li riche rei ad dunc baillé
Dyvelin en garde, la cité :
E le Chastel et le dongun
A Huge de Laci le barun."

² Topography of Ireland, cap. xxxvii.

³ "*The Northmen in the Hebrides.*—The usual monthly meeting of the Society of Antiquaries of Scotland was held last week at Edinburgh. The first paper read was a communication by Captain F. W. Thomas, R.N., F.S.A., Scotland, in which he discussed the question: 'Did the Northmen extirpate the Celtic inhabitants of the Hebrides in the ninth century?' and answered it in the affirmative. Altogether Captain Thomas had examined about 12,700 names and the results of this elaborate inquiry were considered conclusive. In the rentals of Lewis and Harris, for instance, there are 269 entries of place names, and of these 200 are Scandinavian and sixty-four are English, and three uncertain. Thus the Scandinavian names are nearly four times more numerous than the Gaelic. But this by no means represents the relative importance of the places so named, for while on the Norse-named townlands

In Ireland there are but few Scandinavian names of places. The provinces Ulster, Munster, and Leinster have their termination 'ster' from 'stadr;' and there was a Kunnakster.¹ We have also harbours, islands and headlands. Thus there are the five 'fiords' of Carlingfiord, Wexfiord, Waterfiord, Strangfiord, and Ulfrickfiord (so long unknown, till the Rev. W. Reeves, D.D., identified it as Larne Lough). The islands of Lambay, with Skerries and Holmpatrick; the headlands of Hoved (Howth), Wykinlo (Wicklow), and Arclo.

*Ostman place-names in Ireland.*

But the only well ascertained inland Scandinavian name that readily occurs is "Gunnar" a name so distinguished in the Nials Saga or Burnt Nial. In the suburbs of Waterford, on the south, beside the river, lie Ballygunner, with Ballygunner Castle, Ballygunnermore, and Ballygunnertemple, within the parish of the same name.²

I had often wondered in earlier days when at Waterford there are 2,429 tenants there are but 327 on those with Gaelic names. The facts brought out lead to the conclusion that the Northmen extirpated the original inhabitants, and settled upon the best lands to which they gave descriptive names and that the Gaelic names were bestowed after the Gaelic language was reintroduced subsequent to the cession of the Hebrides to Scotland in 1266. In Lewis and Harris there is scarce an important place bearing a Gaelic name. Gaelic names are plentifully written on the Ordnance Maps, but as a rule they belong to minor features. These names are entirely modern in form and are such as would naturally arise in the six centuries which have passed since the islands formed part of the Norwegian kingdom. Captain Thomas intimated that the comparative tables of names he had constructed would be deposited in the library of the Society."—*Scotsman;* in *Times* of 17th March, 1876.

¹ Page 135.

² These lands with Little Island, were the estate of Sir Robert Walsh, of Ballygunner, knight and baronet, and of Sir James Walsh, knight, his father, who died in 1650. They were set out by the Cromwellians, but recovered by Sir Robert in the Court of Claims (5th November, 1663), under a decree of innocence. But he was obliged as a restored Papist to pay a heavy new quit-rent, and he had lost houses in Waterford which as a Papist could not be restored to him. He petitioned the King 9th July, 1682, for a reduction of quit-rent. His father, he said, served till the surrender of the Royal forces in Cornwall. In 1643, he (Sir Robert) went over to Ireland by the King's warrant, and raised horse and foot,

on circuit how such a name could have arisen before the time of guns, gunpowder, and gunnery little thinking that it would afterwards be my chance to know that this was the seat of an Ostman or Dane named Gunnar, and probably called by him and his countrymen "Gunnars stadr" or "Gunnars holt" as the family settlement in Iceland was named,[1] but changed by the Irish into Bally-Gunnar.

*Ostmen and the earliest burgess roll of Dublin.* It is also striking how few Scandinavian names of men are found in a roll of freemen of some guild of Dublin, containing about 1,500 names, made within thirty years after the Conquest.[2]

Except Walter *s.* of Edric, William *s.* of Godwin, Philip *s.* of Harald, William *s.* of Gudmund, Robert *s.* of Turkeld, William Wiking, William *s.* of Ketill, Simund Thurgot, there are no Scandinavian names to be found.

and brought them to England at a charge of £1,000, which force fought at the Castle of Lesleadle in Cornwall, Essex's army being there.—Carte Papers, clxi., p. 2. Ormonde backed the petition and reminded the King 'that H. M. said in his coach going towards Bury St. Edmunds, Lord Bath being also in the coach, that Sir Robert Walsh should have compensation for his services and sufferings,' (*ib.*) Previous to this on March 18th, 1681, he wrote a letter to the King in indignation at being commanded out of his presence as a Papist by Mr. Secretary Lionel Jenkins, reminding H. M. how he had his blessed father's commission to wear a gold medal with his royal effigy, for services rendered at the battle of Edgehill.—(Carte Papers, vol. 216, p. 10.) In a letter to Jenkins he complains that he "with this medal on his breast should be driven out of the royal presence by any upstart suggester like Dr. Titus Oates." (*Ibid.* p. 9). And to Ormonde, recounting the indignity and the warmth of his temper, he says "the best man in the kingdom once told me 'no butter would stick on my bread.' A bedchamber man (he added) once said 'the best man in the kingdom (meaning Ormonde) was my enemy.' I had a mind to Culpepper him." (*ibid.* p. 8); in allusion to this—that about thirty years before, in 1648, when the King (then Prince of Wales), and he and many more were in exile at the Hague, Sir Robert Walsh, by order of the Prince, was imprisoned for a bastinado he gave to Lord Culpepper.

[1] Index of names of places in Iceland. Sturlunga Saga.

[2] Historic and Municipal Documents of Ireland in the Archives of the City of Dublin, by J. T. Gilbert.

But this may arise from the fact recorded by Giraldus, that on the assault and capture of Dublin by Strongbow and the English, "the better part of the Scandinavian inhabitants under their king, Hasculf, embarked in ships and boats with their most valuable effects, and sailed (says Giraldus) to the northern islands," or Orkneys.[1] The rest, there can be little doubt, were driven by the English over to the north side of the Liffey, and compelled to dwell there, and form the Ostmantown, while their conquerors seated themselves in the original city, on the south side. For such was the course taken with the Ostmen of Waterford,[2] and those of Cork and Limerick. *Treatment of Ostmen at the conquest.*

Or perhaps it was the heavy cost to be paid for English liberty that hindered them, amounting it would appear, in some instances to three thousand pounds, an enormous sum, *Ostmen claiming English freedom.*

---

[1] "Conquest of Ireland," chap. xvii.

[2] The Plea Roll, third to seventh Edward II. (A.D. 1319) contains this interesting historical detail concerning Waterford. Robert Walsh was indicted at Waterford for killing John, son of Ivor M'Gilmore, and pleaded that the said John was Irish, and that it was no felony to kill an Irishman. The King's Attorney (John fitz John fitz Robert le Poer), replied that M'Gilmore was an Ostman of Waterford, descended of Gerald M'Gilmore, and that all his (Gerald's) posterity and kinsmen were entitled to the law of Englishmen by the grant of Henry fitz Empress, which he (Mr. Attorney) produced. And issue being joined, the jury found that on the first invasion of the English, Reginald the Dane, then ruler of Waterford, drew three great iron chains across the river, to bar the passage of the King's fleet; but being conquered and taken by the English, he was for this tried and hanged by sentence of the King's court at Waterford with all his officers. They further found that King Henry the second, banished all the then inhabitants of the town (except Gerald M'Gilmore), who joined the English, and dwelt at that time in a tower over against the church of the Friars Preachers, very old and ruinous at the time of the trial, and assigned them a place outside the town to dwell at, and there they built what was then (A.D. 1310) called the Ostman town of Waterford. There can be little doubt but that the Ostmantown of Dublin, and the "cantreds of the Ostmen" of Cork and Limerick, got their names from similar circumstances, i.e., the driving out of the Ostman inhabitants of each to an Ostman quarter.

considering the value of money in the twelfth and thirteenth centuries. Thus Maurice MacOtere, on the 9th December, 1289 (18th of Edward I.), an Ostman dwelling (as he describes himself) at the end (or back) of the world in Ireland (*in fine mundi in partibus Hiberniæ*), petitioned the king in parliament on behalf of himself and 300 of his race, that they might enjoy the liberties of Englishmen, granted him by letters patent, under the King's Great Seal of Ireland enrolled in Chancery "letters by which the king gained three thousand pounds in one day." But as these rights were denied him, he prays to have the Irish patent confirmed under the Great Seal of England.[1]

For the lords of Ireland it seems were very much opposed to these grants, as appears as well by the instance just given as the following petition of Philip MacGuthmund, presented also to the king in Parliament on the 23rd of April, 1296. He describes himself as Philip MacGuthmund "Ostman and Englishman of our Lord the King of the City of Waterford," and complains that for the sake of the five marks payable for every Irish(man) killed, the grasping lords of Ireland, the kings' rivals, would make the petitioner and over 400 of his race Irish. He therefore prays in behalf of himself and 400 of his race, for God's sake, and for the sake of the king's father, that he may enjoy the liberties his ancestors enjoyed, and that of Englishmen and Ostmen, they be not made Irish, adding that it was better for the king, that there should be more English than Irish. And in proof of his claim that he and his ancestors had enjoyed these rights, tenders the letters patent of the bailiffs and commons of Waterford, and prays the king's letters to confirm his English liberty.[2]

[1] Petitions to the King in Parliament (in England) in the eighteenth of Edward the First "Documents illustrative of English History, in the 13th and 14th centuries, from the Records of the Queen's Remembrancer of the Exchequer," p. 69. By Henry Cole, Assistant Keeper of Public Records. Folio, London, 1844.

[2] *Ibid.* Sir John Davys gives many similar instances in his "Discoverie why Ireland was not sooner reduced to complete obedience than in King James the First's reign." The following from the King's

For the laws being personal, that is to say, an Irishman being under Brehon law (unless an Englishman was concerned, when the case was ruled by the law of England), an *eric* or pecuniary mulct was payable to the lord of the fee for any Irishman of his slain; whereas if an Englishman or any one having "English liberty" or the benefit of English law were killed it was punishable with death, and the forfeiture consequent went to the king. It was thus of course a gain to the lords of the fee to have for their tenants Irishmen, and to question the claims of Ostmen such as Maurice MacOtere and Philip MacGuthmund to English liberty.

And it must be understood that the absence of Ostman names from the guild roll above mentioned, was rather for this want of English liberty probably than the want of

<small>Juries of Ostmen.</small>

Bench Rolls and Plea Rolls in Edward the First's reign are further illustrations. Thus in A.D. 1278, John Garget, Seneschal or Prior of the Holy Trinity (now Christ Church), Dublin, was indicted for having sentenced a woman named Isabel, and her daughter, who had murdered Adam fitz Robert and his brother—Isabel, the mother, to be hanged, and her daughter to have her ear cut off—a sentence which was executed according to the said judgment of the court of the Prior. And the said Seneschal admitted the sentence given. The jury being asked if the said girl was English, they said she was Irish. But because it was found by the oath of the members of the Chapter that she was English, the said John and the Court of the said Prior aforesaid were attached.—MS. transcript of the Early Rolls by the Record Commissioners of 1810, Public Record Office, Four Courts. There being no such penalty by English law, she ought to have been hanged as well as her mother. At assizes and jury trials for the county of Limerick, held at Kilmallock on Tuesday next a fortnight after Trinity Day, A.D. 1300, it was found by a jury in an action between Walter Chappel, plaintiff, and John Thebaud, defendant, that the aforesaid Walter, an Irishman of the Offyus (*de cognomine Offyus*) was a miller of the said John's, as was his father before him, at Forsketh in the said county, but not an Irishman of the said John's; and in a late quarrel between the said Walter and a mistress of the said John's (*amicam ipsius Johannis*), she called him a robber, whereupon he called her a common whore (*pupplicam meretricem*). And afterwards the said John ran after him and tore his eyes out (*avulsit oculos ejus*). The said John Thebaud was accordingly committed to gaol and fined in a hundred shillings. But if Walter Chappel had been one of John Thebaud's Irishmen he could not have had an action against him.

Ostman inhabitants, who were numerous enough to form juries of inquest more than fifty years after the Conquest, King John directing his justiciary to inquire by the English and Ostmen of Dublin, if the Prior and convent of the Holy Trinity (now Christ Church) had of ancient right a boat (for salmon fishing) on the Liffey.[1]

It has just been observed that frequent as are the notices of the Scandinavian occupation of Ireland in the Icelandic Sagas, almost all traces of them in the Irish records are lost from the time of the English invasion.

Our early Chancery records to the end of the reign of King Edward I., were all burned in the time of Master Thomas Cantok, Chancellor, when his lodgings in Saint Mary's Abbey took fire, amongst them the very enrolment referred to by Maurice MacOtere. This is recorded on the patent roll of Chancery of the second of King Edward II. (A.D. 1309), when Thomas Cantok's executors delivered up to the Lord Walter de Thornbury, his successor in office, such writs, bills, inquisitions, &c., as had escaped with an inventory or schedule of them.—*Calendar of the Patent Rolls*, p. 12, b.

But few as are the traces of the lives and actions of the Ostmen to be found in the public records, fewer still are the monuments of their past habitation of Ireland, such as castles, towers, walls, and tombs.

Reginald's Tower at Waterford is the only building that remains as a subsisting memorial of their rule. Or, may we say, *was* the only one until Mr. Haliday's energetic zeal in research has revived and brought to light the Thingmount and Long Stone of Dublin, which though swept away by all-devouring time seem to be at length rescued from oblivion, not only through the curious incidents and notices

---

[1] Rot. Litt. Claus., 17° Johann, p. 224 (Folio Record Publications). In the "Registrum Decani Limericensis," there is a curious inquisition concerning lands and churches, on the oaths of separate juries, one of twelve Englishmen, another of twelve Irishmen, and a third of twelve Ostmen or Danes.—*Archæologia*, V. 17, p. 33.

he has collected, but by the drawings which represent them to the eye. So fully has Mr. Haliday done his work, that to this treatise might well be applied, with only a slight change, the title which Richard Verstegan gave to his, namely—a restitution of decayed intelligence in antiquities concerning the renowned city of Dublin.[1]

It appears from Mr. Haliday's commonplace books that before he engaged in the study of the Scandinavian origin of Dublin he had collected all such notices as are to be found concerning the Steyne of Dublin and the Mound of le Hogges in the printed histories and public records. But these sources gave no notice of their Scandinavian origin. Great then was his joy to find what a flood of light was thrown upon these two monuments of the Ostmen through his study of Scandinavian antiquities. The elucidation of the history of the Steyne and Thingmount of Dublin will be found in the third book of the following work. I would only desire further to call attention to the height of the Thingmount over the Steyne, and to show what a lofty aspect it must have presented before the river was banked out from the Steyne, the strand taken in, and the ground raised and built over. It appears from the Ordnance Survey that the base of the Thingmount, which stood at the same level as the base of the present Saint Andrew's Church, was thirty-five feet above the level of low water, so that the mount being forty feet high its summit stood seventy-five feet above the Liffey when the tide was lowest. Hoggen Green was then a pasture for the cows of the freemen, and without any buildings till the year 1603, when Sir George Carey built his hospital.[2]

*The Thingmount.*

At the rere Carey's Hospital was only separated from the river by a lane along the Strand, the present Fleet-street.

---

[1] "A restitution of Decayed Intelligence in Antiquities concerning the most noble and renowned English nation. By the Studie and Travaile of R. V." Small 4to, Antwerp, 1605.

[2] This was afterwards purchased by Sir Arthur Chichester, and thus became Chichester House. From the time of the Restoration the Parliament sat there.

lxxiv      SOME NOTICE OF THE

The water of the Liffey then covered all the lower end of Westmoreland-street and Dolier-street, and was only shut out in 1663 by Mr. Hawkins's wall.[1]

*Gilmeholmoc and the Thingmount, A.D. 1172.*

Standing then on the strand the Thingmount would be seen as a lofty mound, seventy-five feet high, overlooking the level plain of the Steyne, part of which was College-green. From the summit there must have been an extensive view over the Steyne and river on one side, and over Stephen's-green on the other. It was here that Gilmeholmoc and his force sate, at the request of Strongbow, to view the battle between the English and the Ostmen, for the possession of Dublin, with liberty to fall upon the beaten party. And Mr. Haliday always contended that it was considered by all sides as a wager of battle, the event being held as the decree of God, as indeed is stated in this interesting poem.

I shall give here Mr. Haliday's rendering of the Langue d'Oc or Provençal of the Geste into modern French, by which it will be seen how like they are to one another:—

| | |
|---|---|
| Vos ôtages aurez par sí | Vous leur soyez en tout aidant |
| Que tu faces ce que [je] te dis | De nous trancher et occire |
| Par sí que ne soyez aidant | Et nous livrer à martyre. |
| Ni nous, ni eux, tant ni quant | Gilmeholmoc rejouissant |
| Mais que á coté de nous soyez | Dehors la cité maintenant, |
| Et la bataille regarderez : | Ce roi pour vrai s'est assis |
| Et si Dieu le nous consent | Avec les gens de son pays |
| Que soient deconfis ces gens | Desur le Hogges dessus Steyne |
| Que nous, avec ton pouvoir soyez | Dehors la cité en une plaine |
| Aidant pour eux debarater : | Pour regarder la melée |
| Et si nous soyons recréans | Ils y se sont assemblées.[2] |

In the "Geste of the Conquest" the language, as printed is "Desur le Hogges de Sustein," and I cannot easily forget

[1] I have not been able to find in the Assembly Rolls the history of Hawkins' Wall; but I have met occasional notices that show the line of it to be such as is above stated.

[2] The language of this geste is sometimes called "Norman," but wrongly. Of the Langue d'Oc, Littrè says, 'l'ancienne langue qui se parloit au delà de la Loire, dont se sont servis les Troubadours, que l'on connoit sous le nom de Provençal et que dans le temps on appeloit plus ordinairement 'langue Limousine.' (Oc

the pleasure of Mr. Haliday when I showed him that the true reading was 'De sur le Hogges dessus Stein,' the 'de Sustein' being plainly a trivial error of the scribe, in making one word of what ought to be two.

Hoggen-green was only separated from Stephen's-green *Hoggen Green.* in times before the dissolution of religious houses by the Mynchen's fields, or lands of the Nunnery of Saint Mary del Hogges, which ran side by side with the lands of All Hallows Priory, now Trinity College Park, to the full length of the Park. Leinster House and Kildare-place, as we have shown, standing on part of the Mynchen's fields and the Mynchen's Mantle. But as time flew on, and all memory of Saint Mary del Hogges was lost the name was corrupted into Mr. Minchin's and Menson's fields[1], in like manner as we find Hoggen-green made into Hog's-green and Hogan's-green, and Hoggen but made into Hog *Hoggen but.* and Butts[2].

Only for my intercourse with Mr. Haliday, I should probably have no more understood what was meant in Colonel Michael Jones' report of the mutiny of the garrison of Dublin in 1647, by the seizing of the "fortified hill near the College" by the mutineers[3], when I met with it in the Carte Papers, than Lodge knew what was "hoggen but," (which meant the same place)[4] and being unintelligible to him he dropped the "but."

Quitting now the prospect over Stephen's-green, and *The Long* turning round again to the northward, or towards the river, *Stone of the Steyne.*

---

veut dire Oui) ou Langue d'Oil (Oil vent dire Oui) ou langue d'Oui, l'ancien Français—la langue Française qui florissait du xième au xivième siècle, celle dans laquelle on lit les trouvères. Dictionnaire de la Langue Française par E. Littré. 4 vols., quarto, Paris, 1868-1869.

B. III., chap. II., p. 164, *infra*.
[1] Book III., chap. II., p. 193, n., *infra*.

[2] *Ibid.* p. 196, n. ².

[3] B. III., chap. II., p. 165, n.

[4] *Ibid.* p. 169. One is reminded of Pope's lines:—

"No commentator can more slily pass
O'er a learned unintelligible place;
Or in quotations shrewd divines leave out
Those words that would against them clear the doubt."

—Satires of Dr. Donne versified.

there would be seen the Long Stone, standing on the green sward of the Steyne, near the bank of the Liffey. For it appears by the transcript of Petty's map in the Down Survey, made in 1654, that even at that late period there were few buildings on the riverside between Dublin and Ringsend. And there was a covenant, it may be remembered, in the lease of the Corporation in 1607 to Sir James Carrol, of the strand overflown by the sea from the Stain to Ringsend, in order to its being taken in, that he should not erect any building for habitation on the premises.[1]

In this transcript of the Down Survey, if I am not deceived, the Long Stone will be found represented. The scale is unfortunately very small, but the map has been given in facsimile instead of on an enlarged scale (which would have made the stone more conspicuous), that it may be more true and authentic. Mr. Haliday considered it as a memorial of possession taken of the land by the Ostmen at their first landing, just as we now set up an English flag and flagstaff, or perhaps a monument to King Ivar, the first Ostman king of Dublin. For this was a well known landing place, and in early times a port, as appears by a regulation of the reign of King Henry IV., entered on the Exchequer Memorandum Rolls, concerning goods exported from the ports of Clontarf, Dalkey, Stayne, Dodder, and le Kay de Dyvelyne. And in Speed's map of 1610, is shown a pill or small harbour at this spot; which it must be remembered, though now surrounded by streets, was then nearly half a mile east of the walls of Dublin, and has since been obliterated by the building of Hawkins's Wall so far into the river beyond it. It is at this port that Hasculf and his fierce bersaker (or champion) from Norway, are described as landing to attempt the recovery of Dyveline from the English.

"A Steine etoit arrive
Hescul et Johan le devè."

And here therefore the Ostmen probably first landed, and set up the Long Stone as the mark of possession taken.

[1] B. III., chap. I., p. 145, n.², *infra*

After this sketch of Charles Haliday's course of study, we now return to his personal history, first giving a short notice of his father, and of some of his brothers.

The father of Charles Haliday was William Haliday, a medical practitioner, dispensing both medicine and advice, who for many years dwelt in the house on Arran-quay at the corner of West Arran-street, where his son Charles dwelt also for some years, and had it as his house of business to the time of his death. William Haliday the elder.

Mr. William Haliday was born at Carrick-on-Suir, in the county of Tipperary, where some of the family were originally engaged in the business of wool-combing and the making of friezes and blankets.

It was a trade introduced by the Duke of Ormond, about the year 1664, into his own town of Carrick, where he assigned to the workmen half of the houses and 500 acres of land contiguous to the walls, for three lives or thirty-one years, at a pepper-corn rent, and afterwards at two thirds of the old rent.

Mr. William Haliday was apprenticed by his father, in the year 1777, to Thomas Lucas, apothecary, of Clonmel.

He completed his apprenticeship on the 14th of November, 1782, and soon after removed to Dublin. In the year 1792, he purchased from Nicholas Loftus, late Lieutenant-Colonel of the Royal Irish Regiment of Dragoon Guards, the house on Arran-quay where he so long resided, and his son Charles Haliday after him. On 23rd December, 1795, he became a Freeman of the city of Dublin. On the 31st October, 1796, he had a commission from Earl Camden, Lord Lieutenant, as Fourth Lieutenant in the Dublin Infantry Corps, (Yeomanry) commanded by Humphry Aldridge Woodward, esq.; and on 17th September, 1803, he received a commission from Earl Hardwicke, Lord Lieutenant, as Second Captain in the first company of the armed corps in the county of Dublin, called the Barrack Infantry.

A sister of William Haliday's, Esther Haliday, was married

to John Domville, of Clonmel, and the Domvilles were connected with Lord Norbury, Chief Justice of the Common Pleas, a connection which was the means of getting the appointment from Lord Norbury of Deputy Filacer in his court for William Haliday, Charles Haliday's eldest brother.

In a letter to his father, Charles Haliday thus alludes to the death of one of the Domvilles.

"London, 1812.

"MY DEAR FATHER.—To my last letter, sent through the Castle, addressed to you, my mother, to William, and to Dan, I have received no answer. My last letter from you contained a postscript by which I have been informed of the melancholy fate of Henry Domville. His death I had some time looked for as an event not far distant. The nature of his disease had long left one without a hope of his recovery. And yet his death seems to have been sudden. Poor fellow! When last we met, when last we parted little did either of us think we parted for ever. He was leaving town. He came to bid farewell. He was in health, I was but sickly; and could the idea have entered the mind of our friends that either of us was so soon to have quitted this earthly stage, no one could long have hesitated, I believe, to point to me as the destined victim. Quickly indeed the scene has changed. It is but one short year, and I am now as he was, and he is no more. Another year may roll away, and I too may have passed that bourne from whence no traveller returns. I pause to think for what purpose existence was bestowed. I turn to my own breast to ask has that purpose been fulfilled?"

When Charles Haliday left Dublin, it was his father's intention that he should settle in London as a merchant. In a letter to his father, of 8th October, 1812, he says that it would be in vain to enter on any mercantile pursuit whatsoever without more capital than he was possessed of, and he proposes to his father, with evident embarrassment arising from feelings of delicacy, an advance of some capital to be employed in the way of partnership.

Before stating the terms, which he afterwards details with great clearness and minuteness, he apologises for the strict business like form that his letter is obliged to assume, "I can offer," he says, "but one reason for doing so. I have long since vowed to know no distinction of persons in affairs like this. I wish no one to know them towards me. To friendship

I could grant almost anything. Unbending strictness is the soul of business."

In allusion to the advance of capital suggested, he says, "I cannot avoid seeing that I am placing the stepping stone on which my weight must rest, the foundation on which my hopes must rise ; and although (Heaven knows) the structure appears but slight to my eyes, without this basis it must vanish entirely."

It does not appear whether the suggestion was acted on ; but it was of little consequence, for the death of his brother William, in this very month of October, 1812, changed the whole course of his career and brought him to settle at Dublin, at the end of March, 1813, in an already established business.

Among his father's guests at Arran-quay, were Surgeon Benjamin Lentaigne (father of my friend, the present Sir John Lentaigne, C.B.) and Major Sandys, keeper of "The Provo," or Provost Martial's Military Prison, on Arbour-hill, adjacent to the Royal Barracks.

Surgeon Lentaigne was a French Royalist who had escaped from France in the year 1793, after losing two of his brothers by the guillotine. He first fled to Flanders and there joined a regiment of noblesse raised by the French Princes ; but afterwards came to England, and took his degree as a Surgeon, and was, in 1799, appointed to the 1st Dragoons. He had the medical charge of " The Provo."

It was while lying a prisoner for high treason in this prison that Theobold Wolfe Tone attempted to end his life by cutting his throat with a penknife.

He wounded himself badly but did not effect his purpose, and lay for a few days between life and death, though in the end he succeeded in saving himself from a public execution. It was the intention of the Government to try him and execute him by martial law, an act it was contended that could not lawfully be done where the King's courts were sitting and had jurisdiction.

A Habeas Corpus was moved for in the King's Bench by Curran, to be directed to the keeper of the Provo: but Tone died, having contrived to loosen the bandages round his neck placed there by Surgeon Lentaigne.

Haliday, who was at this time a boy and well remembered both Lentaigne and Sandys, often heard his father tell, that while Wolfe Tone was thus lying between life and death, Sandys would say to Lentaigne. "Lentaigne, I will hang your patient to-morrow morning—his neck is well enough for the rope." "No, no, you must not stir him," said Lentaigne, adding in his broken English, "By Gar, if you do, I will not be answerable for his life!" Grim jokes that best bespeak the violent passions prevalent at that period of blood and terror.

Mr. William Haliday passed the closing years of his life at a villa called Mulberry-hill, still to be seen, at the west end of the village of Chapelizod, and was buried in the graveyard of the old church there, where may be seen his tombstone, a large horizontal flag near the east window, with the following epitaph:—"Beneath this stone lie the earthly remains of William Haliday, Esq., late of Arran-quay, in the City of Dublin, who died the 7th day of September, 1830, aged 76. Also of his sister, Margaret Haliday, spinster, who died the 30th of March, 1836, aged 83."

*William Haliday, jun.*

Charles Haliday's eldest brother was named William. Lord Norbury, Chief Justice of the Common Pleas, was his godfather, and having given the patent office of Filacer in the Court to his eldest son, the Honorable Daniel Toler, he made him appoint William Haliday his Deputy.

But the office being one of routine, he probably gave up his leisure more to literature than to law. He could not otherwise have made himself so distinguished a name as a man of erudition, dying as he did at the early age of twenty-four.

He had a passion for languages, and to the ordinary subjects learned at schools, such as **Latin and Greek**, he soon added a knowledge of Hebrew, Persian, Arabic, and Sanscrit. These were the fruits of his own unaided exertions; for there were not then those many books of instruction, and accomplished teachers such as are abundant now. But he made the study of all these tongues only subsidiary to a perfect knowledge of the original language of his own country, Irish, being possessed of a patriotic ardour to revive its ancient glory. In the year 1808, when he was only twenty, he published an Irish grammar under the fictitious signature of "E. O'C."

In the year 1811 he published anonymously the first volume of a translation from the Irish of Dr. Jeffry Keatinge's History of Ireland from the earliest time to the English invasion, a work written in the first half of the seventeenth century. He only lived to execute half the work. A complete translation of Dr. Keatinge's work has been since executed at New York by the late John O'Mahony, and published there in 1857, and it is no small testimony to the merit of William Haliday's work that so complete a master of Irish as O'Mahony, should have selected it as the best translation of Keatinge's history. *Keatinge's Ireland, by W. Haliday, jun.*

In this publication William Haliday gave the original Irish text on one page, and the translation on the other, in the manner since followed by Dr. John O'Donovan, LL.D., in that great work, "The Annals of the Four Masters."

As the mode adopted by William Haliday was then new, he gives the following account of its adoption. "The plan here adopted," he observes in his preface, "has been often suggested and repeatedly wished for, heretofore, and among the rest by our late illustrious countryman, Edmund Burke, who in one of his addresses to General Vallancey, expressed his ardent wish 'that some Irish historical monuments should be published as they stand, with a translation in Latin or English; for until something of this sort be done, criticism can have no sure anchorage.'" "The great Leibnitz,"

*f*

continues William Haliday, "hesitated not to aver that the language of Ireland, as being the most sequestered island in Europe, must be considered as the purest and most unadulterated dialect of the Celtic now in existence . . . . . and the philosophers of Europe," he adds, "seem at length to admit that no progress can be made in the genealogy of language without a previous knowledge of Irish . . .
yet how is it possible" he also adds "to obtain any knowledge of a language, still enclosed within the sooty envelopes of moth eaten, half rotten, illegible manuscripts?"

"Though that inconvenience," observes William Haliday, "had been often felt and lamented since the invention of printing, little had been done through the agency of the press for the Irish language; a complaint which his work, he hoped, would tend to remedy." Nor was he disappointed in his expectations. For as this work of William Haliday's was the first undertaken in this form, it may be considered as the parent of that splendid undertaking, the Annals of the Four Masters, fit rather for a national and governmental project, than for the enterprise of a private firm of booksellers. Since the publication of the Annals of the Four Masters, Parliament has given greater encouragement to the printing of our earlier Irish historical manuscripts, and many have been lately edited under the care of the Royal Irish Academy in a manner worthy of a great country. So that the press has at length done its services to the Irish language. The plan of printing the Irish text on one page, and the literal translation on the opposite, originated by William Haliday, and followed in the Annals of the Four Masters has been since adopted in the specimens of our early national manuscripts, edited by J. T. Gilbert, in the works of the Irish Archæological Society, and in the Annals of Loch Cé, by W. M. Hennessy.

But this translation of Keatinge's History of Ireland, was not William Haliday's only work. In the preface to it he announced that he had then "nearly ready for the press a complete Irish Dictionary," but his death in the following year, interfered to prevent its publication. Charles Haliday always maintained that his brother's work had been appropriated by another, and there is an admission of some portion at least of his labours having been so used, in the following extract taken from the preface to O'Reilly's Irish-English Dictionary, which first came forth in the year 1817, but was republished by the late John O'Donovan, LL.D., in the year 1864. English-Irish Dictionary of W. Haliday, jun.

O'Reilly says, "my collection of words from ancient glossaries is copious, and several of those words which I have added to the collections published in the dictionaries of my predecessors, were collected with a view to publication by the late Mr. William Haliday, junior, of Arran-quay. That young gentleman, after acquiring a knowledge of the ancient and modern languages, usually taught in schools, enriched his mind with the acquisition of several of the eastern languages, and made himself so perfect a master of the language of his native country, that he was enabled to publish a grammar of it in Dublin, in the year 1808, under the fictitious signature of "E. O'C.," and would have published a dictionary of the same language, if death had not put a stop to his career, at the early age of twenty-three."

Such is O'Reilly's admission. But it may well be doubted if the entire obligation is confessed. Probably, Charles Haliday's statement is nearer the truth. The manuscript of the work got into other hands, and Charles Haliday never recovered it. Besides these services rendered to Irish literature by William Haliday, he may be said to be entitled to the further merit of infusing his own zest for Irish history and antiquities into the heart of the late George Petrie, that learned Irish antiquary, whose life has been published by his friend, William Stokes, M.D. Charles Haliday told me, that in the year 1807, Petrie, whose father and mother kept a

*f* 2

curiosity shop in Crampton-court, was engaged by his, Mr. Haliday's, father, who then had a house at Dunleary, to teach him drawing, " And while Petrie was teaching me drawing (said Haliday) William was teaching Petrie Irish, and Irish antiquities."

But whilst this gifted young man was engaged thus zealously in his literary labours, his frame was a prey to that insidious enemy of life, consumption ; and the ardour with which he pursued both learning and pleasure together only hastened the progress of his disease.

In 1812, much to his brother's surprise, he married. The following are portions of Charles Haliday's letters to his brother on the occasion :—

"London, 3rd March, 1812.

"MY DEAR WILLIAM.—From the unvarying round of waste-books, journals, and ledgers, I scarce can steal time soberly to congratulate you on your late change. As to my last letter, an impatient hand just held the pen while a brain nearly turned with joy guided its flourishes over half a sheet of paper. You may conceive with what sensations I read your letter, when I tell you it was the first intimation I had of a thing of the kind. Here is, said I, a revolution. However, like a loyal subject my cry shall be, " Long live William and Mary," and in due time I hope to see their heir-apparent. I got a letter from your father a short time since. It said you were dying. I got a letter from you, it said you were married. Upon my word, said I to myself, he has chosen a queer physician, yet one with whom there will be far more pleasure to die than in the hands of any of that learned body who scribble those big M.D.s at the end of their names."

In the following letter he assumes a jocular tone, to conceal probably the anxieties he felt concerning the state of his brother's health.

"London, 20th April, 1812.

"DEAR WILLIAM.—Your letter, which I received this day from Mr. Martin, informs me that among other reasons for not writing to me, it gives you pain to write. I am truly sorry to hear you continue so unwell, and I sincerely wish you would follow the advice that has been given, and try what the milder air of England can do in such a case. Of this, from experience, I am satisfied that the air is not so moist as that of Ireland, and the respiration of dry air is, I believe, a disideratum in complaints like yours.

"You say you are thin, I am thinner; and no doubt you have heard I am not over corpulent. I believe we belong to Pharoah's lean kine. I have done everything that could make a man fat without improving, and everything that could make him thin without growing worse, that is worse than I was when I came to London. For, since then I have been like the spirit of Loda that Ossian makes appear to Fingall: you can almost 'see the stars twinkle through me.' But I should not complain, for I have lately enjoyed a greater continuance of good health than had for some time before fallen to my lot. I tell you all this to support you during the absence of your fine legs. I never thought fatness in a young person a sign of health, nor the want of it a criterion of the contrary. For I think a house may stand very well for a sixty years lease (all I should ever wish for) without walls five feet thick and Act of Parliament rafters. A comfortable inside is all we want, either as lodging for body or soul. Apply yourself then to the repairs of the inside, which I trust that your going to Rathmines may be a means of affecting. God bless you. And as the whole tissue of our lives is but a scene of self-love, I long for your getting rid of that pain in your side that I may have the pleasure of hearing from you. Farewell."

But all these hopes were vain, William Haliday only survived his marriage six months. He died 26th October, 1812, and was buried in the graveyard attached to the old ruined church of Dundrum, otherwise Churchtown, in the county of Dublin. He was long (indeed ever) deeply lamented by his brother, Charles Haliday, who, after the lapse of fifty years, always spoke of him in most affectionate terms as "Poor William," as if he had only lately lost him. He has said to me at particular seasons, such as Christmas or the beginning of the year, "Yesterday I rode to see poor William's grave." After Mr. Haliday's death, I went to see it. I found a monumental tomb about seven feet high, surrounded by an iron railing, standing on the highest point in the graveyard.

It had evidently been lately painted by his brother's care, and the following inscription said to be the composition of the Rev. Dr. Lanigan, whose Ecclesiastical History of Ireland has been so often cited in the text of the present work, may be easily read. The following is the epitaph:—

*His epitaph.*

"Beneath this stone are deposited the remains of William Haliday, cut off by a lingering disease in the early bloom of life. He anticipated the progress of years in the maturity of understanding in the acquisition of knowledge, and the successful cultivation of a mind gifted by Providence with endowments of the highest order.

"At a period of life when the severer studies have scarcely commenced, he had acquired an accurate knowledge of most of the European languages, of Latin, Greek, Hebrew, and Arabic.

"But of his own, the Hiberno Celtic, so little an object of attainment and study to (Oh! shame) the youth of this once lettered island, he had fathomed all the depths, explored the beauties, and unravelled the intricacies. He possessed whatever was calculated to exalt, to enoble, to endear: great faculties, sincere religion, a good son, and an affectionate husband, a steady friend. Carried off in the twenty-fourth year of his age, his worth will be long remembered and his death lamented.

"Obiit, 26th October, 1812."

To these few memorials of his youthful and lamented genius it remains only to add the following letter from his brother Charles, written shortly after his death.

"CHARLES HALIDAY to THOMAS MARTIN.

"London, 27th March, 1813.

"MY DEAR SIR,—By the receipt this evening of the accompanying volumes from Ireland, I am enabled to gratify the wish you had expressed of having in your possession part of the works of my lamented brother. Unhappily it has fallen to my lot to gratify this wish. Unhappily, I say, for had it pleased the Almighty to have prolongued his life to this time, and had he known your wish, I feel certain from the sentiments I have heard him express that there is no one to whom he would have had greater pleasure in making such an offering.

"From my ignorance of our native language, unfortunately, I am unable to judge of their intrinsic merits; nor, were I gifted with that power would it well become me to panegerize the works of so near a relation. To his friends, for any errors or omissions they may discover in them, it is probable little apology may be made; to his countrymen I would make none. A life spent in the service of Ireland—to redeem the memory of her past glory—again to place her in the list of nations, though unsuccessful in the object, needs no apology for its exertions. To the more fastidious critic, if apology be due, he will find it in the youth of the author (the grammar having been written in his 20th year); in the strong prejudice which prevails with many to pursuits like his, and the little encouragement they meet with from any; in the difficulties attendant on self instruction in the Hebrew, Arabic, Persian, Syrian, Sanscrit and Irish languages. These difficulties were increased by the necessary attendance on an arduous profession and in other obstacles which those by whom they were created have now far too much reason to regret they had ever placed to obstruct his way.

"In elucidation of the motive by which he was influenced to publish the present translation of Keatinge's History of Ireland, in addition to those mentioned in his preface, was the wish to render that respectable historian more familiar to his countrymen."

Besides William, Charles Haliday had a younger brother, Daniel Haliday, who graduated as a physician at Edinburgh, in August, 1819, as appears by his Latin thesis on Apoplexy, dedicated to his father, with another dedication to the memory of his brother William, "optimi, dilectissimi, morte eheu immaturâ, abrepti."

Daniel settled at Paris, and practised his profession principally among the English and Irish residents there. His political sentiments were 'National' and anti-Unionist. He was familiar with all the '98 men living in exile in France.

Mr. Haliday told me an anecdote of him expressive of his feelings. Daniel on returning to his apartments one day found that in his absence some one had called and left his card, with a message to the servant that he would call next day at noon, as he was particularly desirous of seeing Dr. Haliday. It was the card of Thomas Nugent Reynolds, through whose disclosures the plans of the United Irishmen for insurrection in 1798 were defeated, Lord Edward Fitzgerald was arrested, and many of them were convicted and suffered death, and more driven into banishment. Daniel Haliday was indignant. So taking down a cabinet portrait of Lord Edward, and sticking Reynolds' visiting card between the canvas and the frame, he hung it up outside his door with its face to the wall, and bade his servant tell the visitor when he called next day that he would find his answer if he turned the picture. On doing so, he of course found himself face to face with the man he had betrayed, and his card returned.

<small>D. Haliday and Sir Jonah Barrington.</small>

Amongst Daniel Haliday's acquaintances at Paris was Sir Jonah Barrington, then engaged in completing his celebrated "History of the Union, with authentic details of the bribery used to effect that great political measure." Sir Jonah's anti-Union sentiments harmonized with those of Daniel Haliday, and they formed such an intimacy that Daniel Haliday gave him a share of his apartments and even supplied him with money, as appears by unpaid promissory notes found amongst Daniel Haliday's papers after his death. In fact, Sir Jonah's "Historic Memoirs of Ireland" were completed and his "Personal Sketches" written in Daniel Haliday's rooms at Paris.

Francis Plowden in his History of Ireland from 1800 to 1810, a work published in 1812 gives an interesting account of the compilation of the Historic Memoirs by Sir Jonah. Sir Jonah (says Plowden) had been always a devoted servant of the Government up to the time of the debates upon the Union.

For his services he had been made Judge of the Court of Admiralty, at £800 a year, a post which at that time neither hindered his practice at the Bar nor his sitting in Parliament. In the debates upon the Union he was a most violent opponent of the measure, speaking often and with great ability against it.

No sooner was it carried than he proceeded, while the anti-Union fervour was still strong, to collect all the authentic evidence he could of the corrupt means employed to carry it, and was supplied with a great mass of proofs. Amongst the rest, the Right Honorable John Foster, the late Speaker of the Commons, then violent against Pitt and

Castlereagh, on account of the Union, gave him many secret papers of the utmost importance. These Sir Jonah got engraved in fac-simile, the better to authenticate them. Such was his diligence, that, in 1803, he was able to announce that his work, "comprising" (as the notification stated) "secret records of the Union, illustrated with curious letters in fac-simile," was ready for the press. At the same time Sir Jonah went over ostentatiously to London to bring out the work. All the world were eager for its issue, except, of course, the Ministers and those who were to be exposed in its pages. But the work was delayed during Addington's ministry from unexplained but easily imagined causes.

When Pitt succeeded Addington, Sir Jonah became active again, and Foster, the late Speaker, having become reconciled by this time to Pitt, he apprised him and Castlereagh of the documents he had put into Barrington's power. The result was that Barrington was to have a pension of £2,500 a year, and orders were sent to Lord Hardwicke, then Lord Lieutenant of Ireland, to give his warrant for passing it. But at this time Lord Hardwicke was at difference with Mr. Pitt, and he declined, as he said he ought to have been consulted with, and he disapproved of it. He was peremptorily ordered to pass it, and he as peremptorily refused, and soon threw up his office. The business having thus become public, and Pitt dying, the proposed pension dropped.[1]

Sir Jonah now tried what the actual publication might do as a commercial speculation, and there were published, between 1809 and 1815, five parts of the Historic Memoirs, at a guinea each, on the largest and finest imperial quarto

---

[1] "History of Ireland, from its union with Great Britain, in January, 1801, to October, 1810," by Francis Plowden. Vol. 2nd, pp. 229–233. 3 vols., 8vo, Dublin, 1811.

paper, and illustrated with finely etched portraits. And there the work stopped, being about half way (for it was announced as to be completed in ten parts), and so remained for twenty years, when it was taken up by Henry Colburn, and the publication completed in 1835, in the same sumptuous style as the early parts, the unpublished remainder having been purchased by him from Sir Jonah's executors.[1] But, in the meantime, and before the publication of the Historic Memoirs by Henry Colburn, that is to say, in the year 1833, a comparatively mean edition of the work, under another title, appeared at Paris, in one volume octavo, being called the "Rise and Fall of the Irish Nation." It was this work that Sir Jonah prepared for the press in Haliday's rooms. Such was one of Daniel Haliday's anti-Unionist friends.

*D. Haliday and Colonel John Allen.*

Another friend of Daniel Haliday's, of a different stamp from Sir Jonah Barrington, but more decidedly anti-Unionist, was Colonel John Allen. He was son of a woollen draper, in Dame-street, and was deeply engaged in the Rebellion of 1798. He was arrested in the company of Arthur O'Connor and Quigley at Margate, trying to hire a vessel to carry them to France, with an address to the French Directory, encouraging them to invade England. He was tried with them for High Treason, at Maidstone, on the 21st of May, 1798, but had the good luck to be acquitted with Arthur O'Connor, while Quigley was convicted and hanged. The address was found in the pocket of Quigley's great coat, thrown over a chair, at the King's Head, Margate, where they were arrested, and it sealed Quigley's fate. Allen appeared as servant to Quigley, who went by the name of "Captain Jones." He told a friend of

---

[1] "Critical Dictionary of English and American Authors," by S. Austin Alibone. Philadelphia and London. 3 vols., imperial 8vo, 1859.

Haliday's, at Paris, that the address was carried each day by a different one of the party, and it was thus in Quigley's care the day of their arrest. Upon their fortunate escape, Allen returned to Ireland, took part in the Rebellion of 1798, and escaped again ; and, in 1803, was active in Robert Emmet's outbreak.

He escaped arrest and lay hidden with some young friend in Trinity College until he was put into a cask, carried to George's-quay and shipped for France. There he entered the French military service and obtained a commission in the Irish Legion.

This regiment was one of those that in April, 1810, most closely invested the city of Astorga in Spain. The French artillery having made a breach, General Junot, who commanded the besieging army, ordered an assault. The "forlorn hope," consisting of six companies of light infantry, was led by Colonel (then Captain) Allen of the Irish regiment. The breach was obstinately defended by the Spaniards, but Allen succeeded in making with his Voltigeurs a lodgment in the works, and throughout the ensuing night maintained himself there, and kept up an incessant firing to intimate his existence and position. General Junot having next morning determined on a general assault of the town, Colonel Ware (another Irishman, a descendant of Sir James Ware, the antiquary), with his grenadiers was to enter first, but the garrison surrendered.

One who knew Allen well at Paris in the later years of his life, said, a gayer, more light hearted, and agreeable man he never met, and that the same might be said of Colonel Miles Byrne and others of the band of Irish exiles, their companions.

He often looked with admiration, he said, on these men who had so long lived with their lives in their hand, showing such ease and hilarity.

Allen, he said, kept his whole substance in coin in a box, mistrusting all Government securities, being persuaded that there would be a fresh revolution, as there was, but it was only of a dynasty.

For many years Charles Haliday was the hand employed to pay a small annuity to two poor but highly respectable women, Allen's sisters, dwelling in an obscure and mean place called Hoey's-court, near Werburgh-street. And when Captain Allen died he secured for them the property of their brother.

It was, of course, by means of his brother Daniel that Charles Haliday became acquainted with Allen's affairs, for Mr. Haliday differed in political sentiment, as has been already stated, from his brother Daniel. Yet this in no manner diminished his affection for him. Mr. Haliday mingled the sentiments of a loyalist of the old stamp with the more liberal views of a modern Conservative. And thus recurring to the language so common in '98 and 1803, he would sometimes say of him jocularly, "Dan was a rebel; if he had lived he'd have been hanged."

*Death of D. Haliday.* Daniel died in the year 1836, at Paris, but his brother got his remains brought over to Dublin, and buried them beside his brother William at Dundrum. He erected a monument over them within the enclosure encircling William's grave, in the form of a broken column, with the following inscription:

Danielis Haliday
Edinburgensis Parisiensisque
Medicinæ Facultatum Socius;
Academiæ Regiæ Hiberniæ Sodalis
Natus Dublinii 19 October, 1798,
Obiit Die nono Maii, 1836,
Ætatis 38.

Translation:—

Daniel Haliday, Fellow of the Faculties of
Medicine of Paris and Edinburgh, Member of the
Royal Irish Academy.
Born at Dublin 19th October, 1798,
Died 9th May, 1836,
Aged 38.

In 1864 there was a project before Parliament for a central general railway terminus in Dublin. One part of the plan was to run a viaduct diagonally across Westmoreland-street, at the height of about twenty feet above the pavement. It was to pass from near the second house on the east side nearest to Carlisle-bridge, to the middle house on the opposite side, in other words about half-way down that side between Fleet-street and the river. Mr. Haliday, to whom nothing that concerned the port or city of Dublin was indifferent, saw that the finest view in Dublin would be thus sacrificed. He at once organized resistance to the scheme, collecting witnesses of approved character to confront the witnesses of the projectors, writing letters in the public prints, stirring up the Corporation to protect the city. The Corporation took the best way of bringing to the notice of the citizens the disfigurement of the city that would follow the completion of the plan. They erected a wooden frame work, of the size of the proposed viaduct, across the street in the exact line of its direction at the height intended, and kept it there until after the Parliamentary inquiry was over. It was at once plain to every eye that the huge ungainly structure would spoil the finest architectural scene in the city. Just as the only fine view of that noble building of St. Paul's Cathedral in London is ruined by the railway viaduct crossing Ludgate Hill, obstructing the view of Sir Christopher Wren's masterpiece, and cutting its front in half; so by this project, Nelson's column and the bold Ionic portico of the General Post Office adjacent, as viewed from Westmoreland-street would have been ruined, and in like manner, the fine grouping of the Corinthian columns of the Lords' portico in connexion with the front of Trinity College as seen from Sackville-street.

Mr. Haliday proceeded to London with his witnesses, entertained them there, kept them together, attended their examination before the Committee of the Lords, and the bill for the scheme was thrown out, owing in a great degree to his energetic opposition. Lamentable as the effect of the viaduct would have been then, how much more to be deplored would it have been now since the lowering of Carlisle-bridge, and the widening of it to the full breadth of Sackville-street.

*The Wenix.* In the library at Monkstown Park there was a fine panel picture over the fireplace by Wenix, the celebrated Dutch animal painter. The picture had originally been much larger, representing probably a farmyard, but what remained represented little more than a gray and white goose standing on one leg. And a very fine object it was. Mr. Haliday told me that he got it in this way. One morning in passing through Trinity-street he called in at Jones's the auctioneer, father of Jones, the worthy auctioneer of D'Olier-street, so well known and respected, and only just dead. Jones came in with a large roll of dirty canvas under his arm, and on Mr. Haliday's asking him what he had got there, he said it was a piece of old canvas that covered the top of a bed at an old furniture broker's in Liffey-street; that the bed, a miserable one, had belonged to a caretaker of Tyrone House in Marlborough-street. The caretaker it seems had cut the picture out of one of the panels as a tester or cover for his bed. "I'll give you ten pounds for it," said Haliday, "without looking at it." It was handed to him, and at first he feared he had made a bad bargain it was so dilapidated. But he had judged rightly in guessing that nothing worthless or common could come out of that splendid dwelling,[1] a model of architectural taste and elegance It proved to be a Wenix, and what remained was well worth the price paid. In showing the picture to his friends Mr. Haliday used always to say jocularly, "That's a portrait of the head of the family."

---

[1] Tyrone House in Marlborough-street was built in 1740 for Sir Marcus Beresford, Viscount, and afterwards Earl of Tyrone, by Cassels, architect of the Parliament House and Leinster House. It is now occupied by the National Education Commissioners.

I remember well accompanying Mr. Haliday in his carriage to our friend James Frederic Ferguson's funeral, from his lodgings in Rathmines to Mount Jerome Cemetery at Harold's-cross." Talking of his own death, he said, "I often think of what old Herbert the auctioneer said to Henry Harrington, of Grange Con, near Baltinglass, in the county of Wicklow, a gentleman of large fortune, with an extensive collection of objects of vertu of all kinds. "Mr. Harrington," said Herbert, "what a fine catalogue you will make."[1]

Akin to this was an anecdote he had from me of my friend Colonel Robert O'Hara, Lieutenant-Colonel commanding the 88th or "Connaught Rangers." He said to his mother, one day at dinner in Mountjoy-square, "Where is the nice China dinner service you had? Ah! I know it all. It is keeping for the auction." Often afterwards, Mr. Haliday, when he missed something from the table, would say, "Mary! don't let us be keeping it for the auction."

Distant as we were at one time we grew close acquaintances as years flew by, and we were mutually glad of

---

[1] Mr. Harrington was descendant and representative of Sir Henry Harrington, a soldier of Queen Elizabeth's day, who got large grants in the county of Wicklow. It was then "the Tooles' and the Byrnes' country," and was part of the county of Dublin. It was only made into a separate county in the year 1606 by King James I. Sir Henry Harrington was long Seneschal of the Tooles' and Byrnes' country. Henry Harrington, of Grange Con, had literary tastes, was of most temperate habits, unmarried, and was between eighty and ninety when he died, about the year 1842, a prisoner for debt in the Marshalsea. He ruined himself by buying pictures, porcelain, ivories, old curiosities of all kinds, which were all catalogued, seized, and sold in the year 1832.

"What brought Sir Visto's ill-got wealth to waste?
Some demon whispered,—Visto have a taste.
Heaven visits with a taste the wealthy fool"—

Lines applicable to poor Harrington in all but the getting of his wealth, for whatever may be said of being ill-got by his ancestor through confiscation, a possession of 250 years by his descendants had cured at all events any original defect of title.

accidental meetings. Often, on my way home from the courts, by the Southern quays, I have met Mr. Haliday, on his way from the Bank of Ireland, Corn Exchange, or the Ballast Board, to his counting house, on Arran-quay. He would then turn back, and accompany me a good distance for the pleasure of conversing. When we reached the place where we ought to part, I, in return, would accompany him back, but he was a man of such courtesy that he would insist on leaving me to the parting point nearest to my own house, and thus often took a third walk, and so we spent our time in the escorting of each other. Mr. Haliday always walked by the Southern quays, though his house of business was on the other side, as being quieter, and leaving him better opportunity to observe the Liffey. Often was he meditating where "the Hurdle ford" was placed, or contemplating the shelf of rock to be seen at low water, above Essex-bridge, towards the Four Courts (supposed to be the ford where Lord Thomas Fitzgerald passed with his company on horseback to throw down his defiance to the Council, in Mary's-abbey, and renounce his allegiance to Henry VIII., in 1534), whilst he was supposed by the citizens, who knew him, to be occupied with the price of wheat or the rise or fall of public stocks.

When some special business would take him to London his partner, Richard Welch, his wife's nephew (since his death his worthy representative), would say to him, "Now, don't forget to go down at times to the 'Baltic Coffee house,' among the Greeks, and see the Mavrocordatos, the Rallis, the Castellis, the Rodocanachis, and try and pick up a few commissions or some cargoes of wheat." While he was away they could scarce get a word from him, and, when he returned, he was obliged, somewhat ashamed, to confess that he had spent more time at the Public Record Office with his friend Sir Thomas Duffus Hardy, Deputy Keeper of the Records, or at the British Museum, than among the Greeks, at the Baltic Coffee House. But at home no such researches were ever allowed to interfere with his business pursuits.

The Rev. James Graves, Secretary to the Royal Irish Historical and Archæological Society, told me that visiting Dr. Todd, one day at his chambers, in Trinity College, Dr. Todd said to him, "Come here, Graves, and see what that noble fellow, Charles Haliday, has done;" and, opening a box, he showed him some fine prehistoric gold ornaments, amongst others two torques or twisted collars, "the *likes of which*" (said Todd) "I never saw before. They are part," said he, "of a find—a fifth part only—of what five navvies chanced upon while working in a cutting on the Limerick and Foynes Railway track. They agreed to keep the secret of their discovery, and to divide it amongst themselves. One of them sold his share to West, the jeweller, of Dame-street, and Haliday, hearing of it, went there, and West sold it to him for £160, the price he had paid for it, which was only the value of the gold. Haliday did this to secure it for the Royal Irish Academy, and allowing them to select such articles as they desired for their museum of antiquities, sold the rest."

He, Lord Talbot, and Dr. Todd, contributed £25 apiece, and secured for the Academy the Book of Fermoy, an ancient Irish manuscript, sold at Monck Mason's sale. He offered, he told me, £800 for Eugene O'Curry's papers, but the Catholic University would not let anyone have them but themselves.

Between the years 1854 and 1860 Monsieur Ferdinand de Lesseps came over to Dublin, and at a special meeting of the Chamber of Commerce, unfolded his scheme for a canal through the Isthmus of Suez, so run down and derided in Parliament by Lord Palmerston (who got Stephenson, the great engineer, after an inspection of the mouth of the canal, in the Mediterranean, in his yacht, to declare it impracticable), that he would be scarce listened

*Monsieur de Lesseps and C. Haliday.*

to in London. But, as M. de Lesseps stated in his speech at the Vartry Waterworks, when afterwards he came over here in 1871, as one of a deputation sent by Monsieur Thiers, to thank the Irish for their aid of money and surgeons sent to them in the Franco-German war—" In Dublin," said de Lesseps, " I met a more intelligent, a more sympathising audience, than almost anywhere else." Mr. Haliday played a leading part at the meeting of the Chamber of Commerce, and I remember my surprise at his saying, when I met him coming away, and asked him did he think the scheme feasible? " Perfectly feasible," was his answer.

Mention has already been made of his humanity and his efforts to preserve or procure a bathing place for the poor of Kingstown. I am myself a witness of similar efforts of his for the poor of Dublin. They had a bathing place at Irishtown (within the last two years destroyed by the carrying of the great culvert for the drainage of the Pembroke township across the sands), where, for a half-penny, men and boys found a good plunging and swimming bath, long established there as a private speculation, and women and girls had a separate place equally cheap, or both could bathe for nothing on the shore. In the year 1860, finding the soles of my shoes coated with sticky mud in walking across the sands on my way home to Sandymount, I told him I had discovered that it arose from the Ballast Board discharging the dredgings of the Liffey through gaps they had made for the purpose in the walls of the road leading to the Pigeon House Fort, and that it was spoiling the bathing place. He was distressed to hear it, and instantly used his influence at the Board, and had the practice stopped.

Talking with him of the pleasure a man of small means may enjoy with a taste for letters, he said it was true : " A lawyer, a soldier, a clergyman may be poor," said he, " and yet respectable," but a merchant was considered as a poor creature unless he was supposed to have his pockets full of money.

"My brother merchants would think me mad," said he, on another occasion, " if they knew I rose before day to labour at these literary tasks." But the few who knew the zest he felt in these pursuits could not doubt but that from it came his habitual animation, like that of a sportsman in a chase.

In truth one great prescription for happiness in life is to have a hare to hunt. And " the sober sage " who would call this ruling passion madness, might well be answered in the lines of the poet:—

> "Less mad the wildest whimsy we can frame
> Than e'en that passion if it has no aim :
> For though such motives folly you may call
> The folly's greater to have none at all."

Mr. Haliday was never confined to his bed by illness, but his health was impaired about ten years before his death by an event curiously connected with the subject of his studies.

It was the custom of the Ballast Board, twice a year, to send their fine steam yacht on a voyage round the coasts of Ireland to visit and view the several Lighthouses. Mr. Haliday was seized with an ardent desire to avail himself of such an opportunity of visiting the many isles or islets lying off the shores of Ireland, the scenes of the first plunderings of the northern sea rovers from Norway, the Orkneys, and the Hebrides, when they fell upon the small monasteries on these islets, or upon the solitary hermits like him who occupied Skelig Michel, off the coast of Kerry, and carried away, as they found nothing else to take, and he died in captivity with them.[1]

Mr. Haliday had not been long at sea, when he found his constitution so disordered, though he did not suffer from

*C. Haliday attempts a voyage round Ireland.*

---

[1] "Wars of the Gaedhill with the Gaill," xxxv., xxxvi.

sea-sickness, that he was obliged to abandon his scheme, and I have often thought that his ailments had their first origin from this voyage.

He was himself apprehensive of heart disease. "My cough," said he to me one day, sitting after dinner *tete-à-tete* " shakes parts that I do not like."

In the summer of 1865, he came down to Oxford, to visit me there at work over the Carte Papers at the Bodleian Library, bringing with him the first (and greater) part of the vellum Register of Thomas Court Abbey, to compare with the residue or the other part in that library. I remember his waiting with the volume under his arm at the library door, until I brought the Librarian to him, lest he might be suspected when going away of taking the property of the library with him. Later in the day he was on his return thence to London, and while waiting at the station, I observed his necktie with its knot shifted under his left ear—

"Just where the hangman doth dispose,
To special friends, the knot of noose;"

and as his sight had greatly failed, I made a jesting excuse of these lines out of Hudibras, for offering to be his valet. He smiled and said that the throbbing was so violent in his carotid artery, that he was obliged to leave his necktie loose and liable to get out of place.

But all this time he never allowed his family to suppose he was ill, and would never use his carriage when sent, once or twice only, by his wife to the train to meet him of a cold winter evening, who knew too well that he would be annoyed at it, yet was unable to forbear to send it in her anxiety for his health.

*C. Haliday's grave.*

Just outside the western wall of his garden, lying at the foot of the knoll on which his house is built, is one of those small ancient ruined churches and graveyards so common all over Ireland, nothing of the church remaining but an ivied gable or perhaps a chancel arch, and among the mouldering heaps a few old battered or broken tombstones. As often as we passed the scene, he would say "There I am to be laid; and I have left orders that I shall be borne thither by my own servants, and that no stone shall ever be set up over my remains."

He indulged in no complainings or regrets, unless once or twice to say "Don't grow old P., don't grow old," not sadly, but with a smile, and in a jesting tone, as if to tell how he felt the incommodities of age, though he would say no more about it; or on another occasion when he said "Ah, you may do something, but I—I have no time left me at my age to do anything in the literary line!"

He judged very accurately of the length of time he had to live. On the 12th of November, 1865, he said to me after dinner (as I find by a memorandum I made at the time) "Another year will see me down." And he died on the 14th day of September, 1866.

Mr. Haliday married Mary Hayes, daughter of Mr. Hayes of Mountmellick, in the Queen's county. Her uncle was General Hayes of the East India Company's Army, and the following epitaph on the monument set up for him at Mountmellick, is the composition of Charles Haliday : [Mrs. Haliday.]

Erected<br>
To the Memory<br>
of<br>
Major-General Thomas Hayes,<br>
Who departed this life the 2nd of September, 1831,<br>
Aged 72 years.<br>
Distinguished during a long period of<br>
Active Military Service,<br>
By Courage, Decision, and Perseverance.<br>
He was in the retirement of private life beloved<br>
From the Warmth of his Friendship, the Benevolence of his Actions,<br>
and the integrity of his Conduct.<br>
A liberal Benefactor to the Public Works and Private Charities<br>
of this his native town,<br>
He rendered Wealth estimable by the manner in which he used it.

Her mother was Miss Hetherington sister of Richard Hetherington, Secretary to John Philpot Curran, Master of the Rolls, better known as Curran, the great forensic and Parliamentary orator of his day in Ireland. Through this connexion with the Hetheringtons Mr. Haliday was possessed of a vast fund of anecdotes concerning this extraordinary and, in private life, ill regulated character.[1]

Mrs. Haliday was of delicate health and nothing could be more admirable than the chivalrous and devoted attention which her husband paid her, more like that of a youthful lover than of a long-wedded spouse. Their love was mutual. His death was too heavy a stroke for her to bear up against in her enfeebled state and she died on the 10th of April, 1868. Before she was laid beside him in the grave she practised a little pardonable casuistry, evading the directions he gave that no stone should be set up over his grave by placing a tablet to his memory against the wall of the ruined church, hard by but not over him. She could not bear to think that his memory should be forgotten, little knowing how soon such memorials perish—how soon indeed oblivion covers all things.

*Mrs. Haliday's gift to the Royal Irish Academy.* But she raised a more enduring monument to his memory by the sumptuous gift she made of his rich library and all its treasures to the Royal Irish Academy whereby his name will live as long as learning shall live in Ireland. She had heard him sometimes say that he had thoughts of leaving his collections where they would be kept together; but he did not carry out his design; but left her everything he was possessed of by his will, in the shortest and most com-

---

[1] Curran was appointed in 1806, and resigned in 1814. Hetherington was indignant at Curran's concealing from him his intention of resigning, and more especially at his not securing him some provision. Curran had presented Hetherington with his portrait in the days of their friendship. Hetherington after Curran's retirement sent him back the picture in a dung cart to his house called Hermitage, at Rathfarnham, in company with a pig 'the only fit company for such a man,' he said.

prehensive terms. In connexion with this gift there will be found in the proceedings of the Royal Irish Academy[1] the following letter:—

"Monkstown Park, 9th of January, 1867.

"DEAR SIR,—It is with much pleasure I have to announce to you that Mrs. Haliday has decided on presenting intact to the Royal Irish Academy the whole of the late Mr. Haliday's collection of pamphlets, tracts, papers, &c., relating to Ireland. Having been left all his property absolutely she is desirous to pay this tribute to the memory of her late beloved and lamented husband, and at the same time to preserve to the Royal Irish Academy so valuable and unique a collection.

Believe me, &c.,
RICHARD WELCH.
Executor to the late Charles Haliday.

To the Rev. William Reeves, D.D.
Secretary of the Royal Irish Academy.

The extent of this priceless collection has been already mentioned[2] and it can now be seen and judged by the literary world. It is kept as a separate library, the more to honour the name and memory of the donor. And to further perpetuate the recollection of him, the Academy had a portrait of him painted by Catterson Smith and hung it in the library or collection designated by his name.

Mr. Haliday was tall and well proportioned. His countenance was expressive of great animation and energy. He had a fine head and regular features with a brow indicative of capacity. His mien had something haughty, his manners though courteous, were rather distant and forbad familiarity; but to friends he was free and cordial. He was benevolent and ever ready to aid the deserving; to servants he was a good master.

*Characteristics of C. Haliday.*

He spoke with intelligence and precision. He seemed to concentrate all the powers of his mind in discussion, and he thoroughly investigated and mastered every subject he took in hand. The most practised lawyer was not more

---

[1] Proceedings of the Royal Irish Academy, Vol. x.      [2] Page xviii.

diligent than he was in the search for evidence or more capable of testing its value.

In reflecting on the great zeal for learning and accomplishment displayed by him and his brother one is inclined to ask whence came this desire to shine and to excel? His eldest brother William Haliday was a prodigy of learning before he was twenty-four; for he was only that age when he died.

We find the author of the present work giving himself up to study, in a career so inimical to letters, with such zeal as to hurt his health. "I feel it now," said he to me one day not six years before his death. They had no companions winning fame at the bar to stimulate their rivalry; they had no hopes of getting into Parliament; competition for the public service was not yet dreamt of. The family was not moving in so high a circle as to make such accomplishments necessary or even acceptable—yet they both dedicated all their efforts to training and exercising their faculties.

It was a saying of one of the first masters of athletics in ancient Greece that he could distinguish his pupils at a distance even though only carrying meat from the market; so the sentiments of those who have received a polite education exercise a similar influence over their manners.

And thus in the most trivial intercourse with Mr. Haliday one could scarce fail to be sensible of the high training his mind had undergone.

To me who enjoyed so much of his intimacy these characteristics were most strikingly displayed. His reading and recollection furnished him with a fund of anecdote about the public men of his time, particularly of the period of '98; of this era he had read all the literature besides knowing personally some of the families of those concerned in that rebellion. His memory was so retentive and accurate and the style of his conversation was so pointed and animated that our Sunday dinners were to me a feast the day after. He owed none of these brilliant qualities to association with the class he belonged to; they were the product of self-education. But whence the motive? Was it not due to the period when the faculties of him and his brother were opening? May it not be traced to the influence of the era of the French Revolution? This great event awakened and stimulated the minds of men, with the hopes of a new and better world.

Added to this were the agitations of the Irish rebellion and of the Union, which also powerfully exercised the faculties and passions. Though he and his brother were then too young for public life, the houses they frequented were full of the men of that day and their conversation had its influence upon their minds.

Be the cause what it may it is an honour to this city and country to have had such a citizen as the author of the present work, and especially to the Merchants of Dublin, a body he was proud to belong to.

For myself I count it a happy event of my life to have enjoyed the friendship and intimacy of such a man; and I am glad to think that as Editor of his literary remains my name will in future times be thus associated with his.

### Of the Maps in this Work.

Mr. Haliday's original design was to write a history of the port and harbour of Dublin, with a view to trace the progress of improvement in the navigable channel of the Liffey, but he was so seduced from his course by a search into a history of its Scandinavian antiquities, that there would have been left no monument of his proper object only for his essay or paper on Sir Bernard de Gomme's map of the port and harbour of Dublin in 1673.

One can only regret, considering the ability and research he has displayed in this short essay, that he was not able, through the late period of life when he entered on this study, to accomplish as well his original design as that which he substituted for it. The amount of materials to be found in his commonplace books will prove what a supply he had collected for his work. They will yet prove useful to others, and they, not he, will reap the honours.

Whilst the history of the port of Dublin was still in his mind he sought in the Assembly Rolls of the city for the periodical reports made to it by the Ballast Board, which was only a branch or committee of the Corporation.

But, besides searching the Corporation records and other sources already mentioned, Mr. Haliday made inquiry for all such maps as might throw light on the early state of the port.

Sir B. de Gomme's map, 1673. In this manner he obtained from the British Museum copies of Sir Bernard de Gomme's map, made in 1673, of Captain Greenvil Collins's map, made in 1686, and in his own library he had Rocque's map of the city and bay, made in 1756,—all reproduced on a smaller scale in the present volume, except Sir Bernard de Gomme's, which is on the scale of the original.

In addition to these are given three other maps of considerable interest.

Down survey map of harbour, 1654. One is a facsimile from Petty's Down survey, made in about 1655, being the earliest map made to scale of the port and city. It is reproduced on the original scale, and it is to be regretted that the scale is so small. The other is Captain John Perry's map of the bay and harbour of Dublin, engraved in 1728. A notice of this map is given in Gough's "Topographical Antiquities," but as it is not to be found at the British Museum Mr. Haliday inserted a notice in *Notes and Queries*, inquiring for this map, and also for information as to any other map of the city, either in manuscript or printed, between Speed's map in 1610 and Brookin's map in 1728.[1]

Mr. Haliday's queries were never answered, nor were his

[1] Appendix, p. 249, n. 2.

wishes gratified in his lifetime. But since his death I discovered Petty's map, made in the year 1654, in the celebrated Down Survey at the Public Record Office; and it was my good fortune to meet with Captain John Perry's map of 1728 by accident in the hands of my friend Richard Bergoin Bennett, of Eblana Castle, Kingstown. It is a very finely engraved map, printed by Bowles, of Cheapside, London, the great map and print seller of that day. It would have been particularly interesting to Mr. Haliday, as exhibiting the canal (and pier) projected by Captain John Perry as a new entrance to the harbour of Dublin to avoid the bar. The canal was to be carried through the sands of the North Bull, parrallel with the north shore of Dublin Bay. He proposed that the seaward entrance should be in the Sutton Creek, near Kilbarrack Old Church, and the other to come out nearly opposite Ringsend. The third is the ground-plan of Chichester House, made in 1723, which I met with, in the year 1852, when rooting among the Exchequer Records with my friend James Frederic Ferguson, their then keeper, and copied it.[1]

*Capt. J. Perry's map of 1728.*

*Plan of Chichester House, 1723.*

---

[1] *Chichester House.*—In 1602 the city granted a plot of ground to Sir George Cary, knt., Treasurer-at-War for Ireland, to build an hospital for poor, sick, and maimed soldiers, or other poor folk, or for a free school.—(*City Assembly Rolls*). Sir George Cary sold his interest to Sir Thomas Ridgway. In 1611 Sir Arthur Chichester purchased Cary's hospital (*ibid.*), and in 1613 are found despatches and State papers, dated by him from " Chichester House."—*Calendar of State Papers of James I.* (*Ireland*), 1611–1614, p. 336. Sir Arthur did not die till 1625, and, during his lifetime, in 1618, Lord Deputy St. John held councils there, and dated his despatches from " Chichester House " (*ibid.*, 1615–1625, p. 204), as did Lord Falkland, Lord Deputy, on 23rd July, 1623 (*ibid.*, p. 414). On Sir Arthur's death, in 1625, without issue, Chichester House passed to his brother, Sir Edward Chichester, who sold it to Sir Samuel Smyth. The following is a verbatim copy of Sir Edward's letter to Sir Samuel, who had contracted for the purchase:—

" Sir Samuel Smyth,

"I understand, by Sir Thomas Hybbotts, that he hath acquainted you soone after my comeing from

The "Old shore," marked under the present Lords' portico, had the greatest interest for Mr. Haliday, and

Dublin that Sʳ. Fra. Annesley hath relinquisht my promise to him for Chichester House, and that therefore now the bargayne betweene me and yoᵘ for it (is) to goe forward. As soone as the conveyhances shall be drawen and brought to Sʳ Tho. Hibbotts hee will pʳuse them and send them to me to be perfected wᵗʰ I will hasten in respect my occasions are urgent for money whᶜʰ was the cheife cause I sell at such a lowe rate. And thus, not doubtinge of yoʳ. pʳformance herein, I doe for this tyme, wishinge yoᵘ much happiness, bid yoᵘ very hartely farewell.

"Yoʳ. assured friend,
"(Signed), EDWARD CHICHESTER.
"Joymount, 29th Decᵇᵉʳ, 1626.
(Addressed) " To my very good friend Sir Samuell Smyth, knt., give theis."
(*Original with W. Monck Gibbon*, LL.D., *Barrister*.)

Sir Samuel Smyth made a lease of the mansion-house, gate-house, garden, and plantations to the Rev. Edward Parry, D.D., who became Bishop of Killaloe, and died of the plague, the 28th of July, 1650, in his house—"Chichester House." On his death it passed to his son, the Rev. John Parry, D.D., afterwards Bishop of Ossory. On 12th September, 1659, "the Church of Christ meeting at Chichester House," appointed Mr. Thomas Hicks to preach and dispense the Gospel at Stillorgan and other places in the barony of Rathdown as the Lord shall enable him."—(*Book of Establishment, Record Tower, Dublin Castle.*)

In 1661 it was first made use of for the sittings of Parliament. On 5th April, 1661, £30 were ordered to Mrs. Sankey on perfecting the writings on her part concerning Chichester House, " now to be made use of for the Parliament."—Vol. L., *ibid.*) On 26th April, 1661, Richard White, of Dublin. merchant, demised to Sir Paul Davis, knt., Clerk of the Council, the great hall in Chichester House, and one chamber adjoining to the end of the said gallery for H.M.'s use, from 25th March last past, for two years, at £60 per annum; and the said lease having expired on 25th March, 1663, it was thought fit by the Lord Deputy and Council (says their Concordatum Order of April 3, 1669), to continue the lease, and the rent was ordered to be paid him from time to time, half-yearly, beforehand. Signed at head " Ossory ; " and at foot :—" Michael Dublin, Canc. ; Ja. Armach " (and other Councillors). Dated at the Council Chamber, Dublin, 3rd April, 1669.—(*Auditor-General's Records, Records, P.R.O.*). These were portions of the house probably demised by Chichester, Smyth, or Parry. In 1675 (25th of King Charles II.) John Parry, Bishop of Ossory, made a lease of Chichester House to Sir Henry Forde (Secretary to the Lord

he refers to it in his essay on Sir Bernard de Gomme's map.[1]

By the aid of these maps and the information collected by Mr. Haliday, from the Assembly Rolls of the Corporation, a good conception can be formed of the extraordinary changes effected in the channel of the Liffey in the course of 200 years.

In Sir Bernard de Gomme's map, the northern shore of the bay is now represented by the line of Amiens-street and

Lieutenant of Ireland, for the use of His Majesty, for ninety-nine years, at £180 a year, for the use of the two Houses of Parliament. The premises are described as "a large room wherein the Lords sate; two committee rooms for the Lords on the same floor; a robe room; a wainscot room at the stairfoot; a conference room below stairs wherein the Commons sate; a passage leading to the committee room; two committee rooms above stairs for the Commons; the Speaker's room; two rooms below stairs for the sergeant-at-arms; three rooms adjoining for the clerk; two small cellars; a gate-house next the street containing five small rooms; a courtyard, with an entry through the house to the back-yard; a stable-yard (with buildings enumerated); a large garden with an old banqueting house, and all other rooms of the said house as then in His Majesty's possession."—(*Original in the possession of W. Monck Gibbon*, LL.D., *Barrister*.)

The care and preservation of Chichester House, when Parliament was not sitting, was, in 1670, granted to William Robinson, esq., Superintendent of Government buildings, for his life, and the use of the outoffices and gardens, " except a terras-walk, at the east end of the said house, twenty-five feet broad, and a terras-walk, on the south side, twenty feet broad, and a back yard, forty feet deep," on condition of keeping it in repair, and paying the taxes. On 19th May, 1677, the Earl of Essex, being then Lord Lieutenant, he recommended that a lease should be made of the garden and outoffices to Mr. Robinson, on similar conditions, for ninety years, and the use of the house for life, except during the sittings of Parliament.—(*Earl of Essex to Henry Gascoyne, esq.; Carte Papers, vol.* ccxlii., *p.* 128.) In pursuance of which a patent was passed to that effect, dated 2nd June, 1677. This demise to William Robinson serves to explain the interest of him or his representatives mentioned in the return of the surveyors annexed to the ground-plan of Chichester House, made in 1723, given at page 239.

[1] Appendix, p. 239.

the North-strand, the latter still preserving the original denomination.

The site of the terminus of the Great Northern Railway then was still covered by the sea.

*River and harbour in 1673.* The southern shore was Townsend-street, then known as Lazars' (corruptly Lazy) Hill, and Denzille-street. Between Lazy-hill and Ringsend is seen a wide waste of sand, with the waters of the Dodder River spread over it in small streams. It will be easily seen, that the building of Sir John Rogerson's wall, from Lazy-hill towards Ringsend with the making of other walls inland to the Barrack-hill at Beggar's Bush, gained all the strand within them; and that the making of a new and straight channel for the Dodder, which was done in 1796,[1] completed the work, so that the sands previously overspread by the wandering waters of the Dodder, are now meadows or streets, traversed by the Bath-avenue, leading to Ringsend.

If these alterations of the southern side are striking, the changes produced on the northern shore, since the making of Sir Bernard de Gomme's map, are as remarkable. By the making of the North Wall parallel to Sir John Rogerson's Wall, as far as Ringsend, and by running other walls inland, from the North Wall (all the work of the Ballast Board), an equal, indeed a larger extent of land has been gained from the sea.

In Sir Bernard de Gomme's map, all this land, both on the north and south sides of the bay, was then sea. At low water it was dry, with the Liffey divided into two or three branches wandering through this waste of mud and sand, and only uniting again at Ringsend.

And so the river remained until the commencement of the eighteenth century, when the Ballast Board was erected in 1708. The first work this Board designed was, to make an entirely new channel for the Liffey, from Lazy-hill to Ringsend. On looking at the waste of waters, as shown on Sir

[1] Appendix, p. 242.

Bernard de Gomme's map, this was certainly a bold undertaking. The river was to be made to flow in one straight channel to Ringsend.

Their first work was to stake out this channel, and then by piling and wattling in the sand on each side, to confine the river current to that new channel. On this foundation quay-walls were afterwards raised.

### THE BALLAST BOARD AND THE NEW CHANNEL.

The two operations of making a new channel for the river and the walling-in of the river were distinct works, and done by different agencies—the first being done directly by the Corporation through the Ballast Board, for this Board was only a branch of the Corporation; whilst the walling-in of the river was done by the Corporation for the most part, indirectly, by making grants and leases to persons on conditions of building the walls.

It will be found convenient to consider the making of the new channel first.

As this was done by the Ballast Board, the following short summary of the origin and creation of that Board is given. *Origin of the Ballast Board.*

In 1676, Henry Howard having petitioned the Lord Lieutenant for a patent for a Ballast Office in all the ports of Ireland, pursuant to the King's warrant under privy seal, made five years before, the Corporation interposed to prevent it.

By their charter they were owners, they said, of the waters and strand within their bounds, and had lately revived their ancient right to ballast, and by a by-law laid down rules for ballasting, and hoped to have a ballast office themselves, the profits of which were intended for the King's Hospital.[1] And their opposition was so effectual, that in 1682, Howard offered to take a lease of the port of Dublin, of the City at fifty pounds a year, and to surrender this

---

[1] Appendix, p. 244, n. 1.

patent or warrant. The Corporation ordered him a lease for thirty-one years.¹ But Howard having neglected to perfect this lease, the Corporation at Christmas, 1685, prayed for a patent to themselves.²

Thirteen years elapsed apparently without their obtaining their desire, for on 23rd November, 1698, they petitioned the Parliament of Ireland for a Ballast Board to be governed by themselves, to whom the river and strand belonged.³

The river they said was choked up by gravel and sand and ashes thrown in; and that by the taking of ballast below Ringsend the river had carried great quantities of loose sand into Poolbeg, Salmon Pool, Clontarf Pool, and Green Patch, the usual anchoring places, so that barques of any burden must unload, and the citizens bring up their coals and other things by land.⁴

Ten years more elapsed, and then in 1708 an Act of the Irish Parliament⁵ passed, creating the Ballast Board.

*New channel for the Liffey begun, A.D. 1710.*

The Board lost no time, and on 20th of October, 1710, gave orders to stake out the channel between Lazy Hill and Ringsend.⁶ But their first operations were on the north side. For on 21st July in that year they gave orders for dredging the channel and forming a bank on that side.⁷ On 2nd May, 1712, they resolved to enclose the channel and to carry it straight to Salmon Pool. This they effected by laying down kishes filled with stones, on both sides of the river which, was found by experience, so they said, to withstand all the force of the floods.⁸ Full details will be found in the Appendix amongst the notes on Mr. Haliday's paper, on Sir Bernard de Gomme's map.

But this new channel between Ringsend and the present quays, and all this work of enclosing it by kishes would have been useless and never undertaken unless for the sake

¹ Appendix, p. 244 n. 3.
² Ibid.
³ Appendix, p. 245, n. 1.
⁴ Ibid.
⁵ 6th of Anne, chap. xx.
⁶ Appendix, p. 235.
⁷ Ibid.
⁸ Ibid.

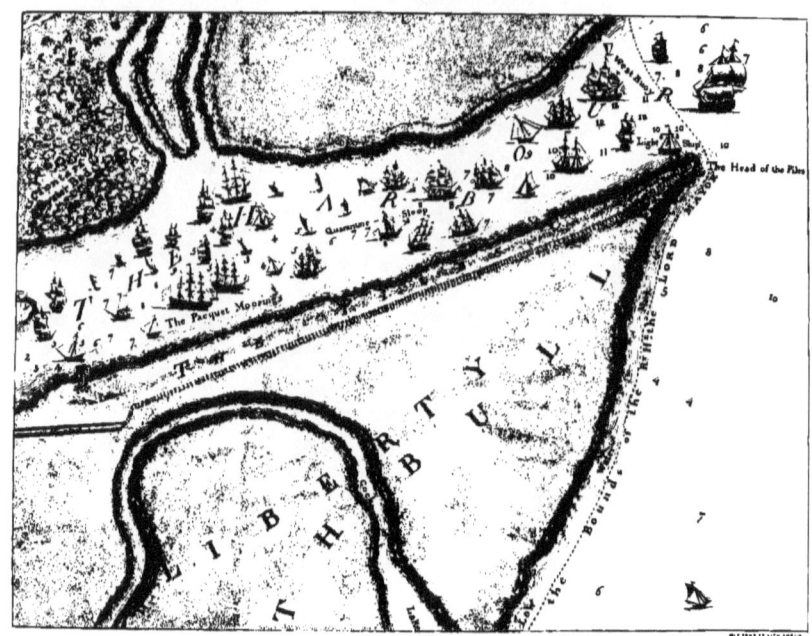

FROM
"Plan of the Town, Harbour Bay, and Environs of Dublin on the same scale as those of London Paris and Rome, by Jean Rocque, Chorographer. A.D. 1757."

of the harbour below Ringsend, that is to say, between Ringsend and the bar.

The earliest printed account of the port and harbour, by Gerard Boate, writing in 1649, describes the harbour amongst "the barred havens of Ireland."[1]

Over the bar there was at that time only six feet water at low tide. "With an ordinary tide you cannot go to the quay of Dublin (he says) with a ship that draws five feet of water; those of greater draught cannot come nearer than the Ringsend, three miles from Dublin Bay, and one mile from Dublin.[2] This haven (he adds) falleth dry almost all over with the ebb as well below Ringsend as above it, so as you may go dry foot round about the ships at anchor, except in two places, one at the north side, half-way between Dublin and the bar, and the other at the south side not far from it, one called the Pool of Clontarf, and the other Poolbeg, where it never falleth dry, but ships can remain afloat in nine or ten foot of water. Besides its shallowness (adds Boate), there is hardly any shelter, so that early in November, 1637, ten or twelve barques were driven from their anchors and never more heard of."[2]

*Harbour in A.D. 1649.*

But these pools, as we have seen by the petition of the Corporation to Parliament, had become greatly filled up in 1698. On both accounts the merchants of Dublin, in January, 1715, gave it as their opinion that the south side of the channel below Ringsend should be piled in, which would raise the south bank so high as to be a great shelter to shipping.[3]

The Ballast Board accordingly began to pile below Ringsend (that is to say, in the line from Ringsend towards the site of Pigeon-house); so that on 19th of October, 1716,

*New channel by piling begun, A.D. 1717.*

[1] " Ireland's Natural History; being a true and ample description, &c. Written by Gerard Boate, late Doctor of Physick to the State in Ireland, and now published by Samuel Hartlib, esq.;" p. 29, 8vo, London, 1652.
[2] *Ibid.*
[3] Appendix, p. 235.

*h*

they were able to report that they had made some progress in piling below Ringsend, adding that they intended going on the South Bull next year—the South Bull being the bank of sand between the Pigeon-house and the Lighthouse, left dry at low water.[1]

*Piling on the South Bull.*

On 19th January, 1717, having continued the piling below Ringsend, according to their report, as far as the sea would permit, they purposed to go on with the South Bull, and for that purpose they had oak timber for one set of piles, but four sets were required.[2] Accordingly in 1717 they began the work. By 19th July, 1717, they had driven 500 piles on the South Bull, and had filled in the spaces between the piles with hurdles and stones, with the expectation, since fully realized, that it would raise the bank and give shelter to ships.[3]

Having carried on the piling of the South Bull till 1720, they found further progress difficult, as the sea scarcely ever left the east or seaward end of the piles. They were therefore forced to change their method. Accordingly on 21st of April, 1721, they report that instead of piling by the engine, which was found impracticable so far at sea, they had used frames made of piles, twenty-two feet in length and ten feet in breadth, twenty-four piles in each frame. These were floated out from Blackrock accompanied by two gabbards filled with stones, and the frames then filled with the stones from the gabbards, and sunk.[4]

Captain John Perry's map of 1728, exhibits these works very clearly.

He shows the piling on the South Bull, then carried but to a certain distance, and at the end of the Bull, towards the sea, "framed spur work," such, evidently, as is above described.

But besides the piling on the South Bull, he shows the piling "below Ringsend," before alluded to. This had

[1] Appendix, p. 235.  [2] *Ibid.*
[3] *Ibid*, p. 236.  [4] *Ibid.*

advanced only as far as "Green Patch" (marked on Perry's map), by reason of the depth of the water, which hindered the piling from being carried to Cock (or Cockle) lake, as intended. On 17th of July, 1731, the Ballast Board sugges- *Pigeon-house-road.* ted, that instead of piles or frames, a double dry stone wall should be built and filled in between with gravel.[1] And such is the origin and history of what is now known as the Pigeon-house-road.

It remains to give some short account of the history of the Pigeon-house itself, of the Lighthouse, and the long low wall of granite from the Lighthouse to the Pigeon-house, nearly three miles in length, through the sea. The piling of the South Bull being completed about 1735, the Ballast Board placed a floating light near the eastern or seaward end of the piles in that year.[2] On 23rd of February, 1744, there appears a notice from the Ballast Board in the *Dublin Chronicle,* for proposals to build a lighthouse at the end of the piles. But it will be seen by Rocque's map, that in 1756 (the date of the map) the light ship was still there, and no lighthouse built. It was in June, 1761, that the Poolbeg Lighthouse, of cut granite, was begun, and at the same time the building of the long stone wall, called the Lighthouse wall.[3]

The progress of the wall was at first slow, for it appears *Lighthouse wall.* by a plan engraved on copper, attached to a proposal to Parliament, dated 5th July, 1784, concerning the erecting of a new bridge at Ringsend, that the length of wall was only like a short spur attached to the Lighthouse at that date. But on 10th January, 1789, there appears the following notice in the *Dublin Chronicle:*—

"The wall to the Lighthouse is now in such a state of forwardness, that it is expected the whole will be completed in eighteen months."[4]

[1] Appendix, p. 237.
[2] *Ibid.* p. 238, n.
[3] *Ibid.* p. 238.
[4] *Ibid.*

And the notice adds :—

"It will then form one of the finest moles in the world. The stone for filling it up is brought from the nearest parts of the eastern coast, but the granite flags to face it are quarrying at Lough Shinney. It is but justice to mention that the indefatigable exertions of Lord Ranelagh to this great undertaking has been the principal means of its present forwardness."

By a notice in the same journal of 2nd June, 1791, it is probable that it was completed in 1792.

This mention of Lord Ranelagh, one of the directors of the Ballast Board named in the Act of 1789, whose abode at Monkstown became afterwards that of Mr. Haliday, leads one to remark on the strange coincidence, that two members of the Ballast Board, so warmly interested in all that regards the port of Dublin, should have successively occupied the same villa. Some of this information will be found in Captain Washington's second report to the Tidal Harbours Commission in 1846; but what appears here was taken as well from Mr. Haliday's copies of entries on the Assembly Rolls of the Corporation of Dublin, as from the information of my friend, neighbour, and brother barrister of the Leinster Circuit, William Monk Gibbon, LL.D., of "The Cottage" Sandymount, who closely succeeded Mr. Haliday as a member of the Ballast Board—sharing at once in Mr. Haliday's earnest interest in all that concerned the port and harbour of Dublin, and with the same historical tastes.

*History of the Pigeon-house.* To him is also wholly due the following account of the Pigeon-house.

It appears from the journal of the Ballast Office that the Commissioners of that Board had a servant, John Pigeon, for on the 8th of June, 1786, he and another were ordered to attend the Board on that day sennight, when the stores adjoining the Pigeon-house were ordered to be cleared out, to accommodate the workmen in working at the Ballast Office wall (as the Lighthouse wall is here called), which was then, as has been shown, approaching its completion.

There had previously been a block-house here for men engaged in watching wrecks and wrecked property. And John Pigeon being one of these men, it probably got its name from him. In the following year (29th August, 1787), the block-house was to be enlarged and improved for the accommodation of the Board, and referring to a ground-plan, they order some rooms for Francis Tunstal, Inspector of Works for the Ballast Board, and others for the housekeeper, Mrs. O'Brien, and her husband, she keeping the Corporation rooms clean, and providing breakfast for any of the members whenever directed, with a liberty of retailing spirits, but without any salary. In the *Dublin Chronicle* of 3rd August, 1790, it is announced that an hotel is to be built there for passengers by sea between England and Ireland. This was Mrs. Tunstal's, so well known to men of a former generation.

In 1798 the Ballast Board sold their property in the Pigeon-house and the newly constructed hotel to the Government, for a place of arms and a military post for £130,000.

The hotel was still continued there, and much frequented by good fellows for gay dinners. But in 1848, in Smith O'Brien's rebellion, the Pigeon-house fort was made a close garrison, and Mrs. Tunstal's hotel thrown down, and she came to Sandymount to reside; and thenceforward to this day the Pigeon-house remains merely as a fort, garrison, and store for guns and ammunition.

### The Walling-in of the Liffey.

The forming of walls to keep out the tide and take in land on the southern side of the river, began probably with the lease to Sir James Carroll, in the year 1607.[1]

Walling the South side.

The limits of the grant are not defined, but it probably included the space between Burgh-quay and Townsend-

---

[1] P. 145, n. 1.

street. In 1656, as appears by the Assembly Rolls, Sir James Carroll's daughter had a remission of arrears of rent at five pounds per annum, on a lease for 200 years of 1,000 acres of the strand,[1] and at this time the strand reached to the ground where the Theatre Royal stands, which is built on the College property, formerly the land of the Priory of All Hallows, and the shore of the Liffey was the limit of the land of the monks in this direction.

In 1661 and 1662 Mr. Hawkins built the great wall to gain the ground from the Liffey near the Long Stone. This may have included part of Aston's-quay, Burgh-quay, and George's-quay; and the ground gained extended inwards to Townsend-street. The name is continued in Hawkins'-street.[2]

The Long Stone stood about where the Crampton monument now stands.

It would seem that Sir James Carroll's lease was surrendered or forfeited, for nothing more is heard of it or of his representatives, and the lands subsequently dealt with must have been included in his lease.

The next extension of the wall in continuation of Hawkins' was in 1683, when a lease was ordered to be made to Philip Crofts, of part of the strand on the north side of Lazy-hill (now Townsend-street), from Hawkins' wall eastward 284 yards behind the houses on Lazy-hill, he walling-in the ground demised from the sea.[3] And in 1713 a lease was made to Sir John Rogerson of the strand between Lazy-hill and Ringsend, he informing the City Assembly that he intended speedily to take in the strand and desiring to be furnished by them with gravel by their gabbards, he paying three pence per ton.[4]

Between Sir John Rogerson's wall and the place called Mercer's Dock, near George's-quay, there was a gap in the

[1] Haliday's abstracts.
[2] P. 147, n. 3.
[3] Assembly Rolls—Haliday's Abstracts.
[4] *Ibid.*

line unbuilt of 606 feet in length. In the year 1715 the City began to build this wall, and hence probably the name of City-quay.

Such being the history of the walling of the southern bank of the Liffey, we now turn to the northern side. The laying down of kishes on that side began, as already stated, in 1710. As this work was to form a foundation for a wall, which is shown in Brookin's map of 1728 as then standing, it would be interesting to fix the date when it was built. But it cannot be fixed very accurately. *Walling of the North side.*

On 22nd July, 1715, the Ballast Board reported that they were laying down kishes to secure the north side of the channel.[1] In October of that year they report they had made good the bank as far as opposite to Mabbot's Mill, and that the remainder would be completed in the following summer.[2] But in 1716, 1717, and 1718, they were still at work laying kishes.[3] It does not appear when this kishing was actually completed. It was probably in 1718 or 1720.

At all events it was so far advanced in 1717 that the Corporation anticipated its early completion, and the consequent building of the North Wall. They also anticipated the gaining of the land behind the wall. For in 1717 they proceeded to a lottery among themselves of the land to be thus gained. And there is a reprint of a map, by no means scarce, showing the various lots as set out in Easter Assembly, 1717, and perfected (by lottery) in the year 1718. Hence the origin of the name of the "North Lots." By this scheme each allottee had a small frontage, but a wide allotment at the rere.

How valuable the whole has become may be judged from this, that three great railway companies have lately built their terminuses there, and the steam shipping have their berths there.

The wall was not completed in 1717, for in 1718 the

[1] Appendix, p. 235.
[2] Ibid.
[3] Ibid.
[4] Ibid, p. 248, n 2.

Ballast Board were still laying kishes; but in 1728 the wall was finished, as appears by Brookin's map of that date. The sea, however, is shown behind it and in front of it. It required the dredging and filling-in behind it with the rubbish and spoil of the river bottom of near 100 years to make land of it as it is now.

In all this long journey about the port and harbour of Dublin it has been my singular good-fortune to have found such a companion as my friend William Monk Gibbon, LL.D.

For, besides his antiquarian and historical tastes,[1] he

---

[1] He was in early life addicted to seamanship. He had four uncles in the Royal Navy, and he passed much of his youth in one or other of their ships. One of them, after the close of the war with France, in 1815, became master of one of his father's merchantmen, and, with this uncle, two years after he was called to the bar, he made voyage to Leghorn with a cargo of Manchester goods. The crew they shipped at Liverpool was so worthless that Gibbon had to act as able seaman. On nearing Leghorn his uncle, seeing the yellow or quarantine flag flying, said, "I'll go in in the boat, and you must take the command, and bring the ship in whenever you see the yellow flag down." He did so; but scarcely had they anchored when a spruce boat, with as spruce a gentleman sitting in the stern sheets, hailed him, and said, " I know the master of your vessel, and what I have to say is, that I want you to take the command of that ship there (pointing to a very fine barque) to-morrow, and take her to London." "Oh, sir," answered Gibbon, " I am not a seaman—I am only an amateur." He replied, "I want no certificate, it is quite enough that a man can handle a ship as you have handled yours. But (said he in conclusion), I'll meet you again in Leghorn." Gibbon and his uncle were at a restaurateur's the same afternoon, when the stranger came in. His uncle said to him, "Let me introduce my nephew Counsellor Gibbon." " Counsellor!" said he, striking the table, and using certain flowers of rhetoric, thought as well by seamen as Cicero to adorn oratory, " Why then, sir, you have mistaken your profession! You are a seaman, and now I repeat my offer, and undertake that you shall have the command of a better ship even than that I have shown you—one of the finest out of the port of London—if you will only join the service of our house."

Soon after this he was engaged for the " Wild Irish Girl," before a bench of magistrates, in the

has known Sandymount all his life, and Sandymount lay in the wash of the Dodder, a river which has had a great influence on the port of Dublin, and has undergone such changes that it required long investigation as well as the aid of his local knowledge to comprehend its former state. Thus when Gerard Boate, writing in 1645, describes the stone bridge, built over the Dodder, in consequence of the drowning of Mr. John Usher, father of Sir William Usher, as upon the way between Dublin and Ringsend,[1] I doubt if it could have been ascertained without his aid that this bridge was where Ball's-bridge now stands, and that the way from Dublin to Ringsend lay over Ball's-bridge. Mr. Haliday even was mistaken on this point, for he makes the way from Ringsend to Dublin, at high water, to be by the line of Bath-avenue, then overflowed by the sea.[2] But it will be seen by Sir Bernard de Gomme's map by how many devious streams, and through what a waste of sand, the Dodder made its way to the Liffey, though now running in one straight stream between the artificial banks made in 1796.[3] He also supplied me, in illustration of Mr. Haliday's statement, that, at the period of Sir Bernard de Gomme's map, "the sea flowed almost to the foot of Merrion-square,"[4] with the curious, and what to many would seem the incredible fact of the Duke of Leinster, so late as in the year 1792, shooting the breach in the South Wall in his yacht, and landing safely at Merrion-square;[5] and the extract from the newspapers of the year 1760 describing the bodies of two murderers as

A.D. 1645, stone bridge built where Ball's bridge stands.

county of Wexford, and succeeded so well that the underwriters of Liverpool, who were interested in the case, made him their counsel-in-ordinary. This brought him into connexion with Mr. James Watt, Queen's Proctor, a member of the great house of Barrington, Hunt, and Jeffares, and thus into equity business.

[1] Appendix, p. 233, n.
[2] *Ibid.*, pp. 241, 242.
[3] *Ibid.*, p. 242, n.
[4] P. 231.
[5] *Ibid.*, n. 1.

having fallen from their gibbets on the river, and lying tossed about by the waves among the piles."[1]

[1] These were two of four pirates, murderers, as he has since informed me, part of the crew of the "Sandwith," bound from the Canary Islands, which she left in Nov., 1765, for London, Captain Cochran, Commander, and Captain Glas, and others, passengers. They murdered the captain and the passengers, and made for the Waterford river. Near the Hook, on the 3rd of December, they left the ship scuttled, as they hoped, and made off in a small boat with about two tons of Spanish milled dollars in bags, and other treasure. They landed two miles from Duncannon Fort, and buried in the sand 250 bags (at a bay since called "Dollar Bay"[2]), keeping as much as they could conveniently carry, with some ingots of gold, jewels, and gold dust. They were soon after arrested, and on Saturday, March, 1766, George Gidley, Richard St. Quintin, Andrea Zekerman, and Peter M'Kinlie, were tried at Dublin, and found guilty, and, on Monday, the 3rd, were executed at St. Stephen's-green.[3] He also furnished the following note from the Dublin papers of March 9, 1766:—

"The bodies of the four murderers and pirates—M'Kinley, St. Quintin, Gidley, and Zekerman, were brought in the black cart from Newgate, and hung in chains, two of them near Mackarell's Wharf, on the South Wall, near Ringsend, and the other two about the middle of the piles, below the Pigeon-house. The bodies of the four pirates remained suspended on the wharf and at the Pigeon-house till the month of March following." The same journal for the 29th March has the following:—"The two pirates, Peter M'Kinley and George Gidley, who hang in chains on the South Wall, for the murder of Captain Coghlan (Cochran), &c., being very disagreeable to the citizens who walk there for amusement and health, are immediately to be put on Dalkey Island, for which purpose new irons are making, those they hang in being faulty. Richard St. Quintin and Andrea Zekerman, the other two concerned in this cruel affair, are to remain on the piles at the Pigeon-house." Accordingly, the same journal, on the 1st and 12th of April, 1767, announces the removal of the bodies from the new wall, and that they were carried by sea to the rock on the Muglins, near Dalkey Island, where a gibbet was erected, and they were hung up in irons, said to be the completest ever made in the kingdom.

[1] P. 238, n.

[2] In the parish of Templetown, barony of Shelburn, near the Hook.

[3] From "A short account of the life of Captain Glas, and execution of the four pirates for his murder, at St. Stephen's-green, Dublin."

The numerous maps have been lithographed on American paper. Its fineness and tenacity, almost equal to that of silk, gives hopes of its enduring the wear and tear of handling and of reference.[1]

[1] From Colton and Co., publishers of maps, atlases, and guide books, &c., No. 172, William-street, New York. The railway maps of this house seem to stand constant use without giving way.

# THE SCANDINAVIANS:

AND THE

## Scandinavian Antiquities of Dublin.

### BOOK I.

THE DYNASTY OF SCANDINAVIAN KINGS AT DUBLIN.

### CHAPTER I.

No cities among the early Irish.—The site of Dublin a place of no distinction amongst them.—Dublin founded by Scandinavians, and made their capital.—Thence became the capital of the English.—Denmark filled by Saxons who escaped thither to avoid forced baptism by Charlemagne.—The Norsemen, infected by these exiles with their hatred, ravage the coasts of France.—Their ravages of England.—They plunder the islands and coasts of Ireland.—Their ravages on the mainland of Ireland.—The Dubhgoill and the Finnghoill.—Aulaff of the Dubhgoill settles at *Dubhlinn of Ath Cliath*, A.D. 852.

IT must surprise those who examine the history of Ireland that so little appears known respecting the social position of those Scandinavians who, under the common name of Ostmen, or of Danes, occupied our principal seaports from the 9th to the 12th century, and that even local historians are silent respecting the civil and religious institutions, the works and monumental remains, of a people, who not only inhabited and ruled over Dublin for more than three hundred years, but who, if not the

*Dublin Scandinavian for its first 300 years.*

\* B

BOOK I.
CHAP. I.

No cities among the early Irish.

founders of the city, were unquestionably the cause of its metropolitan supremacy. For notwithstanding Ptolemy's supposed notice of Dublin under the name of Eblana,[1] and the inflated description of its splendour by Jocelyn,[2] it is almost certain that before the Scandinavian invasion the Irish had no cities or walled towns in any degree resembling those spread over England, France, Germany, and wherever the Romans had penetrated. There were large ecclesiastical establishments at Armagh, Clonmacnois, &c.[3] At Emania, Aileach, Tara, &c., there were cashels, duns, or raths, in which kings and chieftains, with their attendants, resided, the bulk of the population being scattered over the territory inherited by each tribe, moving with their cattle from pasture to pasture, having little tillage, and ever ready to assemble at the call of their chief, either to repel invasion or to invade the territory of their neighbours. But cities they had none. Consequently, in all our annals of intestine warfare, although we have records of the destruction of Armagh and Clonmacnois, of Emania[4] and Aileach,[5] and of duns, fortresses, and fastnesses,

---

[1] Ptolemy, who wrote in the 2nd century, never saw Ireland, but gave from the report of others the supposed latitude, longitude, and names of eight or ten Irish cities.—Ptolemy Geogr. Rome, 1490. Dublin is not mentioned by Strabo, who wrote his Geography in the time of Augustus Cæsar, but he knew little of Ireland.

[2] Jocelin, Vit. S. Patricii, c. 69.—His description is self-refuting. Jocelin wrote in the 12th century.

[3] Around these establishments towns subsequently grew up, but previously the term Civitas was frequently applied to monastic establishments.—Bk. of Hymns, p. 156.

[4] [Anciently the seat of the Kings of Ulster;—" Emania Ultoniæ regum pulcherrima sedes."—Ogygia, Preface, p. 14. Now the Navan fort, near the city of Armagh (a corruption of the Irish "An Emhain"). (J. O'Donovan, LL.D., Ann. 4 Mast.)]

[5] [Now Elagh, in the barony of Inishowen, county of Donegal.]

there is no allusion to the siege of an Irish town, or the destruction of an Irish city.

<small>BOOK I.
CHAP. I.</small>

And not only is there no Irish record of a "City of Dublin" before the 9th century, but before that period there is no record that the place where the city now stands was a place of any importance.[1] Our annals refer to the *Dubhlinn* or harbour, which was the resort of ships, and to the Ath Cliath, or bridge of hurdles, which crossed the river; but if there were a dun or rath near the harbour, that fortress never was the seat of an Irish king, the capital of an Irish territory, or the centre of Irish dominion; and as regards the present metropolitan supremacy of Dublin, it is manifest that Henry the Second made Dublin the metropolis of his royalty, not because he considered it to be the capital of Ireland (over which he only claimed a "lordship"), or because its position was more advantageous than that of either Wexford or Waterford (then the ports of communication with England),[2] but because it was the principal city of the Ostmen he had conquered, and over whose subjugated territories he did claim

<small>The site of Dublin a place of no importance among the Irish.</small>

<small>From being the capital of the Danes became the capital of the English.</small>

---

[1] Colgan gives a list of Bishops of Dublin from the arrival of S. Patrick to the arrival of the Northmen. Most of his bishops died or were martyred on the Continent. The list is evidently fictitious. The only notice of Dublin in the Annals of the Four Masters—at A.D. 765—records a battle at Ath Cliath, and that "Numbers were drowned at the full tide, returning."

The seat of the Kings of [all] Ireland, at an early period, was Tara: the chief residences of the Kings of Leinster were Naas and Ferns.

[2] The communication was chiefly between Bristol and Waterford. It was not until Edward had conquered Wales that there was any communication with England through Holyhead and Dublin. The first notice probably of that line of communication is that in Rymer, vol. iv., p. 524:—" Pro navibus arrestandis ad Holyhead pro passagio regis in Hiberniam."

BOOK I.
CHAP. I.

to exercise regal privileges.[1] Henry found that Dublin was the seat of Ostman sovereignty; it thence became the capital of his Irish dominion, and from the extension of that dominion it has become the capital of Ireland.

*High qualities of the Ostmen founders of Dublin.*

Yet even if Dublin were not founded by the Scandinavians, or that the Ostmen were not the cause of its present pre-eminence, the silence of local and general historians respecting the social position, religion, laws, and monuments of those who occupied Dublin for more than three hundred years on all facts connected with the first Scandinavian invaders, excepting such as relate to their inroads and devastations, has contributed to strengthen very erroneous opinions respecting that remarkable people. And although this silence may be justified, in some degree, with regard to the first invaders, their history being obscure, it certainly cannot be so justified with

---

[1] Henry left Strongbow in possession of the territory he had acquired by marriage with the daughter of the King of Leinster, but he claimed, by right of conquest, the Ostmen cities of Dublin, Wexford, Waterford, and Limerick, and out of the lands which belonged to the Ostmen [kings] of Dublin he formed his four royal manors of Newcastle, Esker, Saggard, and Crumlin.

[McMurrough ruled over the city of Dublin and the town of Wexford, as well as the rest of Leinster. This is evidenced by the following entry of his grief made by one of his followers in the Book of Leinster, on the very day (1st August, 1166) when the king was driven out of Ireland, and went to seek foreign aid:—

"Oh, Mary! It is a great deed that is done in Erinn this day. Dermod, son of Donchadh Mac Murchadha, King of Leinster *and of the Danes*, was banished by the men of Ireland over the sea eastward. Uch! Uch! Oh now, what shall I do?"—War of the Gaedhil with the Gaill, p. xii. "The Danes meant the Danes of Dublin."—Note by Dr. Todd, *ibid.* Yet King Henry took from Strongbow Dublin and Wexford, though equally acquired by marriage with Eva, McMurrough's daughter. He feared probably that they might render him too powerful for a subject.]

respect to the Ostmen who founded the Kingdom of Dublin in A.D. 852, as very slight research would have discovered the high position they held among surrounding nations, and that so far from being a mere band of pirates, who only constructed a fortress as a receptacle for plunder, and who left no monuments which could indicate that either religion or legislation existed among them, there was abundant evidence to show that the Ostmen of Dublin were colonists, who settled in the land they invaded, and that Pagan and barbarian as they were their religion was less idolatrous, their civil institutions not less perfect, and their laws more consonant with human freedom, than the religion, institutions, and laws of those civilized Romans who invaded Britain. *[margin: BOOK I. CHAP. I. Dublin founded by Ostmen, A.D. 852.]*

To the history of these Dublin Ostmen we will presently refer, but previously we will endeavour to mark the distinction between them and those ruthless Pagans who first invaded Ireland, and who, under the name of Northmen or of Danes, ravaged also the coasts of England and France, at the close of the eighth or at the beginning of the ninth century. *[margin: Origin of the Northern sea rovers.]*

According to some French historians, the "barbarians" who sailed along the coasts of France in A.D. 800, were persecuted and banished Pagans, who, with aid from their allies, were in search of new homes, and were seeking to avenge on Christian clergy and Christian churches the destruction of their temples and their idols by the Christian armies of Charlemagne. The statement is, that before the end of the 8th century the Franks had suffered much from the hostility of their Saxon neighbours, and *[margin: Charlemagne forces Christianity on the Saxons, A.D. 772.]*

BOOK I.
CHAP. I.

*Revolt of the Saxons, A.D. 774.*

that Charlemagne, desirous to terminate these hostilities, and influenced by zeal for religion and love of conquest, invaded Saxony in A.D. 772.[1] His first attack was on the fortress of Eresbourg,[2] which contained the temple of Irminsul, the great idol of the nation. He took and destroyed the fortress, pulled down the temple, broke in pieces the idol; and believing that the mild doctrines of Christianity could alone restrain the barbarous habits of the Saxons he had conquered, " he built monasteries and churches, founded bishoprics, and filled Saxony with priests and missionaries."[3] But the Saxons were neither easily conquered or converted. In A.D. 774, and again in 775,[4] they revolted; and although in 776 and 777 many came to Paderborn to be baptized,[5] they again revolted in A.D. 782, and abjuring Christianity as a badge of slavery, they burned the churches, slew the clergy, and returned to the worship of the idols which Charlemagne had overturned. This outbreak, instigated by their beloved chieftain, Witikind, was soon suppressed, and Witikind, with the fiercest of the Saxon idolaters, fled into Denmark, where Sigefroi, his wife's father, then reigned.[6] Enraged by the conduct of the re-

---

[1] Eginhardi de Gest. Carl. Mag. Imp. ap. Du Chesne, A.D. 782; Ann. Franc., A.D. 782.

[2] Eresbourg, now Stradbourg, between Cassel and Paderborn.

[3] Hist. de Charl., vol. ii., p. 246.

[4] Eginhard, A.D. 774, 775.

[5] Ibid., 776, 777. To commemorate this supposed conversion a medal was struck with this inscription, " Saxonibus sacro lavacro regeneratis, 777."

[6] Pontanus, Rer. Dan. Hist., p. 91. Witikind's wife was Geva, daughter of Sigefroi.—Hist. de Danemarc, par Des Roches. Paris, 1782. Vol. ii., p. 20:—" Il y mena aussi sa femme Geva, fille du Roi de Dannemarc." Pontanus, Rer. Dan. Hist., p. 89.

volters, and the escape of Witikind, Charlemagne forgot the precepts of that Christianity he desired to spread, and with unparalleled cruelty he beheaded four thousand five hundred Saxons in cold blood, and in one day.[1] Yet, fearing that even this horrible butchery would not secure the lasting submission of the survivors, "he added to it a secret order to put to death those who would excite the Saxons to revolt."[2] Still revolt succeeded revolt, and revolt was ever accompanied by a return to idolatry, the re-establishment of idols, the burning of churches, and the massacre of priests. Charlemagne, however, had decided that the Saxons should be Christians, but unfortunately he decided on making them Christians by means which Christianity abhors. He ordained that "Every Saxon who refused to be baptized should be punished with death;" and that "those who to avoid baptism should say that they had been baptized should be similarly punished."[3] And subsequently he established a secret council, composed of men whose duty it was silently to traverse the country, to watch the actions and words of the people, and instantly to put to death those who renounced Christianity or excited revolt. Yet even this was insufficient. The Saxons and their neighbours still clung to their Paganism, and Charlemagne ultimately proceeded to banish the idolaters from the scene of their idolatry. He spent part of the years 795, 796, 797 in destroying with fire and sword the countries between the Elbe, Upper Saxony,

*Charlemagne beheads 4,500 Saxons in one day.*

*Banishes the Saxons, A.D. 795-797.*

---

[1] Annales Fuldenses, A.D. 782; Eginhard, 782; Ann. Franc., 782; Hist. de Charl., vol. ii., p. 253.
[2] Hist. de Charl., vol. ii., p. 241.
[3] Hist. de France, par De Mezerai. Paris, 1643, p. 191, A.D. 804.

BOOK I.
CHAP. I.

The Saxons fly into Denmark.

the German Ocean, and the Baltic,[1] the population flying into Denmark and the North. Ten thousand families of the Saxons were transplanted into Switzerland and the forests of Flanders;[2] and in A.D. 795, men, women, and children were transplanted into France,[3] and their lands given to the Abrodites, the inveterate enemies of the Saxons, and the faithful allies of the Franks.[4]

The clergy serve in Charlemagne's armies.

In fact Charlemagne's war was now a crusade. Its object was alike to conquer and convert. The military and religious habit were united in his camp, which was the scene of martial exercises, solemn processions, and public prayers;[5] and hence the clergy, who crowded around his standard, participating in the objects and results of his victories, sharing the gold and silver (plunder of the countries he conquered),[6] and baptizing the infidels he captured

Hence hateful to the Pagans.

and spared, that clergy became hateful to Pagans, who attributed to them and the religion they preached, the destruction of temples,[7] the desolation of homes, and all the means employed to extirpate idolaters and to make Christians.

The Saxons forced out of Denmark.

Nor was Charlemagne's hostility confined to the Pagans he subdued. Those who fled from his arms

[1] Hist. de Charl., vol. ii., p. 267. De Mezerai, p. 208, Medal xii.
[2] Hist. de Charl., vol. ii., p. 268. Chron. St. Denis, lib. ii., cap. 3.
[3] Ann. Bertiniani, A.D. 804.
[4] Eginhard, A.D. 804.
[5] Hist. de Charl., vol. ii. p. 280.
[6] Hoveden, Rer. Ang. Scrip. Lon., 1596, p. 233. Chron. Mailros, A.D. 795.
[7] Montesquieu, Esprit des Lois, liv. xxxi., cap. x.:—"The Normans plundered and ravaged all before them, wreaking their vengeance chiefly on the priests and monks, and devoting every religious house to destruction. For they charged these ecclesiastics with the subversion of their idols, and with all the oppressive measures of Charlemagne, by which they had been successively obliged to take shelter in the north."

were pursued by his policy. Sigefroi could not obtain his friendship, or rather his forbearance, except on condition that the refugee Saxons, Frizons, Soarbes, &c., should be expelled from Denmark,[1] and his successor Godfrey found it necessary to conclude a treaty binding himself to drive out of his states the Pagans who had sought an asylum there.[2]

Thus compelled to seek other homes, these infuriated Pagans, or, as De Mezeray writes, "The banished and their descendants, burning with a cruel desire to avenge their gods and their liberty, made continual sorties, and principally exercised their rage on the priests and on the monks who had destroyed their temples and their superstitions."[3]

The Danes, who saw with uneasiness the progressive conquests of Charlemagne, quickly imbibed the feelings of their homeless kinsmen, and in A.D. 800 "they dared to infest the coasts of France."[4] Sailing

[1] Pontanus. Rer. Danic, p. 90.
[2] Hist. de Charl., vol. ii., p. 273.
[3] "L'Idolatrie, &c., &c., étant vivement pressée par les armes des François, elle s'etait jettée au-delà de l'Elbe et en Danemarc comme en son dernier fort, d'ou ces bannis et leurs descendants brulant d'un cruel désir de venger leurs Dieux et leur liberté, faisoient de continuelles sorties et exerçoient principalement leur rage sur les prestres et sur les moines qui avoient destruit leurs temples et leurs superstitions."—Hist. de France, De Mezeray, Paris, 1685, vol. i., p. 423. "Vitikind (roi de Saxe) alla porter sa haine et sa douleur à la cour de Sigefroi son ami, Roi des Danois ou Normands; démarche importante, première époque d'une grande révolution dans l'Europe. Ce fut cette alliance de Vitikind avec Sigefroi, ce furent ses continuelles instigations qui attirèrent sur les côtes de la France ces Normands," &c.—Hist. de Charlemagne par Gaillard, Paris, 1782, vol. ii., p. 231.
[4] Depping Hist. des Expeditions Marit. des Normands, p. 66. Monachi Sangall De Reb. Bel., lib. ii., cxxii. Montesquieu, Grandeur et Decadence des Romains, cap. 16. : —"The conquests and tyrannies of Charlemagne had again forced the nations of the south into the north. As soon as his empire was weakened

from sea to sea they approached the shores of Languedoc, where Charlemagne, recognising their fleets from the windows of his palace, wept for the misery he foresaw they would bring on his descendants and on France. Nor was it long until the destruction of churches, the slaughter of clergy and of people, justified the fears of the emperor.

On the English coasts the Northmen appeared within five years after Witikind had fled into Denmark and carried the story of Charlemagne's cruelties to the subjects of King Sigefroi.

According to the Saxon Chronicle, "A.D. 787, first came three ships of the Northmen out of Hœretha land," and it adds what is confirmed by every English historian—that these were "the first ships of Danish men which sought the land of the English race."[1] Roger de Wendover says, "It may be suspected they came to spy out the fertility of the land," and therefore sailed along the coast in search of some spot on which to settle. But in 793 and 794 these "heathen men" came with larger fleets and with other objects; for soon "they dreadfully destroyed the churches of Christ."[2] They trod down holy places with their unholy feet; they slaughtered priests and Levites and multitudes of monks and nuns; undermined the altars, and carried off all the treasures of Holy Church." The great monastic establishment at Lindesfarne,

they passed a second time from the north into the south."

[1] Sax. Chron. Mon. Brit., p. 257. Ingram in his Edition of the Saxon Chronicle, translates Hœrethas land "the Land of the Robbers."

[2] Sax. Chron. A. D. 793, 794. Hen. Hunt. Rerum Anglicanarum Scriptores, Lon., 1596, p. 197. Simeon Dunhelmhelmensis Hist. Aug. Scrip. Lond., 1682, p. 11.

celebrated for the sanctity and number of its inmates, lying directly opposite those Scandinavian districts into which the Saxons and other Pagans had fled or were driven, being easily accessible from the creeks of Jutland, from the Baltic and the Elbe, became the first objects of attack from Pagans seeking vengeance on Christian communities. Lindisfarne was totally destroyed in A.D. 793 ; and in 794, after the "heathen men" had ravaged Northumberland, they destroyed Ecgferth's monastery at Weremouth.

The Pagans who invaded Ireland probably sailed from the fiords of Norway about the same time that those from Denmark had sailed for England; but, sailing round the north of Scotland, and passing from island to island, and probably forming settlements in the Orkneys, Hebrides, and Shetland isles, they did not reach the north-east coast of Ireland until A.D. 795.[1] The words of the annals of Innisfallen are: "A.D. 795. The Danes were first seen cruizing on the coasts of Ireland prying out the country." They attacked and plundered the ships of the Irish, and then proceeded to plunder those Irish islands on which the desire for a hermit life had led many ecclesiastics to form small religious establishments.

*Their raids on the coasts of Ireland, A.D. 795-812.*

According to the Annals of the Four Masters in A.D. 795, "The 'heathen men' burned the island of Rechru" (between Scotland and the north coast of Ireland), "and broke and plundered the shrines."[2] In

*They plunder the Hermits' island retreats.*

---

[1] Ogygia, p. 433. Brut y Tywysogion, A.D. 795. Ann. Ulst. give the date 794.

[2] Annals of the Four Masters, translated by J. O'Donovan, LL.D., 7 vols., 4to., Dublin, 1851 (hereafter quoted as Ann. 4 Mast.), vol. i., p. 397, n. [" This was one of the many names of the island of Rathlin, off the north coast of Antrim ;

A.D. 798 they burned St. Patrick's Island (on the east coast), and bore away the shrine of St. Dachonna.[1] In A.D. 807 they burned the churches in the island of Innishmurry on the coast of Sligo;[2] and in A.D. 812 plundered the island of Scelig Michel[3] (off the coast of Kerry), took the anchorites and kept them captive until they perished for want of food.[4]

*Their raids retaliatory.*

From proceedings so closely resembling those of the invaders of France, commenced at the same period, and by the same people, it might be inferred that the invasion of Ireland originated in the same cause, and had the same object; and that the sacrilegious devastations on our coasts, so far from being unprovoked aggressions on Christian lands, were acts of retaliation and revenge for injuries inflicted on a Pagan people by a Christian Emperor, and his propagandist army.

*Not mere piracy.*

Nevertheless, the love of piracy, which characterized the Scandinavians of the 8th and 9th centuries, and the Viking expeditions which closely followed, and which perhaps, in some cases, were contemporaneous with the successes of the first invaders, has apparently influenced the opinion, that they were alike the effect of a desire for plunder and bloodshed.

---

but it was also the ancient name of Lambay, near Dublin, which is probably the place here referred to." J. O'Donovan, *Ibid.* Such also is Dr. Reeves' opinion.— "Wars of the Gaedhil with the Gaill," p. xxxii., n. 5.]

[1] *Id.* 793 (= 798). ["Dr. O'Donovan understood the Inispatrick here mentioned of the island so called on the coast of Dublin. But the mention of Dachonna, who was Bishop of Man, proves that Peel, on the west of the Isle of Man, formerly called Insula Patricii, is intended. See Colgan Actt. S. S. (ad 13 Jan.), p. 50; Chronicle of Man, by P. M. Munch, p. 23, Christiania, 1860."—Wars of the Gaedhil with the Gaill, p. xxxv., n. 1.] This identification is due to the Rev. Dr. Reeves.

[2] *Id.* 807.
[3] *Id.* 812.
[4] *Ibid.*

It is urged that, when we read of clergy slaughtered, of churches plundered, and of relics shaken from their shrines, we should recollect that relics were worthless to Pagans, pirates who only valued the gold or silver shrines in which these relics were enclosed; that churches were the repositories of coveted treasure, and that the slaughter of clergy might not be in all cases a religious martyrdom, as in the 8th and 9th centuries the clergy fought and fell like other soldiers in the ranks of armies opposed to the invaders.

*Clergy not always religious martyrs.*

In France, where the bishops had large territorial possessions, they voluntarily led their vassals to battle, and the inferior¹ clergy followed their ex-

*But slain in fight.*

¹ Cap. Reg. Franc., p. 405. In the first capitulary, A.D. 769, p. 189, the clergy were forbid to fight as soldiers; but apparently they disregarded the ordinance, as, in A.D. 803, the chiefs of the army, and the people solicited Charlemagne to prevent bishops, abbots, and clergy, from joining the army and fighting in its ranks. The Italian bishops and clergy also fought against the Pagans at the close of the 8th century, although not compelled to do so. Epist. ad Fastrad. ap. Du Chesne, p. 187. Concilia Ant. Gall., vol. ii., p. 158. Ann. 4 Mast., A.D. 799, (= 804).

In 832, when King Egbricht was defeated by the Danes, " Bishops Hereferth and Wigfert, with two dukes, were slain in the battle," Hen. Hunt. ap. Twysden, p. 198. In A.D. 868, King Buhred is said to have thanked the bishops, abbots, and others of lower rank, who, although freed from all military services by King Ethelwulf, "yet had joined the army of the Lord against those most wicked Pagans" the Danes. Ingulph. ap. Gall., vol. i., p. 20. Codex Dip. Sax., vol. ii., p. 93. Bishop Heahmund was slain fighting against the Danes. Sax. Chron., A.D. 871. And Cenulf, the Abbot, met the same fate, A.D. 905.

In Ireland, so late as A.D. 915, Archbishop Maelmaedhog was slain fighting against the Danes; and Fergus, Bishop of Kildare, and Abbot Dunchadh, met the same fate, A.D. 885. Cormac Mac Cuileannan, King and Bishop of Cashel, with the Abbot of Trian-Corcaigh were slain fighting against the King of Leinster, A.D. 903, Ann. 4 Mast.; and it is even recorded, *ibid.* A.D. 816, that the monks of one monastery fought

ample. In England and Ireland the clergy were compelled to serve in the armies of their sovereign: and from this military service the Irish clergy were not relieved until A.D. 804; nor was it until A.D. 854 that the English clergy obtained a similar exemption. Yet long after these periods they continued to wield the temporal sword, and alternately to wear the casque and the cowl.

These raids, however, are insufficient to show that all the first invaders were mere pirates, and plunder their sole object. Such a theory requires to be sustained by stronger evidence, opposed as it is to historical statements, supported by incontrovertible facts.

*Raids of the Northmen contemporaneous with Charlemagne's crusades.*

Unquestionably, the invasion commenced almost immediately after Charlemagne had driven Witikind and his Saxon followers into the sterile regions of the North; and whatever might have been the piratical tendencies of the Northmen, they had never invaded a Christian territory, destroyed a Christian church, or slain a Christian priest, until Charlemagne had destroyed the homes, the temples, and the idols of the Saxons. It is questionable, indeed, whether previously they had ever sailed out of the Baltic; but if they did, it is certain that previously they never had attempted to colonize or dwell in Christian lands.

*Raids into the interior of Ireland, A.D. 807.*

Those who came between A.D. 795 and 807, appear

with those of another, "400 of lay and churchmen being slain" in one of these contests. Todd's Life of S. Patrick, p. 158–166. "About this time (1174) Peter Leonis, the Pope's Legate, came to England, and obtained from Henry II., amongst other articles, that clerks should not be compelled to go to war." Roger de Wendover.

to have had no other object than devastation and pillage. They landed, plundered, and departed. But whether these invaders were Norwegians, Danes, Swedes, or Jutes, it is difficult to determine. In A.D. 807 they began to make incursions into the interior of the country.[1] In that year, after burning the Island of Innishmurry,[2] they marched into Roscommon.[3] In 812 they landed again, and entered Connemara, where they "slaughtered the inhabitants." They also entered Mayo, where "they were (defeated) by the men of Umhall;"[4] and in A.D. 813, having again entered Mayo, and defeated "the men of Umhall," they slew Cosgrach, son of[5] Flannabhrad, and Dunadhach, lord of the territory.

Their course can be clearly traced. Issuing from the fiords of Norway, they sailed along the east coast of Scotland to the Frith of Forth, and territory of the Scottish Picts, and thence to Northumbria and East Anglia, where the invaders first became settlers in England. Their course along the west side of Scotland was among the Orkneys, the Hebrides, and Western Isles, to the North of Ireland, and thence by Larne (or Ulfricksford), Strangford, and Carlingford, down to Dublin; the first settlement being in Ulster, and the territory of the Irish Picts. There is no record of any attempts made to settle for twenty years after 795, when the Pagans first came

*Course of the Northmen to Ireland.*

---

[1] Ogygia, p. 433. "Hiberniam primùm incursionibus intrarunt." Ann. 4 Mast., A.D. 802 (= 807).

[2] [An island off the coast of the barony of Carbury, county of Sligo. —J. O'D., LL.D., *ibid.*]

[3] *Ibid.*, Ann. Clonmac., A.D. 804. Ann. Ult., A.D. 806.

[4] Ann. 4 Mast., A.D. 812 [Umhall Lower was the barony of Borrishool: Umhall Upper was the barony of Murrisk].

[5] *Ibid.*, A.D. 813.

to Ireland. During that time they landed, plundered, and departed.

In 819 they plundered Howth, and the islands at the mouth of Wexford Harbour.[1] In 820 they plundered Cape Clear and Cork.[2] In 821 they spoiled and ransacked Bennchoir.[3] In 823 they plundered Dun da-Leathghlas.[4] They defeated "the Osraighi," but were worsted by "the Ulidians." In 824 they burned Lusk,[5] and spoiled all Meath. In 825 they "destroyed Dun-Laighen," and slew the "son of Cuchongelt, lord of Forthuatha."[6] In 826 they were overthrown by the Ui Ceinnsealaigh,[7] and again by the Ulidians."[8] In 827 they "burned Lannlere[9] and Clonmor."[10] In 829 they plundered Conaille, and took "its king and his brother, and carried them with them to their ships." In 830 they plundered "Daimhliag,[11] and the tribe of Cianachta, with all their churches;" and took "Ailill, son of Colgan," and plundered Lughmhadh,[12] and many other churches; and "carried off Tuatal, son of Fearadhach," plundering Ard Macha[13] thrice in one month, as it had never been plundered by strangers before. In 831 they plundered Rath Luirigh.[14] In 832 they plundered Cluain Dol-

---

[1] Ann. 4 Mast.
[2] [Id.]
[3] [Id., Bangor in the county of Down.]
[4] [Id., Downpatrick.]
[5] [Id., Lusk, in the county of Dublin, twelve miles to the north of the city.]
[6] [Id., In the county of Wicklow, near Glendalough.]
[7] [Id., The Hy Kinshelas, now the county of Wexford.]
[8] [Id., The Ulster men.]
[9] [Id., The ancient name of Dunleer.]
[10] [Id., Now Clonmore, a townland in the parish of Clonmore, in the barony of Ferrard, and county of Louth.]
[11] [Id., Dulcek, in Meath.]
[12] [Id., Louth, in the county of Louth.]
[13] [Id., Armagh.]
[14] [Id., rectè Rath Luraigh (Lurach's fort) the ancient name of

cain;[1] and, although they were defeated with great slaughter at Doire-Chalgaigh[2] by Uiall Caille and Murchadh, they plundered Loch Bricrenn,[3] in opposition to Conghalach, son of Eochardh, whom they took prisoner, and afterwards killed at their ships. In 833 they plundered "Gleann-da-locha, Slaine, and Finnabhair,[4] but were defeated by Dunadhach, son of Scannlan, lord of Ui Fidhgeinte, and many of them killed." In 834 they plundered Fearna, Cluain-mor-Maedhog, and Drum-h-Ing,[5] and burned "Mungairid,[6] and other churches in Ormond." In 835 they burned "Cluain-mor-Maedhog on Christmas night, slaying many, and carrying off many as prisoners; they likewise burned the oratory of Gleann-da-locha, desolated all Connaught, plundered Cell-dara,[7] and burned half the church. In 836 Dubliter Odhar, of Teamhair, was taken prisoner, and put to death in his gyves at their ships." They had fleets on the Boyne and the Liffey, out of which "they plundered and spoiled Magh Liphthe[8] and Magh Breagh,[9] both churches and habitations of men, goodly tribes, flocks and herds;" and, after being defeated by the "men of

Maghera, in the County of Londonderry.]

[1] [Id., Clondalkin, six miles S.W. of Dublin.]

[2] [Id., Derry (Londonderry).]

[3] [Id., Loughbrickland, in the county of Down.]

[4] [Id., Glendalough, in the county of Wicklow; Slane, in Meath; Fennor, on the river Boyne, near Slane, in Meath.]

[5] [Id., Ferns in the county of Wexford; and Clonmore, in Leinster; and Dromin (probably), near Dunshaughlin, in Meath.]

[6] [Id., Mungret, in the county of Limerick.]

[7] [Id., Kildare.]

[8] [Id., Magh Liphthe, the plain of the Liffey, now the county of Kildare.]

[9] [Id., Magh Breagh, a great plain in the east of ancient Meath, comprising five cantreds or baronies, lying between Dublin and Drogheda.]

Breagh," they defeated "the Ui Neill from the Sinainn to the sea."[1]

*Arrival of Turgesius, A.D. 815.*

In A.D. 815, however, "Turgesius, a powerful Norwegian chieftain, landed," and from that time it is recorded that the foreigners began to form settlements in Ireland.[2] Nevertheless, the same system of plunder and bloodshed, which marked the earlier invasions, long continued; and, year after year, we find records of outrages by those Scandinavians, whose fleets infested our coasts.

*The "Dubhghoill and the Finnghoill."*

Throughout these records of plunder and devastation there is no intimation who the invaders were, or whence they came. The Irish gave to those invaders who came one common name of "Gaill,"[3] or foreigners, no distinction appearing in the Annals of the Four Masters before A.D. 847, when it is stated that "a fleet of seven score ships of the king of the foreigners came to contend with the foreigners who were in Ireland before them."[4] After the arrival of this fleet, and the commencement of the contest which followed, two tribes are recognised, and as enemies to each other—the "Dubhghoill" (or Black foreigners), supposed to be Danes, and the "Finnghoill" (or White foreigners), supposed to be Norwegians.

*Aulaff of the Dubhghoill founds Dublin, A.D. 852.*

In A.D. 849, "the Dubhghoill arrived at Ath Cliath, and made a great slaughter of the Finnghoill,[5] who had settled there." In the same year there was "another depredation of the Dubhghoil on the Finn-

---

[1] [*Id.*, Sinain, the Shannon.]
[2] [Ogygia, Part iii., c. 93, p. 433.]
[3] Ann. 4 Mast., A.D. 790, 793, 797. In the Annals of Ulster they are termed "Gentiles," or Pagans; subsequently they are called Dubh Lochlannaigh and Finn Lochlannaigh.
[4] *Id.*, A.D. 847.
[5] *Id.*, A.D. 849.

ghoill at Linn Duachaill."[1] In A.D. 850 the Finnghoill, "with a fleet of eight score ships arrived at Snamh Eidhneach to give battle to the Dubhghoill, and they fought with each other for three days and three nights, and again the Dubhghoill gained the victory."[2] But in 852 their hostility was terminated. For in that year "Aulaff, son of the king of Lochlann, came to Ireland (and) all the foreign tribes of Ireland submitted to him."[3]

## CHAPTER II.

The founding of Dublin.—The story of Turgesius discussed.—Aulaff, descended of Regnar Lodbrog, founds Dublin, A.D. 852.—Legend of Aulaff, Sitric, and Ivar, three brothers, founding, respectively, Dublin, Waterford, and Limerick, disproved.—Irish and Danish names of the site of Dublin.—Dublin and Northumbria for a century under the same Danish kings.—Legend of Regnar's death in Northumbria.—Regnar put to death in Ireland by the Irish.—Regnar Lodbrog, the Thurgils, or Turgesius of Irish annals.—Account of Turgesius from Dr. Todd's "War of the Gaedhill with the Gaill."

THIS young chieftain, mentioned at the close of the first chapter as having defeated the Fingoill, and received the submission of all the Scandinavians in Ireland, and settled at Dublin, was known by the

*Aulaf, the White, descended of Regnar Lodbrog, founds Dublin, A.D. 852.*

---

[1] [*Ibid.* Not Magheralin in the county of Down, as at first supposed by J. O'Donovan, LL.D., but (as since ascertained by the Rev. Dr. Reeves) a place near the village of Annagassan, at the tidal opening of the junction of the rivers Glyde and Dee, in the county of Louth. Todd's "War of the Gaedhil with the Gaill," p. lxii., n. 1.]

[2] *Ibid.*, A.D. 850. Snamh Eidhneach or Aighneach is Carlingford Lough. Cearbhall, A.D. 873, assisted by the Danes under Gorm, attacked the Lochlans or Norwegians in Munster. Gorm then went to sea and was killed by Ruaidhri, king of the Britons.—Three Fragments, 133.

[3] Ann. 4 Mast. 851—Ann. Inisf. 853—Ann. Ult. 852, "Aulaiv, king of Lochlann, came into Ireland, and all the foreigners submitted to him, and had rent from the Irish."

20 THE SCANDINAVIANS, AND

BOOK I.
CHAP. II.

various names of Aulaf, Aulaiv, Amhlaeibh, Amaleff, and Amlevus, was "Olaf the White," son of Inguald, king of Uplands, a descendant of Regnar Lodbrog, one of the preceding invaders.[1]

Northern history states that in one of his viking expeditions Olaf took Dublin, and was made king of it, and of the "Dyflinarskidi,"[2] a territory around the city, and this statement is corroborated by Irish annals—that he was made king of Dublin, and "of the land in Ireland called Fingal"—that he built a "Dun" at Clondalkin, and that he "exacted rent (scatt) from the Irish."[3] Fingal being the northern part of the Dyflinarskidi, and Clondalkin being in the southern part, about four miles from the city fortress.

Legend of the brothers Aulaf, Sitric, and Ivar founding Dublin, Waterford, and Limerick, disproved.

Modern history adds that, Aulaf was accompanied by his brothers, Sitric and Ivar—that "they built first the three cities of Dublin, Waterford, and Limerick, of which Dublin fell to the share and was under the government of Aulaf, Waterford of Sitric,

---

[1] Eyrbyggia Saga, p. 5. "Oleifrhinn Hvite," or Olaf the White, was son of Inguald, son of Thora, daughter of Sigurd Anguioculus, son of Regnar Lodbrog.

In Landnamabok, p. 106, he is stated to be "son of King Inguald, son of Helgi (and Thora), son of Olaf, son of Gudrand, son of Halfden Whitefoot, king of Uplands."

[2] Landnamabok, Havniæ, 1774, p. 106, "Dyflina á Irlandi oc Dyflinarskidi." In Magnus Barefoot's Saga, c. xxv., it is called Dyflinarskiri.

[3] Ann. 4 Mast. A.D. 866.—This Dun or residence of Aulaf was burned by the Irish during his absence in Scotland in A.D. 868. ["Amlaff's fortress (Longport) at Clondalkin had been burned by the Irish (865=868, Four Mast.), who gibbeted 100 heads of the slain. The next year his son Carlus fell in battle. These outrages probably excited his thirst for vengeance; and on his return in 870 he plundered and burned Armagh (Four Mast. 867=870)."—War of the Gaedhil with the Gaill, p. lxxx. (Dr. Todd's Note.)]

and Limerick of Ivar;"¹ but of this legend, which apparently originated with Giraldus Cambrensis, there is no trace whatsoever in the Annals of Ulster, of Clonmacnois, or of the Four Masters, or in the Chronicon Scotorum, or in the War of the Gaedhil with the Gaill, or in any Irish manuscript known to us. There is no allusion in any of them to the building of cities by Aulaf or his followers, or to his having had brothers named Ivar and Sitric. On the contrary, they record the building of a fortress at Dublin² twelve years before Aulaf came to Ireland, and do not even mention the name of Sitric until nearly forty years after, when they record the death of a Sitric,³ who was (not the brother, but) the son of Ivar; and while we have an uninterrupted succession of Scandinavian kings in Dublin, there is no record of any Scandinavian king in Waterford until 903, or in Limerick till 940.

In fact, if we except the interpolated Annals of Innisfallen, the only Irish authority for stating that Aulaf had any brothers, is Dudley M'Firbis's "Three Fragments of Irish History," in which it is said that he had brothers named Ivar and Oisile, and that, in a fit of jealousy, he slew the latter.⁴

---

¹ Giraldus Cambrensis,Top.Hib., lib. 3, cap. xliii.—Giraldus was copied by Higden, Polychronicon, lib. 1, Rer. Scrip., vol. iii., p. 182; and Higden was avowedly copied by Keating, Hist. of Ireland; and M'Geoghegan, Histoire d'Irlande, vol. i., p. 387. Ware (Ant. Irel., Lon., 1705, p. 59), also copies from Giraldus the story of the three brothers building the three cities.

² Ann. 4 Mast. A.D. 840. Ann. Clonmac. 838.

³ Ibid. A.D. 891.—"Sitric, son of Ivar, was slain by other Norsemen."

⁴ Ann. 4 Mast. A.D. 861.—"Amhlacibh, Imhar, and Uailsi, three chieftains of the foreigners, and Lorcan, son of Cathal, Lord of Meath, plundered the land of Flann." Ann. Ult. A.D. 861,

While, on the other hand, Scandinavian authorities are not only silent respecting the brotherhood of Aulaf with Ivar, Sitric, and Oisile, but supply conclusive evidence that no such connexion existed: they distinctly state that Ivar, so frequently named in Irish and English history, was the son of Regnar Lodbrog, and thus only allied to Aulaf, the probability being that Ivar came to Ireland to avenge the death of his father (who perished in A.D. 845), and that he came, not with Aulaf in A.D. 852, but that his was "the fleet of the king of the foreigners" which reached our shores in A.D. 847.[1] The difference of age which this implies suggests no difficulty. We know that Biorn Ironsides and another son of Regnar Lodbrog were then invading France, and we know that military life began so early and was continued so long, that three generations frequently fought side by side. Nor did Aulaf subsequently obtain any other Irish territory from which he could have exacted tribute. For although in 857 he invaded Meath with his companion Ivar, and his ally Cearbhall, and plundered it in 860, and again in 861, there is no trace that Aulaf obtained any dominion over it. If it be suggested that it is shown by the statements respecting Ivar and Sitric that Aulaf retained the power which Turgesius possessed, and that he "named a Northman king for each province," it is sufficient to reply that these statements, although very generally adopted, are almost obviously incorrect.

---

"The three *kings* of the foreigners, Aulaiv, Ivar, and Auisle, entered the land of Flann." Here there is no mention of Sitric.

[1] Langebek, vol. 1, pp. 283–344. *Ibid.* vol. i. p. 540; vol. ii. p. 14. Ordericus Vitalis apud Du Chesne, p. 458.

The place where Aulaf fixed his residence the Irish called "Ath Cliath," or "the ford of Hurdles,"[1] from the wicker bridge by which the great road from Tara was continued across the Liffey into Cualann. The Scandinavians called it "Dyflin," a corruption of the Irish name for that inlet at the confluence of the Poddle and the Liffey, which formed a harbour where ships were moored, and which the Irish called "Dubhlinn" or "the Black pool," from the dark colour given to the water by the bog which extends under the river.

The Anglo-Norman charter writers of Henry the Second latinized its Ostman name into "Duvelina," and those of King John brought it nearer the name it has since retained. About ten years before the arrival of Aulaf a body of foreigners, probably Norwegians, landed at "Dubhlinn of Ath Cliath" and erected a fortress near where Dublin Castle now stands, and around this fortress the city grew and continued to be the scourge of their Irish neighbours. Out of it they "plundered Leinster and the Ui Neill, both territories and churches;"[2] nor was their career of spoliation checked until A.D. 845, when they were defeated and "twelve hundred of them slain at Carn Brammit by Cearbhall, son of Dunghal, lord of Ossory."[3]

Weakened by this defeat and the death of Turgesius, they were unable to prevent Maelsechlainn

---

[1] Irish writers celebrated it under various names, while in possession of the Ostmen as "Ath Cliath of ships," "Ath Cliath of swords," and call the harbour "The Dubhlinn of Ath Cliath," &c.

[2] [Ann. 4 Mast., A.D. 840.]

[3] [Id., The situation of Carn Brammit has not been identified.]

and Tighearnach from "plundering Dubhlinn" in 847; but if with the harbour the fortress also was taken, it was not long retained, for new fleets having arrived in A.D. 847, the Foreigners assisted "Cinaedh, son of Conang, lord of Cianachta Breagh,"[1] to rebel against Maelsechlainn and to plunder the Ui Neill from the Shannon to the sea; nor did they permit Maelsechlainn's ally to escape with impunity, they entered the territory of Tighearnach, "plundered the island of Loch Gabhor,[2] and afterwards burned it, so that it was level with the ground."[3]

*Dublin and Northumbria for a century under the same kings.*

But the high position which Dublin held amid the colonies of the Northmen, is more evident from its connexion with Northumberland, which, extending from the river Humber to Scotland, and having York for its capital, was governed for nearly a century by the kings of Dublin, or by kings of the same race.[4]

*Legend of Regnar's death in Northumbria.*

Northern and English historians concur in stating that Ivar, son of Regnar Lodbrog, King of Denmark

---

[1] [The river Ainge (now the Nanny) flows through the middle of the territory of Cianachta Breagh, dividing the barony of Upper Duleek from that of Lower Duleek, in the county of Meath. J. O'Donovan, LL.D., Ann. 4 Mast.]

[2] [Or Loch Gower, now Logore, near the town of Dunshaughlin in the county of Meath. *Id., Ibid.*]

[3] In 849 "The people of King Maelsechlainn and Tighearnach lord of Loch Gabhor, captured Cinaedh, enveloped him in a sack, and drowned him in the Ainge."

[4] Northumberland included Deira and Bernicia "Deira extended from the Humber to the Tyne, Bernicia from the Tyne to Scotland."—Caradoc, p. 26. Northumbria was called in the Sagas "the fifth part of England." Egils Saga, Hafniæ, 1809, p. 266. Northumberland, Westmorland, Cumberland, and part of Lancashire, are omitted in the Doomsday Book as not being part of England. The connexion between Dublin and Northumberland, and the fact that Northumberland was long governed by the kings of Dublin or by kings of the same race, is not mentioned in any English history.

and Norway, invaded England and conquered Northumberland, but they differ widely respecting the cause and consequence of that invasion. The generally received legend is, that Regnar Lodbrog, having invaded Northumberland with a small Danish fleet and army, was defeated and captured by Ella, then the reigning sovereign, and by his orders thrown into a cave where he was stung to death by serpents; and further, that Ivar, to avenge his father's death, invaded Northumberland, seized Ella, inflicted on him the cruelest tortures,[1] and then became King of Northumberland.[2] Yet, generally adopted as this legend is, it chiefly rests on the authority of the Lodbrog Quida, the supposed death-song of Regnar, and on an " Icelandic fragment " not written before the twelfth century. Its story of Ella's victory and Regnar's death in Northumberland is not to be found in more trustworthy Northern history, nor is it to be found in any old English Chronicle or early English history. The Saxon Chronicle has no allusion whatsoever to the supposed events. It neither alludes to the alleged cruelty of Ella, or the consequent vengeance of Regnar' sons. It neither mentions Regnar's name, nor does it assign any cause either for the invasion of East Anglia in 866, or for that of Northumbria in A.D. 867,—neither does Ethelwerd, William of Malmesbury, Simeon of Durham, Florence of Worcester, or Henry of Huntingdon; and Asser, who lived at the period, and wrote soon after it, only mentions Regnar

---

[1] [Islendzkir Annal., p. 5. Turner's Anglo-Saxons, second edition, i., 223. Lappenberg (Thorpe's trans.) ii., p. 30.]

[2] Langebek, Rer. Scrip., vol. ii., p. 278.—Sax. Gram.

Lodbrog as being the father of "Hinguar and Hubba," neither assigning any cause for the invasion of Northumberland, or making any allusion to Ella's cruelty or Regnar's death.

Apparently the first English historian who assigned any cause for the invasion of Northumbria by the Northmen, was Geoffry Gaimar, who wrote about the middle of the twelfth century,[1] but the cause which he assigns has no connexion whatsoever with Ella, or Regnar, or Regnar's sons. His statement is, that the invasion originated from the revenge of Buerno, an English nobleman, for an injury received from King Osbright, and in this story Gaimar is followed by Brompton.

But if Gaimar were the first to assign a cause for the Danish invasion of Northumberland, Roger of Wendover, a writer of the thirteenth century, was probably the first to chronicle the death of Regnar Lodbrog; yet in doing so he also wholly differs from the Northern legend, his story being that Regnar, while hawking on the coast of Denmark, was driven out to sea by a storm and cast on the English coast and murdered, not in Northumbria by Ella, but in East Anglia by the huntsman of its king, Edmund. Nor is it less conclusive of the Northern legend, that although the almost universal testimony of English history is, that Edmund, king of East Anglia, was cruelly martyred by Hinguar and Hubba, the sons of Regnar Lodbrog, there is not a line in English history to show that Ella, king of Northumberland,

---

[1] Monum. Britt. p. 795. Geffri Gaimar, l. 2593, *et seq.*

[2] Brompton, Hist. Ang. Script., apud Twysden, p. 803.

was tortured by them, or anyone else; all testimony being that he was slain in battle in 867.¹ And further, if the Northern legend were true, Ella must have captured Regnar Lodbrog some years before Northumbria was invaded by Regnar's sons. But, there is only one authority for the statement that Ella reigned, except during the years 866 and 867; and, even supposing that Simeon of Durham is correct in stating that Ella's reign commenced in 862, Regnar must have invaded Northumbria, and have been captured by Ella between that year and 866. Yet, not only is there no record of such events, but there is no record of any invasion whatsoever, or any landing in Northumberland by Regnar or any other Scandinavian during that period.²

Northern historians also differ respecting the period in which this celebrated leader lived. Nor do they agree about his death—they either make no allusion to it, or differ about the date of it. And so glaring are their anachronisms that Torfœus suggests the existence of two Regnar Lodbrogs, and Suhm of three, with two successive Ellas, by whom the three Regnars were killed.³

All English history being thus opposed to the story of Regnar's death in Northumberland, and the torture

BOOK I.
CHAP. II.

Regnar Lodbrog put to death in Ireland by the Irish.

¹ Chron. Mailros, A.D. 867.
² Rafer, who was misled by the statements of Turner, says, in a preface to the Krakas Maal, Copenhagen, 1826, p. 40—"Vers la fin du huitième siecle de l'ère chrétienne Regnar Lodbrog, Roi de Danemark, fut fait prisonnier par son ennemi Ella," &c., &c. But Ella did not commence his reign until after the middle of the ninth century, and was slain by Regnar Lodbrog's sons in 866.
³ Torfœus Series Dynastarum, &c., Hafniæ, 1702, p. 346. Suhm, Hist. of Danemark, Kiobch, 1828. Mallet (Hist. Danemarc, Geneve, 1787, vol. iii., p. 35) also supposes that there were two Regnar Lodbrogs.

of Ella by Regnar's sons, and this story having little support from Northern history, we may claim attention for the much more numerous Scandinavian authorities, which state that Regnar Lodbrog perished in Ireland, being captured and put to death by Hella (Ailill), an Irish prince. It is distinctly stated by Saxo Grammaticus[1] that Regnar Lodbrog invaded Ireland, and, having killed its king, Melbricus, besieged and took Dublin, where he remained a year. Unfortunately, Saxo is not equally clear respecting Hella—he says that "the Galli" having expelled Ivar, Regnar's son, and conferred the authority of king on Hella, son of Hamon, "Regnar landed, and after a protracted battle, forced Hella to fly, although supported by the valour of the Galli."

But whether these Galli were the people of Wales or the Welsh of Cornwall, who were in constant communication with the people of the south of Ireland, and Hella, an Irish prince, who then ruled over them, we are left to conjecture. Saxo, however, adds, that "Hella, having repaired to the Irish, put to death all who had joined Regnar;" and that "Regnar attacking him with a fleet," was captured and thrown into prison, where he paid the just penalty for his persecution of Christians.[2]

---

[1] Saxo Grammat., Danica Hist., Frankfort, 1576, p. 158.—"Verum hanc mœroris acerbitatem Ivari regno pulsi repentinus detraxit adventus. Quippe Galli, fugato eo, in Hellam quendam Hamonis filium falsam regis contulerant potestatem, &c., &c.

"Cumque ibidem Regnerus annum victor explesset consequenter excitis in opem filiis Hyberniam petit, occisoque ejus rege Melbrico, Dyflinam barbaris opibus refertissimam obsedit, oppugnavit, accepit; ibique annuo stativis habitis," &c., &c., et seq.

[2] Langebek, vol. i., p. 268, A.D. 826—"Persecutio Regneriana contra Novitios Christianos." Saxo, p. 158, "Superveniens enim Regne-

The "Chronicle of Danish Kings"[1] repeats these statements of Saxo respecting Regnar's invasion of Ireland, his "taking of Dublin," and Hella's actions among the Irish. Nor is the "Lodbrokar Quida"[2] more explicit, for although it states that Regnar's final battles were in Ireland and in Wales it neither names the place where Regnar perished or the kingdom where Ella reigned.

But in the Chronicle of King Eric we find the explicit statement that Regnar having conquered many countries was "at length killed in Ireland,"[3] Hamsfort being equally explicit in stating that Regnar was captured by Hella, an Irish prince, and put to death in prison.[4]

Let us now see how far these statements are consistent with Irish history.

rus inductaque per eum sacra temerans, vera religione proscripta pristino adulterinam loco restituit ac suo ceremonias honore donavit." Pontoppidan Gesta et Vestigia Danorum, 1740, vol. ii., p. 301 et 298, quoting Saxo Gramm., has the marginal note "Gesta Regnari Lodbr. et mors calamitosa in Hibernia." Pontoppidan, vol. ii., and Torfœus Dynast. et Reg. Dan. have collected much respecting Regnar Lodbrog, but were utterly ignorant of Irish history, which, in fact, was almost a dead letter until the publication of O'Conor, Rer. Hib. Script., and the translation of the Four Masters by O'Donovan.

[1] Chron. Reg. Dan. Langebek, vol. 1, p. 110, *et seq.*

[2] Lodbrokar Quida, Copenhagen, 1782. Johnstone, Stroph. xx., trans lates "Lindiseyri" Leinster, which is probably correct, as "Erin's blood" is mentioned immediately after. Others have supposed it to be Lindesness in Norway, or Lindesey in England.— *Vide* Krakas Maal, Rafer., Copenh., 1826, p. 135. Johnstone also surmises that the Irish king, Marstan, of the poem is the Melbricus of Saxo.

[3] Langebek, vol. i., p. 156, Regneri Lothbroki: "Iste subjugavit Angliam, Scotiam, Hyberniam, Norwegiam, Sweicam, Teutoniam, Slaviam, Rusciam, et omnia regna occidentis; ita quod ix. filios suos in singulis terris reges fecit et ipse de uno regno in aliud inter eos pertransivit. Tandem in Hybernia occisus est," &c., &c.

[4] Hamsfort, Series Regum; Langebek, vol. i., p. 36. "Qui Reg-

In our annals we find several princes of the name of Ella, or as written by Irish scribes,[1] Ailill; and one of these, Ailill, son of Dunlang, King of Leinster, is stated to have been "slain by the Norsemen" on the return of Ivar from Scotland in A.D. 870,[2] but with the exception of his having been put to death by the Norsemen there is nothing to identify him with the Ella of Saxo.

*Regnar Lodbrog the Thurgils or Turgesius of Irish Annals.*

Of Regnar Lodbrog there is no mention by any of our annalists, but they celebrate the actions of a Danish or Norwegian king whom they call Turgesius; and the dates and facts in their history of this King Turgesius correspond with and strongly resemble those in the Scandinavian history of Regnar.

Assuming that the authorities quoted by Torfœus are correct,[3] and that Regnar Lodbrog began his reign and conquests between A.D. 809 and 818, and was put to death between the years 841 and 865, we find in the Annals of Innisfallen that, A.D. 815, "the Danish king Turgesius came to plunder and conquer Ireland,"[4] he and his followers being cruel enemies to Christianity.

---

nerus ab Hella Hybernorum regulo captus gravi supplicio afficitur, anno 854." The account given by Peter Olaus of Regnar's capture by Ella, an Irish prince, and his death in Ireland, is nearly similar to that given by Saxo Grammaticus; Meursen and Krœutzer give the like accounts.

[1] That Ella was killed in battle together with Osbright has been already shown. Ella's death in Northumbria is recorded thus in the Annals of Ulster:—"A.D. 866."

Battle upon Saxons of the north, &c., &c., wherein Ailill [Alli] "king of Saxons was killed."— Ann. 4 Mast., p. 503, n.

[2] Ann. Ult., 870.; Ann. 4 Mast., 869.

[3] Torfœus, Scr. Reg. Dan., p. 389.—Huisfeldens gives Regnar's reign 818 and death 865; Lyschander 812 and 841; and Svaninguis 815, and his death 841.— Langebek, vol. 1, p. 268-854.

[4] Ann. Innisf. A.D. 815 et Ogygia, p. 433. Anno 807 Hiber-

The Annals of the Four Masters add that, A.D. 830, the Norsemen "took King Maelbrighde (the King Melbricus of Saxo) and carried him to their ships."[1] That, in 836, they took Dublin,[2] where Turgesius subsequently reigned; and that, in 843, King Maelseachlain captured Turgesius,[3] and put him to death by causing him to be thrown into Loch Uair,[4] where he was drowned; and, further, that, A.D. 846, "Tomhrair, earl, tanist (or chosen successor) of the king of Lochlan, was killed in battle by Ollchovar, king of Munster, and Cellach, king of Leinster."[5]

From this coincidence of dates and facts, it might be inferred that the Irish Turgesius and the Scandinavian Regnar were identical, Turgesius[6] being the Latin form of Thorgils (pronounced Turgils), literally signifying "the servant of Thor;" and Tomar, or Thormodr, signifying "Thorsman," or one devoted to Thor,[7] the Scandinavian deity. Such names might have been assumed by, or applied to, Regnar and his

---

niam primùm incursionibus intrarunt; deinde anno 812. Demùm anno 815 Turgesius Norwegus in Hiberniam appulit et exinde ibidem fixas sedes habere cœperunt. Chronologia Anschariana, Langebek vol. i., p. 531, as to the death of Horrick vel Regnar A.D. 846.

[1] Ann. 4 Mast. 830. Saxo Gram., p. 158.

[2] Ibid. 836.

[3] Ibid. 843. Ann. Ult. 844.

[4] [Lough Owel, in the county of Westmeath.—J. O'D., LL.D.]

[5] Ibid. 846. Ann. Ult. 847.— The story of Turgesius captured by young men disguised as women (see Keating and M'Geoghegan) is the repetition of an old story. See Plutarch—Life of Pelopidas; see also Herodotus, &c.

[6] Thorgils is a common name in Northern history, but there is no mention of any king, prince, or chieftain of the name of Turgesius. It is a name unknown to all history except as used by the Irish.

[7] Thormodr was a very general name of the priests of Thor, vid. Landnam, p. 70: Thormod Godi, p. 19; Thormodr Allsheriar Godi; Thormodr Godi; Thormodr pontifex, &c. Thors Rolf, who fled to Iceland, was Thorlf or Thors Rolf, from being priest of Thor.

successor, as worshippers of Thor and enemies of Christianity, these virulent Pagans being designated as Thorsmen or followers of Thor, in contradistinction to Christsmen or followers of Christ.

This suggestion is rendered more probable when we observe that those who are known to be the descendants and successors of Regnar Lodbrog are called, by the Irish, "the race of Tomar." The name is given to the pagan kings of Dublin who succeeded Ivar, the son of Regnar. Their chieftains are called "Tomar's chieftains," their subjects "the people of Tomar"; the king of Dublin himself being called "Prince Tomar," the badge of his authority "the ring of Tomar," and a wood near Dublin, "Tomar's wood," probably from having been devoted to the religious services of Thor. Nor do the Irish confine the name to pagan descendants of Regnar Lodbrog in Ireland. His descendant, grandson of Gormo Enske, king of Denmark, who renounced Christianity and embraced the religion of Thor, is called "Tomar mac Elchi" (Tomar, son of Enske) in the Book of Rights and other Irish manuscripts.[1]

But there are Irish legends which even more directly tend to identify these individuals. They state that Turgesius had "a lord deputy" named Gurmundus (the Latinized name of Gormo), and Scandinavian history records that Gormo was deputed to rule over Regnar's dominions during the absence of his sons.[2]

---

[1] Gormo Enske was succeeded by his son Harold, and Harold by his son Gormo. Langebek, vol. i., p. 16.

[2] Fragm. Islandica, Langebek, vol. ii., p. 280. "Sigurd Anguioculus (Regnar's son) Blœjam Ellœ regis filiam in matrimonio habuit.

Nor should we omit to observe that the fact of Regnar Lodbrog's death, not in Northumberland but in Ireland, would explain what otherwise appears inconsistent in the proceedings of his son. For if Ivar's object were to avenge his father's death, it would show why Ireland, and not England, was the country he first invaded; and it would not appear extraordinary that when he subsequently invaded England, he landed in East Anglia, having sailed past Northumbria without any attempt to molest its people or their king, a course difficult to account for if it were in Northumbria Regnar perished, and that there his slayer reigned.

BOOK I. CHAP. II.

NOTE.

[The following particulars of the rule of Turgesius in Ireland are from "The War of the Gaedhil with the Gaill," not published till after the death of Mr. Haliday:—

Chapter VI. records the first invasion of Ulster (A.D. 824); Chapter VII. gives the invasion and plunder of Leinster; Chapter VIII. the arrival of a fleet at Limerick (A.D. 834); Chapter IX., is as follows:—

"There came after that a great royal fleet into the north of Erinn with Turgeis, who assumed the sovereignty of the foreigners of Erinn; and the north of Erinn was plundered by them; and they spread themselves over Leth Chuinn" (the northern half of Ireland, as divided by a line drawn from Dublin to Galway). "A fleet of them also entered Loch Eathach (Lough Neagh), and another fleet entered Lughbudh (Louth), and another fleet entered Loch Rae (Lough Ree, a swell of the Shannon, between the counties of Longford and Roscommon). Moreover Ard Macha (Armagh) was plundered three times in the

Account of Turgesius from Dr. Todd's "Wars of the Gaedhil with the Gaill."

Turgeis in the north of Ireland assumes the sovereignty of the foreigners, A.D. 839.

Eorum filius fuit Canutus, Hördaknutus dictus qui in Selandia Scania et Hollandia post patrem suum regnum nactus est. Vikia vero ab illo tunc defecit. Ille filium nomine Gormonem habuit. Hic denominatus est a suo nutritio, filio

Canuti expostititii qui totum regnum pro Regnari filiis administravit, dum illi expeditionibus bellicis occupati erant. Olaf Trygv., vol. i., p. 72. Des Roches Hist. de Danm., vol. i., p. cxxv.

BOOK I.
CHAP. II.

*Turgeis enters Loch Ree, and plunders the monasteries of Meath and Connaught, A.D. 838–845.*

*Invasion under Turgesius.*

same month by them; and Turgeis himself usurped the abbacy of Ard Macha; and Farannan, abbot of Ard Macha, and chief comharba of Patrick, was driven out, and went to Mumhain (Munster) and Patrick's shrine with him; and he was four years in Mumhain, while Turgeis was in Ard Macha, and in the sovereignty of the north of Erinn."

CHAPTER XI. "There came now Turgeis of Ard Macha, and brought a fleet upon Loch Rai, and from thence plundered Midhe and Connacht; and Cluan Mic Nois" (Clonmacnois, on the left bank of the Shannon, five miles south of Athlone), "and Cluan Ferta of Brennan" (Clonfert, in the county of Galway), "and Lothra and Tir-dá-glass" (Lorrha and Terryglas, on the banks of Lough Derg, a swell of the Shannon, in the county of Tipperary), "and Inis Celtra, and all the churches of Derg-dheirc" (the churches in the islands of Lough Derg), "in like manner. And the place where Ota, the wife of Turgeis, used to give her audience was upon the altar of Cluan Mic Nois."—(pp. ix.-xiii).

Dr. Todd, after fixing the dates and series of the earliest ravages of the Scandinavians, says:—

"Finally, in A.D. 815, according to the Chronology of O'Flaherty (or more probably, as we shall see, about 830), Turgesius, a Norwegian, established himself as sovereign of the foreigners, and made Armagh the capital of his kingdom."—(p. xxxvi.) "After this our author says" (continues Dr. Todd), "came 'a great royal fleet into the north of Ireland,' commanded by Turgeis or Turgesius, 'who assumed the sovereignty of the foreigners of Ireland,' and occupied the whole of *Leth Chuinn*, or the northern half of Ireland. In addition to the party under the immediate command of Turgesius, three 'fleets,' probably in connexion with him, appeared simultaneously. One of these took possession of Lough Neagh, another of Louth, anchoring in what is now the bay of Dundalk, and the third, having, as it would seem, approached Ireland from the west, occupied Lough Ree. The chronology of this invasion is fixed by means of the particulars recorded. Armagh was plundered three times in the same month. This, the annalists all say, was the first plundering of Armagh by the Gentiles, and is assigned to the year 832." Dr. Todd then shows that, in A.D. 845, Turgesius was made captive by Malachy, "and drowned in Loch Uair, now Lough Owel, near Mullingar, county of Westmeath."—(*Ibid.*, pp. xlii., xliii.)

This and another event "enables us (Dr. Todd says) to ascertain the duration of Turgesius' dynasty with tolerable certainty." He fixes its commencement with the seizing of Armagh after three assaults in one month, in A.D. 832. " For nine years afterwards he seems to have remained content with his secular possession of the country, or [was] unable to overthrow the power of the ecclesiastical authorities. It was not until the year 841 that he succeeded in banishing the bishop and clergy, and 'usurped the abbacy,' that is to say, the full authority and jurisdiction in Armagh and in the north of Ireland. From these considerations we may infer that the entire duration of the tyranny of Turgesius cannot have been more than about thirteen years, from 831 or 832 to his death in 845."— (*Ibid.*, xliii., xliv.) *Duration of Turgesius's dynasty.*

"The times immediately preceding the arrival of Turgesius and his followers were remarkable for internal dissension amongst the Irish chieftains . . . . It is not wonderful that these dissensions should have suggested to Tugresius the expulsion of the contending parties, for the purpose of taking the power into his own hands. He seems to have had a higher object in view than mere plunder, which influenced former depredators of his nation. He aimed at the regular government or monarchy over his countrymen in Ireland; the foundation of a permanent colony, and the subjugation or extermination of the native chieftains. For this purpose, the forces under his command, or in connexion with him, were skilfully posted on Lough Ree, at Limerick, Dundalk Bay, Carlingford, Lough Neagh, and Dublin. He appears also to have attempted the establishment of the national heathenism of his own country in the place of the Christianity which he found in Ireland. This may be the significance of his usurpation of the 'abbacy' of Armagh. *Dissensions of the Irish chieftains in the ninth century. Turgesius attempts the subjugation of Ireland. Aims at restoring Paganism.*

"Turgesius was not satisfied with the full supremacy he had acquired in the north of Ireland. He aimed at the extension of his power by the conquest of Meath and Connaught, as a step to the subjugation of the whole country; for this purpose he appears to have gone to Loch Ree to take the command in person of the 'fleet' which had been stationed there. From this central position he plundered, as our author tells us, the principal ecclesiastical establishments of Connaught and Meath, namely, Clonmacnois, in [West] Meath; Clonfert, of St. Brendan in Connaught; Lothra, now Lorrha, a famous monastery founded by St. Ruadhan or Rodan, in the county of Tipperary; Tir-da-glas, now Terryglass, in the same county; Inis-Celtra, an island on which were seven churches,

BOOK I.
CHAP. II.

and all the other churches of Lough Derg, in like manner. With this view he placed his wife Ota at Clonmacnois, at that time second only to Armagh in ecclesiastical importance, who gave her audiences, or, according to another, reading her oracular answers from the high altar of the principal church of the monastery."—(*Ibid.*, xlvi.–xlix.) "At this period" (A.D. 839), continues Dr. Todd, "our author says the sea seemed to vomit forth floods of invaders, so that 'there was not a point of Ireland without a fleet.'"

In the same year (A.D. 845) "Turgesius was arrested in his victorious course, and drowned in Loch Uair by Maelsechlainn (Malachy I.), then King of Meath, who soon afterwards succeeded to the throne of Ireland."—(*Ibid.*, li.)]

## CHAPTER III.

Ivar, conqueror and King of Northumbria, identified with Ivar, King of Dublin.—Of the joint career of Aulaf and Ivar—Ivar's successors in East Anglia and Northumbria.

CHAP. III.

Joint invasion by Aulaf from Dublin and Ivar from Denmark of the Scottish Picts, A.D. 865.

TURNING from this attempt to solve the difficulties in Regnar Lodbrog's story we proceed to the easier task of identifying his son Ivar, the conqueror of Northumberland, with that "Ivar, King of the Norsemen of Ireland and Britain,"[1] who reigned and died in Dublin, A.D. 872, and whose descendants were its succeeding kings. Ivar had invaded Ireland before the arrival of Olaf the White, and was subsequently his companion in many expeditions, but did not accompany him in 865, when, with "his chieftains, and followed by all the Galls of Ireland and Scotland," Aulaf went to Fortren, the capital of Pictavia,[2] and spoiled the Picts.[3]

[1] [Wars of the Gaedhil with the Gaill, p. lxxx.]
[2] [Fortren, Fifeshire.]
[3] Ann. Ult., 865. Aulaf was

allied by marriage to Kenneth King of the Scots, who brought the Picts under his government in 843, and whose son Constantine

Ívar was at that time in Scandinavia, collecting there auxiliaries with whom he joined Aulaf in 865, and then assumed the chief command.¹ Hence the invading fleets were termed "the fleets of the tyrant Igwares."²

At the close of A.D. 866 "the Pagans landed in England and took up their winter quarters among the East Angles,"³ who supplied them with horses; and thus "a great part of those who had been infantry soldiers became cavalry."⁴ In 867 they "went from East Anglia over the mouth of the Humber to York, in Northumbria,"⁵ and having defeated and slain the two kings, Osbright and Ella,⁶ "Ivar was made king."⁷

Although Aulaf is not named in those English narratives, we infer that he accompanied Ivar to the end of the campaign, for in A.D. 868, when the army

*Ivar and Aulaf land in East Anglia, A.D. 866.*

*Thence invade Northumbria, and Ivar is made king, A.D. 867.*

obtained the crown in 863. Aulaf's invasion, which was opposed by Constantine, may have originated in some claim to the kingdom of the Picts, the Irish Picts having submitted to Aulaf, and the Picts of the Scottish Isles having been conquered by Regnar Lodbrog's sons. Sax. Gram., p. 74.

¹ The general practice of the Northmen was to place united forces under one leader.

² Ethelwerd, 866, is the only English authority in which the leader of the expedition is named, and the name Igwares is frequently mistaken (from errors of transcribers) for Inguares or Hinguar, Ivar's illegitimate brother. Northern historians write, "Eo tempore collectis Rex crudelisimus Norman-

norum Yvar filius Lothpardi (Lodbrog) quem ferunt ossibus caruisse (Beinlause) ejus fratres Inguar et Ubi et Biorn et Ulf, &c., &c. Igitur Ivar Brittaniam classe petiit et crudele prelium cum Regibus Anglorum conseruit." Langebek, vol. i., p. 374. Anonymi Roskild. Chron.

³ Sax. Chron., 866; Ethelwerd, 866.

⁴ Ibid.

⁵ Sax. Chron., 867; Asser, 867; Ethelwerd, 867.

⁶ Mat. Westm., 867; Hen. Hunt., 867; Flor. Wig., 867; Ethelwerd, 867; Asser, 867; Sax. Chron., 867, all state or imply that Osbright and Ella were killed in battle.

⁷ Langebek, vol. ii., p. 279.

BOOK I.
CHAP. III.

Aulaf returns to Ireland and plunders Armagh, A.D. 868.

"went into Mercia to Nottingham and there took up their winter quarters,"[1] we find Aulaf returning to Ireland, landing in the north, plundering Armagh, and "burning the town and oratories,"[2] his "Dun," at Clondalkin, having been burned by the Irish,[3] and his eldest son, Carlus, slain in battle during his absence.[4]

Ivar and Aulaf's second invasion of the Scottish Picts, A.D. 869.

In 869 the Danish "army again went to York and sate there for a year,"[5] at the end of which Aulaf and Ivar once more sailed for Scotland to join in another invasion, which, like the preceding, was apparently a combined attack by fleets and armies from Dublin and Denmark. According to Roger of Wendover, A.D. "870, an innumerable multitude of Danes landed in Scotland, at Berwick-on-Tweed, under the command of Hinguar and Hubba;" and the Annals of Innisfallen state that in A.D. 870 Aulaf and Ivar sailed from Dublin "with a fleet of 200 ships to assist these Danes in Britain." Berwick-on-Tweed may be here a mistake for Berwick on the Frith of Forth (Mare Pictum), one of those inlets which would have facilitated the attack on the Picts and Strathclyde Britons, whose capital, "Alcluit, was besieged (in A.D. 870) by the Norsemen under these two kings, Ivar and Aulaf, who took and destroyed it after a siege of four months."[6]

[1] Sax. Chron., 868.
[2] Ann. Ult., 868; Ann. 4 Mast., p. 511, n.
[3] Ann. 4 Mast., 865.
[4] Ann. 4 Mast., 866.
[5] Sax. Chron, 869.
[6] Roger de Wendover, 870, who adds, that "they plundered the country about as they had predetermined to do." Neither Sax. Chron., Hoveden, nor Sim. Dunhelm. mention the landing in Scotland, but state that, A.D. 870, many thousand Danes, under Hinguar and Hubba, landed in England. Ann. Innisf., 870, M'Geoghegan

Having plundered the country,[1] and subjected it to tribute, which "they were paid for a long time after, Aulaf and Ivar came again to Dublin out of Scotland, and brought with them great bootyes from Englishmen, Britons, and Picts in their two hundred ships, with many of their people captives;"[2] Hinguar and Hubba being left to carry on the war in East Anglia and Mercia,[3] and Northumbria being placed under the Viceroyalty of Egbert, who governed it until the death of Ivar.[4]

*They return to Dublin with prisoners and plunder, A.D. 870.*

When Aulaf and Ivar returned to Ireland, the "Lords of the foreigners" plundered part of Munster "during the snow of Bridgetmas" in 870. Their ally Cearbhall had plundered both Munster and Connaught in the preceding year; and, in 871, "the foreigners of Ath Cliath" again plundered Munster, and Cearbhall again plundered Connaught.

*They ravage Munster and Connaught, A.D. 870–871.*

The cause of these devastations is no where stated, but they were the last committed by the united forces

Hist. d'Irlande, vol. i., p. 395, Ann. Ult., 870. The Ann. Camb. and Brut y Tyw. record the destruction of Alcluit in 870, but do not name the destroyers.

[1] The siege of Strath Cluaide [Dumbarton] continued for four months, " at length after having wasted the people who were in it by hunger and thirst, having wonderfully drawn off the well they had within, they entered the fort on them." Three Fragments, p. 193.

[2] Ann. Ult., A.D. 870.

[3] Hoveden, 870.

[4] Roger Wendover—" Egbert governed the kingdom six years in subjection to the Danes." "In 872, the Northumbrians expelled from the kingdom their king Egbert:" and Hoveden, 867.

Hinguar and Hubba are never styled kings: their title was that of Earl (Iarl). Whether this arose from their illegitimacy is uncertain. Harold Harfagre subsequently enacted that all his descendants in the male line should succeed to the kingly title and dignity, but his descendants by females only to the rank of Earl (Iarl), A.D. 870. Olavi Trygvisson Saga, cap. 2, p. 5. Scripta Historica Islandorum, 12 vols., 8vo., Hafniæ, 1828–46, vol. i., p. 5.

BOOK I.
CHAP. III.

Deaths of Aulaf and Ivar in A.D. 871 and 872.

of Aulaf and Ivar, for A.D. 870 or 871 terminated the career of Aulaf. He was slain in battle, and Ivar, who succeeded him as King of Dublin, did not long survive, the record of his death in the Annals of Ulster being that "Imhar, King of the Norsemen of Ireland and Britain, died," A.D. 872.[1]

Proofs that Ivar of Northumbria and Ivar of Dublin were the same.

That Ivar, King of the Scandinavians of Dublin, and Ivar, King of the Danes of Northumbria, was the same individual is here clearly stated; but fortunately our evidence of the fact is not confined to Irish annals. Irish annals are here confirmed by one of the oldest and most important of the English chronicles; for it must be admitted that the chronological difference of one or two years between the chronology of different English historians is so general that it may pass unnoticed when the facts agree,[2] and here Ethelward, after stating that King Edmund was defeated and slain by the Danes in A.D. 870,[3] adds that, although "the barbarians gained the victory they soon afterwards lost their king, for King Ivar died the same year," not in battle, but from old age or disease, as stated in the Icelandic saga and Irish history.[4]

[1] Laudnam. says, he was slain in battle in Ireland. On the contrary, Pinkerton Enquiry, vol. i., p. 495, and Innes Apx. iii. Chron. Pict. say—"Tertio iterum anno Amlieb trahens cetum (exercitum) a Constantino occisus est." This would place his death in Scotland in 868, and consequently inconsistent with the statement of his return to Dublin in 870, but would be consistent with the statement of the Annals of Innisfallen, that it was Aulaf, junior, who returned with Ivar, Aulaf being doubtless a mistake for Osten or Eystein, Aulaf's son, as the Norsemen never called the son by the father's name. Ann. Ult., 872. Ann. 4 Mast., 871. Ann. Innisf., 873.

[2] "During long periods of years the northern (English chronicles) differ from those of the south and west two whole years." Codex Dip. Sax., lxxxv.

[3] Ethelwerd's Chronicle, Mon. Britt., p. 513.

[4] Langebek, vol. ii., p. 281, Ivar "in Anglia senex obiit."—Three Fragments, p. 199, "The King of

This, assuredly, is strong evidence to identify Ivar of Dublin with Ivar of Northumbria; yet, strong as it is, we have to add the more conclusive evidence, which must be deduced from the fact, that the sons and descendants of this Ivar succeeded to the thrones of both Dublin and Northumbria, and long continued to govern the two kingdoms.

<small>BOOK I.
CHAP. III.</small>

When Aulaf and Ivar left Scotland, the army under the command of Hinguar and Hubba set sail for "East Anglia, and took up their winter quarters at Thetford" in 870, and the same winter they defeated and slew King Edmund.[1]

<small>Ivar's army under Hinguar and Hubba defeat Edmund, King of the Anglo Saxons, A.D. 870.</small>

"After the death of St. Edmund," East Anglia was governed by Gormo, son of Frotho, King of Denmark, another of Regnar Lodbrog's descendants,[2] and after the death of Ivar, his reputed brother, Halfden and Bœgsec (whose genealogy is unknown) became kings of Deira and Bernicia, the two divisions of Northumbria.

<small>Gormo, son of King of Denmark, rules East Anglia after Edmund's death. Ivar's brother Halfdene succeeds him in Northumbria.</small>

Bœgsec was slain in 871,[3] and in 873 and 874 the Danes subdued the whole kingdom of Mercia, and placed it under the viceroyalty of Ceolwulf,[4] who gave

<small>The Danes subdue Mercia, A.D. 873.</small>

---

the Lochlans died of an ugly sudden disease—sic enim Deo placuit."

[1] Sax. Chron. 870.—Also Asser and Ethelwerd say that Edmund was slain in battle; but Hen. Hunt., Flor. Wig., and Sim. Dun. say he was "martyred." They differ, however, respecting the manner in which he perished. Edmund was canonized.

[2] "Super regnum Estangliæ quidam Dacus, Godrim nomine, post Edmundum primo regnavit." Brompton Chron., p. 807, apud.

Historiæ Anglicanæ Scriptores Antiquæ, London, 1652, folio. Sax. Chron., 875, where he is called Godrum, and subsequently at 878 Guthrum. Frotho, whose name is unknown to English history, is styled "Victor Angliæ" by Danish writers, Langebek, vol. i., pp. 56, 58, 66. He was son of Swen, son of Knut, by a daughter of Sigurd Anguioculus, son of Regnar Lodbrog.

[3] Sax. Chron. 871.

[4] Ibid., 874.

hostages, and swore "that he would be ready to resign the kingdom" on whatever day they would have it.

<small>BOOK I. CHAP. III.</small>

<small>Gormo attempts to conquer King Alfred, A.D. 875.</small>

Elated by this success, and contemplating further conquests, "the three kings, Godrum, Oscytel, and Anwynd, went with a large army from Repton to Grantabridge"[1] to take possession of Wessex. There they remained for a year, and Alfred, unable to expel these invaders, "ratified a treaty of peace with them (in A.D. 876), and gave them money, and they gave him hostages, and swore oaths to him on the holy ring, which they never before would do to any nation, that they would speedily depart his kingdom."[2] Nevertheless these oaths were either violated by some or not considered binding by part of the army, as war again commenced between Alfred and Gormo, who was now assisted by the celebrated Rollo of Normandy.[3] In 878 another treaty was concluded, by which the boundaries of East Anglia were defined;[4] and Gormo, consenting to be baptized, "took the name of Athelstan as he came out of the baptismal font,"[5] being called "Enske," or of England, by northern writers,[6]

<small>Treaty with Alfred, A.D. 876.</small>

<small>Gormo, with Rollo of Normandy, assails King Alfred.</small>

<small>Gormo made King of East Anglia, A.D. 878; hence called 'Enske' or "English."</small>

---

[1] Sax. Chron. 875. Godrum is a corruption of the name Gormo, and Oscytel of Ketell, a name celebrated in the Sagas. Anwynd is called Annuth by Ethelwerd, Amund by Asser, and Anwend in the Saxon Chronicle.

[2] Sax. Chron. 876.—Asser says "they swore oaths on Christian relics." Possibly Alfred required that they should be bound both by the Christian and Pagan form of swearing.—Crymogœa, Hamburg, 1614, p. 76.—Bartholini, De Armillis Veterum, Amsterdam, 1676, p. 101.

[3] Asser, 876.—Wallingford, p. 536.

[4] This treaty is still extant, vide "Ancient Laws and Institutes of England," London, 1840, p. 66, and Lambard "Apxaionomia," Cant. 1644, p. 36. There was another treaty between Edward and Gormo Danus—Ancient Laws, p. 71, and Apxaionomia, p. 41.

[5] Sax. Chron., 890.

[6] Langebek, vol. i., p. 29. "Gorm Kunung-hin Enske, Frothasun."

and "Elchi" or "Elgi"[1] by the Irish. The Christian Gormo now resigned his Pagan kingdom of Denmark to his son, Harald,[2] and, settling in East Anglia, "apportioned it among his followers."[3] Rollo, who refused to be baptized, retired into Normandy with many of the Pagan Northmen,[4] including Oscytel, or Ketell, and Anwynd, of whom we hear no more in England.

*Rollo returns to Normandy.*

When Gormo left Repton with his division of the army, Halfdene, with the remainder, marched into Northumbria "and took up his winter quarters by the River Tyne," and having subdued all that part "of the land" he afterwards spoiled the Picts and Strathclyde Britons."[5] His object may have been to conquer all the territory overrun by Ivar, or he was provoked by the Picts who had attacked the Danes in 874,[6] and by the treachery of the Scots, who had slain Eystein (or Ostin), the son of Aulaf, for it is recorded in the Annals of Ulster that, "Osten Mac Aulaf, King of the Normans, was killed by a stratagem of the Albanaich."[7] In this expedition Halfdene compelled "Ruaidhri, son of Mormend, King of the Britons, to fly into Ireland,"[8] whither the shrine of Colum Cille and his relics in general were brought for safety."[9]

*Halfdene subdues the Picts of Strathclyde, A.D. 875.*

*Columkill's relics brought to Ireland for safety.*

[1] Book of Rights, p. xl. Ann. Clonmac., A.D. 922.
[2] Langebek, vol. i., p. 39.
[3] Sax. Chron., A.D. 880.
[4] Ingulph, "The rest who refused to be baptized left England and sailed to France."
[5] Sax. Chron., 875.
[6] Ann. Ult., 874.
[7] Ibid., 874.

[8] Ann. 4 Mast., 874. Ann. Ult., 876, Ruaidhri returned to Scotland, and "was killed by the Saxons." Chron. P. of Wales, 877.
[9] Ibid. 875.—Kenneth, king of the Scots, had removed the relics of Columba from Iona, in A.D. 850, and placed them in a church built for their reception at Dunkeld, from thence they were brought into

BOOK I.
CHAP. III.

Halfdene attempts to recover Ivar's kingdom in Ireland, A.D. 876.

Is slain at Lough Strangford.

Having thus subdued his enemies in Scotland, Halfdene returned into England, and following the practice of Scandinavian conquerors, "apportioned the lands of Northumbria (amongst his followers), who thenceforth continued ploughing and tilling."[1] In 876 he appears to have sailed into Ireland[2] to claim that dominion over the "Finnghoill" which Ivar possessed; but from thence he never returned, for in a battle between the Danes and Norwegians, or as they are termed "the White and Black Gentiles." Alban, chief of the Black Gentiles, was slain at Loch Cuan.[3]

## CHAPTER IV.

At Ivar's death, his sons, Godfrey and Sitric, were in France.—Cearbhall (Carrol) ruled at Dublin.—Sitric slays his brother Godfrey, and embarks for Dublin.—Recovers Dublin.—His attempt on Northumberland defeated.—Dies, and his son, Aulaf, succeeds.—Aulaf recovers Northumberland.—Dies at York.—Famine in Ireland through locusts.—Emigration of Danes to Iceland.—The Irish expel the Danes from Dublin.

CHAP. IV.
Cearbhall (Carroll) reigns in Dublin, A.D. 872-885.

ALTHOUGH Ivar's successors in East Anglia and Northumbria can thus be traced through English historians, his immediate successor in Dublin can only be discovered through Icelandic history, which

---

Ireland, when Halfdene invaded Pictavia.

[1] The Scandinavians considered their conquests as common property in which all had a title to share as all had contributed to acquire. Asser, p. 479.—Sax. Chron. 876, Mercia was also "apportioned."

[2] Ann. Ult. 876, calls him Alban. Four Masters, A.D. 874, Alband; and Ann. Innisf., A.D. 877, Albhar.

There is no notice of Halfdene in Sax. Chron. Ethelward, &c., after 876 and until 911, when the "three kings, Halfdene, Ecwils, and Inguar," were killed, but probably this was that Halfdene, who was with Ivar's sons, Sitric and Godfrey, at Haslou in 882—Ann. Fulden. ap. Duchesne, p. 574.

[3] [Loch Cone, or Strangford Lough.]

states that, in 874, Ivar's ally, Cearbhall, was King of Dublin,[1] where, possibly, he ruled from 872 until his death in 885,[2] as during that period no Scandinavian king of Dublin is named in Irish annals or elsewhere, and his rank as a sovereign is manifest from the fact, that with the exception of Maelsechlainn, King of Ireland, Cearbhall is the only Irish king named in the Welsh annals throughout the ninth century.[3]

BOOK I.
CHAP. IV.

When Halfdene apportioned Northumbria, Ivar's sons probably went to France, which previously had been invaded by their uncle, Biorn Ironsides, and which was then a field of plunder for the Northmen. There is no trace of them in Ireland or England between the years 872 and 885, nor do the meagre details of French chronicles afford much assistance in tracing them among chiefs of the same name in France during this period. We infer, however, that the brothers, Godfrey and Sitric,[4] who plundered France in 881,[5] and who are called "sons of Regnar Lodbrog," were the sons of Ivar, and grandsons of Regnar,[6] Regnar not having any son named Godfrey.

Ivar's sons Godfrey and Sitric were then warring in France.

---

[1] Landnamabok, p. 4. "Kiarvalus Dublini in Hibernia," &c. Langebek, vol. ii., p. 32, "Dublini in Irlandia Kiarfalus," &c.

[2] Ann. 4 Mast. place Cearbhall's death 885.

[3] Ann. Cambriæ, 887. "Cerball defunctus est." Chron. P. of Wales, 887—Maelsechlainn died 887.

[4] This Godfrey was slain 885, and Sitric left France. But in A.D. 888, the Emperor Arnulf fought against the brothers, " Sigafrid,

Godafrid, and Ivar." Langeb, vol. ii., p. 17. Ann. Esromenses Langebek, vol. i, p. 230.

[5] Ann. Bartholin. A.D. 881.

[6] Langebek, vol. ii., p. 29. Fragmentum vetus Islandicum, and Pet. Olai Excerpt. Normannica et Danica. Ibid., p. 11. Sigefray or Sitric could not have been Sitric Anguioculus, the son of Regnar Lodbrog, as we have his history in various sagas and chronicles. They were the sons of Ivar, and grandsons of Regnar.

BOOK I.
CHAP. IV.

The Danes leave France for a ransom of 12,000 lbs. of silver, A.D. 883.

In 882 the "two kings, Sitric and Godfrey, and the princes Gormo and Half,"¹ conveyed their plunder into the strong fortress of Haslou,² where they were besieged by the Franks under Charles the Fat, but without success, the Northmen refusing to leave France until paid the enormous tribute of 12,000 pounds of silver ;³ on the payment of this sum it was arranged that Godfrey should renounce Paganism and marry Giselda, daughter of the Emperor Lothair.

Godfrey, son of Ivar slain by his brother Sitric, A.D. 885.

Thus subsidized, baptized, and married, Godfrey retired towards the Rhine, and, according to the French annals, was treacherously slain in A.D. 885,⁴ as some say by Count Everhard, but, according to the Annals of Ulster (in which the year 887 corresponds with 885 of the Four Masters), "Jeffrey Mac Ivar, King of the Normans, was treacherously slain by his brother."⁵

Sitric embarks at Boulogne for Dublin, A.D. 885.

When Sitric received his share of the tribute he burned his camp and marched to Boulogne, part of his army embarking for Flanders,⁶ and the remainder, probably, for Dublin, where the throne had become vacant by the death of Cearbhall in 885, Cearbhall's son Cuilen having been slain in the preceding year "by the Norsemen" amid the lamentations of the Irish, "who thought he would be king."

The re-establishment of a purely Scandinavian

---

¹ Ann. Fuldenses, ap. Du Chesne, Hist. Franc., p. 574; they are there called Sigefrid and Godefrid, Wrm. and Half.

² Langebek, vol. v., p. 134.

³ Ann. Rheginon, Hist. Norman. apud Duchesne, p. 11. Ann. Fuldens. say 2,080 livres in gold and silver.

⁴ Ann. Franc. Metenses ap. Du Chesne, vol. iii., p. 321.

⁵ Ann. Ulst., A.D. 887; but it is not said where he was slain.

⁶ Chron. Rheginon. Hist. Norman. apud Duchesne, p. 11. Sitric is said to have been killed in Frisia, 887. Gesta Nord., p. 6.

dynasty was not, however, quietly effected. Flann, King of Ireland, the son of Cearbhall's sister, and a relative of Aulaf, disputed the sovereignty;[1] but "the foreigners of Ath Cliath" defeated Flann, and slew "Aedh, son of Conchobhar, King of Connacht, Lerghus, son of Cruinden, Bishop of Cill-dara, and Donchadh, son of Maelduin, Abbot of Cill-Dearga," "and many others."

<small>BOOK I.
Chap. IV.

Recovers Dublin from the Irish.</small>

This battle affords further evidence of the previous existence of an Irish dynasty in Dublin, as, from the death of Ivar in 872 to that of Cearbhall in 885, it is the only conflict between the Irish and the "foreigners of Ath Cliath" of which there is any notice in the Annals of the Four Masters,[2] although after that period their contests were frequent.

In A.D. 890, Gormo Enske or "Godrum, the Danish king who governed East Anglia, departed this life,"[3] and "the Gaill left Erin and went into Alba under Sitric, the grandson of Imhar,"[4] to claim Gormo's dominions, or to assist Hastings in the invasion of Wessex; but whatever was Sitric's object he failed to attain it, for Ethelwerd says that, "A.D. 894, Sige-

<small>Sitric invades Alba, A.D. 890.</small>

---

[1] Lann, daughter of Dunghal, Lord of Ossraighe, and sister of Cearbhall, married Maelseachlaim, King of Ireland, who died 860, and by whom she had Flann, King of Ireland, who died 916. After the death of Maelseachlaim, 860, she married Aedh Finnlaith, King of Ireland, who died 879, and by whom she had Niall Glundubh, King of Ireland, killed in 919. Aedh Finnliath's daughter married Aulaf, the first king of Dublin.

[2] Indeed the only intervening notice of Dublin is in the statement that, A.D. 878, "Barith, a fierce champion of the Norsemen, was slain and afterwards burned at Ath Cliath through the miracles of God and St. Cianan." Ann. 4. Mast., A.D. 878.

[3] Hen. Hunt., 890; Sax. Chron., 890; Hamsfort Chron., Langebek, vol. i., p. 269, places his death in 894, and adds that he was succeeded in Denmark by his brother Harald, and in East Anglia by Harald's son Gormo.

[4] Book of Danish Wars MSS. [Wars of the Gaedhil with the Gaill, pp. lxxxi. and 29.]

frith, the pirate, landed from his fleet in Northumberland and twice devastated the coast, after which he returned home,"[1] or in the words of the Ulster Annals, "A.D. 894, Ivar's son came again into Ireland;"[2] and in the following year "Sitric mac Ivar was slain by other Norsemen.[3] In the absence of Sitric his son Aulaf governed Dublin until A.D. 891, when he and Gluntradhna, the son of Gluniarain," were slain in battle.[4] Aulaf's brother, Godfrey, then claimed the throne and was opposed by Ivar, son of that Godfrey who had been treacherously slain. Hence arose "great confusion among the foreigners of Dublin (who) divided themselves into factions, the one part of them under Ivar, the other under Godfrey the Erle."[5] In this contest Godfrey was successful, and Ivar fled into Scotland, where he was killed by the men of Fortrenn, or Pictavia.

Godfrey, now King of Dublin, became King of Northumbria also by the death of his father in 895. He then went into England, the Northumbrians having "made a firm peace with King Alfred,"[6] and Godfrey being thus assured of quiet possession. But his reign was short, for, "A.D. 896, Guthfrid, King of Northumbria, died on the birthday of Christ's Apostle, St. Bartholomew, and was buried at York,"[7] leaving three sons, Neale,[8] Sitric, and Reginald.

---

[1] Ethelwerd Chron., A.D. 894.
[2] Ann. Ult., 893 (=894).
[3] Ann. Ult., 895; Ann. 4 Mast., 891. In Chron. Norm. ap. Duchesne, vol. ii., p. 529, it is said that, A.D. 887, Sigfrid, King of the Norsemen, went into Frisia, where he was killed; and Ann. Bartholin. "A.D. 886, Sigfridus Rex in Frisia interfectus." If this were Sitric, King of Dublin, there are six years difference in the chronology of these annals.
[4] Ann. Ult., 892 (=893.)
[5] Ibid.
[6] Sax. Chron., 894.
[7] Ethelwerd Chron., 896.
This name of Niall was intro-

Godfrey's death having left the throne of Dublin vacant, the Irish, who, since the defeat of Flann in 885, had watched an opportunity to restore a native dynasty, considered this a moment favourable to the attempt.

The year of Godfrey's death Ireland was visited by a strange calamity. Wafted by an unusual wind a flight of locusts came to our shores, and spreading over the land "consumed the corn and grass throughout the country."[1]

The dearth thus caused influenced many to emigrate from Dublin to Iceland, and the garrison, further weakened by the departure of numbers who had followed Godfrey into England, and by the loss of those who had joined Thorstein the Red in Scotland, became inadequate to repel the assaults of the Irish.

Our annals record that, A.D. 897, "the foreigners were expelled from Ireland," "from the fortress of Ath Cliath by Cearbhall, son of Muirigen," king of the adjoining territory of Leinster, and that, "leaving great numbers of their ships behind them, they escaped half dead across the sea" to Ireland's Eye, an island near Dublin, where they were "besieged"[2] until, hopeless of regaining their city fortress, they sought a residence on the opposite coast.

duced among the Norsemen by the connexion with the Irish, amongst whom the name was common, and the possession of it by the son of Godfrey shows his connexion with them. Niall Glundubh was son of Aedh Finnliath, by Maelmur, daughter of Kenneth, King of Scots. Niall Glundubh's sister married Olaf, King of Dublin.

[1] Ann. Cambr., 896; Chron. P. of Wales, 896; Caradoc, 897, p. 42; where they are described as "vermin of a mole-like form each having two teeth, which fell from heaven."

[2] Ann. 4 Mast., A.D. 897.

50    THE SCANDINAVIANS, AND

BOOK I.
CHAP. IV.

The exiled Danes fly to Anglesea; driven thence, A.D. 900.

These fugitive "Lochlans (who) went away from Erin under the conduct of Hingamund"[1] or Igmond, landed in Anglesea, and "fought the battle of Ros Meilor," in A.D. 900,[2] and being there defeated, "and forcibly driven from the land of the Britons,"[3] entered Mercia, where Ethelflœd governed during the illness of her husband. "Hingamund," as a suppliant,

Receive lands near Chester.

"asked lands of the queen, on which to settle, and on which to erect stalls and houses, for he was at this time wearied of war," and "Ethelflœd, pitying his condition, gave him lands near Chester, where he remained for some time."[4]

## CHAPTER V.

Gormo, King of Denmark, rules East Anglia.—Reginald and Sitric, sons of King Aulaf, rule in Northumberland.—On the settlement of Normandy fresh fleets of Danes come to England from France.—Part settle at Waterford.—Sitric of Northumberland recovers Dublin.—His brother Reginald sails to Waterford, and rules there and at Limerick.—Defeats of the Irish by Reginald and Sitric.

CHAP. V.

IN England Scandinavian prospects were not much brighter. Hastings and his allies had been repeatedly defeated, and, in A.D. 897, he was compelled to return to France with the remnant of his army.[5] Alfred, the heroic monarch of the Saxons, died in 901,[6] and

---

[1] Three Fragments, p. 227.
[2] Penros near Holyhead, Chron. Princes of Wales, A.D. 900; Caradoc, p. 42.
[3] Three Fragments, p. 227.
[4] Three Fragments, p. 227, Ethelflœd was not queen, but lady (Hlæfdige) of the Mercians.
[5] Sax. Chron., A.D. 897.

[6] Alfred's death is another instance of the discordance of Chronology in English history. This remarkable event Sim. Dun. and Hoveden place in A.D. 899; Ingulph, p. 28; Chron. Mail., p. 146; Higden, p. 259; Mat. West., and others place it A.D. 900; Flor. Wig. and Sax. Chron, 01.

his son Edward, who "was elected to be king," found his right to the throne disputed by Ethelwald, the son of Alfred's elder brother.

*Book I. Chap. V. Ethelwald disputes the right of Edward, son of Alfred.*

Ethelwald, who had carried off and married a nun,[1] first seized the town of Wimburn,[2] but not receiving homage from the Saxons he turned to the Danes, and flying "to the army in Northumbria they received him for their king."[3] This, however, did not satisfy the ambitious Ethelwald; he collected 'a large fleet of ships,"[4] and inducing Eric, King of the East Angles, to join in the invasion of Essex, they conquered it, "and ravaged Mercia"; but, returning laden with plunder in 905, both Eric and Ethelwald were slain.[5]

*Ethelwald joins the Danes.*

*The Danes defeated, and Ethelwald slain.*

Eric, in East Anglia, was succeeded by "Gormo Danus," King of Denmark,[6] with whom "King Edward, from necessity, concluded a peace,"[7] and Northumbria received the sons of Godfrey, who also

*The sons of Godfrey reign in Northumberland, A.D. 907.*

---

[1] Sax. Chron. A.D. 901.
[2] Ibid.
[3] Ibid.
[4] Flor. Wig., A.D. 904; Hen. Hunt., A.D. 904.
[5] Sax. Chron., A.D. 905; Ethelwerd, 902; "Eric king of the barbarians then descended to Orcus." Langebek, vol. i., pp. 157-173. Eric Barn died 902.
[6] Langebek, vol. i., p. 16, says, "Gormo Enski was succeeded in Denmark by his son Harald, and Harald by his son Gormo." Ibid. p. 158, "Gorm hin Enske," then Harold, then Gorm Gamle, "cujus uxor fuit Thyre Danebot," this Thyra being the daughter of Edward. "Hic, Thyram, Edwardi Anglorum Regis filiam, cognomine DaneBot habuit in matrimonio," Lang., vol. i., p. 37.

Langebek, vol. i., p. 14, "Frotho Rex Danorum et Anglorum regnavit 904." English history has no account of this Frotho: he is possibly the same with Eric, King of East Anglia, who was killed A.D. 905. Sax. Chron., A.D. 906; Sim. Dun., 906; Hen. Hunt., 906.

[7] The treaty between Edward and Gormo is printed in the "Ancient laws and institutes of England," p. 71.

Hamsfort Chron., p. 268, says, Gormo left Denmark to his brother Harald. Gormo III. was son of Harald.

E 2

made peace with Edward. This peace, however, was of short duration.

*They invade King Edward's kingdom; are defeated, A.D. 911.*

In 911 "the army among the Northumbrians broke the peace" "and overran the land of Mercia,"[1] but "on their way homewards" were overtaken by the West Saxons and Mercians, "who slew many thousands of them"; among others "King Ecwils (Ulf) and King Healfden, and Other the Earl" and "Guthferth hold" and "Agmund hold."[2] Possibly that Igmond who had gone away from Ireland in 897, and who secretly "prompted the chiefs of the Lochlans and Danes" to invade Mercia, "take Chester, and possess themselves of its wealth and lands."[3]

Contemporaneously with this outbreak of part of the Northumbrian army a new enemy appeared.

*Accession of Danes through settling of Normandy, A.D. 910.*

The Northmen who entered France with Rollo had wrung from Charles the Simple the treaty of St. Clair-sur-Epte, by which Normandy was ceded to their chief, and he apportioned it among his followers according to the custom of Scandinavian conquerors;[4] but there were some unquiet spirits who disdained to be mere cultivators of the soil—chiefs, for whom war alone had attractions, and new conquests a charm; and these they sought in other

---

[1] Sax. Chron., 911.

[2] *Ibid.* 911. Langebek, vol. ii., p. 53, thinks the name Harold; and Ingulph Hist. Croy., p. 21, has it "Hamond." ["Hold," a nobleman who was higher than a thane, governor, or captain. Bosworth's Anglo-Saxon Dictionary.]

[3] Three Fragm., p. 229; Caradoc, p. 45, says that "Chester, which had been destroyed by the Danes, was rebuilt by Ethelflæd."

[4] Rollo submitted to be baptized, and Dudo (apud Duchesne, p. 82) adds, that Charles ratified the treaty by giving his daughter Gisle in marriage to Rollo; but the statement is doubtful.—*Vide* Pontoppidan Gest. et Vest. Dan., vol. i., p. 285, *et seq.*

climes, in conjunction with Scandinavians from that part of Brittany which had been colonized by the Welsh, and which had been the scene of Ketell's exploits.

"A great fleet came from the south from the land of the Lidwiccas" (or Brittany) under the command of Harold, and of Attar,[1] probably the son of Nidby-orga, granddaughter of Rollo by Helgi, a descendant of Cearbhall, and relative of Aulaf of Dublin.[2]

*Danes from France with Reginald of Northumberland invade Scotland, A.D. 911.*

Simeon of Durham says, that in conjunction with Reginald, King of Northumbria, and "Osulf Cracaban,"[3] they first landed in the country of the Picts, and destroyed Dunblane beyond the Forth.

They then landed "at the mouth of the Severn, and spoiled the North Welsh everywhere by the sea-coast;"[4] but being defeated, and Ottar's brother and Harald his companion slain,[5] Ottar "went thence to Dromod (South Wales), and thence out to Ireland, and with a great fleet of foreigners came to Waterford[6] and placed a stronghold there" in A.D. 912. In

*They spoil North Wales.*

*Build a fortress at Waterford, A.D. 912.*

---

[1] The date of this invasion is variously given. Sax. Chron. A.D. 910. Another copy has it A.D. 918. Chron. Princ. of Wales 910 (=911). Ann. Camb. 913. Sim. Dun. 910. Flor. Wig. 915 (adding that they were the same "who had left England xix years before"). Etheword 913. Caradoc, p. 45, 911.

[2] Landnamabok, p. 90. Attar, grandson of Ketell Flatnef, was father of Helgi, "who made war in Scotland, and carried off Nidby-orga, daughter of King Biolan and of Kadlina, daughter of Ganga Rolfr," by whom he had a son Ottar.

[3] Sim. Dun. A.D. 912. "Reing-wold rex et Oter comes, et Osvul Cracaban irruperunt et vastaverunt Dunblene."—By a strange misconception in a note in Lappenburg, Hist. Eng., vol. ii., p. 94, Cracaban has been mistaken for the name of a place (Clackmannan) in Scotland. Cracaban was the cognomen of Osvul, who is called "Gragava" in the Ann. Ulst., A D. 917, *vide* Langebek, vol. ii., p. 153, for Olaf Cracaban, and Adam Brem. p. 67, for "Olaph filium Cracaben."

[4] Sax. Chron. 910; another copy 918.

[5] *Ibid.* Caradoc 911, "Rahald (Harald) was slain," p. 45.

[6] Ann. 4 Mast. 912 "Loch

*Ravage Munster.*

the following year "great and frequent reinforcements of foreigners arrived in Lóch-Dachaech; and the lay districts and churches of Munster were constantly plundered by them."¹ Cork, Lismore, and Aghaboe being likewise "plundered by strangers."²

These proceedings directed the attention of Godfrey's sons to their Irish dominion.

*Reginald spoils the Isle of Man, A.D. 913.*

In A.D. 913, Reginald crossed over to the Isle of Man, where he found a fleet of the Scandinavians of Ulster, and in a "naval battle between Ragnall (the grandson of Ivar) and Barrid mac Octer, Barrid, with many others, was slain," the "navy of Ulster" having previously been defeated "on the coast of England."³ While Reginald was thus engaged Sitric directed his attention towards Dublin, which had remained under dominion of the Irish since the expulsion of the "foreigners" in 897, and was now probably under the dominion of Niall Glundubh, monarch of Ireland, whose sister had married Olaf the White, the nephew of Cearbhall.⁴

*Sitric recovers Dublin, A.D. 919.*

"An immense royal fleet came with Sitric and the children of Imar, i.e., Sitric, the blind grandson of Imar, and forcibly landed at Dubhlinn (the harbour) of Ath Cliath."⁵ Having gained possession of the city, Sitric proceeded to occupy the territory attached

Dachaech," the Irish name for Waterford.
¹ *Ibid.* 913.
² Ann. Ulst. 913.
³ Ann. Ulst. 913, "Ragnall h-Ua Imair," Barid vel Barith. Chron. Princes of Wales, 914, Ireland and Man devastated by the Pagans of Dublin, 914.
⁴ For thirteen years, between 899 and 912, there is no notice in the Annals of the Four Masters of any Ostman King of Dublin, but Cearbhall is called "King of Liffe of Ships." Cearbhall was slain by "Ulf, a black pagan," in 909; during his life there is no record of any battle between the Irish and the Ostmen of Dublin.
⁵ [Wars of the Gaedhil with the Gaill, chap. xxxi., p. 35.]

to it, and, sailing up the Liffey, "encamped at Cenn Fuait," now Confey, near Leixlip, the extreme boundary of the Dyflinarskiri,¹ while "Ragnall, grandson of Imhar, with another fleet went to the foreigners of Loch-Dachaech (Waterford)," over whom and the foreigners of Limerick, Ragnall, or Reginald, apparently claimed dominion. {BOOK I CHAP. V. Reginald settles at Waterford.}

Thus assisted, "the foreigners" of Waterford spoiled all Munster. They slew "Gebennach, son of Aedh," and these pagan descendants of Ivar, who are there termed "the people of Tomar, carried away his head"; "Munster" being so completely ravaged by them "that there was not a house or a hearth from the river Lin [Lee] southward" that year.² {Reginald with the Danes of Waterford spoil Munster.}

It is not to be supposed that the Irish tamely submitted to this devastation of their country. In 915 "a slaughter was made of the foreigners by the Munstermen." "Another slaughter was made of (them) by the Eoghanachta, and by the Ciarraighi," {Irish victories in Munster, A.D. 915.}

---

¹ ["Cenn Fuait," "Fuat's Head." This place, Dr. O'Donovan conjectures (Four Mast. 915, notes, pp. 589, 590) is now Confey, in the county of Kildare, near Leixlip, (the Danish *Lax-lep*, Salmon Leap), in the barony of *Salt* (Saltus Salmonis). But the Annals of Ulster, at 916 (Four Mast. 915), tell us that Cenn Fuait was ı naıpıupı Laızın "in the East, or anterior part of Leinster," and it must have been near the sea, as Sitric " with his fleet" settled there. A poem quoted by the Four Mast. seems to speak of the battle (if it be the same) as having taken place in "a valley over Tigh Moling," which may signify either Timolin, in the south of the county of Kildare, or St. Mullin's on the Barrow, in the south of the county of Carlow. The latter place may have been approached by water, from Waterford, and as it is situated at the foot of Brandon Hill, the battle may have been in some "valley over Tigh Moling," and the Danish fortress called Cenn Fuait on some *head* in the mountain, accessible to light ships by the Barrow.—Wars of the Gaedhil with the Gaill, p. lxxxix., n. 1.]

² [*Ibid.*, chap. xxviii., p. 31.]

or men of Kerry," and Niall Glundubh led the army of the Ui Neill of the south and north to assist in resisting the invaders. On the 22nd of August Niall "pitched his camp at Tobar Glethrach,"[1] and, as if to try their rights by battle, " the foreigners went into the territory on the same day," fought and were defeated; but "reinforcements set out from the fortress of the foreigners," and "the Irish turned back to their camp before the last host, that is, before Raghnall, king of the black foreigners, and his army."[2]

Niall, however, "and a few with him, went against the Gentiles" expecting their "fight by battle," and "stayed for twenty nights after in camp," until the Leinstermen "on the other side with their camp" compelled Sitric to try his rights by the "battle of Cenn Fuait,"[3] on the boundary of the territory he claimed. But this battle was more disastrous to the Leinstermen than that of Tobar Glethrach to the people of Munster. Their army was defeated, Ugaire, King of Leinster, and Maelmordha, brother of Cearbhall, " and many other chieftains, with Archbishop Maelmaedhog, a distinguished scribe, anchorite, and an adept in the Latin learning," &c.,[4] were slain. Leinster being left defenceless by this disaster, the victors plundered Kildare, and in the following year it was again plundered " by the foreigners of Ath Cliath."[5]

---

[1] Ann. 4 Mast. 915. This place has not been identified.
[2] Ibid.
[3] Ann. 4 Mast. 915.
[4] Ibid. 915.
[5] Ibid. 916.

## CHAPTER VI.

Reginald and Sitric, sons of Godfrey, King of Dublin, return to Northumberland.—In their absence the Irish attempt to recover Dublin.—Reginald and Sitric made Kings of different divisions of Northumbria.—Death of Reginald.

These victories were followed by events which left to Sitric the sole dominion of "the foreigners of Ireland." For Reginald sailed into Scotland to assist Ottar in founding a kingdom there, and from thence into England to pursue his own designs on Mercia.

It was in 916 that Reginald, with "Ottar and the foreigners, went from Waterford to Alba'," where they were encountered by Constantine, son of Aedh, King of the Scots, and in the battle Ottar was slain.

Ottar's death terminated the attempt on Scotland. Reginald's attempt on Mercia was equally unsuccessful. Intending to add Mercia to his Northumbrian kingdom, Reginald had privily contracted marriage with Alfwyn, daughter of Ethelflœd, "the Lady of the Mercians." After Ethelflœd's death in 917 the contemplated marriage became known to King Edward (Alfwyn's guardian), who, jealous of the power of the Danes, sent her prisoner into Wessex, and, alleging that the marriage had been contracted

---

[1] Ann. 4 Mast., 916; Ann. Ult. 917.

The Ann. Ult., describing the battle, says, that "the army of the Gentiles" was formed into four divisions—"one commanded by Godfrey O'Hivar (son of Reginald), another by the two Earls (Ottar and Gragava), the third by the young lords, and the fourth by Raghnall" (or Reginald). That night terminated the conflict, in which, according to one authority, both Ottar and Reginald were slain; but others only mention the death of Ottar.

without his consent, "deprived her of her birthright,"[1] and added the Mercian territory to his own.

*Sitric sails from Dublin to support Reginald.*

Either to support the pretensions of his brother, or to assert his own, Sitric then left Ireland, and entering Mercia besieged Devenport, while "Leofrid, a Dane, and Gruffyth ap Madoc, brother-in-law to the Prince of West Wales, came from Ireland with a great army, and overran and subdued all the country (about Chester) before King Edward was certified of their arrival." It was not long, however, until Edward overtook the invaders, and having defeated and slain Leofrid and Gruffyth, he "set up their heads on the town gates of Chester."[2]

*The Irish under Niall Glundubh try to regain Dublin.*

Sitric and Reginald being thus engaged in England, the Irish claimants of the throne of Dublin again attempted to obtain it.

Assembling a large army Niall Glundubh advanced towards the city, near which he was confronted by the Scandinavian garrison, commanded by the sons of Sitric and of Reginald.

Confident of success Niall had promised the plunder of the fortress to his followers, saying "before the battle,"—

"Whoever wishes for a speckled boss, and a sword of sore-inflicting wounds,
And a green javelin for wounding wretches, let him go early in the morning to Ath Cliath;"[3]

but the result was fatal to him and his allies.

---

[1] Caradoc, p. 47; Ann. Ulst., A.D. 917; Sax. Chron., A.D. 918; another copy A.D. 922; Chron. Princes of Wales places Ethelflæd's death A.D. 914.

[2] Lappenburg, vol. ii., page 96; Tyrrell's Hist. of England, vol. i., p. 321.

[3] Ann. 4 Mast., A.D. 917.

"The battle of Ath Cliath, (*i.e.*, of Cillmosamhog, by the side of Ath Cliath), was gained over the Irish, by Imhar and Sitric Gale on the 17th of October, A.D. 919, "in which were slain Niall Glundubh, son of Aedh Finnliath, King of Ireland;"[1] "the King of Ulidia, the King of Breagh,"[2] with many other nobles, including "Conchobhar, heir apparent to the sovereignty of Ireland."[3]

So disastrous a defeat had seldom been sustained. Deeply deplored by the Irish, and lamented by their bards, it was termed a day sorrowful for "sacred Ireland," a battle which

"Shall be called till Judgment's day
The destructive morning of Ath Cliath;"

and one in which

"Many a countenance of well-known Gaeidhil,
Many a chief of grey-haired heroes
Of the sons of queens and kings,
Were slain at Ath Cliath of swords."[4]

Donnchadh, the brother of Conchobhar, partially avenged it in the following year by "an overthrow of the foreigners," wherein "there fell of the nobles

---

[1] Ann. 4 Mast., A.D. 917 (=919). [*Cill Mosamhog.* The Church of Mosamhog, now Kilmashogue, in the mountains, near Rathfarnham, about six miles from Dublin. The remains of a very large cromlech are still to be seen on Kilmashogue mountain, in the grounds of Glen Southwell, near St. Columba's College. This, in all probability, marks the grave of the chieftains and kings slain in the battle. Dr. Todd, Wars of the Gaedhil with the Gaill, Introd., p. xci., n. 1.]

[2] Ann. Ult., 918 (=919); Ann. 4 Mast., 917 (=919). Ogygia, p. 434, gives the date of Niall's death 919.

[3] Conchobhar was son of Flann, who disputed the possession of Dublin with the Scandinavians in 885, and whose mother was now the wife of Niall Glundubh.

[4] Ann. 4 Mast., 919; Ann. Clonmac., 917.

of the Norsemen as many as had fallen of the nobles and plebeians of the Irish in the battle of Ath Cliath." This, however, was the only result; Donnchadh made no attempt to obtain possession of Dublin, but to preserve the sovereignty of Ireland slew his brother Domhnall.

Secure in his Irish kingdom "Sitric forsook Dublin"[1] in 920, and to maintain their English dominions he and his brother Reginald "with the English and Danes of Northumbria and the King of the Strathclyde Britons and the King of the Scots" submitted to the victorious Edmund and "acknowledged him for their father and lord."[2] Secured by this submission Sitric took possession of one division of Northumbria and "Reginald won York"[3] the capital of the other, the claim of their brother Niall to some share of dominion being settled after the barbarous manner of the times, for "A.D. 921, King Sitric slew his brother Niall."

The dates of these events are variously given in English chronicles which contain no further account of Reginald. It is supposed that he went to France,[4] and was that "Ragenoldus Princeps Nordmannorum"[5] who fell in battle in A.D. 925; the

---

[1] Ann. Ult., 919 al. 920.

[2] Flor. Wig. and Math. Westm., give the date 921; also Chron. Mailros., where Sitric is named with Reginald; Hen. Hunt., 923, and Roger de Hoveden, 917.

[3] Sax. Chron., 922; Sim. Dun., 919; "Ingnald irrupit Eboracum." Hen. Hunt., 923; Sax. Chron., 920; Sim. Dun., 914; Hoveden, 923.

[4] Ann. Bartholin. ap. Langebek, vol. i., p. 337. "Ragenoldus Normannus Franciam vastat A.D. 923." Hist. S. Cuthberti ap. Twysden, p. 74, says he died same year as King Edward, A.D. 924.

[5] Chron. Frodoard, ap. Duchesne, Historiæ Franconcm Scriptores, p. 595, vol. ii.

only record in Irish annals being that "A.D. 921 Reginald O'Hivar, King of the Black and White Gentiles, died."¹

## CHAPTER VII.

Godfrey, son of Reginald, through Sitric's absence, assumes the rule at Dublin.—His conflicts with the Danes of Limerick and their allies Canute and Harold, sons of Gormo, King of Denmark.—Sitric dies, and Athelstan annexes Northumberland.—Sitric's sons come to Ireland.—Godfrey vainly attempts to recover Northumberland.—His renewed conflicts with the Danes of Limerick aided by the sons of Sitric.—Death of Godfrey.—Athelstan makes Eric Blod-Ax, Viceroy of Northumberland.

REGINALD's death and Sitric's residence in Northumbria, gave to Reginald's son Godfrey the Kingdom of the Ostmen, and A.D. 921,² "Godfrey, grandson of Imhar, took up his residence at Ath Cliath," and immediately commenced hostilities against the Irish.

He plundered Armagh but spared "the oratories with their Ceile Des (Culdees) and the sick,"³ who appear to have been lepers.⁴ His army then plundered "the country in every direction, west, east, and north, until they were overtaken by (the Irish under) Muircheartach, son of Niall Glundubh," and

---

¹ Ann. Ult., A.D. 920 (=921). "Reginald O'Hivar, King of the Dubhgalls and Finngalls, killed." Antiq. Celt. Norm. pp. 66, 77, "Reginaldus regno Ostmannorum Dublinii defuncto," &c., A.D. 921.

² Ann. 4 Mast., 919; Ann. Ulst., 920 ( 921). At this period there is a difference of two years between the chronology of the Four Masters and that of the Annals of Ulster, the latter being correct, as the eclipse of the moon mentioned, occurred in 921.

³ Ann. Ulster, 920 (=921).

⁴ Ann. 4 Mast., 919 (=921).

so signally defeated, that "the few who escaped owed their safety to the darkness of the night."¹

Nor was it the Irish alone who engaged Godfrey's attention.

"Gormo-hin-Gamle,"² grandson of Gormo Enske, at this time reigned in Denmark and held dominion over East Anglia. He had married Thyra, the daughter of King Edward,³ and when Edward sought to subjugate East Anglia in 921, Gormo's sons, Canute and Harald, went to England,⁴ and, doubtless, were those termed in the Saxon Chronicle "the pirates whom (the East Anglians) had enticed to aid them."⁵ But the East Anglians been defeated, and having accepted Edward as their sovereign, swearing "oneness with him, that they all would that he would,"⁶ Canute and Harald left East Anglia and sailed for Limerick where sons of Reginald and of Sitric then resided.

Their father, Gormo, who had renounced Christianity and returned to the worship of Thor, was called by the Irish "Tomar" or Thorsman, and "Mac Elchi" as the son (recte grandson) of "Gormo Enske."⁷

---

¹ Ann. 4 Mast., 919 (= 921).

² Gormo III., called Gormo Grandævus, or the old: he was son of Harald the grandson of Gormo Enske. Langebek, vol. i., pp. 17–20.

³ Langebek, vol. i., p. 37. She was called Dana Bota.

⁴ *Ibid.* A.D. 923, p. 37, "Canutus et Haraldus, principes juventutis, in Angliam profecti, Gormonis iii., Danorum tyranni, filii, ab avo materno Edwardo, Rege Anglorum morituro heredes scribuntur."

⁵ Sax. Chron., where the date is 921.

⁶ *Ibid.*

⁷ Gormo, "Hic Christianis infestissimus fuit, renovavit Idolatriam, Ecclesiam constructam circa Sleswic funditus destruxit."—Langebek, vol. ii., p. 345, et vol. i., p. 158, Ann. Bartholini, A.D. 934—"Gormoniana persecutio."

When his fleet with his sons Canute and Harald came to the harbour of Limerick in A.D. 922, its arrival was designated as that of "the fleet of Tomar Mac Elchi,"[1] and when Canute and Harald plundered the adjacent county, the record in our annals is, that 'the shipping of Limerick, that is to say, of the Mac Elchi, came to Lochri (Lough Ree) and spoiled Clonmacnois and all the islands (in Lough Ree) carrying away great booty of gold and silver."

The "Mac Elchi" were aided in these depredations by Colla, Lord of Limerick, the son of Barith,"[2] a Scandinavian chief, who had married the daughter of an Irish prince. But their forays were not always successful; "twelve hundred of the foreigners were drowned" at the mouth of the Erne in Donegal,[3] and one of their pagan associates, Tomrar, the son of Tomralt, was slain by the people of Connemara.[4]

Godfrey in vain attempted to check the progress of these plunderers. He "led an army from Dublin to Limerick,[5]" but "many of his men were killed by

---

[1] After that came Tomar, son of Elge, king of an immense fleet, and they landed at Inis Slibhtonn in the harbour of Limerick, and the chief part of Munster was plundered by them. Wars of the Gaedhil with the Gaill, p. 39.

[2] This Barith had another son called after his grandfather Uathinharan, Ann. 4 Mast., 919. Barith's genealogy is unknown. In the Three Fragments, p. 197, we find that "Barith, tutor to King Aedh's son, drew many ships from the sea westward to Loch Ri; and p. 173, that, A.D. 866, "Barith the Earl and Haimer (Ivar), two of the noble race of the Lochlainns, came through the middle of Connaught towards Limerick." The Four Masters, in A.D. 878, record the death of "Barith a fierce champion of the Norsemen," and that, A.D. 888, his son, Eloir, was killed in Connaught, another of the family, "Eric, or Aric mac Brith," being killed at Brunanburg in 937.

[3] Ann. 4 Mast., A.D. 922.

[4] Ibid., 923.

[5] Ann. Ult., 932.

MacAilche,"[1] and he was forced to return to "Ath Cliath," which during his absence had been attacked by the Irish. The garrison, however, was sufficient to repulse the assailants, and "Muireadhach, king of Leinster, with his son Lorcan, were taken prisoners,"[2] and although subsequently released, clemency had little effect, for some years after Lorcan "was slain by the Norsemen as he was plundering" the city.[3] At this time Godfrey's sons had joined the Danish fleet at Strangford, and plundered Dunseverick in Ulster;[4] but this fleet was taken at Magheralin, on the river Lagan,[5] and, at the bridge of Cluain-na-g Cruimhther, Muircheartach, son of Niall, with the Ulstermen, defeated the Scandinavians, slaying "eight hundred men, with their chieftains, Albdarn (or Halfdan), son of Godfrey, Aufer and Roilt (Harold),[6] the other half of them being besieged for a week at Ath Cruithne, until Godfrey, lord of the foreigners, came to their assistance from Dublin."[7]

Such was the situation of affairs in Ireland when Edward, king of the Anglo-Saxons died in 925,[8] and was succeeded by his illegitimate son Æthelstan, who to secure the throne drowned his legitimate brother Edwin,[9] and entered into an alliance with the Northumbrian Danes, then governed by Sitric.

---

[1] Ann. Ult., 932.
[2] Ann. 4 Mast., 923.
[3] Ibid., 941.
[4] Ann. 4 Mast., "Dun Sobhairce," A.D. 924; Ann. Ult, 925 (=926); Ann. Clonmac., 921.
[5] Ann. Ult., 925.—"Linn Duachaill,"now Magheralin. [Perhaps a place near Annagassan at the tidal opening of the rivers Glyde and Dee in the county of Louth. See supra., v. i., p. 19.]
[6] Ann. 4 Mast., 924; Ann. Clonmac., 921, "Alvdon, Awfer, and Harold."
[7] Ann. 4 Mast., 924; Ann. Ult., 925.
[8] Sax. Chron., A.D. 925.
[9] Hoveden, A.D. 924; Sim. Dun., A.D. 933; Hen. Hunt., A.D. 933.

The alliance between the Saxon and the Dane was doubly cemented, for when "King Athelstan and King Sitric came together at Tamworth, on the 3rd of the kalends of February, Athelstan gave him his sister in marriage,"[1] and Sitric consented to be baptized; but neither matrimony or Christianity were ties which could bind Sitric, for, unsteady in his faith and forgetful of his vows, he soon repudiated his wife, "rejected Christianity, and returned to the worship of idols "[2] he had abandoned.

*Athelstan succeeds, and allies himself with Sitric.*

The apostate did not long survive. In 926 Sitric, grandson of Ivar, "lord of the Dubhghoill and Finnghoill,"[3] or as he is called in the Ulster Annals, "Sitric O'Himar, prince of the New and Old Danes,"[4] died, leaving three sons, Reginald, Godfrey, and Aulaf, who came to Ireland, not being permitted to inherit the English dominion of their father, whose brother-in-law, King Athelstan, obtained the kingdom of Northumbria.

*Sitric dies, and Athelstan annexes Northumberland, A.D. 926.*

*Sitric and sons come to Ireland.*

This annexation of Northumbria to the Anglo-Saxon crown was not in accordance with the right of succession claimed by Godfrey, King of Dublin, the son of Reginald. Godfrey, therefore, "with his foreigners left Ath Cliath,"[5] and accompanied by the

*Godfrey, King of Dublin, attempts to recover Northumberland.*

---

[1] Sax. Chron., A.D. 925. Editha was daughter of Edward and sister of Thyra, who had married Gormo.

[2] Matth. Westm., A.D. 925.

[3] Ann. 4 Mast., 925 (=926). Sax. Chron. also gives 926 as the date of Sitric's death.

[4] Ann. Ult., 926. They appear to have landed at Waterford, where their uncle Reginald had been. Ann. 4 Mast., A.D. 926.

"The plundering of Cill dara by the son of Godfrey of Port Lairge." Ann. Clonm., 923 (=928). "Kildare was ransacked by the son of Godfrey of Waterford." Ann. 4 Mast., 929. "Godfrey (son of Reginald) went into Osraighe, to expel the grandson of Imhar" (that is Godfrey the son of Sitric from Magh Roighne).

[5] Ann. 4 Mast., 925 (=926).

F

"foreigners of Linn Duachaill"[1] (probably the remnant of his son Halfden's army), he sailed for England, where for a brief period the King of Dublin became King of Northumbria also.

*Is expelled in six months, and returns to Dublin.*

The Anglo-Saxon monarch, however, was too powerful; "Athelstan expelled King Guthfrith,"[2] who "came back to Dublin after six months,"[3] and renewed his warfare with the Irish. "On the festival day of St. Bridget" in 927[4] he plundered her sacred fane at Kildare, and on the death of Diarmaid (the last of the sons of Cearbhall[4]) "Godfrey, the grandson of Imhar, with the foreigners of Ath Cliath, demolished and plundered Dearc Fearna" in Ossory, "where one thousand persons were killed."[5] Perhaps the people of Ossory had shown some partiality for the sons of Sitric, who were then joined with the "foreigners" of Waterford and Limerick, as we find that in A.D. 928 "the foreigners of Luimneach" entered Ossory and "encamped in Magh Roighne,"[6] under the command of Aulaf Ceanncairech of Limerick, and that in 929 Godfrey went into Ossory to expel the grandson of Imhar from Magh Raighne,"[7] in which he succeeded, and compelled Aulaf to seek another field of action.[8]

*Godfrey ravages Kildare.*

*Defeats the sons of Sitric, and Danes of Waterford and Limerick, A.D. 929.*

---

[1] Ann. 4 Mast., 925 (=926). Linn Duachaille. See supra, p. 19, n. 1.

[2] Sax. Chron., 927.

[3] Ann. 4 Mast. 925 (=926).

[4] Ibid., 927.

[5] Ann. 4 Mast., 928; Ann Ult., 927 (=930). Dearc Fearna, i.e., the Cave of Fearna, probably the ancient name of the Cave of Dunmore near Kilkenny. (See the Dublin Penny Journal, vol. i., p. 73; Dr. J. O'Donovan, Ann. 4 Mast., vol. ii., p. 623, note 3.)

[6] Ann. 4 Mast., 928.

[7] Ibid., 929.

[8] Ann. 4 Mast., 931. "The victory of Duibhthir was gained by Amhlaeibh Ceanncairech of Luimneach, where some of the nobles of Ui Maine were slain."

While Godfrey was thus engaged the sons of Gormo, that is to say, "the Mac Elgi," aided by "the sons of Sitric took Dublin on Godfrey,"[1] an aggression quickly followed by the death of Canute, the eldest of the Mac Elchi, who was slain near the city by the arrow of a native king.[2] As one of the pagan worshippers of Thor, Canute's death is recorded in Irish annals by the statement that "Torolbh the Earl was killed by Muircheartach," son of Niall;[3] and the statement of Northern historians that Gormo, King of Denmark, died of grief for the loss of his son Canute killed in Ireland,[4] is charitably recorded in the Annals of Clonmacnois, by the statement that "Tomar Mac Alchi, King of Denmark, is reported to have gone to hell with his pains, as he deserved."[5]

In 931 Aulaf, son of Godfrey, imitating the bad example of his father, plundered Armagh, and being joined by Matadhan, son of Aedh, with some of the Ulidians, he continued to spoil Ulster until his army was "overtaken by Muircheartach, son of Niall," and defeated with the loss of "200 heads besides

---

[1] Ann. Clonmac., 922 (=927).

[2] Saxo Gram. lib. ix., p. 162, et Langebek, vol. ii., p. 346. "Deinde Hyberniam adeuntes, Dubliniam caput provincie obsederunt. Rex autem Hybernie nemus circa Dubliniam cum sagittariis ingressus, Knutonem inter milites nocturno tempore ambulantem, cum sagitta letaliter vulneravit."

[3] Ann. 4 Mast., 930. He is called "Toroh," Ann. Clonm., 925 (=930).

[4] Langebek, vol. i., p. 37, et vol. ii., p. 346. "Gormo tyrannus, audito mortis Canuti filii in bello Hybernico obtruncati nuncio, in apoplexin incidit et moritur."

[5] Ann. Clonmac., 922 (=927). Northern annals say that Gormo died A.D. 930, and Canute in 930, in which they agree with the Four Masters.

prisoners."[1] In 932 "Godfrey, King of the Danes, died a filthy and ill-favoured death,[2] and Aulaf, King of Dublin, became by right King of Northumbria also. But this claim was not admitted by Athelstan, who, although he permitted Reginald to remain at York, had determined to govern Northumbria by a Scandinavian viceroy of his own selection.

English chronicles do not refer to the facts detailed in Northern history, but there is every appearance of truth in the Saga narrated, that Athelstan was "foster father" to Hakon the illegitimate son of King Harald Harfagre, and that in A.D. 933,[3] Athelstan sent Hakon to Norway where Hakon's legitimate brother, Eric Blodaxe, had become obnoxious to his subjects, it being subsequently arranged "that King Eric should take Northumberland as a fief from King Athelstan," and "defend it against the Danes or other Vikings,"[4] and further that "Eric should let himself be baptized, together with his wife and children and all the people who followed him." "Eric accepted this offer," came to England, received baptism, and took up "his residence at York, where Regnar Lodbrog's sons it is said, had formerly been."[5]

---

[1] Ann. 4 Mast., A.D. 931.
[2] Ann. Ult., A.D. 933 (=934); Ann. 4 Mast., A.D. 932.
[3] Ann. Island., A.D. 933; Lang. vol. iii., p. 32, vol. ii., p. 188. "In Historia Norvegica Hacon 'Adelsteins fostre' appellatur."
Saga Hakonar Goda, cap. i., p. 125.
[4] Heimsk., vol. i., p. 127, Saga Hakonar Goda.
[5] Ibid., p. 128; Torfœus Hist. North., Pars Secunda, p. 184.

## CHAPTER VIII.

Aulaf, King of Dublin, attempts to recover Northumberland.—Is defeated by Athelstan at Brunanburg.—Returns to Dublin.—The Irish besiege Dublin.

WHILE Athelstan was thus providing for the government of Northumbria Aulaf, King of Dublin, was preparing to assert his right to it. "The foreigners of Loch Erne,"[1] under the command of "Amhlaeibh Ceannchairech,[2] had crossed Breifne (Cavan and Leitrim) to Loch Ribh, and had remained there for seven months plundering the country on the banks of the Shannon.[3] Their assistance, however, was now required, and in 936 "Amhlaeibh, the son of Godfrey, lord of the foreigners, came at Lammas from Ath Cliath, and carried off Amhlaeibh Ceannchairech from Loch Ribh, and the foreigners that were with him."[4] Aulaf's preparations being complete "the Danes of the North of Ireland"[5] and "the foreigners of Ath Cliath left their fortress, and went to England,"[6] where they were joined by Howel Dha,[7] King of Wales, "Hryngr" (Eric), son of Harald Blaatand,[8] and

*Aulaf prepares to invade Northumberland.*

*With his allies, sails from Dublin, A.D. 937.*

*They land at the mouth of the Humber.*

[1] Ann. 4 Mast., A.D. 934 (=935); Crymogæa, p. 127.

[2] Aulaf Ceannchairech—that is, "of the scabbed head." Aulaf is called the Red King of Scotland.

[3] Ann. 4 Mast., 934.

[4] During the absence of Aulaf on this or some other expedition, Dublin was burned by Donnchadh, son of Flann, King of Ireland. The Annals of the Four Masters places Aulaf's expedition to Loch Ribh in 935, and the burning of Dublin in 934.

[5] Ann. Clonmac., A.D. 931 (=937).

[6] Ann. 4 Mast., A.D. 937, say-

"The foreigners deserted Athcliath by the help of God and Mactail." Ann. Ulst. A.D. 931 (=937).

[7] Harald Blaatand was son of Gormo Grandævus, King of East Anglia, who died A.D. 931 (=935). Harald reigned fifty years.—Hamsfort Chron.; Ann. Barthelin, 935.

[8] Langebek, vol. ii., p. 148. It adds that Hrynkr (or Herich or Eric) was killed in Northumbria: doubtless he was killed at Brunanburg. See Egil's Saga, and Ann. Ulst., A.D. 931 (=937), where he is called "Imar, the King of Denmark's own son."

Constantine, King of the Scots,[1] whose daughter Aulaf had married, and whose dominions Athelstan had made tributary. Aulaf was also joined by some Irish and Orkney allies, and from the assembled "fleet of 615 ships" he landed "at the mouth of the Humber" A.D. 927.[2] Athelstan was not inattentive to the preparations of the invaders. He also collected a formidable host, having the assistance of his tributary king, Eric, with many of the Danes of Northumbria, and among his foreign auxiliaries Thorolf and Egils, two celebrated Vikings, who joined his standard with 300 warriors on hearing of large rewards offered for such mercenary assistance.[3] Aulaf here showed that he combined the caution of a general with the courage of a soldier. With equal credibility it is told of him, as of Alfred,[4] that on the eve of the battle, and in the disguise of a harper, he entered and examined the camp of his enemy; but fortune was unkind—Aulaf was defeated in the terrific struggle at Brunanburg, and fled

"O'er the deep water
Dublin to seek
Again Ireland
Shamed in mind."[5]

Langtoff's Chronicle says that he returned at

---

[1] Flor. Wig., p. 578, says Constantine urged Aulaf to this attack on Athelstan.

[2] Sim. Dunelm., p. 686; Flor. Wig., 587; Chron. Mailros, p. 147.

[3] Egil's Saga Hafniæ, 1825, pp. 264, 266. Thorolf was killed in this battle, to the success of which he contributed. With his "two-handed sword" he killed Hryngr in the night attack before the battle (Egil's Saga., p. 285), and in the battle was opposed to the Scotch auxiliaries of Aula, and defeated them.

[4] Ingulf, A.D. 872, p. 26; Will. Malmsb., p. 23; Sax. Chron., A.D. 938, p. 385; Ann. 4 Mast., 938, where he is called "Aulaf, son of Sitric."

[5] Hen. Hunt. gives the date 945; lib. v., p. 204.

Easter, and, after the custom of the Northmen, challenged Athelstan to try his right to Northumbria by wage of battle, for which purpose he selected a redoubtable champion; but his champion was vanquished,[1] and "Aulaf turned again, he and all his to their ships," and after plundering the Isle of Man, "Aulaiv mac Godfrey came to Dublin" in 938.[2]

Brunanburg, however, had destroyed his power.[3] The Irish took advantage of his weakness [or were the allies of another line of Ostman kings][4] and "Donnchadh (King of Ireland) and Muircheartach (of the Leather Cloaks) went with the forces of both

*Marginal notes:* BOOK I. CHAP. VIII. King Aulaf returns to Dublin weakened, A.D. 938. The Irish besiege Dublin A.D. 938.

---

[1] Peter Langtoff's Chron.; Hearn's Collect., Oxford, 1725.

"Aulaf sent messengers vnto Athelstan,
And bad him yeld the lond, or fynd another man
To fight with Colebrant, that was his champion,
Who felle to haff the lond, on them it suld be don."

This "trial by battle" continued among the Anglo-Normans in all disputes of title to land, until Henry II. instituted "Trial by great Assize;" yet his son, Richard I., was challenged by King Philip to try his right to the crown of France. Previously Canute fought Edmund in single combat for the crown of England. William the Conqueror challenged Harald for the same purpose. So it was offered between John of England and Lewis of France (*vide* Selden Duello, Lond., 1610). Olaf Trygvesson, with twelve champions, fought Alfen with an equal number.

Heimskr. Olaf Trygvesson's Saga, chap. 34, vol. i., p. 126; and throughout the Sagas we find numerous instances of single combat, or of combats with a stated number on each side, to try not only titles to land, but claims of other kinds.

[2] Ann. 4 Mast., 936; Ann. Ult. 938.

[3] Sax. Chron., A.D. 937, and all English historians describe the battle of Brunnanburgh as one of the bloodiest conflicts of the age. Of Aulaf's allies the slaughter was great. The Ann. Clonmacn. name "Sithfrey, Oisle, the two sons of Sithrick Gale, Awley Fivit, and Moylemorey the son of Cossawara, Moyle Isa, Gellachan, King of the Islands, Ceallach, prince of Scotland, with 30,000, together with 800 about Awley mac Godfrey, and about Aric mac Brith, Hoa, Deck, Omar the King of Denmark's son, with 4,000 soldiers in his guard, were all slain." Ann. 4 Mast., v. ii., p. 633, n.

[4] [Of Godfrey, son of Sitric.]

fully assembled to lay siege to the foreigners of Ath Cliath," and although they failed to take the city, "they spoiled and plundered all that was under the dominion of the foreigners from Ath Cliath to Ath Truisten."[1] Either in retaliation for this aggression or as a mere piratical expedition, the Northmen of the Scottish Isles, the subjects or allies of Aulaf, plundered Aileach and carried Muircheartach prisoner to their ships. The captive, however, escaped, and fitting out a fleet pursued his captors to their island homes from which he returned laden with plunder. Nor was he content with this exhibition of his power, he marched from Aileach with a thousand chosen men, prepared for a winter campaign by sheep skin mantles (an improvement in military costume, which gained for him the name of "Muircheartach of the Leather Cloaks"), and "keeping his left hand to the sea," "he made the circuit of Ireland until he arrived at Ath Cliath," from whence "he brought Sitric, lord of Ath Cliath," or more probably the son of Sitric, "as a hostage."[2]

---

[1] Ann. 4 Mast., 936; Ann. Ult., 937 (=938). *Ath Truisten*, a ford of the river Greece near the hill of Mullaghmast, in the southern part of the county of Kildare.

[2] Ann. 4 Mast., A.D. 939, vol. ii. p. 643.

## CHAPTER IX.

King Edmund dies A.D. 946.—Aulaf Cuaran, King of Dublin, contests Northumberland with King Eadred, Edmund's successor.—Aulaf, after four years' possession of Northumberland, is expelled.—He returns to Ireland.—His extensive Irish connexions.—His throne at Dublin disputed by his nephew.—Aulaf recovers it.—Goes a pilgrimage to Iona.—Abdicates.—Maelsechlain overthrows Reginald, Aulaf's son. —Maelsechlain proclaims the freedom of Ireland.

CONTEMPORANEOUSLY with the death of Blacaire in Ireland was that of Edmund in England. He was assassinated "on St. Augustin's mass-day,"[1] 946, and was succeeded by his brother Eadred, who "subdued all Northumberland under his power."[1] In 947 "Walstan, the archbishop, and all the Northumbrian 'Witan' plighted their troth to" him, with oaths which they did not long remember, for "within a little time they belied it all, both pledge and also oaths" by taking Eric (of Danish extraction) to be their king.[2] Enraged by this perfidy "Eadred ravaged all Northumbria" in 948, and "would have wholly destroyed the land" if the Witan had not "forsook Eric, and made compensation" to their Saxon lord.[3]

The dethronement of Eric left Northumberland again open to Aulaf Cuaran, who since the death of Blacaire had retained undisputed possession of Dublin.

In 948 Aulaf sailed for England,[4] leaving Dublin to the care of his brother Godfrey. Scarcely, how-

*K. Edmund dies A.D. 946.*

*Is succeeded by his brother Eadred.*

*The Northumbrians elect Eric son of Harold for their king.*

*King Eadred expels Eric.*

*King Aulaf sails from Dublin to Northumberland.*

---

[1] Sax. Chron., 946.
[2] Ibid., 947. This was Eric, son of Harald Harfagre.
[3] Ibid., 948.
[4] "Quant il regnout el secund an Idunekes vint Aulaf Quiran." (Geffrei Gaimar, I., 3550).

ever, had he left Ireland until Ruaidhri Ua Canannain, taking advantage of his absence, attacked and defeated Conghalach in Meath. "Plundering all Breagha, Ruaidhri reduced Conghalach to great straits," encamping "for six months" in the midst of the country until "the dues" payable to Conghalach as "King of Ireland, were sent to him (Ruaidhri) from every quarter." Godfrey, with "the foreigners of Dublin," endeavoured to arrest his progress, and a sanguinary battle was fought, in which "the foreigners of Ath Cliath were defeated," with the loss of "six thousand mighty men, besides boys and calones." "Godfrey, the son of Sitric," escaped from the field, but "Imhar, tanist of the foreigners," was slain; and on the other side "Ruaidhri himself fell in the heat of the conflict."[1]

In 949 "Godfrey, the son of Sitric, with the foreigners of Ath Cliath, plundered Ceanannus" "and other churches in Meath," carrying "upwards of three thousand persons with them into captivity, besides gold, silver, raiment, and various wealth, and goods of every description,"[2] which (say the Annals of Clonmacnois) "God did soon revenge on them,"[3] for there broke out great disease, "leprosie and running of blood, upon the Gentiles of Dublin"[4] in that year.

In 949 Aulaf Cuaran arrived in Northumberland,[5]

[1] Ann. 4 Mast.
[2] Ann. 4 Mast., 949; Ann Ult., 950.
[3] Ann. Clonmac., 946 (=951).
[4] Ann. Ult., 950; Ann. 4 Mast., 949.
[5] Sax. Chron., 949. Edmund died in 946, and was succeeded by Eadred, and

"Quant ll regnout el secund an
Idunekes vint Aulaf Quiran
Northumberland scise e prist
Ne trouvat ki le defendist."
(Geff. Gaim., I., 3350.)

and "held it by the strong hand for four years."[1] At the termination of this period the Northumbrians, with their usual fickleness, "expelled King Aulaf, and received Eric, Harold's son,"[2] whose reign was short, for in 954[3] the Northumbrians dismissed him as carelessly as they had received him, and inviting King Eadred, voluntarily replaced him on the throne.[4]

<small>BOOK I. CHAP. IX.</small>
<small>Is expelled, A.D. 953, and Eric elected by the Danes.</small>
<small>They expel Eric and acknowledge Eadred, A.D. 954.</small>

Eric,[5] "with his son Harekr, and his brother Reginald, was treacherously slain in a desolate place called Steinmor, through the treason of Count Osulf, and by the hand of Maccus,"[6] the son of Aulaf; but the Sagas say that Aulaf himself fought Eric, and that "towards the close of the day King Eric, and five kings with him, fell—three of them Guttorm and his two sons, Ivar and Harekr. There fell also Sigurd and Rognvalldr, and with them Tor Einar's two sons, Arnkel and Erland," whom Eric had brought from the Orkneys.

<small>Eric slain in an attempt on Northumberland, A.D. 956.</small>

From this period Northumbria ceased to be a kingdom. "What became of Aulaf, the last king" (says Drake) "I know not. It is probable he died

<small>On Eric's death Aulaf returns to Ireland.</small>

---

[1] Hen. Hunt., "quod in fortitudine tenuit quatuor annis."
[2] Sax. Chron., 962; Hen. Hunt., 953.
[3] Sax. Chron., 954.
[4] Hen. Hunt., 954.
[5] Brompton ap. Twysden, p. 862, "Iricio rege super ipsos Scotos statuto," &c., &c.
[6] Hen. Hunt., 950; Mat. West., 950; Roger Wendover, 950. Hoveden says—"The Northumbrians slew Amaccus, the son of Aulaf, and that the province was then given in charge to Osulf, whose sister had married Aulaf," &c. Saga Hakon Goda, c. iv., p. 129. Saga of Olafi Hinom Helga, c. 99, p. 145. Harald's Saga ens Harfagra, cap. xlvi., p. 12—"Eric was a stout, handsome man, strong, and very manly—a great and fortunate man of war, &c. His wife, Gunhild, was a most beautiful woman; their children were Gamle, the oldest, then Guttorm, Harald, Rangfred, Ragnhild, Erleng, Gudrord, and Sigurd Sleve."

abroad, no author making any mention of him after Edred's last expedition into the North."¹ But if the historian of York had referred to Irish annals, he would have ascertained that, after Eric's death, Aulaf returned to Ireland, where his matrimonial alliances with native royalty had secured to him a safe asylum. To some of these alliances we have already referred, but they deserve more distinct notice, as furnishing a curious illustration of the manners of the times, and of the cause of many of the confederacies and wars between the Ostmen and the Irish.

In the eleventh century Lanfranc, Archbishop of Canterbury, wrote to Turlough O'Brien, King of Ireland, that it was reported to him that within Turlough's dominions "there are men who take to themselves wives too near akin, both by consanguinity and affinity; others who forsake at will and pleasure such as are lawfully joined to them in holy matrimony, and some who give their wives to others in matrimony, and receive the wives of such in return by an abominable exchange."²

If such were the practices in the eleventh century they do not appear to have been very different in the tenth.

Among the Scandinavians repudiation and polygamy were royal privileges. Polygamy continued in Norway down to the thirteenth century, and Harald Harfagre put away nine wives when he

---

¹ "Eboracum, or Hist. and Antiq. of York, by F. Drake: Lond., 1736, p. 81. According to Chron. Mailros, p. 148—"Ericum filium Harold qui fuit ultimus Rex, &c.

² Ware's Bishops, p. 307.

married "Raughill the Mighty."[1] We find no trace of polygamy among the royal families of Ireland; but in their alliances with Aulaf there is evidence that repudiation and divorce were not known to them.

*Princely Scandinavian and Irish intermarriages.*

Maelmhuire, daughter of Kenneth, King of the Scots,[2] married Aedh Finnlaith, by whom she had Niall Glundubh, King of Ireland. After Aedh's death Maelmhuire married his successor, Flann Sinna, by whom she had Gormflaith, who first married Cormac Cuilennan, King and Bishop of Cashel, and being put away by him she married Cearbhall, son of Murigen, King of Leinster, and then married Niall Glundubh, her step-brother, by whom she had Muircheartach of the Leather Cloaks, King of Ireland.[3]

*Aulaf Cuaran's Irish connexions.*

Maelmhuire's daughter, Dunlaith, first married Domhnall Donn, son of Donnchadh Donn,[4] by whom she had Maelseachlainn, and then married Aulaf Cuaran, by whom she had Gluniarain; thus Mael-

---

[1] Harald Harfagre Saga, c. xxi.

[2] Ogygia, p. 484. Maelmhuire, the follower of Mary; she died A.D. 910.

[3] Ann. Clonmac. gives the order of her marriages differently—First, she married Cormac Cuileannain; second, Niall Glundubh; and third, Cearbhall; but this would imply that she was also repudiated by Niall Glundubh, as he lived ten years after Cearbhall. Aedh Finnlaith was also married to Flann or Lan, daughter of Dunlang of Ossory, the widow of Maelseachlainn I., by whom she was the mother of Flann Sinna; and Flann Sinna married Maelmhuire, the widow of Aedh Finnlaith, who was his mother's second husband. Three Fragments, pp. 157 and 179. Flann married a third time Gaithen, by whom she had Cennedigh, and according to Ann. Ult., "in penitentia dormivit," A.D. 889.

[4] Dunlaith was probably in Aulaf's "strong fortress" of Dublin in 939, when her father came to it, and was that "Damsel whose soul the son of Niall was, and who came forth until she was outside the walls, although the night was constantly bad."—Circuit of Ireland, p. 33. (Archæolog. Soc. of Ireland's Tracts.)

seachlainn, King of Ireland, and Gluniarain "were mother's sons,"[1] and Maelseachlainn having married Maelmhuire, Aulaf's daughter, the connexion became closer.

Aulaf Cuaran, however, had other alliances, for Aulaf also married Gormflaith, daughter of Murchadh, son of Finn, King of Leinster, by whom he had Sitric.[2] She then married Brian Borumha,[3] by whom she had Donnchadh, and being repudiated by Brian,[4] who married Dubhchobhlaig, daughter of the King of Connaught.[5] Gormflaith married Maelseachlainn, by whom she became mother of Conchobhar.

Aulaf's royal connexions were further extended and complicated by the marriage of his daughter Radnalt with Conghalach, King of Ireland.[6] Conghalach being the son of Maelmithigh, by Ligach, daughter of Flann Sinna,[7] and step-sister of Niall

---

[1] Ann. 4 Mast., 982; Ann. 4 Mast., 1021—Maelmhuire died; Ann. Clonmac., 1014.

[2 Wars of the Gaedhil with the Gaill. Introduction, cxlviii., n.; ibid., cxlix., n.]

[3 For a history of Gormflaith see "Wars of the Gaedhil with the Gaill," p. cxlviii., n. 88. "The three 'marriages' of Gormflaith are described in some verses quoted by the Four Masters (A.D. 1030), as three 'leaps,' 'or jumps' which a woman should never jump." This seems to hint that three leaps were not legitimate marriages. They were a "leap at Ath Cliath, or Dublin," when she *married* Olaf Cuaran; "a leap at Tara," when she *married* Malachy II., and "a leap at Cashel," when

she *married* Brian. *Ibid.*, p. clxi. n. l.]

[4] Nial's Saga, cap. clv., p. 590, says that Gormflaith had been Brian's wife, but that they were then parted (1012), and that she sent her son Sitric to induce the Norsemen to attack Brian at Clontarf.

[5] Ann. 4 Mast., 1008 Dubhchobhlaig died.

[6] Book of Leinster, MS.

[7] Ann. 4 Mast., "Lighach died," 921. Niall's Saga, cap. clv., p. 590, says she was first married to Brian and then to Aulaf Cuaran, Murchadh, Gormflaith's father, died in 928. If she were born that year and died 1030 she was then 102 years old. It is not improbable that she was first married to Brian,

Glundubh and Gormflaith; and by the marriage of Aulaf's son Sitric with the daughter of Brian Borumha; Brian subsequently marrying Sitric's mother.

While Aulaf Cuaran was in England his brother Godfrey, King of Dublin, was slain by the Dal-cais,[1] and was succeeded by his son Aulaf; but when Aulaf Cuaran was expelled from Northumbria, he again claimed the throne of Dublin to the exclusion of his nephew, and in this as in previous efforts he was assisted by his son-in-law Conghalach.

*Aulaf Cuaran's nephew disputes the throne of Dublin with him, A.D. 951.*

*Aulaf is aided by his son-in-law Congalach.*

On his return to Ireland in 953 Aulaf Cuaran plundered Inis Doimhle and Inis Ulad; and in 954 Conghalach entered Leinster; but the young King of Dublin, Aulaf, the son of Godfrey, laid a battle ambush for Conghalach by means of which stratagem he was taken with many of his chieftains,[2] "and slain with many others."[3]

In 968 Kells was plundered by Aulaf Cuaran and the Leinstermen;[4] and in 979 this Aulaf Cuaran, or, as he is termed, Amhlaeibh, son of Sitric, chief lord of the foreigners of Ath Cliath, went (to Iona) on his pilgrimage and died there after penance and a good life."[5] Our annals do not give the date of his death, but if we could rely on the statement of the Sagas he must have returned to Dublin and survived his pilgrimage many years; for when

*Aulaf Cuaran goes a pilgrimage to Iona, A.D. 979.*

*Date and place of his death uncertain.*

and that divorced by him she then married Aulaf [See note 3, supra].

[1] Ann. Inisf., 951; Ann. 4 Mast., 951; Ann. Ult., 952; the true year being 953.

[2] Ann. 4 Mast., 954; Ann. Ult., 955.

[3] Ibid., 954.

[4] Ann. 4 Mast., 968.

[5] Ibid., 979. The Four Masters record Aulaf's pilgrimages both in 978, recte 979, and in 979 (=980); possibly he went to Iona twice.

messengers were sent from Norway to seek Olaf Tryggvasson they are said to have found him in Dublin, at the court of his wife's brother, Aulaf Cuaran.¹ Aulaf was the first Scandinavian pilgrim from Ireland, and the year in which he abdicated, Domhnall, King of Ireland, died, and was succeeded by Maelseachlainn, Aulaf Cuaran's step-son and son-in-law. On this relationship Maelseachlainn possibly founded some claim to the throne of Dublin, and having defeated the garrison and slain "Ragnall, son of Aulaf, heir to the sovereignty," he laid siege to the city "for three days and three nights," and ultimately succeeded in reducing it to subjection.² It was then Maelseachlainn issued his famous proclamation, "that as many of the Irish nation as lived in servitude and bondage with the Danes (which was at that time a great number) should presently pass over without ransom and live freely in their own countries according to their wonted manner." The captivity of these unfortunate Irishmen being described in our annals as "the Babylonian captivity of Ireland (and) until they were released by Maelseachlainn, it was indeed next to the captivity of hell."³

---

¹ Saga Olafi Tryggva Syni, chap. lii. This was about the year 994.

² Ann. 4 Mast., A.D. 979 (=980), vol. ii., p. 713. See also Ann. Clonmac. *Ibid*, p. 712, n. x.

³ Ann. Clonmac., 974 (=980). ["He carried thence the hostages of Ireland, and among the rest Domhnall Claen, King of Leinster, and all the hostages of the Ui-Neill. Two thousand was the number of the hostages, besides jewels and goods, and the freedom of the Ui-Neill from the Sinainn to the sea, from tribute and exaction. It was then Maelseachlainn himself issued the famous proclamation in which he said, 'Every one of the Gaedhil who is in the territory of the foreigners in servitude and bondage, let him go to his own

This sketch of the connexion, which long existed between Dublin and Northumberland, is given as far as possible in the words of the authorities quoted; and although the narrative may thereby have been made less attractive than it might otherwise have been rendered, yet it must be considered desirable to have distinct reference to well-known authorities, where the subject is one of much historical interest, heretofore unnoticed in any history of England or Ireland.

We trust, however, that the narrative, such as it is, embodies conclusive evidence that Dublin and Northumbria were sometimes governed by the same king, and almost always by kings of the same race. That it not only shows the high position which Dublin held among the Scandinavian colonies, but that it discloses the origin of confederacy and wars between the Ostmen and the Irish, and, as a matter of local interest, it tends to explain why our early Danish coins, although minted for Dublin, were coined by Anglo-Saxon moneyers, and only bear the names of Ivar, Sitric, Reginald, or Aulaf, "the high kings of the Northmen of Ireland and England."

territory in peace and happiness.' This captivity was the Babylonian captivity of Ireland until they were released by Maelseachlainn. It was indeed next the captivity of hell."— Ann. 4 Mast., A.D. 979 (=980), vol. ii., p. 713].

# BOOK II.

OF THE SCANDINAVIANS OF DUBLIN AND THEIR RELATIONS WITH NEIGHBOURING KINGDOMS.

## CHAPTER I.

### DUBLIN AND THE ISLE OF MAN.

Man for the Romans an Irish island.—Man yields tribute to Baedan, King of Ulster, A.D. 580.—Thenceforth said to *belong* to Ulster.—Conflicts between the Norwegians of Ulster and Danes of Northumbria about Man.—Claimed by Reginald, brother of Sitric, King of Dublin, from Barid of Ulster.—Magnus, King of Man, grandson of Sitric, with the Lagmen, sails round Ireland doing justice.—Magnus, one of the eight kings who rowed King Edgar's barge on the Dee.—The ground probably of the forged charter of King Edgar pretending dominion in Ireland.—In the eleventh century intermarriages make it hard to say whether the kings of Dublin are to be called Danish or Irish.—De Courcy's claim to Ulster through his wife, daughter of the King of Man.—King Henry Second's jealousy.—De Courcy's fall.

BUT Northumberland was not the only realm which had been subject to the Scandinavian kings of Dublin; the Isle of Man, with "The Kingdom of the Isles," was also at intervals governed by the descendants of Ivar.

Lying within view of the north-east coast of Ireland, the Isle of Man, like the islands surrounding, was known to the Irish at an early period, and was by Ptolemy considered to be an Irish island.[1]

---

[1] Between Manx traditions and Irish historical legends there is a curious coincidence respecting the early connexion of the Isle of Man, the Orkneys, and Hebrides, with Ulster and Connaught.

Sacheverell* says—"The universal tradition of the Manks nation ascribes the foundation of their laws to Manannan MacLir, whom they believe the father, founder, and legislator of their country, and

\* View of the Isle of Man: Lond., 1702, p. 20.

In A.D. 254, Cormac MacArt drove some of the Cruithne, or Irish Picts, from Ulster into the Isle of place him about the beginning of the fifth century. They pretend he was the son of a king of Ulster, and brother to Fergus II., who founded the kingdom of Scotland, A.D. 422" (recté 503). Johnson[*] adds, "That the Manks in their ancient records call him (Manannan) a paynim, and that at his pleasure he kept by necromancy the land of Man in mists, and to an enemy could make one man appear one hundred."

In Irish historical legends we find four Manannans, three of whom are thus noticed—"Manannan, the son of Alloid," "Manannan, the son of Athgus," and "Manannan, the son of Lir."

Of the last, that is Manannan MacLir, the Book of Fermoy says, that he was a pagan, that he was a law-giver among the Tuatha De Danann, and that he was a necromancer (a Druid), possessed of power to envelope himself and others in a mist (or "Feth Fiadha"), so that they could not be seen by their enemies. (Druids were supposed to possess the power of raising mists.—See Todd's "Life of St. Patrick," p. 425.)

Of Manannan, the son of Alloid (also a Druid), it is said[†] that his real name was Orbsen—that he was a skilful seaman, and traded between Ireland and Britain, being commonly called Manannan Mac Lir—Manannan, from his commerce with the Isle of Man, and MacLir, that is "son of," or "sprung from the sea," from his skill in navigation. The Yellow Book of Lecan[‡] adds "that he was killed in the battle of Cuilleann, and buried in Connaught, and that when his grave was dug Loch Oirbsen burst over the land, so that it is from him Loch Oirbsen (now Loch Corrib) was named."

Of the other Manannan the Yellow Book of Lecan says, "That Manannan, son of Athgus, King of Manain (Man) and the islands of the Galls (the Hebrides, &c.), came with a great fleet to pillage and devastate the Ultonians, to avenge the children of Uisnech," an Ulster chieftain. These children of Uisnech when compelled to fly "from Erinn" had sailed eastwards, and conquered "what was from the Isle of Man northwards of Albain," and "after having killed Gnathal, king of the country," were induced to return to Ireland under a pledge of safety from Conchobhar, King of Ulster. The sons of Gnathal, who also sought the protection of Conchobhar, "killed the sons of Uisnech," in consequence of which Gaiar, the grandson of Uisnech, banished Conchobhar to the Islands of Orc and Cat (the Orkneys and Caithness), and Gaiar having reigned over Ulster for a year, went into Scotland with Manannan, and died there.§

In these Manannans we find a

---

[*] Jurisprudence of the Isle of Man: Edin., 1811, p. 3.
[†] Ogygia, p. 179.   [‡] MS. T. C. Dublin.   [§] *Ibid.*

Man and the Hebrides,[1] and his son, Cairbre Riada having taken possession of the territory from which they had been expelled, it thence obtained the name of Dal Riada, or the territory of the descendants of Riada.[2]

*Fergus of Ulster invades Man, A.D. 503.*
*Man pays tribute to Baedan K. of Ulster, A.D. 580.*
*Man said thenceforth to belong to Ulster.*

Fergus, son of Erc, lord of Dalriada, sailed from Ulster into Scotland,[3] and in A.D. 503, founded a Dalriadan kingdom there.[4] He also visited Man and the Hebrides, and about A.D. 580, Baedan, king of Uladh (or Ulidia) cleared Man of the foreigners, and received tribute from Munster, Connaught, Sky, and Man. From this time it is said that the island *belonged* to Ulster.[5]

While the Romans were in Britain Man was an Irish island,[6] and it will be seen that a connexion long existed between them.

strong resemblance to the Manx legislator, but as they all lived before the Christian era, none of them could have been the brother of Fergus II.

Fergus, the son of Erc (or Eric), king of the Dalriads of Ulster, left Ireland with his brothers, Loarn and Angus, and became King of the Scots, A.D. 503,\* and ruled from "Brunalban" to the Irish Sea, and Inse Gall,† until A.D. 506.

It is likely, however, that the Manx tradition embodies several legends, and that the island having been visited at a very early period by Manannan MacLir, or Manannan MacAlliod, was subsequently formed into a kingdom by Loarn, or Angus, the brother of Fergus.

[1] Tighernach, A.D. 254; Ogygia, p. 335.

[2] Ogygia, p. 332. Dalriada, sometimes written "Ruta," and still called the Route, extended thirty miles from the River Bush to the cross of Gleann-finnaght in Antrim. Dal Aradia joined Dalriada, and comprehended the greater part of the present county of Down. (Reeves's Life of St. Columba, p. 67.)

[3] Ogygia, pp. 323, 466; Ussher Primordia, p. 1117, Dublin, 1639.

[4] Innes, p. 690, says, Fergus, son of Erc began to reign A.D. 503, and died 506.

[5] Reeves's Life of St. Columba, p. 373, extracted from the Book of Lecan, fo. 139.

[6] By Ptolemy (Lib. ii.) called Monada, or the further Mona, to distinguish it from Anglesea, the Mona of the Romans; by Pliny Monabia; Menavia by Orosius and Bede; and Eubonia by Gildas.

\* Innes' Crit. Essay, Tab., p. 690; Pinkerton, Enquiry, vol. ii., p. 88.
† Ogygia, p. 323.

The Scandinavians invaded Mann in A.D. 798. Those who came to Dubhlinn of Ath Cliath in A.D. 836, had doubtless visited Man. In 852 they devastated Mona.

Nevertheless, the earliest notices connecting our Ostmen of Dublin with the island is, that in 913 "a naval engagement was fought at Man between Barid Mac-n-Oitir and Ragnall Mac-hUa Imair, in which Barid, with almost his entire army, was slain."[1]

Ragnal, or Reginald, was king of part of Northumberland, and brother of Sitric, then king of Dublin, and Barid, or Baidr, was chief of the Norwegians who had settled in Dal Aradia, on the north-east coast of Ulster, and probably grandson of that Barid[1] who in A.D. 873, "drew many ships from the sea westward to Loch Ri," and thence sailed down the Shannon to Limerick, where he married the daughter of Uathmharan,[2] and thus their son Colla became Lord of Limerick in A.D. 922.[3]

*Reginald of Northumbria attacks Barid of Ulster, A.D. 913.*

*Reginald was brother of Sitric, K. of Dublin.*

(Rolt's Hist. of the Isle of Man, p. 3, Lond., 1773.)

[1] Ann. Ult., 913, *alias* 914. In O'Connor's Rer. Scrip., vol. iv., p. 247, he is called Barid MacNoitir, and his opponent Ragnall-h-Imair. In Johnston's Antiq. Celto-Norman., p. 66, this sea fight was between Barred O'Hivar and Reginald O'Ivar; and the "black pagans," who devastated Mona in 852, were probably part of the fleet of Aulaf, who came to Dublin in that or the following year.

[2] Ann. 4 Mast., A.D. 878, "Barith, a fierce champion of the Norsemen, was killed, &c."

[3] Uathmharan was son of Dobhailen, Lord of Luighne in Connaught, and died 920 (Ann. 4 Mast.). Barith, who married his daughter, had by her a son named Uathmharan, who came with a fleet of twenty ships to Ceann Maghair in 919 (Ann. 4 Mast.). He had another son, Colla, who was Lord of Limerick, and had a fleet on Loch Ree in 922 (Ann. 4 Mast.). By an earlier marriage Barid had a son named Elir, who was killed in Mayo in 887 (Ann. 4 Mast.). The Scandinavians transported their light-built ships overland from the sea to inland waters, and the Irish followed their example. In A.D. 953, "Domhnall, son of Muircheartach," carried boats from the River Bann over the

*BOOK II.*
*CHAP. I.*

*Reginald, K. of Man, invades Ulster, A.D. 940.*

The cause of warfare is not stated, but "the fleet of Ulster" had made a descent on the Danes of Northumberland, of whom Reginald was king; and Reginald, perhaps for himself, or for his brother, Sitric, claimed the Isle of Man from the Scandinavians of Ulster, of whom Barid was chief.

The son of Reginald, however, remained *de facto* King of Man, and in A.D. 940, he landed from thence on the opposite coast of Ulster, the territory of Barith, and plundered Downpatrick, "for which deed," the "Four Masters" say, that "God and Patrick quickly took vengeance of him, for foreigners came across the sea, and attacked him and his people on their island, so that the son of Raghnall, their chief, escaped to the mainland (where), he was killed by Madudhan, King of Ulidia, in revenge of Patrick, before the end of a week after the plundering."[1]

*Plunders Downpatrick and is slain.*

The immediate succession of the son of Reginald is uncertain.

*Magnus or Maccus, K. of Man, A.D. 971.*

Shortly after this period, however, a king of the name of Maccus, or Magnus, was sovereign of Man. The signature "Ego Maccus rex insularum" appears to a charter of King Edgar in 966. This charter, however, is alleged to be a forgery;[2] but the signature of "Maccusius Archipirata" appears to a charter of

Dabhall (Blackwater), and over Airghialla to Loch Erne, and Loch Uachtair.—Ann. 4 Mast.

[1] Ann. 4 Mast., A.D. 940. The foreigners here mentioned were probably from the fleet of King Eric, son of Harald Gœfeld, who had left Northumberland in A.D.

947, "on a Vikingr cruise to the westward," and had visited the Orkneys, Hebrides, and isles of Scotland, before he steered for Ireland.

[2] Codex Diplomaticus Anglo Saxonicus, vol. ii., p. 412. J. T. Kemble.

971,[1] the latter title being that of admiral or chief of seamen, derived from the command of some portion of the fleet which Edgar had organized[2] for the protection of his kingdom, and which annually sailed round its coast. Maccus, however, was one of the eight tributary kings who attended Edgar at Chester in A.D. 973, and rowed his barge on the Dee,[3] the name being placed next after that of "Kenneth, King of the Scots, and Malcolm, King of Cumberland, as Maccus, King of Man, and many other isles;"[4] nor can there be much doubt that the connexions of this tributary king with Dublin, Waterford, Limerick, &c., and his exploits in Meath and on the Shannon, were the grounds for Edgar's forged claim to dominion over "all the kingdom of the islands of the ocean, with their fierce kings, as far as Norway, and the greater part of Ireland, with its most noble city of Dublin." Maccus, like Reginald, was a descendant of Ivar. He was the grandson of Sitric, King of Dublin, and "son of Harald, Lord of Limerick," who was slain in 938. Nor would he have been unjustly styled "archi-pirata," supposing that title synonymous with the Scandinavian term "Vikingr," for, according to Welsh historians, "Mactus, the son of Harald, with an army of Danes, entered the island of Anglesea (Mona), and spoiled Penmon" in 969,[5] and although he could not retain possession, "being forced to return home,"[6] yet in the following year

*Maccus attends K. Edgar at Chester, A.D. 973.*

*Forged claim of K. Edgar to dominion in Ireland.*

*Maccus grandson of Sitric K. of Dublin.*

---

[1] Ego, Maccusius, Archipirata, confortaoi. Codex Diplomaticus Anglo Saxonicus. J. T. Kemble, vol. 3, p. 69.

[2] Spelman, Glossar. in voce *Pirata* p. 460.

[3] Will. Malmesbur., cap. viii.

[4] Matth. Westmonast., A.D. 964, p. 375; Flor. Vigorn., p. 78.

[5] Caradoc, p. 57. Chron. Princes of Wales, A.D. 969.

[6] *Ibid.*

his brother, "Godfrey, the son of Harald, devastated Mona, and by great craft subjugated the whole island."[1]

In 972 "the son of Harald sailed round Ireland with a numerous fleet,"[2] and visiting his father's territory in Limerick, carried off the reigning chieftain, this expedition forming a remarkable record in the Annals of the Four Masters, as again referring to "the Lagmanns of the islands,"[3] and showing that Magnus, claiming to be supreme chief, accompanied by the "lawmen," or judges, made the "circuit" of Ireland, according to the Scandinavian custom, for the settlement of rights or punishment of criminals;[4] and, as in the former case to avenge the murder of Ain, so in this case "Magnus, the son of Aralt, with the Lagmanns of the islands along with him," came to Inis Cathaigh, one of the islands in the Shannon, "and Imar, lord of the foreigners of Luimneach, was carried off from the island, and the violation of (St.) Senan thereby."[5] He was, however, soon released from captivity, for in 974 the celebrated Brian Borumha went to Limerick and "slew Ivar, King of Luimneach, and two of his sons,"[6] and Harald, another of Ivar's sons, being then elected king, "Brian slew Harald also, and returned home loaded with immense spoil."[7] Maccus probably died about this time, or may have been slain in the battle of

---

[1] Chron. Princes of Wales, A.D. 970.
[2] Ann. 4 Mast., 972.; Ann. Inisfal., A.D. 973.
[3] Ann. 4 Mast., A.D. 972.
[4] It was customary in Scandinavia for a chief and his Lagmen to make a circuit at stated intervals round the province to dispense justice, whence these circuits obtained the significant name of "Circuit Courts." Hibbert's Tings, p. 182.
[5] Ann. 4 Mast., A.D. 972.
[6] Ibid., A.D. 974.
[7] Ibid.

A.D. 978, which Maelseachlainn gained "over the foreigners of Ath Cliath and of the islands,"[1] and was succeeded by his brother Godfrey.

*Godfrey his brother becomes K. of Man.*

In 979 Godfrey, son of Harald, devastated Llyn and Mona;"[2] and again in 981 "Godfrey, son of Harald, devastated Dyved and Menevia,"[3] his services having been "hired" by Constantin, son of Iago, against his cousin Howel.

But the Isle of Man, although now under the dominion of Scandinavians, was not exempted from Viking ravages. The Sagas relate that Olaf Trygvesson, to dissipate grief for the loss of his queen, sailed on a Viking expedition, and after plundering in England, Scotland "and the Hebrides, he sailed southwards to Man, where he also fought, and thence steered to Bretland (Wales), which he laid waste with fire and sword."[4]

*Olaf Trygvesson spoils Man, A.D. 985;*

This expedition, which occupied Olaf four years, is apparently confirmed by the agreement of Icelandic Sagas with English chronicles and Irish and Welsh annals. The coincidence of dates and facts furnishes strong grounds for supposing that the "three ships of pirates" which, according to the Saxon chronicle, landed in Dorset and ravaged Portland, in 982,[5] was the fleet of Olaf Trygvesson, and were "the three ships of Danes" which, according to the Annals of Ulster, came to the coast of Dalriada in 986,[6] and sailing thence to the Scottish isles, plundered Hi-Choluim-chille, and in the following year, according

*also Dalriada of Ulster and Hy-Colum-Kill.*

---

[1] *Ibid.*, A.D. 978 (==979).
[2] Chron. Princes of Wales, A.D. 979.
[3] *Ibid.*, A.D. 981.
[4] Olaf Trygvesson's Saga, chap. xxxi.
[5] Anglo-Sax. Chron., A.D. 982.
[6] Ann. 4 Mast., A.D. 985, *note* ".

to the chronicle of Wales, the pagans "devastated Llanbadarn, Menevia, Llanilltut," &c.,[1] having previously (that is, in 986) visited the Isle of Man, when "the battle of Manann was fought by Mac Aralt and the foreigners."[2]

*Godred s. of Sitric K. of Man, A.D. 1066.*

For later events we are generally referred to the "Chronicle of Man," an authority which cannot be implicitly relied on, either for facts or dates. This chronicle, which commences A.D. 1000, contains nothing relating to the island until A.D. 1065, when it states, that "Godred Crovan, son of Harald the Black of Ysland (Ireland), fled to Godred, the son of Sytric, at that time King of Man,"[3] and after his death Godred Crovan is said to have conquered Man, and

*His apocryphal conquest of Dublin and Leinster.*

in A.D. 1066 (=1075), to have "reduced Dublin, and a great part of Laynester."[4] Godred Crovan probably was son of Reginald (whose son was elected King of the Galls in A.D. 1046),[5] as many of the Scandinavians of Ireland had been at the battle of Stamfordbridge with Earl Tostig and King Harald Hardraad, in A.D. 1066[6]; but whoever he was, or whatever conquests he may have made elsewhere, there is no allusion in Irish annals, or contemporary history, to any conquest of Dublin, or of any portion of Leinster.

*Intermarriages of Danish and Irish in 11th century.*

When the Ostmen of Dublin were converted to Christianity, their intermarriages with the Irish became so frequent, and the morality of the period was so lax, in repudiation, divorces, and marriage of

---

[1] Chron. Princes of Wales, 987.
[2] Ann. Ulst., 986 in Ann. 4 Mast., vol. ii., p. 720, n. n.
[3] One copy was published, Camden, 1607, another by Johnstone,
Antiq. Celto-Norm., Copenhagen, 1786.
[4] Camden's Britt., vol. iii., p. 705.
[5] Ann. 4 Mast., A.D. 1046.
[6] Anglo-Saxon Chron., A.D. 1066.

kindred, that it is doubtful whether the kings of Dublin during the eleventh century should be called Irish or Scandinavian.

Hence hard to say if the kings were Danish or Irish.

Thus we find that Aulaf Cuaran, whose double connexion with Conghalach, King of Ireland, has been already noticed, was also married to Gormflaith, daughter of Murchadh, son of Finn, King of Leinster, by whom he had a son, Sitric.[1] Gormflaith then married Brian Borumha, and by him had a son, Donnchad, step-brother of Sitric, who was succeeded by Diarmid, subsequently "King of the Danes of Dublin,"[2] and Brian having repudiated Gormflaith, she married Maelseachlainn, King of Teamhair, by whom she had a son, Conchobhar,[3] Maelseachlainn having been previously married to Maelmary, daughter of Aulaf Cuaran,[4] Gormflaith's first husband.[5]

Aulaf Cuaran was succeeded by his son Sitric, and Sitric, mindful of the example of his father (who had been a pilgrim at Iona), and urged by the clergy, undertook a pilgrimage to Rome (now become the frequent practice of Christian kings) in A.D. 1028.[6] In his absence his son Aulaf was taken prisoner by Mathghamhain Ua Riagain, but regained his liberty by payment of a heavy ransom.[7]

Aulaf also undertook a pilgrimage, but "was slain by the Saxons on his way to Rome," A.D. 1034.[8] He

---

[1] Supra, p. 78, and notes 3 and 7, *ibid.*, Ann. 4 Mast., A.D. 1030.

[2] Ann. Clonmac., A.D. 1069 (=1072) in Ann. 4 Mast., vol. ii., p. 904, *n.* ᵇ.

[3] Wars of the Gaedhil with the Gaill. Introd., p. xlviii., *n* ᵃ.

[4] Ann. Clonmac., A.D. 1014 (recte 1021) in Ann. 4 Mast., vol. ii., p. 800, *n.* ʰ.

[5] Gormflaith died A.D. 1030 (Ann. 4 Mast.), which supports the statement of the Sagas that Aulaf Cuaran was King of Dublin until after A.D. 994. Olaf Trygvesson's Saga, chap. lii.

[6] Ann. 4 Mast., A.D. 1028.

[7] *Ibid.*, A.D. 1029.

[8] *Ibid.*, A.D. 1034.

was succeeded by his son Sitric, who endowed Christ Church, Dublin, A.D. 1038.¹ Sitric, too, "went beyond the seas, and was succeeded by Eachmarcach, son of Raghnall," in A.D. 1036.² Eachmarcach also "went beyond the seas," A.D. 1052³ (probably to aid Earl Godwin), and "Diarmid, the son of Maelnambo, assumed the kingship of the foreigners,"⁴ in right of his descent from these kings, he having married "Dearbhforghaill, daughter of Donnchadh,"⁵ son of Brian Borumha by the widow of Aulaf Cuaran.

When the sons of Earl Godwin were restored to the Earldom of Northumbria, "Eachmarcach, the son of Ragnall,"⁶ retired to the Isle of Man, of which his brother Godfrey is said to have been king. Possibly alarmed by this, Diarmid, son of Maelnambo, sent his son Murchadh to the island, A.D. 1060, and "Murchadh carried tribute from thence, and defeated the son of Ragnall."⁸ Eachmarcach died A.D. 1064, and Diarmid, son of Maelnambo, who is styled "King of Leinster, of the Innse Gall (Danish isles), and of Dublin," was slain in battle A.D. 1072,⁹ and his sons, Gluniarn and Murchadh, having died previously, "Godfrey, son of Ragnall,"¹⁰ apparently he who was King of Man, assumed the sovereignty of Dublin. Godfrey was banished beyond the seas by

*Marginalia:* BOOK II. CHAP. I. — Man yields tribute to Diarmid K. of Dublin, A.D. 1060. — Diarmid slain, A.D. 1072. — Godfrey K. of Man becomes K. of Dublin also, A.D. 1073.

---

¹ Sitricus, King of Dublin, son of Ablef, Earl of Dublin, gave to the Holy Trinity and Donatus, first Bishop of Dublin, a place to build a church to the Holy Trinity, &c. Ware, Antiquities (from the Black Book of Christ Church).
² Ann. Tigern., A.D. 1035.
³ Ann. 4 Mast., A.D. 1052.
⁴ Ibid.
⁵ Ogygia, p. 437.
⁶ Ann. 4 Mast., A.D 1060.
⁷ Ann. Inisf., A.D. 1072; Ann. Clonmac. calls him "King of Leinster, Wales, and Danes of Dublin."
⁸ Ann. 4 Mast., A.D. 1070.
⁹ Ibid., A.D. 1072.
¹⁰ Ann. Ulst., A.D. 1075 in Ann. 4 Mast., vol. ii., p. 904, n. ᵇ.

Turlogh O'Brian, but returned soon after with a great fleet, and died A.D. 1075,[1] whereupon "Mortogh, son of Turlogh O'Brian, became King at Athcliath,"[2] and Godfrey's son, Fingal, became King of Man.[3]

Here we can trace a connexion between the Kingdom of the Isles and that of Dublin, but we can find no trace of Godred Crovan's conquest of the city, on the contrary, there is much to justify an opinion that the Godred, or Godfrey, whom Lanfranc styled " King of (the Ostmen of) Ireland" (while at the same time he styled Turlogh O'Brian " the mighty King of Ireland "), was that Godfrey, the son of Ragnall, who died A.D. 1075, the year after Lanfranc's letters were written. It was this connexion between the Kings of Dublin and Man which induced the Manx nobles in A.D. 1089 to request Murchard O'Brian to send one of his lineage to reign over them during the minority of Olave, Godred's son,[4] and which subsequently led De Courcy to emulate the example of his leader, Strongbow, and by marrying the daughter of Godred, King of Man,[5] to acquire a claim to Godfrey's Irish territory, the yet un-

*Manx nobles ask Murchard O'Brian to send them a ruler, A.D. 1089.*

*De Courcy weds a daughter of Godfrey K. of Man.*

---

[1] Ann. Ulst., A.D. 1075 in Ann. 4 Mast., vol. ii., p. 908, n. *.

[2] Chron. Scotorum., A.D. 1072.

[3] Chron. of the Kings of Man. Camden, vol. iii., p. 705. Gough's edition, London, 1789.

[4] Ibid. Camden has this under the date of 1089. Chronicon Manniæ, by Johnstone, has it A.D. 1075.

[5] Lodge's Peerage of Ireland, Dublin, 1789, vol. vi., p. 139. He married in A.D. 1180; was created Earl of Ulster 1181, and in 1182 entered the territory of Dalriada, and defeated Donald O'Loghlin.

Godred was *legally* married in 1176 by the Pope's Legate, Cardinal Vivian, to Fingala, daughter of Mac Lauchlan, son of Muircheard, King of Ireland.—Chron. Man., Johnstone. Vivian came to Down in 1177, met De Courcy there, and endeavoured to render it tributary to the Anglo-Normans.

conquered territory of the Scandinavians around Strangford, Carlingford, &c. Nor is it improbable but that this alliance gave to De Courcy the title of Earl (Jarl) of Ulster, and led De Courcy after he had entered Dalriada, and conquered the territory of the Northmen, to avow pretensions and claim privileges which provoked Henry to seize his person and his property, as he had previously done with Strongbow.

*Marginalia: BOOK II. CHAP. I. In her right claims Ulster. Henry II. jealous seizes his person and territory.*

## CHAPTER II.

### DUBLIN AND NORWAY.

Notices of Dublin frequent in Norwegian and Icelandic history.—Constant intercourse between Dublin and Norway.—Ostmen from Dublin fight for Norwegian liberty at the battle of Hafursfiord.—Led by Cearbhall, King of Dublin, or his son-in-law, Eyvind Austman.—Every King of Norway (almost) visits Dublin.—Biorn, son of Harold, King of Norway, visits Dublin as a merchant; also King Hacon.—Dublin the port for sale of Scandinavian prizes, or cargos of merchandise.

If the rank of Aulaf's colony among surrounding kingdoms were to be judged by reference to English chronicles and English historians, a very low estimate of its importance should be the result.

Until after the commencement of the eleventh century there is not a single record relating to Dublin in the Saxon Chronicle, even the name is not to be found, except in the poem on the battle of Brunnanburg, in A.D. 937, and then only in the statement that the Northmen fled " Dublin to seek."

Yet it must not be supposed that because Dublin is unnoticed, it therefore was unknown. Ireland itself is seldom named by the Saxon monks who wrote this chronicle, although from the number of Irish monks taught in England, their disputes with

*Marginalia: CHAP. II. Silence of the Anglo-Saxon Chronicle as to Dublin.*

the Irish clergy, who dissented from the doctrines or practices of the Church of Rome in the celebration of Easter, the form of tonsure, the consecration of bishops, &c., they must have been well acquainted with the state of the country.

*BOOK II. CHAP. II.*

If, however, we cannot estimate the importance of Aulaf's colony from English chronicles, we have abundant evidence respecting it in Icelandic Sagas and Irish annals, nor can the importance of Dublin be more strongly marked than by this, and it is worthy of observation, that although Dublin is frequently named, and in almost all the Sagas, yet throughout this entire range of Icelandic literature and history, with one or two exceptions, Limerick is the only city in the British Isles that is named as one with which the Northmen had intercourse or connexion. We find that between Dublin and Norway the intercourse was frequent and varied. In 872 the Ostmen of Dublin fought for Norwegian liberty at the fatal battle of Hafursfiord, where the Irish allies, or "Westmen," distinguished by their "white shields,"[1] were probably led by Eyvind Austman,[2] son-in-law of Cearbhall, King of Ossory, or by Cearbhall himself, as after their defeat Cearbhall was met in the Hebrides, and accompanied to Ireland by Onund, surnamed "Trefotr," from his wooden substitute for the foot or leg he had lost in the engagement.[3]

*Constant mention of Dublin in Icelandic Literature.*

*Ostmen of Dublin at battle of Hafursfiord, A.D. 872.*

*Led perhaps by Carroll, K. of Ossory.*

---

[1] Hcimsk., vol. i., p. 95. The Valsera, or people of Valland, also named the Galli-Bretons, or West Welch, inhabiting Bretagne, Cornwales (Cornwall).

[2] Landnamab., p. 374.

[3] Grotte's Saga, cap. i.; Landnamab., Part II., chap. xxxii., p. 168. "Trefotr," wooden foot. This is not a singular instance of

*BOOK II.
CHAP. II.*

*All the Kings of Norway (almost) visit Dublin.*

Subsequently, either as friends to the colonists, or as foes to the natives, almost every King of Norway visited Ireland, or sent his sons there. King Harald Harfager, who was of the same family as Aulaf, gave ships to his sons Thorgils and Frode, with which they visited Dublin.[1] His son, Eric,[2] and Eric's sons[3] after him, marauded in Ireland. Kings Trygve Olafson,[4] Harald Grafeld,[5] Olaf Trygvesson,[6] and Magnus Barefoot,[7] all visited Ireland. Olaf Trygvesson married a sister of Aulaf Quaran, King of Dublin, and was in Dublin when he was called to the throne of Norway. Barefoot attempted to take possession of Dublin, and after remaining a year in Ireland, was killed there. His son, King Sigurd, was to marry Biadmynia, daughter of the King of Connaught.[9] King Harald Gille was born and bred in Ireland, and Guttorm,[10] King Olaf the Saint's sister's son, had "his winter quarters at Dublin, Ireland being to him a land of rest." Although it must be admitted that the quietude he enjoyed was of a very ambiguous character, as the Saga adds that "in summer Guttorm went with King Margad (Murchadh) on an expedition to Bretland (Wales), where they made immense booty," for which they

*Their visits enumerated.*

---

supplying the loss of a limb. The Eyrbyggia Saga, p. 67, mentions Thorèr Vidlegg, or wooden leg, from the substitute he used for a leg lost in battle.

[1] Heimsk., vol. i. Harald Haarfager's Saga, cap. xxxv.
[2] *Ibid.* Hakon's Saga, cap. iv.
[3] *Ibid.*, cap. v.
[4] *Ibid.*, cap. ix.

[5] Kormak's Saga, cap. xix.
[6] Heimsk., vol. i. Olaf Trygvesson's Saga, cap. xxxi.
[7] *Ibid.* Olaf Trygvesson's Saga, cap. xxxiv.
[8] *Ibid.* Magnus Barefoot's Saga, cap. xxv., xxvii.
[9] *Ibid.* Cap. xii.
[10] *Ibid.* Harald Hardrada's Saga, cap. lvi.

quarrelled, the Irish king claiming the whole, and only giving his ally the choice to resign it or fight for it, an alternative which, after three days' consideration, Guttorm decided by fighting his Irish friend, killing him, "and every man, old and young, who followed him." Thus relieved from a claimant, Guttorm made his own division of the "booty," for having registered a vow to his uncle the saint, and believing that victory was due to miraculous interposition, the Saga further adds, that "every tenth penny of the plunder was given to St. Olaf's shrine; and there was so much silver that Guttorm had an image made of it, with rays round the head, which was the size of his own, or of his forecastle man's head; and the image was seven feet high," and long remained in St. Olaf's church "a memorial of Guttorm's victory and the saint's miracle."[1]

Nor were these friendly or hostile visits the only intercourse between Dublin and Norway. The two countries had also commercial relations, many of the chief men being both traders and warriors. Biorn, King Harold's son, had merchant ships, and was called "the Merchant."[2] "Lodin, rich, and of good family, often went on merchant voyages, and sometimes on Viking cruises."[3] Plundering in one country, these "merchant princes" sold the produce of their piracy in another, and Dublin was frequently

*Dublin the mart of the Vikings for cargoes of merchandise and prizes.*

---

[1] Heimsk., vol. i., Harald Hardrada's Saga, chap. lvii. The Chronicle of the Princes of Wales says "A.D. 1042, Howell, son of Edwin, meditated the devastation of Wales, accompanied by a fleet from Ireland;" and that Howell was killed there. The Annals of the Four Masters and those of Ulster state that Murchard was killed in 1042, but killed by Gilpatric Mac Donogh.

[2] Harald Harfagr's Saga, chap. xxxviii.

[3] Olaf. Tryggv. Saga, chap. lviii.

their place of sale. Hence we find that Thorer, the friend of King Hacon, who had long been on Viking expeditions, went on a merchant voyage to Dublin, "as many were in the habit of doing."[1]

## CHAPTER III.

### DUBLIN AND ICELAND.

*Iceland visited by Irish previous to its discovery in A.D. 870 by Lief and Ingolf, Norwegians.—Lief bringing captives from Ireland is saved by their device from perishing of thirst.—Many descendants of Cearbhall, an Irishman, King of Dublin, follow his son-in-law, Eyvind Ostman, and settle in Iceland.—Auda, widow of King Aulaf, founder of Dublin, retires thither.—Auda becomes a Christian like her brother-in-law, an emigrant from Ireland.—Descendants of Aulaf and Auda settlers in Iceland.—Other emigrants from Ireland.—America discovered long before Columbus by Norsemen connected with Dublin.—Ari, a descendant of Cearbhall's, wrecked on the coast of Florida A.D. 983.—Gudlief from Dublin driven by storms to America A.D. 936.—Is addressed in Irish.—Finds it is Biorn, long banished from Iceland.*

But the importance of Dublin as a Scandinavian kingdom is more strongly marked in its connexion with other colonies of the Norsemen.

Of these one of the most celebrated was Iceland, an island which, although known to the Irish at an early period, was not discovered by the Norwegians until ten years after Aulaf had become King of Dublin,[2] nor did they attempt to settle there until

---

[1] Olaf Tryggv. Saga, chap. li.

[2] Dicuil De Mens. Orb. Terræ, Letronne, Paris, 1814, cap. vii., s. ii., gives the statement of Irish monks who spent six months in Thule (Iceland) about A.D. 795, or thirty years before Dicuil wrote, and (cap. vii., s. iii.) he says, other Irish isles were inhabited by Irish eremites nearly a hundred years previously (in 725), in consequence of the incursions of the Northmen (quere, Picts). Island. Landnamabok, Havniæ, 1774, p. 5, *et seq.* Naddad, a Norwegian pirate, in a voyage to the Fœroe islands was driven by a tempest on the coast of Iceland, A.D. 861. It was again seen by Gardar, a Swede, in A D. 864, and subsequently by Floki.

A.D. 870, when Ingolf and Lief landed, and found that some Irish Christians called "Papæ,"[1] had left behind them "Irish books, bells, and croziers."

Ingolf returned to Norway to prepare for the intended settlement, and Lief sailed on a Viking cruise to Ireland, where, in pursuit of plunder, he entered a dark cave or underground retreat, and there discovered one of the natives by the glittering of his sword; killing the sword-bearer, and seizing the bright weapon, he thence obtained the name of Hior Lief, or Lief of the Sword.[2]

Ingolf and Lief did not meet again until A.D. 874, when Lief brought to Iceland ten Irish captives,[3] to whom he owed his safety during the voyage, as the stock of fresh water in the ship being exhausted they

*Lief brings ten Irish captives to Iceland, A.D. 874.*

---

another pirate. Crymogœa, Arn. Jonas, Hamburgi, 1614, p. 20. Specimen Islandiæ, Amstelodami, 1643, p. 4. Heimskringla. Havniæ, 1777. Harald's Saga, vol. i., p. 96, says that in the discontent at Harald's seizing the land of Norway (after the battle of Hafursfiord) great numbers fled from their country, and the out-countries of Iceland and the Fœroe islands were discovered and peopled. This refers to later colonization, as, according to Schoning's chronology, Harald began to reign in 863, and the battle of Hafursfiord was in 885.

[1] Landnamab., p. 2 ; Crymogœa, p. 21. Every bishop was styled papa, or father, and the books, bells, and croziers belonged to some of this order, this island, lying to the east of Iceland, being called Pap-ey after its Irish Christian inhabitants. Irish missionaries or anchorites had given their names to many of the islands, as Papa Stronsa, or Papa Westra.

[2] Landnamabok, p. 13. "The plundering of the caves" by the Norsemen is mentioned by the Four Masters in A.D. 861, and Ann. Ult., 862, out of their navy; but these appear to have been subterranean chambers, such as those under the Tumulus at New Grange and elsewhere. Lief's adventure some years later may have been in some of these chambers, of which there are many still in Ireland.

[3] [Multis in Hiberniœ locis piraticam exercuit et magnam prædam reportavit; ibi decem servos cepit quorum nomina sunt Dufthakus, Grirrandus, Skiardbiörn, Hallthor, Drafdritus; cæterorum nomina ad nos non pervenerunt.] Landnamab., p. 13.

BOOK II.
CHAP. III.

taught the crew to allay thirst after the manner of the Irish, by the use of meal and butter kneaded into a substance termed "Mynnthak;"[1] yet the life they had saved they did not preserve, for not long after their arrival in Iceland they slew their captor, and flying to neighbouring islands, yet called Westmen's, or Irishmen's, islands, were pursued and slain by Ingolf.[2]

*Westmen's or Irishmen's islands of Iceland.*

The Landnamabok, which minutely describes the colonization of Iceland, states that when the Norwegians took possession of the country Alfred the Great reigned in England, and "Kiarval was King at Dublin."[3] Through the disguise of Icelandic orthography there is no difficulty in discovering that this King Kiarval was Cearbhall, King of Ossory, who governed Dublin from the death of Ivar in 872 until his own death, and the restoration of a Scandinavian dynasty in 885. His children had intermarried with the Scandinavians; and the voyage of Lief having attracted the attention of the Ostmen of Dublin and their Irish friends, the family of Cearbhall furnished many emigrants to the new settlement.

*Descendants of Carroll, Irish K. of Dublin, settle in Iceland.*

Of these, Snœbiorn, who inhabited Vatnsfiord,[4]

---

[1] Landnamab., p. 15: from the Irish kijn, meal. ["Dufthaksker nomen est loco ubi ille mortem appetiit: plures per saxa precipites se dederunt, quæ ab iis nomen trahebant, insulæ autem ab illo tempore Westmanna-eyar appellantur, quia ibi occisi Westmanni erant," &c.]

[2] Ibid., p, 17. "Vestmanneyar," the island where the "Vestmenn" were slain by Ingolf.

[3] Ibid., p. 3. It also names the other sovereigns of Europe, and by including Kiarval of Dublin among them, marks the importance of that kingdom. The Landnamabok was begun by Ari Froda about the year 1075, and may be termed the Doomsday Book of Iceland. Ann. Clonmac., A.D. 929, calls him Cerval.

[4] Ibid., p. 159.

and his brother Helgi Magri, who took possession of a large tract of the country, were grandsons of Cearbhall, being sons of Eyvind Austman by Rafarta, Cearbhall's daughter,[1] Helgi being more closely connected with Dublin by marrying Aulaf's wife's sister.[2]

*(margin: Grandsons of King Carroll, Icelandic colonists.)*

Thorgrim was another of Cearbhall's grandsons, his father Grimolf having married " Kormlöd," or Gormflaith, Cearbhall's daughter.[3] His brother's son Alfus, with his uterine brother Onund, both settled in Iceland,[4] and his daughter having married his slave, or freedman, Steinraud, son of Maelpatric, an Irish noble, Steinraud also formed a settlement, to which he gave his name.[5]

Among the great grandsons of Cearbhall who settled in Iceland were Vilbald and Askel Hnokkan.[6] They were the "sons of Dufthach, son of Dufnial, son of King Kiarwal,"[7] and had large possessions, which their descendants continued to occupy.

*(margin: Carroll's great grandsons settlers in Iceland enumerated.)*

Baugus, also a great grandson of Cearbhall, settled at Fliotshild. He was "the son of Raude,"[8] son of Cellach, who succeeded his father Cearbhall as King of Ossory, and was killed in the same battle with the King of Cashel A.D. 903.[9]

---

[1] "Eyvindus postea in Hibernia Rafortam, filiam Karvialis Regis Hiberniæ, uxorem duxit." Landnamab., p. 228.

[2] Ibid., p. 229. Helgi married Thorunna Hyrna, Ketel Flatnef's daughter, and sister of Auda, wife of Aulaf, King of Dublin.

[3] Ibid., p. 375.

[4] Ibid., pp. 372, 374.

[5] Ibid., pp. 372, 373. His settlement was Steinraudarstad.

[6] Ibid., p. 312. Vilbald came from Ireland in his ship Kuda, and the river, at the mouth of which he landed, was thence called "Kudafliotsos."

[7] Ibid., p. 350. Askel's settlement was Askellshofda. The Icelandic Dufthack is the Irish Dubhthach, &c.

[8] Ibid., p. 334. Baugus was father of Gunnar of Gunnarsholt, and foster-brother of Ketel Hengs.

[9] Ann. Four Mast. A.D. 839, 900, 903.

BOOK II.
CHAP. III.

Another of the great grandsons of Cearbhall was Thordus, who settled at Hofdastrondam.¹ He was fifth in descent from Regnar Lodbrog, and married Fridgerda, the daughter of Thoris Hyrno by Fridgerda, Cearbhall's daughter.² Thordus, son of Viking, who settled at Alvidro, married Theoldhilda, daughter of Eyvind Austman;³ Ulf Skialgi, who colonized the whole promontory of Reykeanes, married Beorgo, another of his daughters,⁴ consequently both were great grandsons of Cearbhall; and Thrandus Mioksiglandi, who colonized the country between Thiorsa and Laxa, was son of Biorn, the brother of Eyvind Austman.⁵

Auda widow of K. Aulaf of Dublin, retires to Iceland.

The family of Aulaf, the Ostman king, no less than that of the Irish Cearbhall, contributed to connect Iceland with Dublin. After Aulaf's death his widow and her son, Thorstein, left Dublin, to which kingdom Ivar and the Irish Cearbhall succeeded. The Laxdæla Saga⁶ relates that "Auda while in Caithness heard that her son Thorsteinn the Red was betrayed by the Scots and killed, and her father, Ketill Flatnef, being also dead, she deemed that her prosperity was at an end. She (Auda) therefore caused a ship to be secretly built in a wood, and when the ship was completed she furnished it, placed all her wealth on board, and, with all those of her kindred who remained alive," she sailed away to the Orkneys, thence to the Fœroe islands, and ultimately to Iceland, where her ship was wrecked.⁷

¹ Landnamab., p. 219.
² Ibid.
³ Ibid., p. 149.
⁴ Ibid., p. 132.
⁵ Ibid., pp. 228, 363.
⁶ Laxdæla Saga, p. 9; Landnamab, p. 107, et seq.
⁷ Landnamab., p. 106, et seq.

Her brothers, Biorn Austman and Helgi Beola, with her brother-in-law, Helgi Magri, had previously settled in Iceland. There Auda fixed her residence at the head of Huammsfiord, in the Dale country,[1] and influenced by the example of Helgi Magri, who had been educated in Ireland,[2] and who, with his family, had become Christians,[3] Auda also became a convert, and opposite the Pagan temple she set up the emblem of her faith on the hill still called "Krossholar," where she and her household worshipped.[4] Although her descendants relapsed into Paganism,[5] Auda died firm in her faith, and unwilling that even her bones should lie in heathen ground, she directed her burial to be on the sands[6] below high-water mark, and, after the manner of her Viking forefathers, her ship was turned over her, and "a standing stone" (yet visible) was raised to mark the place of her interment.

*Auda becomes a Christian, like her brother-in-law bred in Ireland.*

*Has her grave under the water, not to lie in heathen soil.*

Nearly all the grandchildren of Aulaf and Auda also settled in Iceland, and established large families there. Olaf Feilan, son of Thorstein the Red, married Asdisa Bareysku, daughter of Konall.[7] Their son, Thordus Geller, became one of the most distinguished of the Icelanders, and their daughter Thora, having married Thorsteinn Thorskabitr, son of Thorolf Mostrarskegg (the priest and founder of the first

*Aulaf and Auda's grandchildren settlers in Iceland.*

---

[1] Eyrbyggia Saga, p. 15, gives the date A.D. 890.
[2] Landnamab., pp. 229.
[3] Ibid., 231.     [4] Ibid., p. 110.
[5] Ibid., p. 117.
[6] Kristni Saga, Hafniæ, 1773, p. 17. Fridgerda was a violent opponent of the Christian missionaries. Hakon's Saga, cap. xxvii. King Hakon made many of the ships be drawn up to the field of battle. He ordered that all the men of his army who had fallen should be laid in the ships, and covered with earth and stones, &c.
[7] Landnamab., p. 116.

**BOOK II.**
**CHAP. III.**

Pagan temple in the colony), became the mother of Thorgrim, whose son was Snorri, the celebrated lagman and priest.[1] Of Thorsteinn the Red's daughters, Oska married Haltsteinn, also a son of Thorolf Mostrarskegg, and another daughter, Thorgerda, married Kollus, who took possession of the whole of the Laxdœle, and thence obtained the name of Dal-Kollus.[2] After Dal-Kollus's death, Thorgerda married Herjolf, and became mother of Hrut, a patriarchal chief, whose family may be estimated from the statement that he rode to the "Althing" meeting attended by fourteen full-grown sons on horseback.

Other Irish settlers in Iceland.

Such were among the emigrants furnished by the royal families of Aulaf and Cearbhall; but, added to these we find a large number of settlers of Irish extraction. According to the Landnamabok, one of the slaves brought to Iceland by Auda was "Erps, son of Meldun, a Scotch earl, slain by Sigurd the Powerful." The mother of Erps was Mirgeol, daughter of Gljomal, King of Ireland. Sigurd took Mirgeol and Erps and enslaved them,"[3] but being enfranchised by Auda, Erps married, and fixed his residence at Saudafels, where a numerous progeny sprung from this mixture of Irish and Scandinavian blood.[4]

Thormodr Gamli and Keltic, sons of Bresii, came

[1] Landnamab., 95. Niall's Saga, p. 385, says she married Thorolf himself.
[2] Ibid., 113.
[3] Ibid., p. 108.
[4] Ibid., p. 112. Gliomal was probably Gluniaran, who reigned in Dublin with Aulaf in 890. His son, Gluntradhna, and Aulaf were killed in battle in 891. Mirgeol is the Irish Muirghael. One of that name was wife of the King of Leinster in A.D. 852, and Gluniaran, connected with the Irish, may have given the name to his daughter.

from Ireland, and colonized the promontory of Akranes.¹ Edna, the daughter of Ketil Bresii, was married in Ireland to "Konall," or Conal, and their son, Asolfus Alskek, came to Osas, on the east coast of Iceland.²

Avangus, an Irishman, settled at Bötn.³ Kalman or (Colman) came from the Hebrides and took possession of a large tract of country.⁴ His brother, Kylan, was another settler, and we may assume from their names that Kylan and Kiaran were also Irish.⁵

The connexion between Dublin and Iceland thus cemented by family ties continued throughout the ninth, tenth, and eleventh centuries, and the voyages for friendly intercourse, or commercial objects, led to the discovery of America by Norsemen connected with Dublin centuries before it was seen by Columbus.

*Norsemen connected with Dublin discovered America in 10th century.*

About the year 983 Ari, the son of Mar, a descendant of the Irish king Cearbhall,⁶ was wrecked on the coast of Florida, which he called "Irland er Mikla," or Great Ireland, it being also termed "Hvitra Manna Land," or Whitemens Land.⁷ Subsequently Gudlief, sailing from Dublin, landed on another part of the American continent, the incidents of his voyage forming one of the most interesting episodes in the Eyrbyggia Saga.

Bork the Fat and Thordis, Sur's daughter, had a daughter named Thurida, who married Thorbiorn,

¹ Landnamab., p. 30.
² Ibid., p. 31.
³ Ibid., p. 29.
⁴ Ibid., p. 51.
⁵ Ibid., p. 52.

⁶ Landnamab., p. 132. Ulf Skialge, the father of Mar, married Beorgo, daughter of Eyvind Austman, son-in-law of Cearbhall.
⁷ Ibid., p. 133.

who dwelt at Froda.[1] Thorbiorn, with many of his followers, was slain by Thorar.[2] Thurida then became the wife of Thorodd,[3] a Viking merchant, who, coming from Dublin,[4] had fixed his residence in Iceland;[5] but unfortunately for the matrimonial happiness of Thorodd, Biorn Asbrand, "the hero of Breidviking,"[6] a military Lothario, becoming enamoured of Thurida, an intimacy ensued, which led common fame to assert that he was the father of her son Kiartan.[7] After a desperate effort of the husband to destroy the lover,[8] Snorri, scandalized by the conduct of his sister, attempted also to assassinate Biorn, but failing in this, made a compact under which Biorn left Iceland in A.D. 908,[9] and it was supposed that overtaken by storms, he had perished at sea.

Some years after these events Gudlief, a merchant, who traded to Dublin and occasionally resided there, being on his return from thence to Iceland, was driven by contrary winds to an unknown land, where he and his companions going on shore were surrounded by people speaking a language which Gudlief could not understand, but which he thought "resembled Irish." While the natives were deliberating on the fate of the Icelanders, a number of horsemen approached with a banner, and headed by an old man of noble mein, to whom the subject of

---

[1] Eyrbyggia Saga, p. 43.
[2] Ibid., p. 61.
[3] Ibid., p. 141.
[4] Ibid., p. 141.
[5] Ibid., p. 143.
[6] Ibid., ibid., and p. 198, et sequ.
"Breidvikinga Kappi." "Kappi" a hero. Landnabok., p. 85.
[7] Ibid., pp. 203, 287.
[8] Ibid., pp. 147, 141.
[9] Muller's Bibliothek., vol. i. p. 193.

discussion was referred.¹ To the astonishment of Gudlief, the old man addressed him in Norse, and, after various disclosures, which left no doubt that he was that Biorn whom Snorri had induced to leave Iceland, he gave Gudlief a gold ring for Thurida, and a sword for her son Kiartan, at the same time requesting that, as he was an old man, neither friends nor relatives would incur the danger of seeking him in this foreign and savage land. Biorn had previously decided that the strangers should be freed, and Gudlief thus saved from captivity or death, returned to Dublin, where he passed the winter, and in summer sailed for Iceland, the bearer of Biorn's presents and message.²

*Book II. Chap. III.*
*Discovers Biorn then old.*
*Biorn refuses to return.*

Passing over the narratives of other voyages to America by the Norsemen,³ we will extract from the Laxdale Saga another episode connected with the history of Dublin, and illustrative of the manners and customs of the period.

Early in the tenth century Hoskulld, a great grandson of Aulaf, first King of Dublin, went from Iceland to the Brenneyar Islands, where King Hakon had convened that popular assembly denominated a "Thing."⁴ The meeting combined festivity with business, political and judicial labours being en-

*Story of Melkorka and her son Olaf Pa, A.D. 936, 962.*

---

¹ Eyrbyggia Saga, chap. lxiv. p. 328, *et seq.*

² *Ibid.* The closing chapter of the Eyrbyggia Saga is altogether occupied with this tale.

³ America was visited by Eric the Red in A.D. 986, by Lief, Eric's son, in A.D. 1000, and by Thorwald Ericson in A.D. 1002.

⁴ "A fragment of Irish history or a voyage to Ireland undertaken from Iceland in the tenth century." Fragments of English and Irish history in the ninth and tenth centuries. Translated from the original Icelandic by Grimes Johnson Thorkelin, 4to.: London, 1788.

livened by all the attractions of a Norwegian fair. Slaves were then articles of commerce in Scandinavia, as they long after continued to be in England; and Hoskulld, desirous to purchase a female slave, entered the tent of Gille, a wealthy slave merchant, who was distinguished by a "Russian hat."[1] Behind a curtain which divided the tent twelve young maidens were arranged for sale. Eleven of these were valued at one mark each, but the twelfth, who was valued more highly, was purchased by Hoskulld. As money had not yet been coined in Norway, he paid for her from "a purse which hung at his girdle" three marks of silver, "weighed in a scales."[2] The girl was beautiful, but apparently dumb, and Hoskulld gave her to his wife as a handmaid, having by her a son, whom he called Olaf, after his grandfather, Olaf the White,[3] and "Pa," or the Peacock, from his stateliness and beauty. After a lapse of years Hoskulld was surprised by overhearing the supposed dumb mother speaking to her son. The discovery led her to confess that, from a sense of degradation she had remained mute, that her name was Melkorka, and that her father was Miarkartan, King of Ireland, from whence she had been carried captive when fifteen years of age.[4] Hoskulld, by repeating

---

[1] A Russian hat appears to have been a valuable article. It was one of the presents made by King Harold to Gunnair. Niall's Saga, p. 90.

[2] In the Museum of Antiquities of the Royal Irish Academy at Dublin may be seen several pairs of small scales, found with Danish armour, used probably for this purpose.

[3] Hoskuld was son of Thorgerda, daughter of Thorstein the Red, son of Olaf the White, otherwise Aulaf, King of Dublin. Landnamab., p. 43.

[4] "Many were the blooming, lively women, and the modest, mild, comely maidens, &c., whom they carried off into oppression

this story to his wife, so far excited her jealousy that she struck her attendant, who indignantly returning the blow, rendered it necessary that Hoskulld should provide a separate residence for Melkorka and her son. As soon as Olaf had passed the age of Scandinavian manhood, Melkorka became anxious that he should visit his Irish relations, and Hoskulld declining to assist in this project, she clandestinely married another, on condition that he would provide means for the prosecution of Olaf's voyage. The stipulation was fulfilled, and Olaf, then eighteen years old, sailed for Norway, where he was graciously received by King Harald Grœfeld and Queen Gunhild, who gave him a vessel, which had the appearance of "a ship of war, having a crew of sixty men."[1] Sailing for Ireland they lost their course during a storm, and came to a part of the Irish coast "which strangers could not frequent with safety," not being in possession of the Ostmen. Here they anchored, but when the tide ebbed the Irish came towards the vessel intending "to draw her ashore;" and we thus obtain an idea of the size of their ships, for it is added that "the water was not deeper than their armpits, or the girdle of the tallest," but yet deep enough to keep the ship afloat. Olaf, who had been taught the Irish language by his mother, began to parley with the assailants, who insisted that, according to their laws, vessels in such a position could be claimed as

*Is driven from her master's house.*

*Sends her son to Ireland.*

*Olaf Pa is driven on the coast.*

*He addresses the natives in Irish.*

and bondage over the broad green sea."—Chap. xxxvi., p. 43, Wars of the Gaedhil with the Gaill.

[1] Each Fylki furnished twelve ships, having each sixty or seventy

well-armed men. Olaf Tryggvason's Saga, c. xli. Turner's Hist. of the Anglo-Saxons, vol. i., b. iv., c. i., p. 425.

wreck. Olaf admitted that such might be the law if foreigners had not an interpreter on board, but as he spoke Irish, his property was not liable to seizure, and he was prepared to defend it. Olaf and his companions, therefore, seized their arms, "and ranged them along the sides of the vessel," which "they covered with their shields as a bulwark." Olaf himself ascended the prow, "having on his head a golden helmet," in his hand a spear, his breast being covered with a shield "on which a lion was emblazoned," and thus prepared, awaited the attack. At this critical moment the King of Ireland arrived, an explanation ensued, as evidence of identity Olaf produced "a gold ring" which Miarkartan had given to his daughter Melkorka "on the appearance of her first tooth,"[1] and the King recognising the token, acknowledged his grandson, and invited Olaf and his companions to land, having first appointed proper persons to take charge of his ship, and "draw it upon the beach," the usual practice when the voyage was ended.

Olaf, now in favour with the king, accompanied him everywhere. Miarkartan being desirous to punish the Vikings, who continued to ravage the coast of Ireland, Olaf attended the king on board his own ship in pursuit of these pirates. He also accompanied him to Dublin, and the citizens on being informed of his parentage received him with joy.

---

[1] The appearance of the first tooth was celebrated in Scandinavia by a feast. "It appears to have been a solemn occasion when the child received its first tooth, at which time the friends and relations presented it with a gift called Tandsel." Baden's Hist. Norw., p. 78.

In spring "a Thing" was assembled, at which Miarkartan proposed to make Olaf heir to his kingdom, as being fitter to maintain its dignity than his own sons. Olaf, however, declined the honour, and loaded with presents, returned to Iceland, where "he drew his ship ashore," and was visited by his mother, who during his absence had given another son to her new husband. Nial's Saga adds that Olaf brought from Ireland an Irish dog of huge size, equal to a second man as a follower, and endowed with sagacity which enabled him to distinguish friends from foes. This dog, which he called "Samus," Olaf gave to his friend Gunnar,[1] but, like the celebrated Irish dog "Vig," which Olaf Tryggvasson had brought from Ireland,[2] Samus was killed defending his master. Thorkelin says that the facts here related "took place between 936 and 962,"[3] and if his chronology be correct, there is little difficulty in deciding that the King Miarkartan of the Saga was Muircheartach, King of Aileach, or the northern part of Ireland, and his daughter Melkorka, the Irish Maelcorcah. Our annals state that the fortress of Aileach was plundered by "Foreigners" in A.D. 900,[4] and again in A.D. 937,[5] when Muircheartach himself was captured and carried off to their ships, from which he was redeemed. But the foray in which Melkorka was carried off may have been that of the

*Muircheartach wishes to make him heir to his kingdom.*

---

[1] Niall's Saga, p. 217, chap. 82.
[2] Olaf. Trygg. Saga, chap. xxxv.
[3] Niall's Saga, p. 237.
[4] Thorkelin's Fragments, Lond., 1788, p. x. Schöning Chronology in Heimskringla, vol. I., p. 411, says Harald Greskin was born 934, and died 977; other chronologies place his death in 969.
[5] Ann. Four Mast., A D. 900.
[6] Ann. Ulst., A.D. 931 (=937).

[BOOK II. CHAP. III.

*Muircheartach's offer consistent with the law of Tanistry.*

foreigners who came to Loch Foyle, and plundered around Aileach, in A.D. 919.[1] According to the Saga, about twenty years after the capture of Melkorka, Olaf, then eighteen or nineteen years old, landed in Ireland, and attended King Miarkartan on board his own ship in an expedition against the pirates who had infested the coasts of Ireland. This date corresponds with A.D. 939 of the Four Masters, when Muircheartach fitted out a fleet, and pursued the Scandinavian pirates into the Hebrides, from which "he carried off much plunder and booty,"[2] and the visit to Dublin in the same year by Olaf and Miarkartan may have been that in which "Muircheartach and his Leather Cloaks" entered the city, where

*The Ostmen of Dublin would have willingly had Olaf for king.*

Olaf must have been "joyfully received" by the Scandinavian citizens, as a descendant of their founder, King Aulaf, Muircheartach's proposal that Olaf, one of his family, should succeed to the throne, being consistent with the Irish law of Tanistry.

[1] Ann. Four Mast., 919
[2] Ann. Four Mast., 939.

## CHAPTER IV.

### DUBLIN AND THE SCOTTISH ISLES.

The Hebrides and Orkneys visited by Irish ecclesiastics long before their occupation by the Scandinavians.—Saint Columba retired from Ireland to Hy (one of the Hebrides), A.D. 563.—Founded a monastery there.—The Scandinavians plunder Hy-Colum-Cille, A.D. 802.—From the Orkneys and Hebrides they plunder in Ireland, Scotland, and Norway.—Harald Haarfagr, King of Norway, sends Ketill Flatnef against them.—Ketill becomes their leader.—Allies himself with Aulaf, the White, King of Dublin.—Marries his daughter.—Scandinavian ravages in Spain and Africa.—They land their Moorish captives in Ireland.—Spanish, Irish, and Scandinavian histories confirm this account.

THE intercourse between Dublin and Iceland necessarily increased that previously existing between Dublin, the Hebrides, Orkneys, and Scottish isles. Like Iceland, the islands to the west and north of Scotland were known to the Irish, and had been visited by Irish ecclesiastics long, prior to the earliest accounts of Scandinavian invasion. St. Columba, one of the royal family of Ireland, and allied to that of the Dalriada of Scotland, being banished from Ireland, went to the Hebrides, and in A.D. 563 founded a monastery at Hy, where his monks peacefully resided until the close of the eighth century, when "the Pagan Norsemen laid waste the islands between Ireland and Scotland," and in A.D. 802 again plundered and burned "Hy-Colum-Cille," and slew sixty-eight of the clergy."[1] Lying in the track of the invaders, the Hebrides and Orkneys became the resort of all who sought new homes or the excitement or plunder of Viking expeditions. Before

BOOK II.
CHAP. IV.

The Scottish isles occupied by the Scandinavians.

---

Colgan, Actt., S.S., p. 241, concerning St. Albens.

Adamnan's Life of St. Columba by William Reeves, D.D., 1857.

Dicuil De Mensura Orbis Terræ,

c. vii., s. ii., pp. 38, lxxv., Letronne, Paris, 1814.

[1] Ann. Four Mast., 801, 802; Ann. Ult., A.D. 801.

the close of the ninth century the Scandinavian pirates of the isles, being joined by kindred spirits from Scotland and Ireland, "made war, and plundered far and wide,"[1] wintering in the Orkneys and Hebrides,[2] and in summer infesting the coasts of Ireland, Scotland, and Norway."[3] King Harald Haarfagr attempted to terminate their depredations, and having fitted out a great fleet, pursued these plunderers to their island fastnesses. Many he slew, but scarcely had he returned to Norway ere those who had escaped by flight returned to their old haunts, and Harald, tired of such warfare, sent Ketill Flatnef[4] to reconquer the islands, and expel the Vikings. But when Ketill had subdued all the southern isles he made himself king over them, and refusing to pay Harald the stipulated tribute, endeavoured to sustain his usurpation by alliances with neighbouring chieftains, of whom one of the most influential was Olaf, the White, King of Dublin, who married Auda, Ketill's daughter.

Prior, however, to the Vikings being driven from the isles they had brought into Ireland a race of people previously unknown to the Irish. In one of their expeditions from the Orkneys they landed among the Moors in Spain, and having defeated and captured a number of these Moors, they retired to their ships, and sailed for Ireland, where they landed their swarthy captives. This curious incident, which

---

[1] Landnamabok, p. 22. Skottar oc Irar heruindu oc ræntu vida.

[2] The Hebrides were termed the "Sudreyar," or Southern Islands, in contradistinction to the Orkneys or Northern Isles. The name still survives in "Soder and Man."

[3] Harald Haarfagr's Saga, cap. xx.

[4] Landnamabok, p. 22. Ketill Flatnef means Ketill Flatnose.

is not alluded to in any modern Irish history, we find recorded in one of the "Three Fragments of Annals" preserved in the Burgundian Library at Brussels,[1] and it appears to be corroborated by various statements of Scandinavian, French, and Spanish writers. The words of the Annals are that—" Not long before this time" (A.D. 869)[2] "the two younger sons of Albdan (Halfdan), King of Lochlann, expelled the eldest son, Raghnall, son of Albdan, because they feared that he would take the kingdom of Lochlann after their father; and Raghnall came with his three sons to Innsi Orc (Orkney), and Raghnall tarried there with his youngest son. But his elder sons, with a great host, which they collected from every quarter, . . . . rowed forward across the Cantabrian Sea, *i.e.*, the sea which is between Erin and Spain, until they reached Spain, and they inflicted many evils in Spain, both by killing and plundering. They afterwards crossed the Gaditanian Straits,[3] *i.e.*, where the Mediterranean Sea goes into the external ocean, and they arrived in Africa, and there they fought a battle with the Mauritani, in which a great slaughter of the Mauritani was made." "After this the Lochlanns passed over the country, and they plundered and burned the whole country; and they carried off a great host of them [the Mauritani] as captives to Erin, and these are the blue men [of Erin], for Mauri is the same as black men, and Mauritania is the same as blackness." And "long indeed were these blue men in Erin."

Confirmed by Irish and other Annals.

The Moorish prisoners the blue men of Erin.

[1] Three Fragments, p. 159, Irish Archæological Society, 1860.
[2] This time "the capture of York by the Danes," A.D. 869.
[3] The Straits of Gades in the south of Spain. The modern Cadiz preserves the name.

*Blue men the Norse name for Africans.*

The term blue men here applied to the Moors affords some evidences of a Scandinavian connexion with parts of the narrative. The term, which is not Irish, was doubtless adopted by the Irish from those Scandinavian Vikings who first brought these coloured men into Ireland, for in the Icelandic Sagas and Swedish history Bluemen is the name always given to Moors or Africans,[1] and "Great Blueland" the name by which Africa[2] is designated.

*Identification of King Halfdan.*

The very confused history and unsettled chronology of the reigns of the early kings of Scandinavia, and the number of kings of the name of Halfdan, renders it difficult clearly to identify the King Halfdan referred to in the Annals. It may be asserted, however, with some degree of confidence that he was Halfdan the Mild,[3] son and successor of King Eysteinn. According to Schöning's chronology[4] Halfden was born in A.D. 738, and was succeeded by his son Gudrod, who died in A.D. 824. The names of his other sons are not recorded, but there are reasons to suppose[5] that one of them was called Rognvald, or Raghnal, and, if the supposition be correct, it is not improbable that he may have been driven into the Orkneys by his brothers when they

---

[1] Ynglinga Saga, cap 1.—"Blaland hit Mikla," or Great Blueland, being the name of Africa, and Blae men the name for Africans.

[2] Sigurd Jorsalafain Saga, cap. 24.—Blalande, Saracen's land, and Blamenn, Saracens. Tuyell's Sweden, Blamenn, negroes, &c.

[3] Ynglinga Saga, cap. 411—Halfdan "had been long on Viking expeditions." "He died on a bed of sickness, and was buried at Borre." He was called Halfdann hinn Mildi oc hinn Malar illi (the bad entertainer).

[4] Schöning's Chronology, Heimskringla, vol. i., p. 411.

[5] The Norsemen never named the son after the father, but generally after the uncle, granduncle or grandfather, and Gudrod's grandson was named Rognvald (Raghnal), the son of Olaf, the son of Gudrod.

saw their father suffering from that sickness of which he died.

But whatever difficulty there may be in identifying the King Halfdan who was the father of Rognvald, there is none in establishing the fact that at the time mentioned in the Annals a fleet of Scandinavians came to the coast of Spain, and after plundering the country, captured and carried off a number of Moors, the blue men of the narrative. The French Chronicle of Bertiniani states that the Norsemen invaded Spain in A.D. 844.[1] Depping more explicit says that they plundered the coasts of Galicia, Portugal, and Andalusia, made a descent on Cadiz, and infested the borders of the Mediterranean. "That it was in the month of September, 844, they sailed up the Guadalquiver," and having defeated the Moors who opposed their attack on Seville, they burned the faubourgs, pillaged the city, and retired to their ships, "bringing with them much booty and a crowd of prisoners, who perhaps, never again beheld the beautiful sky of Andalusia."

*Expedition to Spain confirmed by Bertiniani's Annals,*

The Spanish history by Mariani is equally in accordance with our annals. It relates that the Normans "overran and pillaged all the coasts of Galicia till near Corunna"; "that in A.D. 847, having gathered new forces, they laid siege to Seville, plundered the territory of Cadiz and Medina Sidonia, taking great numbers of men and cattle, and putting many Moors to the sword." "They then left Spain, having gained much honour and great riches."[3]

*and by Mariani.*

---

[1] Annals Bertiniani apud Duchesne, vol. iii., p. 201, A.D. 844.

[2] Depping Hist. des Expeditions Maritimes Des Normans, Paris, 1844, pp. 107, 108.

[3] Mariani Hist. Spain, Lond. 1699, p. 112.

## CHAPTER V.

### DUBLIN AND THE MAINLAND OF SCOTLAND.

Difference between the Scandinavian invasions of Scotland and Ireland.—In Scotland they were as conquerors.—The Scandinavians at Dublin, colonists.—Aulaf, King of Dublin, intermarries into the families of Irish Kings.—Enumeration of Aulaf's connexions with Irish royalty.—His connexions with the Scandinavian Lords of the Isles.—Marries Auda, daughter of Ketill, Lord of the Hebrides.—Keneth M'Alpin, King of Scots, calls to his aid, Godfrey, Chief of Ulster.—Godfrey becomes Lord of the Isles.—Aulaf's expedition with his son Ivar, against the men of Fortrenn.—Aulaf slain there, A.D. 869.—His son, Ivar, returns, and reigns at Dublin.—Ivar dies, A.D. 872.—Ivar's grandson driven out of Dublin by the Irish, A.D. 962.—Invades Pictland, and is slain at Fortrenn, A.D. 904.

BOOK II.
CHAP. V.

*Intermarriages of Ostmen with Irish.*

BUT the connexion between Dublin and the Mainland of Scotland was of a different character from that established between the Ostmen of that port and the inhabitants of Ireland. In Scotland the Scandinavians of Dublin were conquerors, not colonists, as the Ostmen of Dublin quickly became in Ireland by intermarriage with the Irish. Thus shortly after his arrival, Aulaf became closely con-

*Aulaf, King of Dublin marries the daughter of Aedh King of Ireland.*

nected with Irish royalty. Aedh Finnliath, King of Ireland, had married Maelmurrie, daughter of Cinnaedh (Kenneth), King of the Scots and Picts;[1] and Aulaf having married another of Kenneth's daughters,[2] he thus became brother-in-law to the reigning monarch. Subsequently Aulaf also married one of Aedh Finnliath's daughters,[3] and thus became

---

[1] Ogygia, seu Rerum Hibernicarum Chronologia. Roderic O'Flaherty. 4to: London, 1685. p. 484.

[2] Three Fragments of Irish Annals, edited by J. O'Donovan, LL.D., p. 173. Irish Archæological Society. 4to: Dublin, 1860.

[3] *Ibid.*, p. 151.

that king's son-in-law, and brother-in-law of Neal Glundubh, the succeeding monarch. Nor was these his only connexions with Irish royalty.

Scandinavian kings were polygamists, marrying and repudiating without controul. And notwithstanding their Christianity, some of our Irish monarchs were tainted by the manners of the age, as even Charlemagne, the anointed champion of the Church, was a bigamist, and worse. Certain it is that their matrimonial connexions were of a most complicated character. Thus Aedh Finnliath, who had married Maelmurrie, had (possibly after her death) married Flauna, daughter of Dunlaing, and sister of Cearbhall, Lord of Ossory.[1] This Flauna had previously been the wife of Maelsachlain, King of Ireland, by whom she became the mother of Flann Sinna,[2] and likewise had been the wife of Gaithen, by whom she had Cennedigh,[3] Lord of Laighis, her brother Cearbhall[4] being married to a daughter of her first husband, Maelsachlain.[5] Nor was this all. After the death of Aedh Finnliath, his widow, Maelmurrie, married Flann,[6] the son of Maelsachlain,[7] by whom she had King Donnchadh,[8] Aedh's sister[9] having been married to Conaing, Lord of Breagh, *i.e.*, Meath.[10]

[1] Three Fragments, p. 179.
[2] Annals of Four Masters, A.D. 886.
[3] Three Fragments, p. 179.
[4] Annals of Four Masters, A.D. 862.
[5] Three Fragments, p. 129.
[6] Ogygia, sen Rerum Hibernicarum Chronologia, by Roderic O'Flaherty, p. 435. 4to: London, 1685.
[7] Three Fragments, p. 179. Annals of Four Masters, A.D. 886.
[8] Annals of Four Masters, A.D. 942. *Ibid*, A.D. 919.
[9] Three Fragments p. 177.
[10] *Ibid.*

Thus allied to the Kings of Scotland and Ireland, Aulaf also connected himself with the Lords of the Isles. He married Auda,[1] daughter of Ketil Flatneff,[2] Chief of the Hebrides; and their son, Thorstein the Red,[3] married Thurida,[4] whose Scandinavian father, Eyvind Austman,[5] was husband of Rafarta, one of Cearbhall's daughters.[6]

We have already seen that the Picts of Scotland had a common origin with those on the sea coast of Ulster, where the Northmen first settled.[7] While they were thus plundering and settling among the Irish and Irish Picts, they were pursuing the same course with the Scots and Picts of Scotland.

The Northern Picts had been the victims of the early invaders; so had been the Scots, or Men of Alba. In A.D. 835, Cinaedh, son of Alpin, King of the Scots, sought assistance from his kindred in Ireland, and Godfraidh, son of Fearghus, Chief of Orghialla (Ulster), went to Alba to strengthen the Dalriada,[8] and thence, perhaps, at the request of Cinaedh, son of Alpin, became Chief of the Hebrides also.

In A.D. 839 the Southern Picts were invaded, and in "a battle by the Gentiles against the Men of Fortren, Eogannen M'Œngus (King of the Picts), and his brother Bran, were slain with a multidude

---

[1] Olaf Trygvasson's Saga. Scripta Historica Islandorum Latine reddita, vol. i., p. 224, cap. 95. Twelve vols., 12mo: Hafniæ, 1828–1832.

[2] Landnamabok, p. 107.

[3] Nial's Saga, p. 389. Harald Harfagr's Saga, cap. xxii.

[4] Landnamabok, p. 109.

[5] Ibid, ibid.

[6] Ibid, p. 228.

[7] Supra, pp. 83, 84.

[8] Annals of Four Masters, A.D. 835.

of others,"[1] this being possibly the expedition mentioned by Saxo Grammaticus, in which Regnar Lodbrog slew the Chiefs of Scotia, Pictavia, and the Western Isles.[2]

It might be suggested that when "all the foreign tribes of Ireland" had submitted to Aulaf,[3] he may have desired to extend his dominion over the Picts of Scotland also. Certain it is that he proceeded to subdue them in A.D. 865; for in that year according to the Annalists of Ulster, "Amlaiv and his nobility went to Fortren together with the foreigners of Ireland and Scotland, and spoiled the Cruithne (the Picts), and brought all their hostages with them."[4]

In A.D. 869, Aulaf in conjunction with Ivar, again invaded Pictland, and after a siege of four months took and destroyed its capital; but Aulaf being slain while leading an army against Constantine, King of the Scots, Ivar returned to Dublin, where he died, A.D. 872.[5]

The sons of Aulaf, however, did not abandon the conquests of their father. Oslin remained in Pictland, where he was slain by a stratagem of the Albanenses, in A.D. 875.[6]

But though the Kings of Dublin ceased to have a

---

[1] Bellum a gentilibus contrà viros Fortrenn in quo ceciderunt Eoganam MacŒngusa et Bran MacŒngus, et Aedh MacBoanta et alii pene innumerabiles ceciderunt. Ann. Ulton. See Reeves's Adamnan, p. 390. (Wars of the Gaedhel with the Gaill. Pref. p. li., n. 1.)

[2] Saxo Grammaticus Hist. *Lib.* ix., p. 154, line 33.

[3] *Supra*, p. 19.

[4] Annals of Ulster, cited in the foot note of J. O'Donovan, LL.D., in the Annals of the Four Masters, vol. i., p. 502.

[5] *Supra*, pp. 38–40.

[6] Annals of Four Masters, A.D. 874. *Ibid*, A.D. 865, p. 519. Citing Annal Ulton.

BOOK II.
CHAP. V.

Ivar's grandson falls in Pictland, A.D. 904.

dominion in Scotland, their connexion with it continued throughout the tenth century. Nor is it impossible that when the foreigners were driven out of Dublin, in A.D. 901,[1] Ivar, the grandson of Ivar, attempted to reconquer Pictland; but was killed by the men of Fortrenn with a great slaughter about him, in A.D. 904.[2]

About this period it is somewhat difficult to decide whether the Kings of Dublin should be termed Ostmen or Irish. After their conversion to Christianity, intermarriages with the Irish became much more frequent, but not less irregular.

## CHAPTER VI.

### RELIGION OF THE OSTMEN OF IRELAND.

Few details in Irish Annals concerning the form of Paganism of the Ostmen of Ireland.—Date of their conversion to Christianity.—The conversion of King Aulaf Cuaran in England.—The first Ostman bishop of Dublin consecrated there.—King Aulaf Cuaran's conversion in England decides the religion of many of his subjects in Ireland.—The rest remain worshippers of Thor.—Proofs of this worship in Irish Annals.—Whether the prefix Gille be Scandinavian or Irish discussed.—Deductions drawn from its use in Scandinavian and Irish names.—The division of Ireland into four provinces, not Scandinavian, but of ecclesiastical origin.—The Dyfflinarskiri or Scandinavian territory around Dublin.—Its bounds co-extensive with the early Admiralty jurisdiction of the Mayor and citizens of Dublin.

BOOK II.
CHAP. VI

OF the form of paganism professed by the Ostmen of Ireland, Irish annals furnish no direct evidence. They do not even inform us of the religious tenets of

---

[1] *Supra*, p. 49. Annals of Ulster. This date in the Annals of the Four Masters, in A.D. 897.

[2] Annal. Ulton. O'Connor's Rerum Hibernicarum Scriptores, vol. iv., p. 243.

the Irish previously to the introduction of Christianity; nor are they singular in this respect, Saxon chronicles being equally silent respecting that which existed in England until the 11th century, when Canute prohibited heathenism by law. To the Christian Monks who wrote their annals and chronicles (and they were almost the only writers and Latin their only language), it seemed profane to mention the names of Thor or Frega or of any heathen deity, or to allude to their temples or worship. We are told only that our Ostmen were pagans, and they remained pagans for 500 years after all Europe was christianized. The Welsh chronicles state that they were pagan to the middle of the 11th century, the Annals of Cambria and Brut y Tywysogain recording that "A.D. 1040 Grufudd (King of Wales) was captured by the pagans of Dublin."[1]

*Conversion of the Ostmen of Dublin.*

This statement of the Welsh chronicle however would prolong the existence of Scandinavian paganism in Dublin much beyond the period usually assigned for its termination; for although it was not until A.D. 1038 that the first Ostman bishop of Dublin was consecrated, we may confidently assert that some of our Ostmen had been previously converted; and that they had been converted in England; and hence their connexion with Canterbury and Rome instead of with Armagh and the Irish Church, and thence also it was that their bishops were consecrated in

*First Ostman Bishop of Dublin*

*Consecrated at Canterbury A.D. 1038.*

---

[1] Ancient Laws and Institutes of Wales, Record publication, 1841. There were some remnants of pagan superstition among the Irish in A.D. 1014, "War of the Gaedhil with the Gaill," p. 173.

England after the Roman formula and that an Ostman bishop was the first Papal Legate in Ireland.¹

*Sitric, King of Dublin, converted in England, A.D. 925.*

Among our Ostmen, the first recorded conversion is that of Sitric, King of Dublin, who was baptized in England, and then married to King Athelstan's sister in A.D. 925,² but the influence of his conversion did not extend to Dublin, for unsteady in his faith and forgetful of his vow he soon abjured Christianity, abandoned his wife, and died pagan where he had been baptized. His successor, Aulaf the son of Godfrey, was opposed to Athelstan and remained pagan until death ;³ but Sitric's son, Aulaf Cuaran,

*Aulaf Cuaran, Sitric's son converted there.*

on visiting England was there converted and in A.D. 943 was received at baptism by King Edmund,⁴ Aulaf's sister, Gyda,⁵ being subsequently married to Olaf Tryggvasson in England, where Olaf also had been baptized.⁶

*His subjects conversion, A.D. 944.*

It was this conversion of Aulaf Cuaran and his family⁷ which decided the religion of his subjects in A.D. 944. When Aulaf returned to Dublin,⁸ his example, aided by the efforts of the Anglo-Saxon

---

¹ Sir James Ware's Works, vol. ii., p. 306. *Ibid*, vol. i., p. 504, "Gilleor Gillebert, Bishop of Limerick, and first Apostolic Legate in Ireland A D., 1139."

² Sax. Chron., 925.

³ Flor. Worcest., 938, calls him "rex paganus Aulafus," he died 942, Sax. Chron.

⁴ Sax. Chron , 943.

⁵ Erat autem illa potens domina (Gyda) soror Olavi, Scotorum regis, qui Kuaran est nominatus, Hist. Olavi Trygvii filius, vol. 10., p. 236. Scripta Historica Islandorum, Studio Sveinbiornis Egilson 12 vols. 12mo, Havniæ, 1841.

⁶ Heimsk Olaf's Saga, cap. XXXIII., Torfæus Hist. Norv., vol. 2., p. 340. Olaf, like many of the Northmen, was baptized several times.

⁷ Aulaf remained steady in his faith, and in A.D. 980 "went to Hi on his pilgrimage, and died there after penance and a good life." Ann. Four Mast., A.D. 980.

⁸ Sax. Chron., 944.; Ann. Ulst., 944.

monks (who followed him from Northumberland), led to that "conversion of the Danes" which Irish writers date from about A.D. 948.¹ There is no proof, however, that this conversion was general, and the progress of Christianity among the Scandinavians elsewhere, would lead us to infer that it was partial, as we find, that although Hakon (Athelstan's foster son) introduced Christianity into Norway in A.D. 956;² and although Olaf Tryggvasson established it there by law, in A.D. 1000 (it being legally established in Iceland the same year),³ yet many Norwegians remained pagan at the close of the 11th century, refusing to submit even to the nominal Christianity then required, districts and armies being baptized without any instruction whatsoever.⁴ The forms of pagans and Christians were in some respects similar, pouring water over the head and giving a name, being ceremonies of Odinism ;⁵ "Thor's hammersign" being used like that of the cross (and sometimes mistaken for it) in religious rites and blessings.⁶

Our evidence therefore only proves that the Ost-

*Marginalia:* BOOK II. CHAP. VI. — This conversion only partial. — Some Pagan and Christian forms alike.

---

¹ Ware's Antiq., p. 61. Lanigan Eccl. Hist., vol. i., p. 75, says, Sitric had three sons, Reginald, Aulaf, and Godfrid, "and it is very probable that Godfrid followed this example of his father and became Christian," but Lanigan probably overlooked the fact, that Godfrid's son, Reginald, was a pagan until A.D. 943, when he also was converted in England; Sax. Chron., 943.

² Heimsk, vol. i.; Chronologia, p. 411.

³ Kristni-Saga, Hafniæ, 1773,
cap. xi. ; introduced A.D. 981.

⁴ Heimsk, vol. ii., p. 340.

⁵ Heimsk, vol. i. p. 72. Saga Halfdanar Svarta, cap. vii.

⁶ Ibid, vol. i., p. 143. Saga Hakon Guda, c. xviii. "The king then took the drinking horn and made the sign of the cross over it. What does the king mean? said Kaare of Gryting"—Earl Sigurd replied—"He is blessing the full goblet in the name of Thor by making the sign of his hammer over it."

men of Dublin were not exclusively pagan in A.D. 1040, as the Welsh chronicles seem to imply.

*Thor worship in Ireland.*

But that those who remained pagan adhered to the worship of Thor, then the religion of Norway, can only be inferred from the few events, which are recorded in our Annals. For instance, we know that the Scandinavians sometimes sacrificed their prisoners to Thor or Odin, by "crushing the spine" (or "breaking the back on a stone"),[1] or by plunging the victim head foremost in water, and auguring from the sacrifice future victory or defeat. Such sacrifices may be alluded to in the statements, that, "A.D. 859, Maelgula Mac Dungail, King of Cashel, was killed by the Danes, *i.e.*, his back was broken with a stone;"[2] and A.D. 863, that, "Conor Mac Dearmada, half King of Meath, was stifled in water at Cluain Iraird, by Aulaf, King of the foreigners" of Dublin.[3]

*Ring of Tomar and sword of Carlus.*

Again, we find it stated, that after the death of Aulaf Cuaran, which is supposed to have occurred in A.D. 992, there was a contest for succession between Imar and "Sitric, the son of Aulaf,"[4] and taking advantage of this dispute in "A.D. 994, the ring of Tomar, and the sword of Carlus were found carried

---

[1] Thordus Gallus mentions the Thorstein on which men were sacrificed (broken), and where also is the circle of stones, "Domhring," or place of justice. Landnamabok, p. 94. And the Eyrbyggia:— "Here (at a spot in Iceland) was set up (A.D. 934), the place of judgment; and here is seen to this day (A.D. 1250), the judicial circle of stones where human victims were offered up to the gods; and conspicuous in the centre of the circle, Thor's Stone, where the backs of the victims were broken, still showing signs of blood." Eyrbyggia Saga, cap. x., p. 27; 4to, Havniæ, 1787.

[2] Ann. Four Mast., A.D. 857. "Was stoned by the Norsemen till they killed him." Ann. Innisfall, A.D. 859. Ann. Four Mast., A.D. 867.

[3] Ann. Four Mast., A.D. 862.

[4] Ann. Four Mast., A.D. 992, 993.

away by Maelseachlain from the foreigners of Ath Cliath."[1]

It has been already observed that the 'godar' were princes, judges, and priests. The emblem of military jurisdiction being a sword, and the marks of the 'godi's' sacredotal dignity being a massive ring,[2] generally kept at the temple of Thor, but sometimes worn attached by a smaller ring to the armilla of the godi, and having some mystery connected with it.[3]

When the "godi" acted in his judicial capacity, witnesses were sworn on this "holy ring," and the "godi" gave solemnity to the oath by dipping the ring in the blood of a sacrifice. Such was "the great gold ring" which Olaf Trygvasson, when he became a Christian, took from the temple door of Lade," and sent to Queen Sigrid,[4] and such was "the holy ring" whereon the Danes "swore oaths" to King Alfred.[5] Of these "great gold rings with the smaller ring attached" there is a splendid specimen in the museum of the Royal Irish Academy.[6]

We therefore infer that the "ring" and sword which Maelseachlain carried away, had been preserved by the Ostmen as tokens of the investiture, spiritual and temporal, of their two races of kingly

*Significance of rings.*

*Ring and sword, emblems of spiritual and temporal investiture.*

---

[1] Ann. Four Masters, A.D. 994.
[2] This ring was sometimes of silver weighing "two ores or more," and was placed on the altar of Thor. For its use in judicial and religious matters, see Landnamabok, p. 299, also Eyrbyggia Saga, cap. x., p. 27.
[3] Bartholinus De Armillis Veterum, Amst., 1676, p. 47, et seq.
[4] Heimsk. vol. i., p. 204. Saga af Olafi Tryggvasyni, cap. lxvi.
[5] Sax. Chron., A.D. 876.
[6] This ring with a large number of other gold articles was found in the county of Clare, and purchased by me for the Academy.

*BOOK II.*
*CHAP. VI.*

*Vicissitudes of the ring and sword.*

worshippers of Thor, Carlus, slain in A.D. 866, being the eldest son of Aulaf, then King of Dublin, and Tomar (Thormodr or Thorsman), " Earl tanist of the King of Lochlann.[2] After A.D. 994, when the power of the Ostmen kings was restored, the sword of Carlus again came into their possession. But in A.D. 1028,[3] Sitric abandoned his kingdom, and with Flannagan Ua Cellaigh, King of Bregia, went to Rome. In their absence Sitric's son was captured by Mathgainhain Ua Riagain, then Lord of Breagha, who exacted for his ransom " the sword of Carlus," and other articles of value.[4]

*Last notice of the sword of Carlus.*

Again, however, the sword of Carlus was restored to the Ostmen of Dublin, but soon again they were deprived of it; the last notice of this emblem of temporal sovereignty, being, that it " and many other precious things were obtained by the son of Maelnambho" in A.D. 1058.[5] But the "ring of Tomar"[6] never reappeared among the regalia of the Ostmen. Christianity had severed the authority of the priest

---

[1] Ann. Four Mast., A.D. 866.

[2] Ibid, A.D. 846.

[3] Ann. Four Mast., 1028. Sitric's son, Aulaf, also commenced a pilgrimage, but "was slain by the Saxons on his way to Rome." Ibid, 1034.

[4] Ibid, 1029.

[5] Ann. Four Mast., A.D. 1058.

[6] "A bull of excommunication was given to William's messenger, and to it was added a consecrated banner of the Roman Church, and a ring containing one of St Peter's hairs set under a diamond of great price. This was the double emblem of military and ecclesiastical investiture." Thierry. Conquest of England by the Normans, vol. i., b. iii., p. 159. (Bohn's Translation, 12mo, London, 1847.) "By a bull in favour of Henry, and another ring, a valuable emerald, &c." Macaria Excidium, being a secret (allegorical) history of the War of the Revolution (1689-1691) in Ireland, by Colonel Charles O'Kelly, edited by John Cornelius O'Callaghan, for the Irish Archæological Society: 4to, Dublin, 1850.

from that of the prince; the spiritual and temporal jurisdictions were no longer united in the same individual, and the pagan relic of priestly office ceased to be used by the Ostman kings of Dublin.

*Of the Scandinavian term Gille.* We think that the appearance of the name "Gille" in Irish Annals, also affords evidence that the worship of Thor was the paganism of our Ostmen. Heretofore, Irish scholars have considered the word Gille to be of Irish origin, notwithstanding the opinion of an eminent etymologist, who, in recently tracing the derivation of the modern Scotch term "Gilly," assumes as "more than probable that the term has been borrowed from the Scandinavian settlers in Ireland and the Isles, as there is no similar term in Cambro Britannic, and as the Icelandic Gilla and Giolla both signify a boy (servant), it is more likely that the Irish received it from their Norse conquerors than that they borrowed it from them, and incorporated it into the Gothic language."[1]

*Gille as a name among Scandinavians.* Our suggestion, however, extends a little farther. There can be no doubt the word 'Gille' was used by the Scandinavians as a proper name, as we read of "Gille the Lagman [or Law maker] of the Faroe Islands,"[2] "Gille, Count of the Hebrides,"[3] "Gille

---

[1] Jamieson's Etym. Dic. Supplement, Edinburgh, 1825, on the word Gillie. At a later period the term Gille was also used by the Irish to signify a boy, servant, *see* Ann. Four Mast., 1022. "Muiren was slain by two Gillies of the Luighni."

[In Cleaseby and Vigfusson's Icelandic English Dictionary at the word Gilli "Gilli, [Gaelic, Gillie], a servant, only in Irish proper names." 4to, Clarendon Press, Oxford, 1874. The statement of Jamieson's as to the use of the words Gilla and Giolla in the Icelandic language does not seem to be borne out by any other dictionary.]

[2] "Gille Lögsogomadr," Heimsk, vol. ii., p. 208.

[3] Niuls Saga. Havniæ, 1809, p. 590.

K

the back thief of Norway,"¹ "Gille the Russian Merchant,"² and we might even add to our list " St. Gille of Caen in Normandy," whose history appears to have perplexed the Bollandists.

And the Scandinavians not only used the name in this manner, but they also used it as a religious adjunct, in the same sense in which it is used among the Irish, as it appears, that many Scandinavians who dedicated themselves to Thor, and were "godar" in his Temples, took the name of the deity they served adding to it some epithet indicative of their connexion with him. Among others they added the words, Kal or Gil, that is to say "man" or "servant of," as Thorkel or Thorgil the man or servant of Thor. We therefore venture to suggest, that not only is the term Gille, of Scandinavian origin, but that it was introduced into Ireland by the Scandinavian worshippers of Thor.⁴

Northern Archæologists assert that when Christianity was established in Scandinavia, the "godi in some degree renounced his Hof and built and endowed upon his demesne a Christian Church of which his

---

¹ "Gilli Bakrauf." Heimsk, vol. iii., p. 204.

² "Gilli enn gerzke," Laxdla Saga Hafniæ, 1816, p. 28.

³ Acta Sanct, Antw., 1746, vol. i. p. 280." St. Ægidio Abbate "vulgo St. Gilles." " In 940 Danish was still spoken by the Normans of Bayeux." Gibbon, Dec. and Fall, Lon. 1807, vol. 2, p. 230.

⁴ [In Cleasby and Vigfusson's Icelandic — English Dictionary, Thorgil is stated to be " the same as Thorketil (by contraction). " In poets of the 10th century the old uncontracted form was still used ; but the contracted form occurs in verses of the beginning of the 11th century, although the old form occurs now and then. The frequent use of these names, combinations of Ketil, is no doubt derived from the holy cauldron at sacrifices as is indicated by such names as Vekell (holy kettle). Compare Kettleby in Yorkshire." P. 337. 4to, Clarendon Press, Oxford, 1874.]

herred became the parish."[1] Over this (apart from the temple) he continued to exercise a civil jurisdiction, and we suppose that when the worship of Thor was abandoned in Ireland, Scandinavian chiefs renounced the name of the deity, to whom they and their hof had been dedicated, each chief building a Christian Church and dedicating it to a Christian saint, took the name of the patron saint,[2] affixing the same mark of devotions to his service, which had been added to the name of the pagans' object of worship.

And that the Gall Gaedhl (Irish who had become Pagans)[3] and Irish hereditary chiefs, who occupied, to some extent, the position of "godar" within the territories of the Ostmen, followed the example of their Scandinavian lords, and hence the names of Gilla Mocholmog, Gilla Colm, Gilla Chomghaill, &c. Nor can we doubt the readiness of Irish chiefs to adopt Scandinavian customs and Scandinavian names in the 10th century, as we find many of them called Magnus, Ragnal, Imar, &c.[4] The difference in the manner of using the term Gille in Scandinavia and in Ireland, arising from the construction of the languages, the Irish prefixing the patronymic mark which the Scandinavians affixed,—the "Mac" or "O" always preceding the Irish name, while the equivalent "Son" of the Northmen always followed, and hence when the Irish adopted the adjunct "Gille" it was placed

*Gille as an adjunct to Irish names.*

---

[1] Hibbert's Tings of Orkney, Archæologia Scotica, vol. iii., p. 153, 4to, Edinburgh, 1829.
[2] Ann. Four Mast., 984, Gilla Phadraig, son of Imar of Waterford. Taking a name was considered one of the strongest proofs of conversion.
[3] Three Fragments, p. 128.
[4] Book of Rights, J. O'Donovan, LL.D., Dublin, 1847, p. xli.

before the Saint's name in Ireland, the "Gil" having been placed after Thor's name in Scandinavia. This is exemplified in the life of Harold who succeeded his father, Magnus Barefeet, on the throne of Norway, for, when he landed from Ireland, where he was born, "he said his name was Gille Christ but his mother Thora (who accompanied him) said his other name was Harold,"[1] and hence Norwegian historians always call him "Harold Gille," the Gille which was prefixed to his name in Ireland being affixed to it in Norway.

*Gille first used as an Irish adjunct in Ostman districts,*

The suggestion may be strengthened by observing that the name "Gilla," as a religious adjunct, is first found in or adjoining the territories of the Ostmen, and at the period when the Ostmen began to be converted. In the Annals of the Four Masters the earliest notice of the name Gilla is A.D. 978, recording the death of "Conemhail, son of Gilla Arri, and the orator of Ath Cliath." The first notice of Gilla Mocholmog, chief of the O'Byrnes, in the southern district of Dublin, being A.D. 1044, and of Gilla Chomghaill, chief of the kindred sept of O'Tuathail (O'Toole), being A.D. 1041; nor can we trace anywhere, before the year 981, the name of Gill Colen,

*and not until the 10th century.*

who appears to have been the chief of the Scandinavian district of sea-coast north of Dublin.[2]

And this argument derived from the period and

---

[1] Heimsk. vol. iii., p. 280, "Gilli, Kristr." *Ibid,* " Saga af Magnusi Konongi Blinda oc Haralli Gilla."

[2] The earliest notices of the name Gilla in the Index Nominum of the Four Masters, are:—
979. Gilla son of Arrin died.
981. Gilla Caeimhghen, son of Dunlag, heir of Leinster.
982. Gilla Phadraigh, son of Imar, of Port Large (Waterford).
991. Gilla Chommain, son of the Lord of Ui Diarmada.

place, when and where, the name first appeared, may be enforced by the question, If the name Gilla were of Irish origin, why did it not appear among the Irish in the first instance, and appear at an earlier period, the Irish having been converted 500 years prior to the conversion of their invaders? Nor should it be unobserved, that although the term Gille is not found among the Irish until the tenth century, the nearly synonymous Irish term "Mael" was in use among both their clergy and laity as early as the sixth century,[1] and continued to be used long after the term Gille came into use in Ireland.[2]

Mael as an Irish religious affix used in 6th century.

The names Maelphadriag and Maelbrighde are of frequent occurrence. The name Maelbrighde, in particular, appears in A.D. 645,[3] and subsequently in almost every page of Irish history, having connected with it the remarkable circumstance (seemingly corroborative of our theory of the Scandinavian origin of the term Gille), that although the Gillephadraig, Gillechommain, &c., frequently occur, there is no early trace of the name Gillebrighde in the territories of the Ostmen; doubtless owing to the well-

---

993. Gilla Cele, son of Cearbhall, heir of Leinster.

995. Gilla Phadraigh, son of Dunchad, Lord of Ossraighe.

Gill-Colom is the name given to the chief of Clonlyffe, Ratheny, Kilbarrock, &c., in a grant of part of his lands made by Strongbow to Vivian de Curcy.—Register of All Hallows.

In the Pocock MSS., Brit. Mus., No. 4813, he is called Gill Moholmoe, a blind chief, who, with Maelseachlain, king of Meath, is said to have built St. Mary's-abbey, Dublin, on having his sight restored. The name is rendered more uncertain by finding Gill-Cacimhghin, son of the heir of Leinster, blinded in A.D. 981, the period when Maelseachlain was king of Meath.

[1] Ann. FourMast., A.D. 538—Tuathal Maelgarbh slain by Maelmor.

[2] Ibid.—Maelbrighde, bishop of Cill dara, died, 1042; Maelbrighde, son of Cathasach, fosoirchinneach of Ard Macha, died, A.D. 1070.

[3] Ann. Four Mast., A.D. 645.—Maelbrighde, son of Methinchlen.

known fact, that the Anglo-Saxon Church and its Scandinavian converts utterly ignored the Irish Virgin,[1] and other Irish saints.

*Division of Ireland into four Provinces.*

Having these details relating to the religion and laws of Iceland and Norway, it remains to support by facts the conjecture that the same laws and religion were introduced into Ireland, the settlers modifying their civil institutions from the peculiar circumstances of the country. For instance, notwithstanding the allegation of Irish historians, that Turgesius had absolute dominion over all Ireland, it is not likely that the Scandinavians could partition hostile Ireland in the manner in which they had divided Iceland; and that because Ireland, like Iceland, is divided into four districts, that division was Scandinavian.[2]

*Irish division was into Fifths.*

We know that it was not made by the Irish, for they divided Ireland into five cuige (or fifths), of which Meath was one.[3] We also know that the termination of the names of three of the provinces

---

[1] A St. Bridget was subsequently canonized for the Scandinavians, and the very curious "Revelationes St. Brigidæ, alias Brigettæ de Suetia," were printed at Nuremberg in 1521, and at Rome in 1556.

[2] "In Iceland, the whole land was politically divided into fiordungar or quarters, a division made A.D. 964, and existing to the present day. Thus Austfirdinga, Vestfirdinga, Nordlendinga, Sunnlendinga fiordungar; or East, West, North, and South quarters."— Icelandic-English Dictionary, by Cleasby and Vigfusson.

See also "The Story of Burnt Nial; or, Life in Iceland at the End of the Tenth Century." From the Icelandic Sagas, by George Webb Dasent. Introduction, p. lxi. 2 vols., 8vo, Edinb., 1861.

[3] Keating, Hist. Irel. (W. Haliday's Edition), Dublin, 1811, p. 123, says that Ireland was divided by the Irish into five fifths or provinces, Thomond, Desmond, Leinster, Ulster, and Conacht; but the later division was Munster, Leinster, Ulster, Connaught, and Meath.

is Norse, the Norse word "ster"[1] being added to the Irish name, as Mumha-ster or Munster, Ulad-ster or Ulster, and Leighin-ster or Leinster; and that Connaught had a similar termination, although it was not retained by the Anglo-Normans, the Scandinavian name being Kunnakster.

Nevertheless, it is much more likely that the division retained by the Anglo-Normans, and now used, was an ecclesiastical one, and that it originated with Pope Eugenius III., when he sent four "Palls" into Ireland in A.D. 1151. This Roman investiture was then a novelty to Irish archbishops, and had been first solicited in A.D. 1124, and subsequently in 1148,[2] by St. Malachy, whose preceptor Ivar[3] (probably connected with the Ostmen and Anglo-Saxon monks) had inculcated the opinions on which Gille, the Ostman bishop of Limerick, and first Papal legate in Ireland, was acting, and which, according to Dr. Lanigan, led Malachy, "instead of Irish practices to introduce Roman ones."[4]

When Malachy undertook his mission to Rome, Ireland was, ecclesiastically, divided into two Archdioceses—Armagh and Cashel, and for these only Malachy solicited Palls,[5] but after the death of

*The four Provinces from the four Palls sent from Rome A.D. 1151.*

---

[1] Stadr, locus. "The plural stadir is frequent in local names of the heathen age, as Haskieldsstadir, Aloreksstadir, &c. Landnamabok, *passim.* See also map of Iceland."—Cleasby and Vigfusson's Icelandic-English Dictionary.

[2] Lanigan, Ecc. Hist., vol. iv., pp. 111-129.

[3] Ibid, p. 60:—Ivar O'Hegan, who died on a pilgrimage to Rome, 13 August, 1134.

[4] Ibid, p. 87.

[5] St. Malachy also applied (to Pope Innocent II.) for the confirmation of the new Metropolitan see of Cashel," Lanigan Ecc., His., vol. iv., p. 112., although Cashel had been previously recognized by the Irish Church, *ibid* 37, and "many of the Irish were displeased at Palliums being intended for Dublin and Tuam." *Ibid*, p. 140.

BOOK II.
CHAP. VI.

Malachy, Pope Eugenius sent four instead of two, yet why he sent more than the two solicited, or why he divided Ireland into four archbishoprics instead of five (the number of the Irish divisions[1]) cannot be discovered. Nor can it be denied that if there had been any fourfold division by the Ostmen he might have known it, for when he sent Cardinal Paparo with these four Palls to Ireland, Nicholas Breakspeare, an English monk, was his Cardinal Legate in Norway, and in the same year brought the first Pall into that country, Breakspeare, assuming to know so much of the state of Ireland also, that in two years after, when he became Pope Adrian IV., he conferred the lordship of the Island on Henry II., in order to, as his bull states, "extirpate the vices which (had) there taken root,"[2] and to enlarge "the bounds of the church" of Rome, or as decreed at the synod held by the Pope's Legate at Cashel, that "all divine matters (might) be henceforth conducted agreeably to the practices of the

[1] "Thence also arose the long pre-eminence of the diocese of Meath. 'The Bishop of Meath,' says De Burgo, "is always first of the suffragans of the province of Armagh; for although he may be junior in consecration among the other bishops of Ireland, he has precedence of them." Hibernia Dominicana, p. 86. Also, "Diocese of Meath, Ancient and Modern," by the Rev. A. Cogan, vol. i., p. 2. Two vols., 12mo, Dub., 1862. The Rev. Dr. Moran, Bishop of Ossory, says, " As regards Meath, when the Archiepiscopal Palls were granted, there were five provinces in (the civil divisions of) Ireland—Meath being the fifth. The Palls, however, and consequent pre-eminence were accorded to four provinces only, an ordinary pre-eminence *inter pares*, in recognition of her former greatness, being the only privilege granted to Meath. This, however, has long since been abolished, and Meath now ranks according to seniority as all the other bishops." (Communicated to Sir Bernard Burke, C.B., Ulster King of Arms, A.D. 1874.)

[2] Pope Adrian's Bull, Littleton's Hen. II., vol. iv., p. 45.

holy church as observed by the Church of England,"[1] a decree, among others, so offensive, as disclosing the real cause of the invasion, that the synod is not even alluded to in the Annals of the Four Masters.

Rejecting then the idea of any general division of Ireland by the Scandinavians, can we discern the appearance of organization in their settlements on the eastern coast. Doubtless, it is there we find the only four " Fiords " marked on the map of Ireland—Wexford and Waterford on the south of Dublin, and Carlingford and Strangford on the north, Dublin being the chief settlement, as it was when Wexford and Waterford, Cork and Limerick were the settlements occupied. It is also true that the names of these four inlets of the sea are wholly Scandinavian, and that the Northmen who occupied them sometimes acted in concert, supplying ships and men as "Shiprathes" might have been required to do, and uniting these ships into one fleet and invading England, Scotland, and Wales under one king or military chief.[2]

Nevertheless, we think, that it is only in the Ostman territory around Dublin we should seek for analogy to the government of Norway and Scotland.

We do not refer to the adjoining district called

*The four Fiords.*

*The Dyfflinars-kiri.*

---

[1] Lanigan Ecc. Hist., vol. iv., p. 207.—Dowling's Annals, Arch. Soc., Dub., 1849, p. 12, has it, "That the Church of Ireland is to observe uniformity with the Church of England according to the rites and ceremonies, &c., of the Church of Salisbury."

[2] In the " Saga af Olafi Hinon Helga," cap. lxxxvii., p. 117., we find the name of another Fiord, at which a battle was fought, but there is no record of any settlement, nor was the position of it known until Dr. Reeves (Down and Connor, p. 265) showed that, " Ulfricksfiord " was a name for Larne Lough. The Irish name

BOOK II.
CHAP. VI.

Fingal, or to the district of Ostmantown, which was like "the cantred of the Ostmen" at Limerick,[1] "the cantred of the Ostmen" at Cork,[2] and "the cantred of the Ostmen" at Waterford,[3] but to the more extensive territory frequently mentioned in the Sagas under the name of "the Dyflinarskiri,"[4] from Dyflin the Scandinavian name of the city.

Bounds of the Dyflinarskiri.

The boundaries of this territory are not defined, but occupying the central position between the four fiords the Dyflinarskiri extended from Arklow on the south to the small river Delvin, above Skerries on the north, and conformable with the Norwegian law extended inwards along the Liffey "as far as the salmon swims up the stream," that is to the Salmon Leap at Leixlip, the name "Laxlöb," or (Salmon Leap) being purely Scandinavian, and most of the names of places along the coast as Skerries, Holmpatric, Hofud (now Howth), Blowick (now Bullock), Bre, Wicklow (the Wikinglo of our old records),

of Wexford is Loch Garman, of Waterford Loch Dachaech, of Carlingford Snamh Eidhneach, and of Strangford Loch Cuan. The Anglo Normans, in almost all cases, adopted the Scandinavian instead of the Irish names of places.

[But this termination "ford" must not be confounded with "fiordanger," or fourths. It is from flordr. "Fiordr," say Cleasby and Vigfusson, "is a frith, or bay, while a small crescent formed inlet, or creek, is called Vik, and is less than fiordr. Hence the saying 'let there be a frith (flordr) between kinsmen, but a creek (Vik) between friends,' denoting that kinship is not always so trusty as friendship." —Icelandic-English Dictionary.]

[1] Rot. Chart. Turr. Lond., 2 John, m. 15.
[2] Littleton's Hen II., Dub., 1768, vol. iv., p. 408.
[3] Davys (Sir John), Hist. Relat. Dub., 1733, p. 60.
[4] Island. Landnamabok, Hafniæ, 1774, p. 106, calls it Dyflinarskidi, and it is so called in Egils Saga, Hafniæ, 1809, p. 15, but in the "Saga-Magnusar Konongs-ins-Berefœtta, Heimsk., vol. iii., p. 226, and most of the other Sagas, it is called Dyflinarskiri, the Danish being "Dublins Herret."

Arklow, &c., &c., and all the names of islands and headlands evincing a Scandinavian origin.¹

*Admiralty of Dublin and Dyfflinarskiri had the same bounds.*

But these limits are chiefly assigned to the Dyfflinarskiri from other circumstances connected with them. In the first place, we find that the specified extent of the sea coast became the maritime jurisdiction of the mayors of Dublin. We are unable to trace the origin of this jurisdiction or to ascertain why it was defined by these limits, unless by supposing that it had previously belonged to the Ostmen.

It is not alluded to in the early charters of the city, and could not have been exercised before the thirteenth century, owing to the power and hostility of the Irish; but, in 1332, we find Sir Anthony Lucy, and a party of the citizens taking possession of the castle of Arklow; and in 1375, a grant made to the city of the customs of all ports between "le Skerry and Alercornshed, otherwise Arklow;"² other records showing that it was an ancient duty of one of the sheriffs, accompanied by two citizen merchants, to ride to all the creeks and inlets, and take cognizance of all offences along this line of coast.³ This extent of maritime jurisdiction was also recognised

---

¹ The Irish name of Dalkey is Delg Inis; of Ireland's Eye, Inis Erin; of Lambay, Inis Rechra, the Norse "ey" being used instead of the Irish word "Inis" for island. The Irish name of Wicklow is Cill Martin, and of Arklow, Inbher Mor, the Norse termination (Lue a flame, a blaze) being from the use of these headlands for beacon fires, which every district like the Dyfflinarskiri was required to maintain.—Landvarnar Bolkr., cap. iv., Leges Gulathingenses Havniæ, 1817, p. 85.

² Lett. Pat 49 Ed. III, Chart. Dub. MS.

³ Municipal Records, 3 Eliz., A.D. 1561.

BOOK II.
CHAP. VI.

by a charter, granted by Queen Elizabeth, to the citizens in 1582, when they petitioned for "authority to exercise the rights of Admyral within (their) streams, as far as (they) recyve custom."[1] The charter constituted the mayor, &c., "Admiral between Arklow and Nannie water," the boundary river below Skerries;[2] and Edward II, apparently referred to some such district when commanding the mayor, &c., in A.D. 1324, "to make ready all ships in the port and liberties of Dublin," for the war in which he was then engaged with France, and "to arrest all the ships and goods of the men of the king of France within the bailwick aforesaid."[3]

Bounds of the diocese of Dublin and Glendalough same as the Dyfflinarskiri.

We find that the boundaries of the united diocese of Dublin and Glendalough, are the same as those here assigned to the Dyflinarskiri. Originally ecclesiastical jurisdiction was concurrent with that of the civil ruler. We have seen that the Scandinavian chief was both priest and king; in this case, however, we find two bishops in the one territory. This originated in the decrees of the Irish Synod of Rath Breasail, by which dioceses were defined, in A.D. 1110. For the Ostman bishops, not being consecrated as Irish bishops were, but consecrated according to the Roman ritual by the archbishops of Canterbury or York, the Irish clergy refused to recognize their authority, and part of this Ostman territory being inhabited by Irish Christians, the synod decreed that the whole should be placed under

---

[1] Brit. Mus. Cotton MSS., Vesp. F. XII., fo. 107.

[2] Charter 24 Jan., 1582, the 24th Eliz. The Irish name of the Nannie water was Inbher Ainge.

[3] Rot. Claus 18. Edw. II., m. 10, in Canc. Hib.

the Irish bishop of Glendalough; the Ostman bishopric of Dublin not being even named, and when subsequently mentioned, only mentioned as being in the diocese of Glendalough.

*Origin of two bishoprics in the district of Dublin.*

The diocese remained until A.D. 1151 in this state, when it was certified to Pope Innocent III., that "Master John Papiron, the legate of the Roman church, coming into Ireland, found a bishop dwelling in Dublin, who at that time exercised his episcopal office within the walls. He found *in the same diocese* another church in the mountains, which likewise had the name of a city, and had a certain Chorepiscopus." But the legate delivered the Pall to Dublin, "which was the best city," and doubtless, also, because its bishop was already in connexion with Rome. "And he appointed that *that diocese in which both cities were*, should be divided; that one part thereof should fall to the metropolis." "And this he would have immediately carried into execution, had he not been obstructed by the insolence of the Irish, who were then powerful in that part of the country," and who denied the authority of the Roman legate.[1]

It is also to be observed that the ecclesiastical jurisdiction of the united bishoprics still extends from beyond Arklow, along the sea shore, to the Delvin rivulet, a little south of the Nanny water, and inwards along the Liffey, to the "Salmon Leap," at Leixlip. The church, "De Saltû Salmonis," being its limit in that direction.

That this ecclesiastical jurisdiction has been made

[1] Harris's Ware, Vol. I., pp. 376, 377. 'Bishops of Glendalough.'

concurrent with that of the civil ruler is confirmed by finding that all grants of land made by the Ostmen and subsequently by the Anglo-Normans, of land "which was of the Ostmen," were within the diocese ; nor do we find any possessions of the Ostmen outside its boundary.

The residence which Aulaf had at Clondalkin in A.D. 866, and Sitric's town and lands of Baldoyle, Portrane, and Ratheny, in 1038, were all within it. So was the territory "from Ath Cliath to Ath Truisten,[1] which Donnchad, king of Ireland, and Muircheartach spoiled and plundered, A.D. 936, as being "all under the dominion of the foreigners of Ath Cliath." So, likewise, was Swords, Luske, and all the country of Fingal,[2] which we find in the possession of the Northmen, in A.D. 1035 ; and in 1135, devastated by the king of Meath, to revenge his brother, "killed by Donnough Mac Gill mo cholmoc, and the Danes of Dublin."[3]

---

[1] "*i.e.* from Dublin to Ath Truisten, a ford of the river Griece, near the hill of Mullaghmast, in the south of the county of Kildare." Ann. Four Masters, Vol. II., p. 635, n.

[2] A.D. 1052, a predatory excursion into Finn Gall, by the son of Mael na mbo, and they burned the country from Ath Cliath to Albene. Reeves' Life of St. Columba, p. 108, fixes the Delvin Rivulet (Irish Albene) as the boundary of Fingal.

[3] Ann. Clomac A.D. 1135.

END OF BOOK SECOND.

# BOOK III.

## THE SCANDINAVIAN ANTIQUITIES OF DUBLIN.

## CHAPTER I.

### OF THE STEIN OF DUBLIN.

Bounds of the Stein.—Priory of All Hallowes, founded on the Stein.—Neck of land at the Stein formed by the confluence of the Liffey and the Dodder.—The favourite landing-place of the Northmen of Dublin.—Bridge and mill of the Stein.—Long Stone of the Stein.—Site of the Long Stone.—The Stein (or Stain) named from this Stone.—References to the Long Stone in city leases.—Scandinavian tombs on the Stein.

If the preceding statements do not show that the laws[1] and religion of Norway governed the Northmen of Ireland, they may be found a desirable introduction to the following description of hitherto unnoticed monuments, which monuments in themselves are evidence of the social position of the Ostmen of Dublin, and of the civil and religious institutions which prevailed among them.

Fortunately, in describing these monuments, we have not to encounter difficulties which elsewhere impede the identification of Scandinavian remains. In Ireland there is no admixture of Roman and Saxon earthworks, nor are we embarrassed by the greater obstacles which the affinity of Danish and Saxon customs and language present to the identification of Danish monuments and names of places in England.

It is now acknowledged that the charter of Edgar (A.D. 964), on which alone rests the claim of Anglo-

*Charter of Edgar (A.D. 964) spurious.*

---

[1] Mr. Haliday meditated a chapter on the Laws of the Northmen, but had scarcely commenced it.

BOOK III.
CHAP I.

Saxon conquest of the greater part of Ireland, "cum suâ nobilissimâ civitate Dubliniâ,"[1] is one of those forgeries by which Anglo-Saxon monks not unfrequently sought to obtain, or retain, possession of lands which they coveted for their monasteries; and as regards language, we have the authority of the sagas for stating that, although the Northmen could communicate with the Saxons in England, the language of the Irish was so wholly dissimilar that they could only trade in Ireland through an interpreter.[2] This absence of Saxon monuments, and of the Saxon language, are facts of much importance to the elucidation of our antiquities, and should be held in recollection throughout the following statement.

The Stein.

Our oldest Anglo-Norman records frequently refer to an extra mural district, east of Dublin, denominated "The Stein," or "Staine," a flat piece of ground extending southwards from the strand of

---

[1] Tyrrell's Hist. of England, vol. i., p. 12, Folio, Lond. 1698. Chartœ Anglo-Saxonicœ, Codex Diplomaticus Ævi Saxonici, J. M. Kemble, 4 Vols., London, 1839-1848. (It is marked by Kemble as spurious).

[2] When Olaf, who was born in Iceland, was embarking for Ireland to visit his grandfather, Miarkiartan, King of Ireland, his mother, Melkorka, thus addressed him:— "I have brought you up," she said, "with the greatest care at home, and have taught you Irish to be of use to you wherever you land." Laxdœla Saga, 73, 74, et sequ, 4to,

Hafniœ, 1826. On reaching the coast two men approaching the ship in a boat called out, "Who is in command of this ship?" Olaf answered in Irish, "Norwegians." The Irish thereupon claimed the ship. But Olaf said, "That might be if there was no interpreter with the merchants." Ibid. See also "Commentary of Paul Vidalin, Jurist of Iceland, concerning the Danish Language translated out of Icelandic into Latin. Appendix to Gunlaugi Saga, pp. 259, 260, 4to, Hafniœ, 1775.

the Liffey to "the lands of Rath," and eastward, from near the city walls, to the river Dodder.[1]

BOOK III.
CHAP. I.

It was on this plain the priory of All Hallowes and other religious establishments were founded before the arrival of Strongbow,[2] whose followers took possession of all that the Church could not claim. About the year 1200, Theobald Walter, pincerna (or butler) to Henry II., and ancestor of the Butlers of Ormond, exercised ownership by granting to Radulf and Richard Clut "all his land of Stayn, except what the canons of All Saints ought to have."[3]

All Hallowes stood on the Steyne.

From these tenants a portion of it soon reverted to the Butler family, as, about the year 1223, the

Grants of parts of the Steyne.

---

[1] This word seems formerly to have been pronounced stain, stane, the Scotch for stone. Thus in 17th & 18th Chas. II., chap. 7 (Irish Statutes), 1665, "Whereas the parishioners of St. Andrew's and of Lazers alias Lazie Hill have no place of worship, St. Andrew's Church being long ruinous, be it enacted that the ambit and tract of ground commonly called The Stane alias Lazars alias Lazie Hill be made part of the parish of St. Andrew.

[2] In 1607 Sir John Carroll petitioned the city for a grant of so much land as is overflown by the sea between the point of land that joineth the Staine near the College and the Ringsend, and reacheth southward to the land of Bagot Rath. Granted. But petitioner not to erect any building for habitation on the premises, and that the land shall not extend but to the Dodder water on the east. Acts of Assembly, Easter 1607, Memo. 13, Corporation Records.

[3] The Charter of Henry II. confirms to the Church of All Hallows at the east of Dublin, and to the canons serving God there, all their lands with their tithes and ancient boundaries and their other free customs, as fully and freely as Dermot, King of Leinster, gave the said lands to the said Church before his, King Henry's, arrival in Ireland. Confirmation and Inspeximus of King Edward I., A.D., 1290, in which this charter is set forth. Registrum Prioratûs Omnium Sanctorum juxta Dublin. By Rev. Richard Butler, M.R.I.A., p. 12, 4to, Dublin, 1845, Irish Archæological Society. See this charter in Historic and Municipal Documents of Ireland, A.D., 1172-1320, edited by J. T. Gilbert, F.S.A., p. 206, n. i., 8vo, Dublin, 1870.

L

second Theobald Walter granted to the priory of All Saints the whole of the tithes, together with that part of his land of Stein which was near the said Church;[1] a patent of Henry IV., also, reciting that James Bottiler, Earl of Ormond, then granted the pasture called the Stein, near Dublin, to Robert Lughteburgh for life, the said pasture being held of the king in cápite.[2] At a later period, a portion of the Stein must have belonged to St. Mary's Abbey, James I. having granted it, among other possessions of the suppressed monastery, to William Taaffe;[3] but forty acres of the Stein, which lay on the south side of the road, now called Townsend-street, remained in the king's hands in 1626, and in 1659

[1] By this charter Theobald Walter gives to the Church of All Hallowes "a certain part of my land of Stein lying to the east of the said church, containing two acres and a half, together with the tithes and issues of the whole of the Stein." Inspeximus of King Edward III., A.D. 1349. Registry of All Hallows, by Rev. Richard Butler, p. 16. These two acres and a half got the name of the "Little Steyn"; the rest was called the "Great Steyn." A lease to Giles Allen, made Easter Assembly, A.D. 1572, refers to "the Little Steyn part of the possessions of All Hallowes." Corporation Records. A decree of John Allen, Judge of the Metropolitan Court of Dublin, concerning tithes of the Steyn, speaks of "the Great Steyn." Registry of All Hallowes, by Rev. Richard Butler, p. 82.

[2] Patent Rolls of Chancery, 26th of July, 4th Henry the IV. Record Commission Publication, folio, Dublin, 1826, p. 171.

[3] Grant to W. Taaffe of a field called the Staine, part of the possessions of the House of the B.V.M., near Dublin, demised 1st March, 17th Elizabeth (A.D. 1575), to Thomas, Earl of Ormond and Ossory, for sixty years, at 20s. (within the franchises of the city of Dublin), 20th January, 1° Jas. I., Art. ix., Callendar of Patent Rolls, Jas. I. Record Commission Publication, folio, p. 2.

These forty acres "of land, called Stayne," had been held by Abbey of St. Mary's from the City of Dublin, at the annual rent of 44 shillings, and were taken by the Crown at the dissolving of religious houses. Inquis. 32nd Hen. VIII. See MS. additions, &c., Archdale's Monasticon in Royal Irish Academy.

were held by Dowcra, Brooke, and others as heirs to Lord Dowcra.¹

*{BOOK III. CHAP. I.}*

We further find that the Decrees of Innocence in 1663 adjudged to Lord Dungan, of Clane, nineteen acres of ground " commonly called Staine, being upon the strand side of the College ;" for previously to 1607 the whole of the north side of the Townsend-street, now covered with streets and quays, was the tidal strand of the Liffey, and, as such, was granted in that year to Sir William Carroll, under the description of " the strand overflown by the sea between the point of land joining the Staine, near the College, and Ringsend ;"² and by him this strand was partly reclaimed.

*{The taking in of the strand adjoining the Steyne.}*

Another portion was taken in in 1663, when Mr. Hawkins built a great wall, carrying the shore further towards the centre of the river.³

*{Hawkins' great wall.}*

The embankments raised by Sir William Carroll, Mr. Hawkins, and Sir John Rogerson, together with subsequent encroachments on the strand of the river, have so greatly altered the outline of the

---

¹ Inquis. Lageniæ, 20 Car. I. Com. Civit., Dublin. Record Commission Publication, folio, Dublin, 1826, and Registry of All Hallows, p. 107. Acts of Assembly, Midsummer, 1659. Corporation Records.

² Acts of Assembly, Easter, A.D. 1607, memb. 13, Corporation Records.

³ [" July, 1663. This year and the precedent year the great wall was built to gain in the ground from the River Liffey, near the Long Stone, on the east side of the city of Dublin, by Mr. Hawkins."

Brief occurrences touching Ireland, began 25th March, 1661, Carte Papers, Bodleian Library, vol. 64, p. 446.] The city, on 16th April, 1708, demise to Thomas Singleton, all that ferry over the river Anna Liffey, at Hawkins's wall, near Aston's quay; from the said Hawkins's wall to the new slip near the watch tower on the north side of the said river, and from thence [back again] to the said Hawkins's wall. Register of City Leases "Ancient Revenue." City Records.]

Stein on the north side, that, without reference to maps, it is impossible to convey an accurate idea of its state previously to the seventeenth century; but the point of land here referred to may be described as an elevated ridge near the confluence of the Liffey and Dodder, forming what the Scandinavians termed a "Nœs," or "neck of land between two streams," and was the place where the Dublin Northmen generally landed.

*Lazers'-hill on the Steyne.*

On this elevated ridge, about the year 1220, an hospital is said to have been founded for pilgrims intending to embark for the shrine of St. James of Compostella, the patron saint of lepers, and from which the termination of Townsend-street received the name of Lazar's-hill. Pope Innocent III., when confirming the union of Glendalough with the See of Dublin, enjoined an appropriation of revenues to the support of an hospital, and Archbishop De Loundres, therefore, with the assent of the chapters of the Holy Trinity and St. Patrick's, assigned the lands of Killmohghenoc and other lands, with the church of Delgany, &c., to maintain this hospital "on the sea shore outside Dublin, called Steyn, where pilgrims to St. James' shrine awaited an opportunity to embark,"[1] Theobald Fitzwalter granting two acres of "his land of Stein" as a further endowment. But if this hospital were ever built no remains of it can now be discovered, the Lepers' hospital of Dublin, which was dedicated to

[1] There were to be ten chaplains to perform Divine service and superintend the household; they and the brethern to wear black cloaks with a white cross on the breast. "Chartæ, Privilegia et Immunitates," p. 18. Record Commission Publication, folio, [about 1826].

St. Stephen, having been built on another part of the Stein, between Stephen's-street and Stephen's-green.

*BOOK III. CHAP. I.*

The point of the Stein, however, long continued to be used for landing and embarking passengers, and for purposes of trade, the Memoranda Rolls of Henry IV. mentioning, "the Stayne and Dodyr," with "the key of Dublin," as places from whence merchandise was exported.

*The port of Steyne.*

But the Northmen had a peculiar object in selecting their landing place. Their ships were long and shallow, lightly built, and for the greater part without decks. These they ran ashore, when about to land, and in winter drew them up the beach, there to remain until summer enabled them " to keep the sea." The bank of a river, a flat sandy strand, such as the north side of Stein presented, was, consequently, best adapted for their purposes, and at all times was preferred to a deep-water anchorage.[1]

On the west side of this landing place was a creek, the mouth of a little river which there entered the Liffey. This was the river of the Stein, and on it was built the mill of the Priory of All Hallows. The mill was of early date as we have on record a grant made to the Prior in 1298 of "four large oaks from

*The river and bridge of the Steyne.*

---

[1] It is to this landing place that the old Norman French poem "The Conquest of Ireland" refers, when relating that Hasculf Mac Torkil having returned to Dublin with his "Berseiker," or furious champion (called in the Ulster Annals "John of the Orkney's):—

"A Stein crent arivé
Hescul et Johan le Devé."

They there left their ships to combat Milo de Cogan who had treacherously taken the City during a truce. Anglo-Norman poem on the Conquest of Ireland by Henry II. Edited by Francisque Michel, p. 108, 12mo, London, 1837.

BOOK III.
CHAP. I.

The Mill of the Steyne.

the king's forest of Glencree to repair his mill and bridge of Stein,"[1] and a grant which I have found, and to which I must refer for another purpose, also very clearly fixes the position of the mill.

This grant made in 1461 when the mill was rebuilt recites that, "Whereas the Prior and Convent of All Saints besydes Dyvelin of old times had a mill near the gate between the Green bank and the Long Stone on the Stayne, it is granted that they have it lyke as they had it of old time, provided that the said mill be made within a year next following the Act made, and that all men go over into the Stayne dry on the said war (weir) of the mill without any let or other impediment."[2] The mill stream which is marked on Speed's map as of considerable extent in 1610, but is now greatly diminished, runs in a covered sewer in front of Trinity College, and until flood-gates were affixed at its entrance into the Liffey the tide flowed as far as Grafton-street, where, not many years since, a female servant was drowned in the basement story of a house, the water having burst up during a flood in the river, and more recently, in preparing to build at this part of College-green, a high tide flooded the foundations which were with difficulty cleared. But the original importance of the rivulet is shown in the statement of Lodge that, in A.D. 1394, William Fitzwilliams, the sheriff of the county, had custody of the Staine near Dublin, in order to

[1] Placita Parliamentaria, 27th of Edward I. Records of Birmingham Tower. Sir William Betham's Origin and Hist. of the Constitution, and Early Parliaments of Ireland, p. 272, 8vo, Dublin, 1834.

[2] Acts of Assembly. City Records.

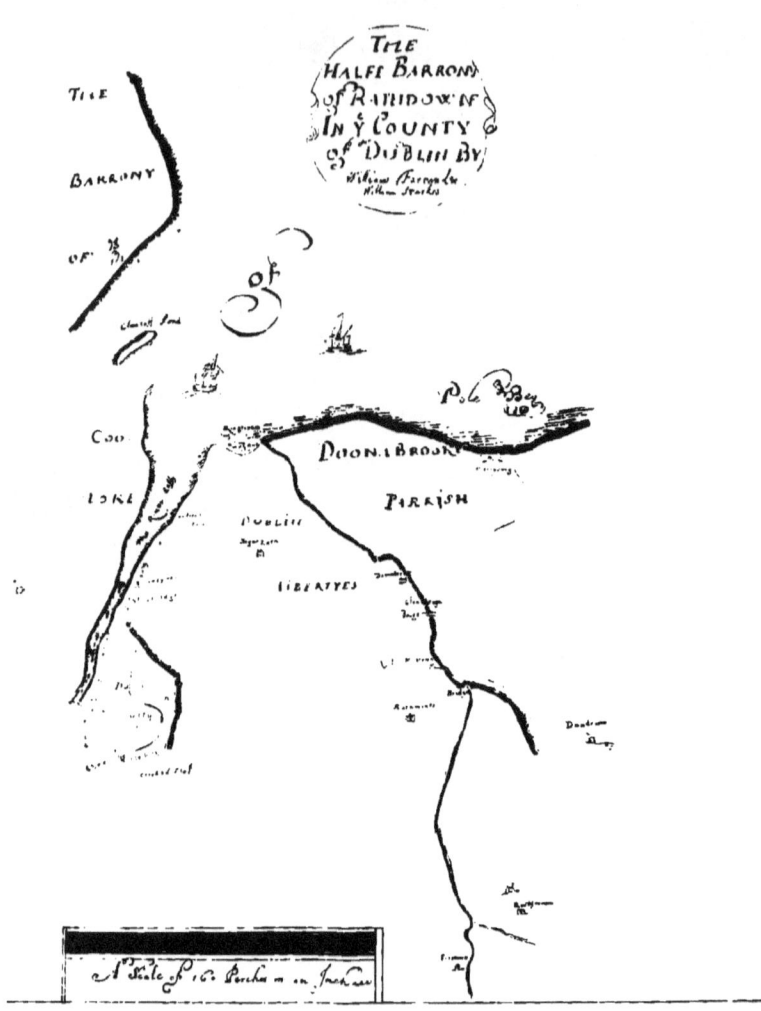

FROM
The Down Survey made A.D. 1654.

preserve the watercourse free and clean, "for the benefit of the City."¹ These minute references to the Stein and its possessors, become necessary to show, that anciently it was a well-known place of considerable extent although not even the name is now to be found on any of our maps, or any reference to it in any modern history of the city.

But the document referring to the mill of the Stein points to another fact more intimately connected with our subject. It was from the "Long Stone," mentioned in this record, that the Stein derived its Scandinavian name. This remarkable pillar stone stood not far from the landing place near where Hawkins-street and Townsend-street now join. From the rough outline drawing which I possess it does not appear that the stone was in any manner inscribed, but it appears to have stood about twelve or fourteen feet above ground,² and it remained standing until the surrounding district was laid out for streets and houses when it was overturned to make room for them. That it continued to be an object of some interest, long after the Northmen were expelled from Dublin, we find from municipal records and from reference to it when the citizens began to build on the adjoining strand. We have a lease made by the City in 1607 to James Wheeler, Dean of Christ Church, of "void ground at the Long Stone of the

*The Long Stone of the Steyne.*

---

[1] Peerage of Ireland by John Lodge, vol. iv., p. 307, 8vo, Dublin, 1789.

[2] This sketch has not been found among Mr. Haliday's papers, but on the annexed fac-simile of a portion of Petty's Down Survey of the Half Barony of Rathdown (made about A.D. 1655), may be observed what is plainly meant to represent the Long Stone at the point above assigned for it.

**BOOK III.
CHAP. I.**

Stein,"¹ another in 1641 to William Kirtly, of "a small plot near the Long Stone of the Stein,"² again in 1679 to William Christian of ground at Lazers Hill, "near the Long Stone of the Stein,"² and from the Earl of Anglesey of "a parcel of the strand at the Long Stone of the Stein over against the College."³

*Scandinavian origin of the Long Stone.*

The name of "the Stein" connected with the pillar stone may not be considered sufficient evidence of Scandinavian origin, that name not being found in Irish manuscripts, or in any record earlier than the Anglo-Norman invasion. But it should be recollected that there are no Hiberno-Danish writings extant, and that the Irish who called it "the Green of Ath Cliath," and allude to it as a place of council,⁴ never used the Scandinavian name for it, or for any part of Ireland, while on the contrary the Anglo-Norman monks, the charter writers of their countrymen, rarely, if ever, used an Irish name when any other existed, and invariably called the city, and even the provinces by their Scandinavian names.

As we proceed, however, to the other monuments

---

¹ Acts of Assembly. Corporation Records.

² *Ibid.*

³ Acts of Assembly. Easter, 1602. *Ibid.*

⁴ " Brian was then on the plain of Ath Cliath in council with the nobles of the Dál Cais (Wars of the Gaedhil with the Gaill, chap. lxxxviii., p. 155), and again "After this the men of Mumhan and of Connacht came to the Green of Ath Cliath and made a siege and blockade round Ath Cliath." *Ibid*, chap. lxxxvi., p. 151. [Mr. Haliday cites "Book of Danish Wars, MS. T.C.D.," and obtained this information no doubt from his friend the Rev. Dr. Todd, then editing this MS., published only in 1867 after Mr. H.'s death. It is only right to say that the latter passage in full is "and he (Brian) came to Cill-Maighnenn (Kilmainham) to the Green of Ath Cliath." Mr. H. had never seen this.]

on the Stein, it will be perceived that such evidence of Scandinavian origin is not indispensable.

Of these monuments the tumuli are the first to claim attention.

In 1646 an attempt was made to fortify Dublin by earthworks, at which Carte says the Marchioness of Ormonde and other noble ladies "condescended to carry baskets of earth." To procure this earth they levelled one of the tumuli on the Stein, of which there is an engraving in Molyneux's Discourse on Danish Mounds in Ireland,[1] and another with the following description which we copy from Ware's Antiquities.

"In November, 1646, as people were employed in removing a little hill in the East Suburbs of Dublin, in order to form a line of fortification, there was discovered an ancient sepulchre, placed S.W. and N.E., composed of eight black marble stones, of which two made the covering, and was supported by the others. The length of this monument was six feet two inches, the breadth three feet one inch, and the thickness of the stone three inches. At each corner of it was erected a stone, four feet high, and near it, at the S.W. end, another stone was placed in the form of a pyramid, six feet high, of a rustic work, and of that kind of stone which is called a millstone. The engraving given is a draught of the monument taken before it was demolished. Vast quantities of burnt coals, ashes, and human bones, some of which were in part burned, and some only scorched were found in it,

[1] Discourse concerning Danish Mounds, &c., in Ireland: 4to, Dublin, 1725.

which was looked upon to be a work of the Ostmen, and erected by that people, while they were heathens, in memory of some petty prince or nobleman."[1]

*The Long Stone perhaps marks the sepulchre of King Ivar, A.D. 872.*

This so closely resembles descriptions given of the burial places of Scandinavian kings[2] as to leave little doubt that it was the tumulus of some distinguished Northman, and we might almost venture to identify him if we could rely on the statements of northern historians, that Ivar, the son of Regnar Lodbrok, who reigned and died in Dublin A.D. 872, had ordered his body to be buried at the landing place, and that his orders were executed, and a mound so reared on the spot.[3] But without entering into the question of identity it may be observed that the custom of burying near the landing place prevailed among the Northmen, the greater number of their tumuli being found on the sea shore or in places commanding a view of the ocean, and that several Danish or Norwegian kings were slain in the neighbourhood of Dublin to whom sepulchral mounds had doubtless been raised. Of these tumuli we have not any description, but we find traces of them in late discoveries.

---

[1] Works of Sir James Ware, by Walter Harris, vol. ii., p. 145, folio, Dublin, 1745.

[2] Odin established a law that for men of consequence a mound should be erected to their memory; and for all warriors who had been distinguished for manhood, a standing stone, which custom remained long after Odin's time. Ynlinga Saga, cap. viii.

[3] There is some difference between the Nordymra sive Historia rerum in Northumbriæ a Danis Norvegisque sæculis ix°., x°., pp. 8, and 29 Grimr. Johnson Thorkelin, 4to, London, 1788, and the Fragmenta Islandica De Regibus Danicis, Norvegicis, &c. Langebek, vol. ii., p. 281.

In Suffolk-street, formerly part of the Stein, a skeleton was recently exhumed, the skull of which being stained by contact with metal supposed to be a helmet, gave rise to the opinion that the owner had been buried in his armour. In the same locality an urn was subsequently found, and previously they had dug up one of the most valuable Danish swords discovered in Ireland, the gold ornaments of the handle having been sold for £70 ; and, according to the Saga, a gold hilted sword[1] was a distinguishing mark of a Scandinavian chieftain, and a chieftain's arms and armour being frequently buried with him.[2] In excavating the foundations of the Royal Arcade, in College-green, where the National Bank of Ireland now stands, several weapons and other relics of the Northmen were thrown up. Two of the swords, which are of iron, and of a form marking them to be Scandinavian, are now in the museum of the Royal Irish Academy, and two spear heads, the rembo of a shield, and some silver fibulæ, said to have been found in the same place, were sold in 1841 with the late Major Sirr's collection of antiquities.

*Scandinavian swords dug up in Suffolk-street, part of the Steyne.*

---

[1] "Kvernlstr," the sword of Hakon, king of Norway, had both hilt and handle of gold. Heimskringla of Snorro-Sturleson, vol. i., p. 121, 3 vols., folio, Havniæ, 1777–1826. "Hneitn," the sword of King Olaf the Saint, had the handle wrought with gold. *Ibid*, vol. ii., p. 352. Olaf's sword was gold hilted. Laxdœla Saga, p. 79.

[2] In the Icelandic Dictionary, lately published, Haugr (pronounced Hogue), is translated a how, a mound, a cairn over one dead. It is there said "The cairns belong to the burning age as well as to the later age, when the dead were placed in a ship and put in the how with a horse, hound, treasure, weapons, and the like," and in proof various references to works are there given. Icelandic and English Dictionary, by Cleasby Vigfusson, 4to, Oxford, Clarendon Press, 1874.

# BOOK III.
## CHAPTER II.

### OF THE THINGMOUNT OF DUBLIN.

The monuments of the Stein shown to be Scandinavian.—Custom of the Northmen to set up a Stone at their first landing place.—And to erect temples to Thor and Freija adjacent.—Also a Thingmount or place of public meeting and judicature.—The Thingmount of Dublin erected on the Stein.—Remained till A.D., 1682.—Account of its removal.—Church of St. Andrew Thengmotha. –Built probably on the site of a Temple of Thor or Freija.—Meeting of King Henry the 2nd with Irish princes on the Stein near the Church of St. Andrew.—Understood probably by the Irish as either a Thing-mote or a Festival meeting.—Not as a submission or surrender of independence.—Hoges.—Hoge-Tings.—" Hoggen Green," " Hogen butts," and " St. Mary del Hogges," all called from this adjacent Hoge or Tingmount.

*Thingwall mount and Pillar Stones in Isle of Man.*

THE Isle of Man retains many relics of the Northmen. We find the Thingwall mount with its "doomsters," or "lagmen." On the sea-shore at Dalby-point is a large tumulus said to be that of a king of the Island, and on other parts of the sea-shore other tumuli. Near Kirk Stanton is a pillar stone above ten feet high. Two more near Mount Murray, and two more at the landing place on the sea-shore near Port Erin. Others stand in various parts of the island, some having Runic inscriptions, undoubted memorials of the Northmen. But the Orkneys being longer subject to Norway and comparatively uncultivated and thinly peopled, their Scandinavian monuments remain much more distinct, and comparing their monument with those of the Stein, and referring to the topography and name of the place where they are found, we have all the evidence we could require to prove that both were works of the same people, and that people, Scandinavian.

The publications of Wallace, Brand,[1] Barry,[2] and Hibbert inform us that in Romona, the chief island of the Orkneys,[3] there is a parish called Steinnis[4] bordering a lake of the same name into which the sea flows from Steinness. On a point of land jutting into this lake is a pillar Stone standing nearly sixteen feet above ground,[5] from which stone the district attained the name of Steinness, compounded of the Icelandic or old Norse words Steinn a stone, and "ness" a tongue (or nose[6]) of land.

This pillar, probably a stone of memorial, or mark of possession taken by the first settlers, was, according to Hibbert, a stone raised to Thor the Scandinavian Deity, the custom of these Northmen being to set up a Stone, and to erect temples to Thor and Freyja at their landing place.[7] Olaus Magnus, however, mentions another purpose, thus, he says, there are high stones without writing, set up by the industry of the ancients to inform mariners that they may avoid shipwreck,[8] and we find that the custom of placing pillar stones at the landing place, for whatever object or design was not peculiar to the

[1] A new description of Orkney, Zetland, Pightland firth, and Caithness, by John Brand, Edinburgh, 1700, 8vo.
[2] History of the Orkney Islands, by the Rev. George Barry, D.D., Minister of Shapinshay, 4to, Edinburgh, 1805.
[3] Heimskringla edr Noregs Koninga Saga, vol. ii., p. 147, Hafniæ, 1777. In Nial's Saga it is called Rossy. pp. 267-587.
[4] In the Sagas called "Steinsnessi."
[5] Memoir on the Tings of Orkney and Shetland, by S. Hibbert, M.D., Archæologia Scotica, vol. iii., p. 118, Edinburgh, 1828.
[6] Icelandic and English Dictionary, by R. Cleasby and Gudbrand Vigfusson, M.A., 4to, Oxford, Clarendon Press, 1874.
[7] Description of the Shetland Isles, by Samuel Hibbert, M.D., p. 109, 4to, Edinburgh, 1822.
[8] Compendious History of the Goths, Swedes, and Vandals, translated, Book I. chap. xviii., p. 12.

Scandinavians, as there was a monument of the kind, the "Lapis tituli," or Folkstone, at the landing place of the Saxons in Kent;[1] and some fancy that the antiquity of the custom may be carried back to the days of Joshua, who caused stones to be set up to mark the landing place of the Israelites, when they went dry over Jordan, and first set foot on the land they were to conquer and dwell in.[2] Near the pillar stone at Steinness were tumuli, in one of which were found nine silver fibulæ.[3] Not far from these tumuli was another artificial mount of two feet in diameter, and thirty-six feet high, of a conical outline, occupying the centre of a raised circular platform, which formed a terrace around it. This was the Thingmount for which the Scandinavians generally selected a plain near their landing place, the terrace or steps being used as they yet are in the Tingwall mount of the Isle of Man.[4] Within view of the Thingmount was a circle of upright stones alleged to have been a temple dedicated to Thor, and a semicircle of similar stones, a temple dedicated to the Goddess Freyja, or the moon.[5] It is unnecessary at the present moment to discuss the various opinions respecting these circular temples, or to enter into the labyrinth of Celtic and Northman mythology to ascertain the form of worship to which

*Thingmount Temples and Pillar Stones at Steinness in Orkneys.*

---

[1] Antiquitates Rutupinæ, Oxoniæ, 1745, p. 17.

[2] Borlase's Antiquities of Cornwall, p. 164.

Joshua, chap. iv., verses 6, 7, Holy Bible.

[3] Description of the Isles of Orkney, by the Rev. James Wallace, D.D., p. 53, 8vo, Edinburgh, 1693.

[4] Hibbert's Memoir on the Tings of Orkney and Shetland, Archæologia Scotica, vol. iii., p. 197.

[5] Ibid, p. 106.

they belonged. It has been observed already that near to the Lawhill in Iceland there yet remains a circular range of stones which is unmistakably described in the Eyrbyggia Saga as the Temple of Thor, this circle having within it one larger stone than the rest which was the Thor Stein, and our chief object here is to show that some place for religious ceremonies was an inseparable adjunct to the place of legislative and judicial assembly, and either that the Thing itself, with its circular enclosure was used as a temple, or that a temple was erected near it.[1]

If this description of the monuments at Steinness were not sufficient for our purpose we might refer to the standing stone and tumuli of the Island of Shapinshay, another of the Orkneys, to its wait or watch hill and adjoining church, and to the "Blackstone of Odin," at the landing place on its sandy beach,[2] but the similarity is so apparent, and the evidence so strong in favour of the Scandinavian origin of our mount, that we may proceed to describe the Thingmount on the Stein of Dublin, which like the mount at Steinness we find in proximity to the pillar stone and tumuli.

*Black Stone of Odin in the Orkneys.*

It is scarcely necessary to state that every act of the Northmen from the election of a king and the promulgation of a law to the trial of a criminal, or the decision of a title to land, was governed by the judgment of the people assembled at a Thing. Hence we read in the Sagas of Court Things, House

*Scandinavian Things or Tings.*

---

[1] Hibbert's Memoir on the Tings of Orkney and Shetland, Archæological Scotica, vol. iii. p. 143.

[2] Statistical account of Scotland, vol. xvii., pp. 234, 235. Description of the Orkney Isles, by the Rev. George Barry, D.D., p. 51, 4to, Edinburgh, 1805.

Things (the origin of our Hustings), and of District Things, and of the Fimtardom being the fifth supreme court or Althing. At Things, assembled on an emergency, the chieftain then present presided, but at the permanent court a "godi," or hereditary magistrate sat.[1] The form of the court also varied with circumstances.

*Stone Circles round Thing-mounts.*

On sudden emergencies an open space was fenced by stakes round which the verbond, a sacred chord, was tied. Sometimes the fence was a circle of stones, the centre being reserved for those who were to be the "Lagmenn," and who alone were permitted to enter. But all permanent settlements appear to have had fixed places of judicature raised on plains like the Stein accessible by water, a facility for attending meetings of primary importance with a maritime people in countries where roads were yet unformed or but few. On such plains a mound of earth was sometimes raised whereon the godi sat with his "lagmen," the armed "bonders," and freemen standing around. Not far from this mound

---

[1] "Godi, a priest, and hence a liege lord or chief of the Icelandic Commonwealth. The Norse chiefs who settled in Iceland finding the country uninhabited solemnly took possession of the land (Land-nam), and in order to found a community they built a temple and called themselves by the name of Godi or Hof-godi, 'temple-priest'; and thus the temple became the nucleus of the new community, which was called 'Godard.' Hence Hof-godi, temple priest, and Hof-dingi, chief, became synonymous.

"Many independent Godi and Godard sprung up all through the country, till about A.D. 930, the Althingi was erected, where all the petty sovereign chiefs (Godar) entered into a league, and laid the foundation of a general government for the whole island. . . . On the introduction of Christianity the Godar lost their priestly character, but kept the name. Icelandic-English Dictionary, by Cleasby and Vigfusson; word Godi; 4to, Clarendon Press, Oxford, 1874.

was another hill used as a place of execution, for when these Things were used for criminal trials, and that "capital punishments were doomed it was ordered that the criminals should be conveyed for this purpose to a stony hill, where there should be neither arable land nor green fields. In Unst, one of the Shetland Islands, such a place is still seen near the site of "three Things." It is a barren serpentine rock where scarcely a blade of grass will grow, and is named the Hanger Hoeg.[1] To the south of the island is a similar place of execution, with the more modern name of the Gallows Hill. In another of the Shetland Isles, on a tongue of land at Loch Tingwall, is the "Law ting" from which it is stated that according to the "custom of the Northmen it was allowed to the condemned criminal to endeavour to make his escape to the kirk of Tingwall; in attempting this his way led through the crowd of spectators, and if he effected his escape, either by their favouring him or by superior swiftness or strength, and reached the kirk he was freed from punishment, this was a kind of appeal to the people from the sentence of the judge."[2]

Of these Thingmounts or places of judicature on the sands of rivers or lakes, or near the sea-shore, we have many examples in Scandinavian settlements connected with Dublin, besides that already described at Steinness, such as the Logbergit or Law mount of Thing vollr in Iceland.[3] The Law mount

*Thing vollr in Iceland.*

[1] Hibbert's Memoir on the Tings of Orkney and Shetland. Archæologia Scotica, Vol. iii., p. 195.
[2] Statistical account of Scotland, Vol. xxi., pp. 274 and 284.
[3] Iceland, or a Journal of a Residence in that Island during 1814-1815. Vol. i., p. 86; 8vo, 3 vols. Edinburgh, 1818.

at Tingwall in the Isle of Man; the terraced mount of Isla;[1] the Mount of Urr;[2] and such I hope to show was the Thingmote of Dublin. But here again we must enter into minute details in collecting facts from original documents, for strange as it may appear there is no known publication which mentions this ancient relic of Scandinavian law.

*St. Andrew's Thengmotha.*

In the register of the Priory of All Hallows we have some indication of the site of the Thingmote of Dublin. It records a grant made to the priory about the year 1241, the land granted being described as situate in "Thingmotha, in the parish of St. Andrew Thingmote,"[3] and an enrolled deed of 1575 gives a further clue by describing the property conveyed, as bounded by the road leading to Hoggen Green, called Teigmote,[4] thus showing that the Thingmotha of the preceding document was that part of the Stein called Hoggen Green. If then we assume that Thingmotha had its name from the Thingmote these records show that the Thingplace of Dublin was on Hoggen Green in the parish of St. Andrew. But other documents leave no doubt that the precise position was at the angle formed by Church-lane and Suffolk-street nearly opposite the present church of St. Andrew, and about 40 perches east of the old edifice. It was here this remarkable

---

[1] M'Cullagh's Western Isles. London, 1819, p. 234.

[2] Grose's Antiquities of Scotland. London, Vol. 2, p. 181.

[3] Sciant presentes, &c., quod ego Johannes Thurgot dedi, &c Deo et domui Omnium Sanctorum, &c., quandam terram meam, &c., in Suburbio Dublin. scilicet in Thengmotha in parochia S. Andree de Thengmotha. Registrum Prioratus Omnium Sanctorum juxta Dublin. By Rev. Richard Butler, p. 26, 4to, Dublin, 1845.

[4] Enrolled 22nd of James I., Calendar of the Patent Rolls of K. James I., p. 585.

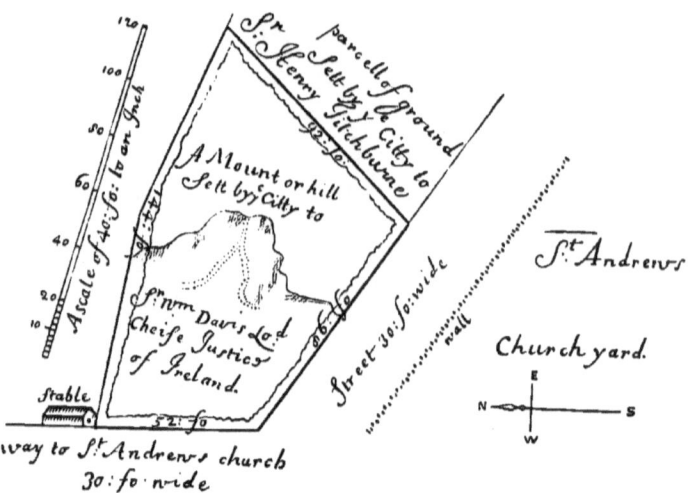

The above Plott is a Survey taken of the Mount neer
St Andrews Church, pursuant to an order from ye Rt Honbt
the Lod Major, the Sherriffs Comons and Cittizens of the
Citty of Dublin      Jo Groone citt Surv:

mount the Thingmote of Dublin stood until the year 1685. From the drawing and survey, which I have been so fortunate as to discover, the mount is shown to have been a conical hill about 40 feet high and 240 feet in circumference.

The drawing of which a facsimile is here given forms part of a survey made in 1682, and it may be observed that the indented outline gives to the mount the appearance of having had those terraces or steps already described on some other Thingmounts. That this mount remained so long undisturbed was partly attributable to its position within the line of fortification for which the tumulus was levelled, but chiefly to the care of the municipal authorities for the health of the citizens. Down to the year 1635 there were numerous edicts decreeing that "the common pastures of the city (among which Stanihurst places the Stein[1])" should be reserved for the citizens to walk and take the air by reason as the last ordinance adds that the "city was growing very populous."[2] These ordinances preserved the ground, surrounding the Thingmote, uninclosed until 1661.

Drawing of the mount or Thingmote of Dublin.

---

[1] Holinshed; Chronicle, vol. vi., p. 28.

[2] "An Act established at Easter Assembly, A.D. 1635, to be publickly reade every Michaelmas Assemblie Daie. Whereas the Commons petitioned unto this Assembly praying that some course might be taken in the said Assembly whereby no part or parcel of the Greens and Commons of this Cittie, viz.:—Hoggin's Green, St. Stephen's Green, and Oxmantown Green, might not from henceforth be sett or leased to any person, but that the same may be wholly kept for the use of the Cittizens and others to walk and take the open aire by reason this Cittie is at this present growing very populous." The Mayor is not to give way to the reading of any petition for the leasing or disposing of any of the said Greens or Commons under pain of 40 pounds. City Records.

BOOK III.
CHAP. II.

*Covenants to preserve the mount for the use of the city.*

In that year Dr. Henry Jones (then Bishop of Meath) obtained a portion of this ground, on lease from the Corporation of Dublin, for a small rent and the somewhat curious consideration that he should give for the use of the city the "Book of Ancient Statutes of the Kingdom," but the lessors, anxious for the recreation of the citizens to which the Thingmount was ancillary, inserted a proviso that " a passage six feet wide and thirty feet square from the top to the bottom of the hill should be reserved to the city for their common prospect, and that no building or other thing should be erected on the premises for obstructing of the said prospect."[1] When this lease was made, St. Stephen's-green also being uninclosed and few buildings erected in the neighbourhood of the Stein, the prospect from this mount, like that from the mount at Steinness, must have been extensive, particularly over the Bay of Dublin,[2] and gave this Thingmount the advantages which the watch mounts or

---

[1] Michaelmas Assembly, A.D. 1661. City Records.

[2] [It is on this mount that the Norman Geste of the Conquest represents Gylmeholmoc, a chief of the O'Byrnes, who had given hostages to Milo de Cogan to be at peace with the English, as seated by Milo's appointment thence to watch the impending battle between him and the Danes, newly landed on the Staine, in order to recover Dublin from the English. " You shall have back your hostages (says Milo) if you do what I say: that is, be neither aiding them nor us, but stand aside with your people and look on at the battle. And if God grants us to defeat these people (the Danes) do you help us to follow them; if we be recreant do you join them in cutting us up and killing us."

" Vos ostages averez par si
Que tu faces ço que tu di ;
Par si que ne sëez aidant
Ne nus, ne euz, tant ne quant :
Mès que encoste de nus sëez,
E la bataille ugarderez :
E si Deus le nus consent.
Que scient deconfiz icele gent ;
Quo nus sëez od tun pöer,
Eidant pur euz debarater :

SCANDINAVIAN ANTIQUITIES OF DUBLIN.   165

ward hills of the islands possessed, rendered it a fit station from whence the city could be warned of the approach of an hostile fleet. But in 1671, the foundation of the new church of St. Andrew having been laid, and the Bishop of Meath having surrendered his lease, a new lease was made to William Brewer, without any reservations of "prospect" from the mount which shortly after was encompassed with buildings.[1]

In 1682 the mount itself was demised to Sir William

E si nus seimiz recrëant,
Vus lur sëez del tut cidant,
De nuz trencher e occire
Le noz livrer à martire."
Gylmeholmoc having granted this and pledged his faith and oath, quits the city to take up his post on the mount:—
"Gylmcholmoth äitant
Dehors la cité meintenaat,
Se est cil reis pur veir asis
Od cel gent de sun päis,
De sur le Hogges, desus Steyne
Dehors la cité en un plein
Pur agarder la mellé
Se sunt iloque asemblé."
That is, Gylemcholmoc gaily (went) out of the city, and now is this king for a truth seated with the people of his country upon the Hogges, over Steyne, on a plain outside of the city, to view the melée, pp. 109, 110, Anglo-Norman Poem on the Conquest of Ireland by Henry the Second. Edited by Francisque Michel, 12mo, London, 1837. This Gylmchomoc ruled over the territory between Bray and Dublin. It was he that granted Kilruddery to the Abbot of St. Thomas's for his country seat, and from this abbey it passed at the Dissolution of Religious Houses in the reign of King Henry VIII. to the ancestor of the Earls of Meath. See the grant in the Register of S. Thomas's Abbey, R. I. A.]

[1] [This was the "fortified hill near the College," referred to in the following:—On the 6th of July, 1647, the Commissioners of Parliament, to whom the Marquis of Ormonde had just then surrendered Dublin, give an account to the Parliament of a mutiny. "On Friday last (they write) many of the soldiers fell into a high mutiny, and, cashiering their officers, marched directly to Damass Gate, adjacent to the place where we have our usual meetings for despatch of public affairs." They then describe Colonel Jones, the new made Governor of Dublin, as marching with several troops of his own regiment of horse against the mutineers, "the greatest part of them being of Colonel Kinaston's regiment, accustomed to like practices in North Wales, and after some skirmishing and coming to the push of pike, wherein some of them were killed, several hurt on both sides, the Governor endangered, and Colonel Castles's horse shot

**BOOK III.
CHAP. II.**

*The mount levelled.*

Davis; he had been Recorder of the city, and was then Chief Justice of the King's Bench. He had a suburban residence adjoining the mount and a fee-farm grant was made to him with the avowed object of clearing the ground. His petition for this grant states that "the ground on which the mount stands, being very small and the mount itself being very high the cost of levelling it and carrying it away would be a vast charge." A mass of earth, 40 feet high and 240 feet in circumference, could not be removed without great expense,[1] but the site was valuable and the earth was useful in raising Nassau-street, then called Saint Patrick's Well-lane, the street being elevated 8 to 10 feet above it. Although these documents indisputably fix the position of the mount within the district of Thingmotha, a doubt whether the word Thingmote in 1241 designated a mount, or merely a place of meeting, the want of early records to identify the mount I have described with the ancient Thingmote and the ambiguity of modern descriptions of the vicinity leave room for controversy, which we must endeavour to anticipate.

*Hoggen butt.*

Harris in describing Hoggen Green says that "a place on this Green was anciently called Hoggen butt, where the citizens had butts for the exercise of archery,"[2] and Daines Barrington, in his "Observations on

under him, the mutineers betook themselves to a place of advantage, a fortified hill near the College, and with them many of those called out to subdue them. After they had defended the said hill till midnight they were received to mercy upon their humble submission and promises of amends." (Signed) Arthur Annesley, Robert King, Michael Jones. Carte Papers, Bodleian Library, vol. lxvii., p. 133.]

[1] Michaelmas Assembly, A.D. 1683. City Records.

[2] History of Dublin, p. 108.

the Statute for the Encouragement of Archery,"[1] says "That the butts erected for archery may have been the occasion of some of those round hills of earth near towns which have often amused and puzzled antiquaries." Barrington's observation coupled with Harris's reference to archery butts might lead to the supposition that the mount here described had been raised for archery practice, and particularly as there is an Irish statute of 5th Edward IV., which ordains that in every English town in this land of Ireland there shall be " one pair of butts for shooting, within the town or near it, and every man of the same town between the ages of 60 and 16 shall muster at said butts and shoot up and down three times every feast day " between March and July.[2] There is also the curious coincidence that one of what are proved to be tumuli at Steinness is also said to have been raised for archers to shoot at " for while Edward was encouraging archery in Ireland, James I. of Scotland was similarly employed in his dominions, the Scotch Act of 1425 requiring every man from 16 to 60 years of age, to shoot up and down three times every holyday at bow marks erected near the parish churches."

It is, however, manifest that Harris did not mean that the mount which he calls Hoggen butt had been used for a target. His words clearly imply the reverse. He says that at Hoggen butt the citizens had butts for archery and that near them (that is the archery butts) was a place called Tib and Tom where possibly the citizens amused themselves at

*Tib and Tom.*

---
[1] Observations on the most ancient Statutes, p. 426, 4to, London, 1775.
[2] 5th Edward IV., cap. 4, A.D. 1465.

leisure times by playing at keals or nine pins.[1] It is manifest also that the Thingmount would not meet the requirements of the statute, which enacts that there shall be not one but a pair of butts and that there was more than one of what are termed butts is rendered probable by an ordinance made for the preservation of "Hogges butts," about three years after the Act of Parliament. This ordinance of A.D. 1469 decrees in the quaint language of the times, that "no manner of man take no clay from Hogges butts upon pain of XX. shillings as oft as they may be found so doing."[2] A stronger argument however may be deduced from the size of the mount. We find that the city forces were periodically mustered on Hoggen Green, that the mayor and principal citizens sat at these musters under a pavilion or tent erected on the top of Hoggen butt,[3] and we know that after the mount was levelled this tent was annually set up in Stephen's-green for these military reviews. Now it is utterly irreconcilable with any description given of archery butts elsewhere to suppose that a high circular mount on the top of which a pavilion could be erected had been piled up for the mere purpose of archery practice.

But in addition to these arguments there are circumstances connected with the mount which strongly tend to identify it with the Scandinavian Thingmote.

---

[1] History of Dublin, p. 108.

[2] Acts of Assembly. Midsummer, A.D. 1469. City Records.

[3] Harris's MSS., p. 115, Pococke Collection, Brit. Mus., MSS. 4823. "Forasmuch as the City is destitute of a tent to serve upon occasion of a general hosting, the Sheriff to cause a new tent to be made, &c., and Mr. Bellew to be answerable for the old tent if he be found chargeable." Acts of Assembly, Christmas, 1593. City Records.

The customs of a people frequently survive their dominion. Those of the Northmen of Dublin were not all abolished by the Anglo Normans. And we find that the Bowling Green, the archery butts, the place for those games, which Harris calls Tib and Tom, and for the miracle plays and pageants were at the mount, and that on this mount the Mayor of Dublin sat with his jurats under a tent, presiding over the armed musters of the citizens.[1]

*Mayor and jurats on the mount.*

We should recollect that it was at the Thing-mount the public games of the Northmen were always held,[2] and that on the Althing, under a tent, the "Godi" or chief magistrate of the district sat with his "lagmen," surrounded by armed freemen. Nor should we forget that this custom apparently preserved in Dublin continued until recently in the Isle of Man where the chief of the island or his representative sat under a canopy on the Thingwall mount with his

*The mount like the Thing-wall of the Isle of Man.*

[[1] At this mount, too, was held the election for the Parliament, which met in A.D. 1613. "The 27th of April the Mayor (Sir James Carroll), taking the first election to be void, about 10 o'clock in the forenoon gave directions for proclamation to be made in several parts of the City that at 2 o'clock in the afternoon of that day he would proceed to election at a place called Hoggen but near the City and within its liberties, which was made accordingly, at which time and place in a great assembly of the inhabitants as well free of the City as not free the Mayor nominated Richard Bolton, Recorder of the City, and Richard Barr Alderman." Calendar of State Papers of King James I., A.D. 1611–1614, p. 441. The editor of Desiderata Curiosa Hibernica having no knowledge of this mount or these butts, and the enrolment with the account of this election having no capital letters nor punctuation, he could not understand "hoggen but," and dropped the latter word and wrote "at a place called Hoggen." Vol. I., p. 244, 8vo, Dublin, 1773.]

[2] Histoire de Suède par Erik Gust. Geyer traduit par J. F. de Lundbhad, p. 31, 8vo, Paris, 1840.

"doomsters" or "lawmen," the armed attendants standing around, and that a like custom long prevailed at the "hill of pleas," the Thingmount of the Norwegian settlers in Iceland.

*Hangr Hoeg or Gallows Hill near the Dublin Thingmount.*

These facts and circumstances we think may be safely relied on as proof of the identity of the mount here described with the Scandinavian Thingmote. And we have now to add that about 200 perches eastward of the mount was the Hangr Hoeg or Gallows hill of Dublin, the usual accompaniment to the Thingmount. Here on a rocky hill, surrounded by a piece of barren ground, the gallows was erected and here criminals were executed until the beginning of the last century, when the gallows was removed farther south to permit the rock to be quarried for building purposes, the city then rapidly extending in this direction. The "Gallows hill" is marked on the maps of Dublin until after 1756,[1] and the quarry is yet to be traced between Rock-lane and Mount-street, both places being very probably named from this rocky gallows mount.

*Search for a pagan höf or temple near the Thingmount.*

If we could now discover the site of any höf or temple connected with the Thingmount, the similarity of the Scandinavian monuments of the Stein and Steinness would be complete, but here great difficulties occur. No vestiges of such temples remain, nor have we the local indications which else-

[1] In the "Survey of the City and Suburbs of Dublin," by Jean Rocque, Folio, London, 1756, the road leading from Stephen's-green to Bull's-bridge (now known as Lower Bagot-street) is styled "Gallows Road." On the north side of this Gallows-road near Lower Pembroke-street is shown a Quarry and over it a Windmill; opposite on the south side of the road is the Gallows.]

where show where the religious ceremonies connected with the Thingmount there performed.¹

The Venerable Bede has preserved a letter from Pope Gregory to the Abbot Mellitus, directing him to tell St. Augustin in England that he (the Pope) had on mature deliberation determined "that the temple of the idols in that nation ought not to be destroyed but let the idols that are in them be destroyed; let holy water be made and sprinkled in the said temples, let altars be erected and relics placed," "That the nation seeing that their temples are not destroyed may more familiarly resort to the places to which they have been accustomed. And because they have been used to slaughter oxen in sacrifices to devils, some solemnity must be exchanged for them on this account, as that on the day of the dedication or the nativities of the holy martyrs, whose relics are there deposited, they may build themselves huts of the boughs of trees about those churches which have been turned to that use from temples, and celebrate the solemnity with religious feasting, and no more offer beasts to the devil, but kill cattle to the praise of God in their eating, and return thanks, &c., &c."²

Almost universally the Christian missionaries everywhere pursued this course. At Upsala, in A.D. 1026,³ the great temple of Odin was converted into a Christian Church, and in Scandinavian settlements, where

---

¹ In each temple was a ring of two oras or more. Such a ring each Godi had. He dipped it in the blood of the victim sacrificed, and all parties were sworn on it before there could be any proceedings at the Thing. Landnamabok, p. 299.

² Bedæ, Historia Ecclesiastica. Lib. I., cap. xxx., p. 141.

³ Laing's Sea Kings of Norway. Vol. I., p. 88.

no enclosed temple existed, churches were dedicated to St. Michael, to St. Magnus, to St. Olave, or to the Virgin Mary, at the places previously consecrated to the worship of Thor and Freyja, other pagan memorials or monuments being sanctified with Christian emblems. Hence we frequently find the pillar stones or bowing stones either marked with a cross, or overthrown and stone crosses raised where they stood, and the sacred wells of Baldur, the son of Odin, with the sacred wells of other heathen deities, becoming the holy wells of St. John or St. Patrick.[1] With similar views the great Saxon and Scandinavian festivals were exchanged for Christian festivals occurring at the same period of the year, the slaughter of oxen to idols, and the feasts which followed, being exchanged for innocent banquets and revelry. Nevertheless the pagan practices which Gregory endeavoured to turn to Christian purposes were not wholly eradicated.[2] The Christian converts still knelt at the *holy wells* and went southwards round them, following the course of the sun, and yet continue to do so in many parts of Ireland, where they still place bits of rags as votive offerings on the sacred ashtree or hawthorn which overhang these wells.[3] They

---

[1] Ancient Laws and Institutes of England from Æthelbert to Cnut, p. Glossary. Record Publication, Folio, 1840. Pigot's Scandinavian Mythology, p. 290.

[2] Thus in the Laws of Canute— "5th. And we forbid every heathenism. Heathenism is that men worship idols, and the sun or the moon, fire, or rivers, or water wells, or stones, or forest trees of any kind." Ancient Laws and Institutes of England, &c., p. 162.

[3] The learned Dr. Charles O'Connor says, "That well worship was a part of the Pagan system which prevailed in Ireland before the introduction of Christianity is clear from Evinus, or whoever was the author of the Vita Septima S. Patricii . . . He expressly states that the Pagan

continued and still continue to light their May fires and to pass through or leap over them. They continued to place boughs of evergreen trees in their places of worship at Christmas, and in some instances, they even continued to the Christian commemoration the pagan name. The great feast of Yiolner or Odin was superseded by the Christmas festival, yet to this hour there are many parts of England and Scotland, as well as of Denmark and Norway, where Christmas is termed Yioletide. The Paschal festival of other

*Yiolner or Odin-tide made Christmas.*

Irish adored fountains as divinities, and his authority is confirmed beyond a doubt by Adamnan.

"I have often inquired of your tenants what they themselves thought of their pilgrimages to the wells of Kill-Aracht, Tubbar-Brighde, Tubbar-Muire, near Elphin, Moor, near Castlereagh, where multitudes annually assembled to celebrate what they, in their broken English, termed Patterns (Patron's days), and, when I pressed a very old man to state what possible advantage he expected to derive from the singular custom of frequenting in particular such wells as were contiguous to an old blasted oak or an upright unhewn stone, and what the yet more singular custom of sticking rags on the branches of such trees and spitting on them, his answer, and the answer of the oldest men was, that their ancestors always did it, that it was a preservative against the Geasa-Draoidecht, *i.e.*, the sorcery of the Druids . . . and so thoroughly persuaded were they of the sanctity of these pagan practices that they would travel bareheaded and barefooted from ten to twenty miles for the purpose of crawling on their knees round these wells and upright stones and oak trees westward as the sun travels, some three times, some six, some nine, and so on, in uneven numbers, until their voluntary penances were completely fulfilled." Columbanus' Third Letter on the Liberties of the Irish Church or a Letter from the Rev. Charles O'Conor, D.D., to his brother, Owen O'Conor, esq., pp. 82, 83, 8vo, London, 1810, vol. i.

Dr. O'Connor adds, "A passage in Hanway's travels (Lond., 1753, vol. i., pp. 177 and 260) leads directly to the oriental origin of these druidical superstitions, 'We arrived at a desolate Caravanserai where we found nothing but water. I observed (continued Hanway), a tree with a number of rags on the branches. These were so many charms which passengers coming to Ghilan had left there,'" Columbanus, *ibid.*, p. 85.

countries is with us called after the goddess Easter, whose festival was coincident, and the days of the week dedicated to Woden or Odin, to Thor and to Freyja, retain their names nearly unchanged in Wednesday, Thursday, and Friday. But at Steinness, Hibbert asserts that the early missionaries proceeded much farther in their anxiety to conciliate the prejudices of converts, inducing them to give to a portion of the Christian church the outward form of the pagan temple for it appears that not only did they build their church adjoining the semicircular temple but they built the belfry of that church in the extraordinary form of a semicircle.[1] It may be reasonably doubted whether the hypothesis on which this assertion is founded be correct, although its advocates might attempt to support their theory by showing that at Egibsly and Birsa (two other of the Orkney Islands) the churches had round towers close to them,[2] which round towers are supposed to have been erected by Irish monks introducing Christianity, only the theory may be supported by pointing out that a large number of churches in Norfolk and Suffolk built before the Conquest, and ascribed to the Danes, were built with circular belfries,[3] that it was a favourite

*Semicircular belfries in imitation of pagan temples.*

*The circle a favourite form for Scandinavian temples.*

---

[1] Description of the Shetland Isles, 4to, Edinburgh, 1822.

[2] Celtic antiquities of Orkney, by F. W. L. Thomas, R. N. Archæologia, vol. 34, p. 117.

[3] Gale's History of Suffolk, Preface, p. 24. Worthing, Norfolk: the steeple which was round is in ruins. Essay towards a Topographical History of the Co. of Norfolk, by Rev. Francis Bloomfield, continued by Rev. Charles Parkin, London, 1805-1810, ten vols. Roy. 8vo. Hist. of Norfolk, vol. viii., p. 198. Grynhoe, at west end, a tower of flint, round to roof, and then octagon. *Ib.*, vol. vi., p. 103. St. Ethelred's, Norwich round steeple, vol. x., p. 280.

form in Scandinavian buildings, and that Torsager (the field of Thor) in Jutland and at Bornholm, where the pagan temples of Thor and Odin stood. For present purposes, however, we need not refer to any peculiarity in the form of the buildings or to the motives for it. It is only necessary to observe that among efforts to attract the pagan from his old superstitions to a pure worship was that recommended by Pope Gregory, of either converting the temple into a church or of placing the church in proximity to it, a practice which is said to have originated the Gallic term, used in the Orkneys, of going to the "Clachan" (or stones), for going to the church, connecting this fact of the church being placed where the temple stood,[1] with the statement of northern Archæologists, that religious ceremonies preceded all legal or legislative acts of the Scandinavians, and that the Thingplace itself was used as a temple, or that a temple was erected near it, we should expect to find the site of the "hof" or temple near that of a church adjoining the Thingmote, where the heathen rites which attended the election of a chief or a trial by combat were exchanged for the Christian ceremonies of an inauguration and of an ordeal. At the Tingwaldmount of the Isle of man, and we believe invari-

*Churches placed near stone circles or "Clachans."*

---

[1] From this circle of stones the Highlanders, when speaking of the kirk of Aberfayle (Co. of Perth), uniformly make use of the term Clachan, *i.e.*, the circle of stones; and the same term is used when speaking of many other places of worship both in the Highlands and the Low Country, places where it is probable that such circles did or do still exist. Statistical Account of Scotland, vol. x., p. 129. The place where the Parish Church stands was probably the site of a Clachan or "circle of stones." *Ibid.*, vol. viii., p. 135.

*Temples always near Thingmounts.*

ably at every other Thingmount, remains of such churches are found.¹ In some places we can trace both the church and the temple. Close to the Thingmount of Upsala we find the temple of Odin converted into a church. At Thingvollr in Iceland, the church retains the name of "the hof." At Balliowen in Man, we see the circle of stones, the church, and the mound, and at Steinness, the church close to the semicircular and circular temples adjoining the watch mount.

*If St. Michael's and St. Bridget's superseded temples to Thor and Freyja?*

If then it be suggested that, as at Steinness, there were two temples on the Stein, and that the churches built near these supposed temples of Thor and Freyja were the churches of St. Michael and St. Bridget, we are met by the denial that these churches could have been built by the Scandinavian converts or by the clergy who converted them, as neither the one nor the other would have dedicated a church to St. Bridget. For it has not escaped observation that when the Northmen in Ireland dedicated a church to a female saint, they never dedicated to the Irish St. Bridget or to any Irish virgin, but always to the Virgin Mary. Whereas the Irish clergy who were not so intimately connected with Rome, if they called any church except by the name of the founder (and they called many after St. Bridget) never dedicated a church to

*The idea dismissed.*

the Virgin Mary until after Northmen set the example²; indeed, St. Bridget is styled "The Mary of

---

¹ "The stones forming this temple, called in Gaelic 'Clachan' are large irregularly shaped masses of granite." "A little to the south of the temple is a mound, 100 feet in diameter, which had probably some connexion with the circle." Train's Isle of Man, vol. ii., p. 26.

² "The earliest record of a dedication of a church to St.

the Gaeidhil" or Irish, in one of the oldest manuscripts of her life, nor has the research of any Irish scholar, so far as I can ascertain, as yet discovered a single church dedicated to the Virgin Mary in Ireland until the middle of the tenth century, when the Northmen converted to Christianity, began to dedicate churches to her within their own territories, the earliest being that of St. Mary's Ostmanby,[1] better known as St. Mary's Abbey Dublin, alleged to have been founded about the year 948.

<small>BOOK III. CHAP. II.</small>

<small>The Ostmen did not invocate St. Bridget.</small>

As regards the Anglo-Saxon missionaries who converted the Northmen, they were not likely to dedicate a church to an Irish Saint, their connection being with Canterbury and Rome, but not with Armagh and the Irish Church. For it is to be recollected that the Northmen did not acknowledge the authority of the Irish Church until the Irish archbishops received the palls from Rome through Cardinal Paparo, in 1152; Laurence O'Toole in 1163 being the first Bishop of Dublin (under the Ostmen) who was consecrated by the Archbishop of Armagh, all previous bishops of the Ostmen being consecrated by the Archbishop of Canterbury.[2]

<small>The Ostmen did not recognise the Irish Church.</small>

Mary in Wales is that of a church near the Cathedral of Bangor, A.D. 993, by Edgar, king of England. About 140 churches were afterwards built to her honour (chiefly in the 12th century, and chiefly in the parts of Wales subject to English and Flemings)." Ecclesiastical Antiquities of the Cymry, by the Rev. John Williams, M.A., p. 184, 8vo, London, 1844.

[1] "Et deinde usque ad Ecclesiam Sancte Mariæ de Osmaneby." Confirmatio Civitat, Dublin. 7 November, 2° Johan. (A.D. 1201) Rotuli Chartarum in Turre Londinensi asservati, p. 788, folio, London, 1837.

[2] Lanigan says that Waterford and Limerick had been placed under the Archbishop of Cashel by the Synod of Rathbreasil, A.D. 1118; but admits that the Danes of Limerick, in opposition to that decree, succeeded in getting their Bishop consecrated at Canterbury. Ecclesiastical History of Ireland, vol. iv., p. 42.

On the other hand if it be suggested that such temples stood on the east side of the Thingmount, we are reminded that All Hallows and St. Mary del Hogges were built between the years 1146 and 1166,[1] and although many of the Northmen retained pagan customs until nearly that time, yet it is scarcely possible that their temples remained objects of so much veneration in the middle of the twelfth century as to induce the Christian clergy to erect churches near them.

*St. Andrew's Thengmotha stands (perhaps) on the site of a temple of Thor.*

Rejecting these suppositions there is yet another which may be offered; it is, that if there were temples to Thor and Freyja on the Stein as at Steinness, the Christian missionaries as they built only one church at Steinness, only built one church at Dublin, and that church may have been the church of St. Andrew Thengmotha. We do not find any notice of this church before the arrival of the Anglo-Normans, but it is mentioned in a Charter of John, while lord of Ireland, and the name of Thengmotha attached to it, apparently justifies the conjecture that it was built prior to that period, and may have been then dedicated to some other saint, as we have the names of several churches in the east suburbs of Dublin of which we cannot now find any other trace. It may also strengthen the conjecture, to observe that at this

---

[1] In the Annals of Leinster there is mention made of this Priory; how it was founded by Dermot M'Murrough, king thereof; and that he came to Dublin in the year 1166, when he fell sick, and, calling all his priests about him on the eve of the Feast of All Saints, made a vow, if he recovered, to build a religious house where he lay sick; so it is probable that Dermot lay there when the Priory was first founded. Robert Ware's Collections, Pococke MSS., No. 4,813, Brit. Museum. St. Mary le Hogges was founded by one of the kings of Leinster, a predecessor of Dermot M'Murrough. *Ibid.*

churchyard the ceremonies, attending the election of the "mayor of the bullring"[1] were performed; and to this may be added the remarkable fact that when the church was rebuilt it was built in an elliptical form which gave it the name of "the Round Church." Whether this form, singular as regards the churches of Dublin, was adopted on any tradition respecting the form of the old edifice, we cannot ascertain, but Speed's map of 1610 although it marks the old church (then standing) like all other churches, yet unlike any other church, shows a semicircular enclosure attached to it, and this form of the pagan temple given to the new church of St. Andrew, and given to the outward wall of the old church, as it was to the belfry of the church of Steinness, is one of those curious coincidences which sometimes are adduced in support of a theory but to which no importance should be attached without strongly corroborative circumstances. Disappointed in this attempt to discern the site of the pagan temple on the Stein, I revert to monuments previously described for the purpose of obviating doubts which might arise respecting them.

With regard then to the Long Stone of the Stein, it is not to be supposed that the "Long Stone" had reference to any boundary or jurisdiction of the city. This is particularly to be observed lest it might be inferred that because the celebrated stone at Staines

[1] A.D. 1575. The Mayor and Sheriffs did not go to Cullen's-wood on Black Monday according to custom, the weather was so foul; and the Mayor of the Bullring, who used to be elected in St. Andrew's Churchyard was now chosen in the Tholsel. Walshe and Whitelaw, History of Dublin, p. 200.

near Windsor now marks the jurisdiction of London on the Thames, the "Long Stone of the Stein" might have marked the jurisdiction of Dublin on the Liffey. To support an inference of this kind there is no perceptible evidence. There is no allusion whatsoever to the "Long Stone of the Stein" in any charter wherein the metes and bounds of the city are described, nor is there any existing boundary or jurisdiction which it could have defined. The evidence is really on the other side, for there are facts clearly showing that "London Stone" was neither set up at the alleged time nor for the alleged purpose,[1] and circumstances connected with it support the opinions respecting the Long Stone of the Stein and tend to show that the Stone at Staines was also a stone of memorial raised at a Scandinavian landing place and probably mark of possession taken. Unquestionably Staines near Windsor was so named from some pillar stone erected there long before the year 1285, the date inscribed on London Stone. It was called "Stane" in the Domesday Book 200 years prior to that date,[2] the first notice of the place combined with an event, in which the name probably originated, being found in one of the manuscripts of the Saxon Chronicle,[3] which states that A.D. 993

*The Long Stone a mark of Scandinavian possession taking.*

[1] On the pedestal is, "This ancient stone above this inscription is raised upon this pedestal exactly over the spot where it formerly stood, inscribed ' God preserve y⁶ City of London, A.D., 1285,' and on the other side, 'To perpetuate and preserve this ancient monument of the jurisdiction of the City of London, &c.'" By Mr. Haliday's notebook it appears he visited this stone to take the inscription the 20th of August, 1855. He has given a very good sketch of this monument.]

[2] Domesday Book, p. 128, London, 1816.

[3] Monumenta Historica Britannica, Folio, London, 1848.

"came Aulaf with ninety-three ships to Stane and ravaged thereabout," the Aulaf who thus sailed up the Thames and made "Stane" his landing-place being the Norwegian Olaf Tryggevesson who was married to a sister of the king of Dublin.¹ To this we may add that the plain of Runymede, famous in connexion with Staines, was like the Stein of Dublin, the title of a Scandinavian Althing, probably so made by Aulaf and Swein, and so remaining while Canute and other Danish sovereigns governed England. Mathew of Westminster tells us it was called "Runymede, that is, the Meadow of "Counsel," because of old times councils about the peace of the kingdom were frequently held there,² Staines apparently being the general name of the place, the letters of safe conduct from King John when the Barons demanded his assent to the laws subsequently embodied in Magna Charta specifying "Staines" and not Runymede as the place of meeting.³ But if the inquiry be pursued it will be found that all the places called Stane in the Domesday Book were on the banks of rivers, and that most of them had been Scandinavian landing-places, and it is of some importance as connected with the name of the Stein of Dublin that we should do so.

It will be found that Humber Stane, at the mouth of the Humber, was the landing-place of the brothers Hinguar and Hubba in A.D. 800, Aulaf, "the pagan king of Ireland," also landing there A.D. 927, and

*Side notes:* BOOK III CHAP. II. Staines near Windsor perhaps site of an Althing. Runymede (or Staines) "The Meadow of Council." The various "Staines" in England.

---

¹ King Aulaf Cuaran.
² Flores Historiarum, A.D. 1215, Folio, London, 1567.
³ Rotuli Litterarum Patentium in Turri Londinensi asservati. A.D. 1215, 17th Johan., Mem. 14

Aulaf in 993 when returning from Staines near Windsor. So Mede Stane (now Maidstone), on the Medway, where the Danish fleet came A.D. 839, and again A.D. 885, "The Mote" being on one side of the river and Pennenden Heath, "a place of counsel" being on the other.

Stanes, at the head of Southampton water, where the Danes came A.D. 860, and where Aulaf, the king of Dublin with his fleet passed the winter of A.D. 993.

Stanes (Estanes), at the mouth of the Thames near Swanscomla (Swinescamp), where Swein landed and encamped in 994, when he and Aulaf were about to besiege London.

Stanes, Hertfordshire, where the Danish fleet came A.D. 896, forming a work twenty miles above London on the River Lea.

Stanes, Herefordshire, A.D. 1055, Earl Elgar, assisted by the Danes of Ireland with eighteen ships, landed here and burned Hereford.

Stanes, Buckinghamshire, hundred of Stanes on the River Thame.

Stanes, Worcestershire, on the River Stour.

Stane, Northamptonshire, near Staneford, all places which had been frequented by the Danes, and we may add to these their landing-places at Stane in the Isle of Oxney (Kent) Stane in the marsh division of Lindsey.

Stane, near Faversham, having on the opposite side of the river "the Mote."

This meeting of John with the English Barons at Stanes for the purpose of sanctioning the laws by which he was to govern England, introduces our notice of the meeting of his father, Henry II., with the Irish chiefs on the Stein of Dublin, A.D. 1172, an event bearing on previous statements that this was the place where the Scandinavian kings were elected and the laws which governed their territories promulgated.

When, therefore, as Hoveden tell us, Henry "ordered to be built, near the Church of St. Andrew, without the City of Dublin, a royal palace, constructed with wonderful skill, of peeled osiers, according to the custom of the country,"[1] and that there, that is, at Thengmotha, he held the festivities of Christmas, feasting the Irish chieftains, entertaining them with military spectacles, and dismissing them with presents, we are not to suppose that his only object was pleasure, or that the Irish chieftains came to do homage to Henry, and considered it a badge of servitude to partake of his festivities or to accept his gifts. It has been already noticed the Irish had widely intermarried with the Northmen, hence they were accustomed to attend the Yuletide feasts, to accept the Yuletide presents, and to join in the warlike exercises of their Scandinavian kinsmen, who, in pagan as well as in Christian times, celebrated Yuletide with feastings, games, and gifts; and, at this Thingmount, annually

---

[1] "Ibique fecit sibi construi, juxta ecclesiam Sancti Andreæ apostoli, extra civitatem Divelinæ, palatium regium miro artificio de virgis levigatis ad modum illius patriæ constructum. In quo ipse, cum regibus et principibus Hibernicis festum solenne tenuit die Natali Domini."—"Rerum Anglicanarum Scriptores post Bedam," p. 302, Folio, London, 1595.

erected these palaces of peeled osiers, which Henry "built after the custom of the country." Henry and his advisers were well aware of this, and that the Irish chieftains would not hesitate to come to the Green of Ath Cliath to join in the similar festivities of a Norman king, yet, if we can believe the statement of Cambrensis, the meeting assumed a very different appearance to Henry's followers. Neither party understood the language of the other. Probably the only interpreters were the clergy called "Latiniers"[1] from their language of intercommunication; and the clergy were the devoted friends of the Anglo-Normans, bound by Pope Adrian's and Alexander's Bulls actively to promote Henry's designs on the lordship of all Ireland. From Norman times it had been the custom of English monarchs to receive the homage of the great tenants of the Crown at Christmas, and to feast them for eight days, and then courteously to bestow presents. Henry's barons and retainers may have considered this the chief object of the meeting, and much was not required to induce the belief that the Irish chieftains had come for the like purpose. But, although the clergy may have bowed before Henry in obedience to the command of their ecclesiastical superior, although Strongbow may have done homage for his Irish lands, although the

---

[1] The Anglo-Norman poëm on the conquest of Ireland begins thus—

\*     \*     \*     \*     \*

" Par soen demeine latinier
Que moi conta delui l'estorie.".
p. 1, 12mo, London, 1837.

Again,
" Morice Regan fist passer,
Son demeine latinier."
*Ibid.*, p. 21.

Ostmen may have acknowledged their conqueror, and the Norman barons their feudal lord, yet that any Irish chieftain who came to the meeting and took part in the ceremony (except possibly those of Leinster) supposed that he thereby " did yield himself to King Henry," as Cambrensis says, is rendered more than doubtful by the facts disclosed.

BOOK III. CHAP. II.

It is manifest that Henry himself had no idea that he had been elected king of Ireland by the chiefs assembled at the Thingmote or that they had yielded to him dominion over the country. The most diligent research has not discovered a single charter, granted by him in Ireland or in England (not even in that by which he granted to his men of Bristol his new gotten city of Dublin), nor a single instance in any other record in which he has styled himself "King" or even "Lord of Ireland" although he rarely if ever omitted his minor titles of Duke of Normandy and Aquitaine and Count of Anjou. While he remained in Ireland he exercised no legal prerogative except over that territory the royalty of which Strongbow had surrendered to him, and over that from which the Ostmen enemies of Dermot M'Morrough had been driven, and where it was indifferent to the Irish, whether the Ostmen or the Anglo-Normans were the rulers. The only laws he made were for his English subjects[1] and for the

No submission intended by the Irish chiefs.

[1 In the confusion of races that followed the irruption of the northern barbarians, and introduced the feudal system, the laws administered were not territorial as in more modern times, but personal, each race in actions between one another, being ruled by its own code: Thus Roman, Frank, Burgundian, had each his law. (See Robertson, Hist. of Charles V., Von Savigny on

Ostmen towns, and these he promulgated at the Thingmote, and possibly after the manner of the Scandinavians.

There is no trace of an attempt to make laws for all Ireland. Even at the Synod of Cashel the only proceeding was to modify the Irish ecclesiastical law in accordance with that of the Church of Rome; and this was done through the introduction of the clergy, who were his supporters. The Irish chiefs and people retained their Brehon laws, and acknowledged no other, and according to these laws they continued to elect their own magistrates, and to judge, punish, or pardon all criminals.[1] Neither did Henry coin money in Ireland or for Ireland, although the Ostmen had mints in Dublin, Waterford, and Limerick.[2] Nor had he a seal for Ireland, nor has there been discovered a single record on which the word "conquest" is used by him, although Strongbow's barons, who had conquered the Ostmen, used that word in grants of their thus acquired lands.[3]

Roman law, &c.) And in Ireland the English did not admit the Danes or the Irish to use English law unless they paid largely for the privilege. Between themselves the latter were ruled (even before English seneschals) by Danes' law or Brehon law, which last was only abolished in the 12th year of King James I., That the laws of England were not given to the meere Irish, was one of the defects of English rule in Ireland.

[1] Sir John Davy's "Discoverie of the State of Ireland and the true causes why it was never entirely subdued till the beginning of H. M. (K. James the First's) most happie raigne;" 12mo, London, 1613.]

[2] Simon on Irish Coins, p. 10, Dublin, 1749.

[3] "Sciant presentes et futuri, &c., quod ego Thomas le Martre dedi, &c., ecclesiæ S. Thomæ apud Dublin, &c., quandam terram de conquestu meo, &c." Chartulary of S. Thomas Abbey, M.S., R.I.A., Nicholas St. Laurence granted

The claim to dominion over Ireland on which Henry relied was evidently Pope Adrian's bull, and even had the title of Lord of Ireland which it granted been then admitted Henry was not ignorant of the limited authority which it conferred, for in his own person he had but recently done homage to the King of France, acknowledging the King as his feudal Lord for Normandy, Aquitain, and Anjou; and subsequently received the homage of William, king of Scotland, who acknowledged Henry to be his Lord.¹

In meeting the Irish Kings at the Thingmote of the Stein it was doubtless Henry's great object to ascertain how far the authority extended. But that even this claim was not fully recognised at the Thingmote, and that Henry did not assume this title of "dominus Hiberniæ" might appear extraordinary if it were not observed that when he came to Ireland with Adrian's bull, Adrian was dead, and the question arose whether for so great a charge there should not be authority from a living Pope. This authority Henry subsequently obtained from Pope Alexander III.,² and sent by William Fitzaldelm and the Prior of Wallingford to a synod of bishops at Waterford.³ How far this served, as

*Death of Pope Adrian IV. made his title doubtful,*

*till confirmed by Bull of Pope Alexander III.*

to his son Almeric his lands of "Houvede" and "all my conquest in Ireland," Hardiman's Irish Minstrelsy, vol. i., p. 390. ["Conquest" here means acquest as opposed to title by inheritance.]

¹ "Conventio, &c., quæ Willielmus Rex Scotorum fecit cum Domino suo Henrico, Rege Angliæ, &c., A.D. 1174." Rymer Fœdera, vol. i., part i., p. 30, London, 1818.

² "Bulla Alexandri III., papæ, de adsistendo Anglorum regi," &c.— Rymer Fœdera, &c. Ibid, p. 45.

³ "On their arrival" (says Dr. Lanigan) "a meeting of bishops

Dr. Lanigan says, " to convince these prelates that the king was the rightful sovereign of the island we are left to conjecture, but the next year O'Connor (the king of Connaught) sent the Archbishop of Tuam to Windsor, where a treaty was concluded by which O'Connor acknowledged Henry as lord of Ireland, and Henry acknowledged O'Connor to be king of Ireland, except the parts occupied by Strongbow and the Ostmen towns and territories."[1]

*Second Bull of Alexander II. to his Legate, the Ostman Bishop of Limerick.*

Lest, however, one bull should not be sufficient to induce obedience to Henry in temporal matters Alexander sent a second bull to his Cardinal Legate, the Ostman Bishop of Lismore, directing the bishops of Ireland to assist the King of England, while Vivian, another Cardinal Legate sent from Rome, and who, according to the Abbé Mac-Geoghegan, " seems to have come to Ireland only to hasten its subjugation,"[2] not only enjoined the Irish, under pain of excommunication, to acknowledge and obey the King of England, but, in a synod which he convened at Dublin, decreed permission to the English soldiers to take whatever victuals they might want in their expeditions out of the churches, into which as sanctuaries the Irish used to remove them, and thus be enabled to traverse the country.

*The Irish Church to preach submission to England.*

was held at Waterford, in which those precious documents were publicly read. This is the first time that they were so in Ireland; and although Henry, undoubtedly, had Adrian's bull in his hands when he was in Ireland, he thought it unadvisable to announce it publicly." Ecclesiastical Hist. of Ireland, vol. iv., p. 222.

[1] By which O'Connor was to hold his land in the same manner as before "dominus rex Angliæ intraverat Hiberniam" (not subdued Ireland). *Ibid.*, p. 30.

[2] Histoire d'Irlande, par l'Abbé MacGeoghegan, vol. ii., pp. 19, 21, Paris, 1762. Lanigan's Ecclesiastical History of Ireland, vol. iv., p. 233.

It was this active interposition of the clergy in carrying out the Pope's bull for the subjugation of Ireland which led to the appointment of John Earl of Moreton, who immediately assumed the title of Dominus Hiberniæ, had a seal, and coined money with that title.[1]

*Prince John confirmed Lord of Ireland by the Pope.*

Nor was the Pope in promoting Henry's interests unmindful of his own. The tribute which the Irish previously paid to the see of Armagh by "The Law of St. Patrick"[2] was now to be paid for the first time to the see of Rome as "Peter pence," and we find Henry III. urging his tenants in Ireland to send the money to him, being, as he says, indebted to our lord the Pope in our annual tribute of 300 marks due to him from our realm of Ireland which yet remains unpaid for the two last years.[3]

Neither was the Pope ignorant of the limited extent of authority which this lordship conferred. He knew that the early kings of England could exercise no legal authority until their claim to the crown was acknowledged by the ceremony of a coronation, and recently discovered documents show that Richard I. merely styled himself " dominus Angliæ" between the decease of his father and the day on

---

[1] " Et in generale Concilio ibidem celebrata Constituit Johannem filium suum, regem in Hibernia concessione et confirmatione Alexandri Summi pontificis " Roger de Hoveden: Scriptores post Bedam, p. 323. See also p. 316, *ibid.*

[2] Archbishop Colton's Visitation of the Diocese of Derry, A.D. 1397, by Rev. W. Reeves, D.D., 4to, Dublin, 1850. Preface, p. v., Irish Archæological Soc. Publications.

[3] Rotuli Litterarum Clausarum in Turri. Londin. 2° Hen. III., memb. 14, dors. Calendar of Documents relating to Ireland in the Public Record Office, London, by H. S. Sweetman, p. 191; 8vo, London, 1875.

*Pope Paul IV. makes Philip and Mary K. and Q. of Ireland, and why.*

which he was crowned.¹ This distinction between the lordship and the kingdom of Ireland was acted on at Rome at a subsequent period, as appears from the course pursued by Pope Paul IV. in A.D. 1555. For when at the Reformation Henry VIII. renounced his allegiance to Rome, and was by an Act of Parliament declared king of Ireland, and that his successors, Philip and Mary, although Roman Catholics, continued to use that title, the Pope refused to see their ambassadors under that title until he had first prepared and published a bull making Ireland a kingdom and had authorized Philip and Mary to assume the legal title, and thus for ever surrendered his asserted claim to the land. The importance of such a bull was well known to the Privy Council of England, for it is stated by the eminent Roman Catholic historian, Dr. Lingard, that " as the natives of Ireland had maintained that the kings of England originally held Ireland by the donation of Adrian IV. and lost it by their defection at the Reformation, the Council delivered the bull to Dr. Cary, the new (Roman Catholic) Archbishop of Dublin, to be deposited in the treasury, after copies had been made and circulated throughout the island."² This is strong evidence, but yet more conclusive testimony is to be found among our unpublished statutes that the cause of Henry's anxiety to meet the Irish kings and chieftains at the Thingmount of Dublin was to impress

---

[1] Rotuli, Chartarum in Turri. Londin., asservati. Introduction by Thomas Duffus Hardy, p. 17. Folio, London, 1837. Record Publications.

[2] History of England, vol. vii., p. 255.

## SCANDINAVIAN ANTIQUITIES OF DUBLIN.       191

upon them the religious claim he had acquired to their obedience and the right to the lordship of Ireland, a title which he wished to assume. Here we find the Act of Parliament held at Dublin, 7th of Edward the IV. (A.D. 1467), which recites, " As our holy father Adrian, Pope of Rome, was possessed of all the sovereignty of Ireland in his demesne as of fee in right of his church of Rome and to the intent that vices should be subdued he alienated the said land to the king of England for a certain rent, &c. by which grant the said subjects of Ireland owe their obedience to the king of England as their sovereign lord as by said bull appears." It enacts that all archbishops and bishops shall excommunicate all disobedient Irish subjects, and that if they neglect to do so they shall forfeit £100.[1]

BOOK III.
CHAP. II.

This meeting of Henry II. with the Irish Chieftains is too important in connexion with the history of the Thingmount and the Stein to be passed over; but to refer to all the memorable events in which the Stein is connected with the history of Dublin would far exceed the limits of a paper like this; and I have yet to notice the Scandinavian origin of the Scandinavian name of Hoggen butt, Hogshill, and Hoggen green in connexion with the nunnery of St. Mary del Hogges.

The nunnery of St. Mary del Hogges stood near the church of St. Andrew, and Harris asserts that it took its name from " Ogh " in the Irish language, which signifies a " virgin," and he adds, " that removing the aspirate ' h,' the word, by an easy cor-

Meaning of name "St. Mary del Hogges."

---

[1] Parliament Roll, 7th Edward IV., Public Record Office, Ireland.

ruption, may pass into Hogges, as much as to say the place of the virgins."¹ Stevens in his Monasticon² gives the authority of Llhuyd for his derivation, which Archdale also gives,³ and that learned ecclesiastical historian, Dr. Lanigan, says, "that Hoggis was not originally the name of the spot, but that it signified virgins through an English corruption of the word Ogh, a virgin, so that St. Mary de Hogges was the same as St. Mary of the Virgins."⁴ Hitherto this derivation has been implicitly adopted, nor can we discover a single objection made or the shadow of a doubt cast on it; we feel some hesitation, therefore, in questioning its correctness, and can only expect to justify ourselves by the strong evidence we are about to give. In the first place I find that the nunnery was not exclusively for virgins. A manuscript in the British Museum states that "the nuns were not of the younger sort but of elderlike persons, and for those who desired to live single lives after the death or separation from their husbands," and the manuscript adds, "that Alice O'Toole, near to the Archbishop of Dublin, in one night's time left her husband and conveyed all his wealth into this abbey, and it was not known for seven years' time where she went or how she conveyed away his wealth" till Laurence O'Toole's death, when she appeared at the funeral, and so was discovered.⁵ The Alice O'Toole here mentioned was

---

¹ History of Dublin, p. 109.
² Monasticon Hibernicum, 12mo, London, 1722.
³ Archdale's Monasticum Hibernicum, p. 172, 4to, London, 1783.
⁴ Ecclesiastical History of Ireland, vol. 4, p. 187.
⁵ Pococke Collection, MSS., No. 4,813, British Museum.

the sister of the archbishop, married to the profligate Dermot M'Murrogh, the founder of the nunnery, who abandoned her and married the daughter of O'Carroll. And the statement respecting the class of females inhabiting the nunnery is supported by the fact that ground on which the nunnery stood was called "Mynechens mantle" and its possessions, Mynechens fields[1] thereby making it as the residence not of young nuns but of those elderly nuns of the superior class termed "mynechens" by Du Cange. And, secondly we find that the old churches in the eastern suburbs of Dublin were almost invariably distinguished by local names, and those names Scandinavian. St. Andrews was called Thengmotha, from proximity to the Thingmote, St. Peters del Hulle, or "of the Hill" from its situation on the rising ground above Ship-street, St. Michaels del Pol from "the pool" or puddle adjoining, and St. Mary's "del Dam" from the dam or mill-pond close to which it stood. This latter derivation nevertheless is rejected by Harris, who denies that the place took its name from the mill-dam near it, as some have conjectured, and avers

*St. Mary del Hogges a nunnery of Mynchens.*

*St. Mary del Dam, meaning of.*

---

[1] Johannes Cosgrave .... seizitus de nuper abbatiâ de le Hoggs et de unâ shoppâ et camerâ in Mensions fields juxta Hoggen Green ... et de peciâ terræ vocatæ Mensions mantle. Inquisitiones Lageniæ, 19th February, 15th James 1st (A.D. 1618), Folio. Record Publication. [Joseph Leeson in 1735 demises to Edward Knatchbull for lease of lives renewable for ever, part of his (Leeson's) garden, 40 feet wide from east to west, and 231 feet in depth, which said premises are part of Minchin's Mantle, near Stephen's-green (Registry of Deeds). In a rental of sale of the estate of Christopher O'Connell Fitzsimon, owner and petitioner, to be sold in the Landed Estates Court, on 21st November, 1871, is named a perpetual annuity of £11, "issuing out of part of Menson's fields, being part of Kildare-street and Kildare-place near Stephen's-green, including part of the grounds of Leinster House and Shelburne-place."]

that the church was called "St. Mary les Dames," but Harris probably was in error. In all ancient documents the church is called " St. Mary del Dam,"[1] the south gate of the city being called " Pol gate " or gate of the pool, and the eastern " Dam gate " or gate of the dam. Even on the opposite side of the river St. Mary's Abbey was called " St. Marys del Ostmanby" from its situation in Ostmans town. From these facts it might be inferred not only that St. Mary del Hogges was not so called from being the residence of virgins, but that it was so called from connection with the place where it stood. Of this we now adduce evidence. If those who alleged that the name came from the Irish word " ogh" had suspected that, like the neighbouring churches, it might have been called from the Scandinavian name of the [hogue or] place where it stood, any glossary would have guided them by a correct derivation. Du Cange and Spelman[2] refer to places so called in that

[1] " De quâdam placeâ vacuâ contra portam del Dam." White Book of Dublin. "De quâdam particulâ terræ, ex opposito ecclesiæ B. V. M. del Dam, concessa Ricardo de Horham." *Ibid.* King Edward II. (8 June, 1319), by writ to Walter de Islip, Treasurer of Ireland, being informed that the belfry of S. Mary's church adjacent to the Castle had been, on the invasion of the Scots, taken down and the stones used to fortify the Castle, directs that it be rebuilt at the king's cost. It is there called " Ecclesia B. V. M. del Dam." Historic and Municipal Records of Ireland, A.D. 1172–1320, p. 406. J. T. Gilbert, 8vo, Dublin, 1870. An Inquisition of the same date speaks of the " predicta porta del Dam," *Ibid.*, p. 445. " Dam Street, anciently le Dom Street. Here was molendinum castri Episcopi." Hist. and Antiquities of Lichfield, p. 503, Gloucester, 1806. [Del dam is masculine, of the dam. " B. V. M. la Dame " (which would be the proper form) is tautologous.

[2] Voce Hoga, Hoghia, et Hogum. Henrici Spelman Glossarium, folio, London, 1626.

part of England which the Northmen had inhabited as Grenehoga in Norfolk and Stanhogia, the gift of Canute to Edwin; and on the borders of the county of Dublin we find a townland having on it a remarkable mound or moat called Greenoge, the derivation of Hoga and Haghia being from " hogue " or " hog," a hillock or mount, the Icelandic and Norwegian " Hauge" (Hogge), a mound or Tumulus " being in this case the direct derivation, and St. Mary del Hogges being really St. Mary's of the hogges or Mount, close to which it stood.

Olaus Wormius tells us that the Scandinavians distinguished three ages by the mode in which the dead were treated. The first was the Roisold or age of Burning. The second was the Hoighold or age of tumuli, in which the body of the chieftain with his arms and ornaments was placed under a mount. And the third was the age of interment or Christian burial.[1] Hence the name of Hogges so frequent in all the settlements of the pagan Northmen. Their descendants, the Anglo-Normans, in whose records we first find the name of St. Mary del Hogges, were not ignorant of its meaning. In their own settlements, in the Channel Islands, the name is given to such mounds of earth as " La Hougue Hatenas" and " La Hougue Fongue," in Guernsey, and in documents relating to La Hogue in Normandy it is spelled " Le Hogges "[2] precisely as we find it in their Latin documents relating to

---

[1] Monumentorum Danicorum, &c., p. 40.

[2] Rex Thesaurario, &c. : Quià dilectus et fidelis noster Ricardus Damory nobiscum . . tempore quo apud Hogges in Normanniâ guerræ nostræ Franciæ applicuimus &c. Close Roll 36ᵉ Edw. III., m. 6. (Engl.), 22 November, A.D. 1362. The following is from

the nunnery on the Stein. But more remarkable authority is found in the dictionary De Trevoux :¹ there Hogue is stated to be an old word signifying a "mound or tumulus," and a port in Normandy, the name of the place being "Hoga, Hogo, or Oga, Ogo," thus removing the aspirate "h," and leaving the name, as our Irish authorities have done, when stating that the nunnery of St. Mary del Hogges was so called from the Irish word "Ogh, a Virgin."

We might rely on this evidence as conclusive against the derivation heretofore given for St. Mary del Hogges, Hoggen Green,² Hogs Hill,³ Hoggen

---

the Proceedings and Ordinances of the Privy Council, 28 November, A.D. 1423. "Et auxi pur les gages de luy mesmes, xxxix. homes d'armes, et lxxx. archiers . . . pur salve conduer les niefs et veissells en les queux le Count de Marche et autres sieurs se transfreterent d'Engleterre jesques le Hogges en Normandy." Proceedings and Ordinances of the Privy Council of England, 10 Richard II.—33 Henry VIII. Vol. iii., p. 125. 7 vols. royal 8vo. (1834-1837). Record Publication.

¹ Hogue ; Collis, tumulus, locus editus. Vieux mot qui signifie une colline, un lieu élevé. Dictionnaire Universel, Francois et Latin, vulgairement appelé Dictionnaire de Trevoux, Paris, 1752. "Haugr; a How, a mound, a cairn over one dead: Names of such cairns,—Korna-Haugr, Melkorka-Haugr. Hauga-thing, an assembly in Norway." Icelandic—English Dictionary by Gudbrand Vigfusson, M.A., 4to, Oxford, Clarendon Press, 1874.

² "Hogges" changed for the Saxon plural became Hoggen (as oxen, hosen, &c.), hence "Hoggen Green." Reconverted into modern English it became "Hog's Green," as in the following order of the year 1615: "Ordered that the Provost and Fellows of Trinity College, Dublin, shall have the precinct of a house called Bridewell, upon Hog's Green, at yᵉ rent of 2 shillings, to be converted by them to a Free School only." Easter Assembly, 1615, City Records. The memory of the origin of Hoggen Green being lost it became "Hogan's Green": Thus the City having demised (6 November, 1764) a lot of ground near Hogan's Green, for three lives renewable for ever, to Garret Earl of Mornington, the said Garret (13 May, 1766) sold his interest to Peter Wilson, bookseller, (Registry of Deeds).

³ In A.D. 1605 a lease is ordered to be made to Jacob Newman of a lot near the end of Hog-lane. Assembly Roll. In Brooking's

Butt,[1] and all those places situate in the vicinity of the Hogges or Tumuli of the Stein, nevertheless we must add from its bearing on the Thingmount of Dublin that the Scandinavians not only called their Tumuli Haugr or Hogs; but sometimes using these mounds of earth as Thingmounts they gave to the mounds or tumuli so used the name of Tinghoges.

In Peringskiold's "Monumentorum Sveo Gothicorum" we find that the great Althing the judicial mount where the national councils of Sweden were held was called the Tingshoge. This mount stands outside Gamla Upsala, on the plain near the river close to the Temple of Odin, and to what he calls the Kings Hogges (the three great Tumuli of the kings). Peringskiold states that it was raised originally for the Tumulus of Freyer "and on account of the community being anciently congregated there to elections, and to sacred and judicial business, it was called the judicial mount or Tingshoge."[2] The Sagas frequently refer to this practice, and mention several instances of Tings held on tumuli or hills which from thence were called Tingshoge, nor are we without traces of the prevalence of this custom

*Meetings held at burial mounds and called Tingshoges.*

---

[1] In 1662 Hoggen Butts had become the Hogg and Butts: Thus Alderman Bladen, King's (and previously Commonwealth) Printer in Ireland, by his will, made 26 April, 1662, bequeaths to his wife "a piece of ground in Dublin near the Hogg and Butts." (Prerogative Probate, Public Record Office, Ireland.)

map of Dublin, 1728, the continuation of Trinity-street towards William-street is Hog-hill. In 1779, when Curran came to practice at the Bar at Dublin, he had his "lodging on Hog-hill." Phillips's Recollections of Curran, 8vo, London, 1818.

[2] Monumentorum Sueo-Gothicorum, Liber Primus, Johannes Peringskioldi, pp. 217, 219, folio, Stockholm, 1710.

amongst the Northmen in England. Gale in his History of Suffolk states that the Hundred of Thinghoge was so called from "the spot within its limits where the placita for the whole jurisdiction were held, Thinghoge," he adds, "signifying the Hill of Council," being the artificial Mount near which the Church of St. Edmundsbury had been erected.[1] In the Domesday Book[2] and in Ely Inquisition the name is spelled variously Tingoho, Tingohan, and Thinghow, &c., the Saxon or Norman scribes endeavouring to give a Latin form to the Scandinavian word, but throughout we can trace the derivation to the Tinghoge or Thingmount, this mount at the Church of St. Edmundsbury, giving the name of Tinghoge to the Hundred as the mount near the Church of St. Andrew gave the name of Thengmotha to the district in which it stood.

Nor is it improbable that the Thingmount of Dublin also may have been a Tumulus from the remains found close to it if not on the spot where it stood.

On these details I fear I have dwelled too long, and in the effort to compress within a moderate space so many facts and statements connected with the Scandinavian remains of Dublin, I may have rendered the description of its monuments of the Stein less clear than could have been wished, and have omitted to refer to doubts and objections which further statements would have removed. I trust, however, that the novelty of the subject will

---

[1] History and Antiquities of Suffolk, Introduction, pp. ix., x., 4to, London, 1838. [2] *Ibid.*

be some apology, and that, even apart from antiquarian objects, it will be considered interesting that, at a moment when the ancient Laws of Ireland are about to be published,[1] we should have before us some of those facts which show that the Scandinavian settlements of Ireland were governed by Scandinavian Laws, and continued to be so governed until Anglo-Norman conquest extinguished Scandinavian dominion. England has preserved the written code under which Canute ruled the amalgamated nations of Britons, Saxons, and Danes.[2] We do not believe that the Irish and the Northmen at any time obeyed the same Laws. But in the Gragas of Iceland,[3] and embodied in the Leges Gulathing of Norway,[4] we apparently possess the Code which governed the Scandinavians of Ireland. We see that the popular assembly of the Thingmount was the source of all political power, and the trial by jury the protection of civil rights, and we have now to learn how far our Celtic institutions were modified by the spirit of freedom which characterized their Ostmen neighbours, that remarkable nation who for three centuries occupied the principal seaports of Ireland, and, as allies or enemies, were ever in contact with the native inhabitants.

---

[1] [Since published under the title " Ancient Laws and Institutes of Ireland or Senchus Mor, 3 vols., imperial 8vo, 1865-1873.]

Ancient Laws and Institutes of England; comprising Laws enacted under the Anglo-Saxon Kings, from Æthelbirht to Cnut, &c. Edited by Benjamin Thorpe, 1 vol. folio (1840), or 2 vols. royal 8vo, cloth. Record Publication.

[2] Grágás Lögbok Islendinga seu Codex Iuris Islandorum, 2 vols, 4to, Havniæ, 1829.

[4] Gulathings laus, Magnus Lagabaeters, seu Regis Magni Leges Gula Thingenses, sive Jus Commune Norvegicum, 4to, Havniæ, 1817.

# APPENDIX.

I. ON THE ANCIENT NAME OF DUBLIN.

II. OBSERVATIONS EXPLANATORY OF SIR BERNARD DE GOMME'S MAP, SHOWING THE STATE OF THE HARBOUR AND RIVER AT DUBLIN IN THE YEAR 1673.

# APPENDIX.

## I.

### ON THE ANCIENT NAME OF DUBLIN.[1]

Shallowness of the navigable channel of the Liffey in early times—Fords at Dublin—Bally-Ath-Cliath, the Town of the Hurdleford, the original name of Dublin—Mistakes of Stanihurst, Ware, and others as to the origin and meaning of the name—Circumstances misleading them—The true meaning of Bally-Ath-Cliath stated in the Dinn Seanchus—Nature of the structure of the Hurdleford—Tochers or wooden causeways distinguished from Droichets or bridges— Droichets or regular bridges distinguished from Droichet-Cliaths— A regular bridge at Dublin before the English Invasion—Bridge of the Ostmen or Dubhgall's bridge—Early bridges in England—Rebuilding of London bridge in stone in King John's reign—Site of the Hurdleford of Dublin discussed—Dr. Petrie's identification of the five great Slighs or roads leading from Tara in the first century of the Christian era—The Hurdleford at Bally-Ath-Cliath shown to be in the line of the Sligh Cualan.

AT the request of my colleagues in the Commission for Preserving and Improving the Port of Dublin, I undertook sometime since to collect materials for a history of the harbour, principally with a view to trace the progress of improvements in the navigable channel of the Liffey, and to preserve some record of the various plans proposed and of the effect of works executed for deepening the river and rendering the port commodious for shipping.

In pursuit of these objects it became necessary to contrast the ancient with the present state of the river and harbour.

*Sites of early Custom Houses.* It is generally known that until 1791, when the new Custom House was opened on the north side of the river, there was a custom house and quay at the south-east side

---

[1] The text of this paper without the notes was printed in the Transactions of the Royal Irish Academy, vol. xxii., having been read there on the 12th of June, 1854.

of Essex-bridge,[1] where vessels trading to our port discharged their cargoes; and previously to 1620 vessels unloaded at Merchants'-quay and Wood-quay, the custom house or crane being then opposite to the end of Winetavern-street.[2] Hence it might be inferred that when vessels ascended the river nearly a mile above the wharfs where they are now moored, the channel must have been deeper than at present; but independently of the facts that the ships which formerly

[1] [At the accession of James I., the customs were for the most part in the hands of the several port (or walled) towns of Ireland under grants from the Kings for the purpose of walling them and defending them against the "Irish Enemy." King James I., resumed them. (Calandar of State Papers (Ireland) of King, James I., A.D. 1611-1614, pp. 140, 194.) By letter under Privy Seal of 29th of July, 1619, the King ordered ground to be purchased in the different ports for cranes and wharfs. (Printed Patent Rolls, 17th of James I., p. 435, cxxviii., 36.) By letter of 20th September, 1620, he directed a lease of ninety years to be taken from James Newman, of 120 feet in front to the Liffey, and in depth from north to south about 160 feet for a crane and wharf. (Ib. Roll 18th James I., xxxv., 18, p. 483.) The lease in pursuance is dated 10th November, 1620. (Ib. xxxvi., 19, p. 483. Enrolled also in Communia roll of the Exchequer, 1626.) In 1639 the premises were enlarged and the New Custom House built. For by indenture between the Corporation and King Charles I., in order that the King might have room convenient for building of a New Custom House and the enlargement of the wharf, the Corporation grants to the King a plot for that purpose therein described. (Exchequer Communia roll, Michaelmas 1640.) The house then built would seem to have been taken down and rebuilt in 1707. (City Annals, Thom's Directory.) A view of the Custom House is given among the vignettes round "Brooking's Map of Dublin," published in 1728.]

[2] In 1651, Richard Heydon and four others pray a lease from the Corporation for sixty-one years from Michaelmas 1652, of the plot of ground on Wood Kea formerly demised by the city for an Exchange thereon to be builded. (Acts of Assembly, Michaelmas, 1651.) In 1701, amongst the properties sold after the route of the Boyne, at Chichester House in College-green was 'one backside and garden, commonly called 'the Royal Exchange,' claimant John Weaver, executor of Daniel Hutchinson; Proprietor Christopher Fagan by lease dated 20th April, 1648, for ninety-nine years to Daniel Hutchinson. (Book of claims at Chichester House, No. 178, p. 19.)

traded to the port were not only differently constructed but were much smaller than those now employed, there are historical incidents which show that at an early period the Liffey was so shallow near the city that it presented no great obstacle to predatory incursions from the southern parts of Leinster into Meath.

Unfortunately, however, no map could be found older than the small outline of the city published under the date of 1610, in "Speed's British Theatre"[1] and as it gives no information respecting the position of the fords or shallow places in any part of the river it becomes necessary to seek that information from documents of another kind.

*Shallowness of the Liffey in 1590.*

In the State Paper Office, London, there is a report, made about the year 1590, which very minutely describes the circuit of the city walls, with its other defences, and states that the depth of water in the Liffey opposite Merchants'-quay and Wood-quay varied from 3 to 6½ feet.[2] This survey, however, only refers to that part of the river fronting the city walls. But among our unpublished records I found two with more important information respecting the state of the river, and in the preceding century. Apparently these documents had been heretofore unnoticed. Their contents are not specified in the list of unpublished statutes made by the Record Commissioners, nor are they to be found in the list printed in the "Liber Hiberniæ."[3]

---

[1] Theatre of the Empire of Great Britain, by John Speed, London, folio, 1610.

[2] A note of the whole circuit of the City walls of Dublin from the tower called "Bremegham's Towre" of the Castle unto the East gate called "Dame is Gate" of the said City according to the direction of the Lord Deputy. Calendar of the State Papers (Ireland) of Elizabeth, A.D. 1574-1585, by Hans Claude Hamilton, Assistant Keeper of H. M. Pub. Records, 8vo, 1867, pp. 590-592.

[3] Liber Munerum Publicorum ab anno 1152 usque ad 1827, or the establishments of Ireland from the 19th of King Stephen to the 7th of George IVth . . . Extracted from the Public Records by special Commission, being the Report of Rowley Lascelles of the Middle Temple, Barrister-at-Law, pursuant to an address of the Commons ordered to be printed A.D. 1824, 2 vols., folio.

The first is an ordinance of a Great Council held in April, 1455, before Thomas Earl of Kildare (Deputy to Richard Duke of York) enacting that the landholders of the barony Castleknock and of the cross of Finglas shall stop all the fords on the Liffey between the bridge of Lucan and city of Dublin—the landowners of the baronies of Balrothery and Coolock and the crosses of Lusk and Swords stopping the fords and shallow places between the bridge of Dublin and the island of Clontarf.[1] The other is an Act of a Parliament held Friday before the feast of St. Luke, being October in the 34 Hen. VI. This Act recites in French that many Irish enemies and English rebels coming by the ford at the pier of St. Mary's Abbey, &c. ("la vade par le pier de Sēint Mary Abbay") enter Fingal by night and rob and destroy the liege people of the King, and for remedy enacts that a wall 20 perches long and 6 feet high and also a tower shall be built at Saint Mary's Abbey to stop the ford there ("une toure ove une mure del XX. perches de longour et vi pees del hautesse soient faitz par le mure de Sēint Mary Abbay avantdit"), and that 140 marks shall be levied on lands in the vicinity to defray the expense of this and similar works.[2] It appears, however, that these measures were not effective, as we find it elsewhere stated that in 1534 Lord Thomas Fitzgerald, the celebrated Silken Thomas, with a troop of armed men rode through Dublin and passing out at Dame's Gate went over the ford to St. Mary's Abbey. Some of his adherents who had besieged the Castle subsequently effecting their escape by fording the river at the same place.[3] This decisive evidence of a ford nearly opposite the city momentarily diverted attention from the immediate subject of investigation by creating doubt

*Ford near St. Mary's Abbey in 1456.*

---

[1] Thirty-third of Henry VI., chap. 4. [See also translations of the early Statute Roll of Ireland made by the Record Commissioners of 1810, MS. Public Record Office Ireland.]

[2] Thirty-fourth of Henry VI., chap. 28, *Ibid.*

[3] Holinshed's Chronicle, 4to, London, 1807, vol. vi., p. 292.

APPENDIX.

*whether* the derivation very generally given of the ancient name of Dublin might not be erroneous.

'Bally-Ath-Cliath,' wherefore the name.

Almost without exception every published history of Dublin asserts that the Irish name "Bally-Ath-Cliath, or the town on the ford of hurdles," originated in peculiarities of the site on which the city was found, and that it had no reference to a ford or passage across the Liffey.

Mistakes of Stanihurst.

Stanihurst, writing in 1570, says that "the Irish called Dublin 'Bally-Ath-Cliath,' that is a town planted upon hurdels, for the common opinion is that the plot upon which the city is builded hath been a marsh ground, and that by the art or invention of the first founder, the water could not be voided and he was forced to fasten the quakemire with hurdels and upon them to build the Citie," and adds "I heard of some that came of building of houses to this foundation."[1]

Camden.

Nearly the same derivation is given by Camden; who states that "the Irish call it the town on the Ford of Hurdles, for so they think the foundation lies, the ground being soft and quaggy like Sevile in Spain, that is said by Isidore to be so called because it stood upon piles fastened in the ground which was loose and fenny."[2]

Speed.

Speed says that the Irish name was "the Ford of Hurdles" for it is reported that the place being fennish and moorish when it first began to be builded the foundation was laid upon hurdles."[3]

Ware.

That great authority on Irish History, Sir James Ware, says it was called "the town on the ford of hurdles because being on a marshy or boggy soil the town was first raised on hurdles."[4]

[1] Stanihurst, *Ibid*, p. 21.

[2] Camden, 'Britannia,' vol. ii., p. 1366, London, 1733.

[3] Theatre of the Empire of Great Britain, by John Speed, London, folio, 1676, b. iv., chap. 3, p. 141.

[4] Disquisitions upon Ireland and its antiquities, by Sir James Ware. "Of places of Ancient Ireland mentioned by Ptolemy, chap. x." "Second edition, London, 1658. Reprinted among a collection of tracts illustrative of Ireland prior to the present century," by Alexander Thom, 2 vols., 8vo, Dublin, 1860, p. 193.

Harris differs in some degree by stating that "before the Liffey was embanked by quays people had access to it by means of hurdles laid on the low marshy parts of the town adjoining the water, from which hurdles it took its name and not from the foundation of it having been laid on piles or hurdles as some have asserted."[1]

<small>APPENDIX.
Harris.</small>

Whitelaw and Walsh in this as in many other instances adopt the words of Harris without any acknowledgment of their source of information.[2]

O'Halloran is singular in the opinion that it was the north side of the river which was called "Ath Cliath," and that it communicated with Dublin, which was on the south side, by a ford of hurdles,[3] and Vallancey asserts that the name was "Bally Lean Cliath" from being built in or near a fishing harbour where certain weirs made of hurdles were used.

It thus appears that with the exception of O'Halloran these historians concur in ascribing the name "Ath Cliath," to some peculiarity in the site of the city differing on the manner in which hurdles were employed whether in the foundations of houses or in roads on the river banks or in fishing weirs but agreeing in not tracing the name to any passage across the river, and that they are correct in one portion of their statement, that is, in asserting that Dublin

<small>O'Halloran singular and correct.</small>

---

[1] History and antiquities of the city of Dublin, by the late Walter Harris, pp. 10, 11, 8vo, Dublin, 1766.

[2] History of the City of Dublin, by the late J. Warburton, Rev. John Whitelaw, and the Rev. Robert Walsh, 2 vols. 4to, Dublin, 1818.

[3] Dubhlin, for so this city was called in those days, lay on the south side of the Liffey and seemingly at some distance from the river, and would seem was so called from 'Dubh,' black, and 'lin,' a port, because built down Patrick-street and Kevin's-port, and the Poddle, which last probably got its name from its low, dirty situation, *quasi* Puddle. The north side was called Atha Cliath or the Ford of Hurdles, communicating with Dubhlin by that means, and from its contiguity to the water was more convenient for traffic. 'General History of Ireland,' by Silvester O'Halloran, 2 vols., 4to, London, 1778. 'Introduction,' p. 120.

APPENDIX.

Dublin of late found built on bog.

is built on a marshy soil, was recently placed beyond doubt.

At the close of the last year, in making a large sewer through High-street, Castle-street, Winetavern and Fishamble-street, the ground was opened to the depth of 8 to 14 feet, and a section was thereby exposed of the elevated ridge and one side of the hill on which the old city stood.

The work was nearly complete before my attention was directed to it, but Mr. Neville, the city Engineer, having kindly accompanied me I had facilities for examining a part of the excavation and of hearing from him and the contractor for the work an account of its progress.

From the middle of High-street to the Castle wall, at depths varying from 8 to 10 feet, the workmen found a stratum of black boggy soil, generally soft but in some places so compact that one of the labourers asserted that he had used it for fuel during the time he was employed in the work. Above this stratum was found one of leaves, and branches, &c., of trees (to which I will presently refer) the stratum immediately under the roadway being soft clay or mud intermingled with shells.

In Fishamble-street, at the depth of 12 to 14 feet, was found a quantity of squared oak timber apparently portions of frame work with piles 4 to 5 feet long, and in Christ Church-place were found foundations of houses, and below those soft mud mixed with shells, leaves, pieces of trees, and black boggy stuff or peat.

The stratum of peat terminated near St. Audoen's Church, where blue or yellow clay (the very general substratum of bogs in Ireland), was found below the roadway, the foundations and vaults of Newgate being discovered a short distance westward, thus marking the portion of High-street, &c., within the city walls.

From proprietors of houses in the same district I ascertained that nearly similar results had followed excavations for new buildings.

When rebuilding part of the "Irish Woollen Warehouse" in Castle-street, in 1838, the ground was excavated about 20 feet, but foundations so deep did not secure the superstructure, the front wall fell, the stack of chimneys sank nearly 4 feet and ultimately it became necessary to place a frame of timber with concrete to build on. In this excavation the workmen found black turf covered by a stratum of leaves and portions of trees, the upper stratum being soft clay or mud with shells intermixed. APPENDIX.<br>Houses on bog in Castle-street.

When rebuilding the Artists Warehouse in Fishamble-street, it was likewise found necessary to lay the foundations on a frame of timber. The soil had been excavated or pierced with boring rods upwards of 30 feet without touching firm ground. The under stratum was nearly pure black turf and above it loose clay, the upper stratum being soft and intermingled with shells, but the shells found here were of cockles and muscles which appeared to have been opened for food being probably the refuse of the ancient fish shambles which occupied this site and from which the street is named. In Fishamble-street.

During alterations in the basement of No. 3, High-street, it was ascertained that the house had been built on a frame of timber and other houses in that and Castle-street were ascertained to have been erected in the same manner. There can be no doubt therefore that Dublin, within the old walls, stands on a plot of marshy ground and that in laying the foundations of houses it is necessary to fix the quagmire with hurdles or frames of timber. Previously however to observations on these facts so connected with the name Ath Cliath, the evidence obtained respecting other peculiarities of the site may be stated. In High-street.

Harris, in his "History and Antiquities of Dublin," says, the site on which the city was founded was called "Drom Choll Coill" (the Brow of the Hazelwood),[1] and a considerable quantity of hazel nuts having been found intermingled Drom Choll Coill, or Brow of the Hazelwood.

[1] Pp. 10–11.

with the stratum of leaves and portions of trees already mentioned, I had ten specimens of trees which had been dug up in different parts of Castle-street excavation, submitted for the inspection of Professor Allman. Dr. Allman found the fibre of one of these specimens so much injured by lying in the wet bog or otherwise, that the species of tree to which it belonged could not be determined; but he ascertained that three of the others were willow and five hazel—this, and the number of hazel-nuts found, supplying presumptive evidence that at a remote period a hazel-wood grew on this hill, and that Harris, or rather the Irish authority on which he relied, was probably correct in stating that "The Brow of the Hazelwood" was a name for the ridge of the hill on which Dublin was built.

But as regards the name of the city itself, although these excavations furnished incontrovertible evidence that Stanihurst and others had correctly stated that Dublin is built on a marshy soil, where some security is necessary to the foundations of modern houses; it did not follow that they were equally correct in asserting that the Irish name "Ath Cliath" originated from the use of hurdles in building the city.

"Ath Cliath" is a name of high antiquity. We find it in connexion with transactions anterior to the fifth and sixth centuries, and we are aware that prior to that period the dwellings of the natives were almost universally constructed of timber, or of timber and wickerwork, plastered with clay.[1] As such habitations did not require the firm

[1] ["The poorer Irish who follow 'creaghting,' or running up and down the country after their herds of cattle, dwell in booths made of hurdles or boughs covered with long strips of green turf instead of canvas, run up in a few minutes, and even the higher classes in Ulster, who, some of them, follow the same custom; for such are the dwellings of the very lords amongst them." Fynes Moryson, p. 164, London, folio 1617. The following description was written in 1644. "The towns are built in the English fashion; but the houses in the country are in this manner: two stakes are fixed in the ground, across

foundations indispensable for the brick and stone, or high cagework, houses of the period when these histories of Dublin were compiled, is it not doubtful that previously to the sixth century the city should have been named from the use of hurdles in the foundation of houses? Is it not much more probable that the statements of Stanihurst and Ware originated in the very common practice of deriving ancient names from modern facts? The suburbs of the city furnish a remarkable instance of this mode of proceeding. Ringsend is alleged to be so called because the mooring rings for shipping in the Liffey ended there;[1] the more probable derivation being from the Irish word (Riñ) Rinn, a point or tongue of land, corrupted into ring, as in Ringrone, Ringagonal, Ringhaddy, or other points of land jutting into rivers or into the sea. Another instance may be found in the alleged origin of the name Pill-lane, which is stated by De Burgho (in his "Hibernia Dominicana") to be from some fancied connexion with the English Pale,[2] instead of being from a way leading to the "Pill" or little

<small>APPENDIX.</small>

<small>Of Ringsend.</small>

<small>Of Pill-lane.</small>

---

[1] "And whereas . . . the place where ships do ride at anchor . . . is so far from our Custom House that many goods . . . may be conveyed from said ships at night without the knowledge of our Officers of Customs, . . . which is a transverse pole to support rows of sloping stakes, on the two sides, which are covered with straw and leaves. They are without chimneys. . . ."—Travels of the Sieur De La Boullaye le Gouz, 'Gentilhomme Angevin,' in Italy, Greece, Anatolia, Syria, East Indies, Great Britain, and Ireland, &c., &c. 4to, Paris, 1657. Edited by Crofton Croker for Camden Soc., 1837, p. 40.] which inconvenience might be avoided if there were an house built for an officer . . . at the place called 'the Ringsend.' "—Letter of King James I., under Privy Seal, 29th October, 1620. Printed Patent Rolls of King James I. Art. i., p. 506. *Ibid.*, 12th Oct., Art. cxxxii., p. 512.

[2] "On the north side (of the river) is Pale-lane (Viculus Pali), commonly called 'Pill-lane,' being a corruption of the word Pale, meaning enclosure, as I have already explained when treating of the English Pale in Ireland."—Hibernia Dominicana, Thomas De Burgo, Colonia Agrippina, p. 189, 4to, 1762.

harbour of St. Mary's Abbey,[1] where the Bradogue river[2] entered the Liffey. Nor should we feel much surprise at Stanihurst, a citizen of Dublin, unacquainted with the Irish language, and knowing nothing of Irish manuscripts, should think that he had sufficient authority for his derivation of the name of "Ath Cliath," when he saw the houses around him built on hurdles or frames of timber; neither should it excite surprise if Harris, the biographer of King William III., knowing that the king's troops, like those of Cromwell under

[1] This Pill was filled up, and Ormond Market occupies the site, as appears from the following entries on the Assembly Rolls:—

"Michaelmas, 1617.—The Eight Corporations prayed for a lease for 99 years upon the Pill beyond the water, at the yearly rent of ten pounds. Midsummer, 1619.—The Commons petitioned that forasmuch as the void ground called the Pill is long void, and might yield rent—Ordered, that if the Eight Corporations do not take a lease it may be let to the best advantage. It seems to have been afterwards leased to James Barry and others. 20th June, 1657—Committee appointed to compromise a long suit between the City and James Barry (made Lord Santry in 1661), Sir Robert Meredith, Alderman Charles Forster, and others, for arrears of rent due for the land called the Pill, near St. Mary's Abbey. 22nd January, 1674.—Jonathan Amory, merchant, to have a lease of that part of the strand on the north side of the Liffey, between the wall of the Pill in the possession of Lord Santry, and the watermill lately built by Gilbert Mabbot. Easter, 1684.—Sir John Davys being interested in the ground lying on the Pill laid out for Ormond market, and the city having lately taken in some of the bed of the river adjacent, he prayed for a lease for 99 years of the ground thus taken in; but the city resolved to have the new ground for a quay, and considering that the fish market there would hinder the beautifying of the quay, and ought to stay where it was, would only grant the lease on condition of Sir John keeping it as a quay, and further undertaking to flag the market"—City By-Laws, Haliday MSS. R. I. Academy.

[2] "It rises in the suburban districts and enters the city boundary where Grangegorman-lane joins the Circular-road, continues under Upper Grangegorman-lane, under the Penitentiary, the canal near the terminus of the Midland Great Western Railway, along the rear of the houses at the west side of New Dominick-street, and by Bolton-street, South Halston-street, Boot-lane, East Arran-street, to the Liffey. A branch of the stream also passes under the Richmond Hospital, and joins the Red Cow-lane sewer." Neville's Report to the Corporation of Dublin on the Sewers, 1853.

Ludlow,[1] had laid hurdles along the marshy banks of the Shannon, should suppose that similar means had been used to pass along the banks of the Liffey, and that from this "fording of hurdles" the town was named.

*Appendix.*

But it should not be necessary to resort to conjectures, for, apart from any consideration arising out of the antiquity of the name, or from the fact that the word "Ath" is almost invariably connected with the Irish name for fords of rivers, the "Dinn Seanchus" (one of the oldest of the Irish topographical tracts) distinctly asserts that the City was named from a contiguous ford on the Liffey, which ford was called "Athcliath," or the ford of hurdles, because hurdles were placed there in the reign of King Mesgedhra to enable the sheep of Athairne Ailgeaseah to pass over the river to Dun Edair, a fortress on Howth.[2]

*Origin of the name Athcliath.*

There are few countries in which an ancient authority of this kind would not be preferred to the surmises of a recent historian, or where such a manuscript would not be considered sufficient to establish an etymology, but Irish authorities on the ancient state of Ireland are not so freely received. The Chronicles of Bede, Hoveden, William of Malmsbury, or Mathew of Westminster, although burdened with enormous fictions, prodigies, or miracles are, notwithstanding, implicitly relied on as the groundwork of English history, while the statements of the greater portion of our Irish Annalists are utterly rejected, because these annalists, like the early historians of all nations, embellish narratives of fact with tales of romance, and ascribe to the founders of National royalty some remote and seemingly fabulous origin. I will, therefore, adduce other authorities to corroborate that of the "Dinn Seanchus," at least so far as to show that at a very early period there was an artificial passage across the Liffey at Dublin.

---

[1] Memoirs of Edmond Ludlow, folio, London, 1751; pp. 133, 134.

[2] John O'Donovan, LL.D.,

"Dublin Penny Journal," 17 November, 1832., vol. i., p. 157.

214    THE SCANDINAVIANS, AND

APPENDIX.

Being without those aids which coins and medals elsewhere supply, it is difficult to discover the precise character of many of our ancient structures. Our early writers are seldom explicit in their descriptions of Irish structures, and in the present instance we have no information from them what this "Ford of Hurdles" really was. It is probable, however, that it was a passage formed by hurdles and stems of trees laid on piles of stone placed at intervals in the stream. Vestiges of such rude structures yet exist, and whether across rivers, swamps, or bogs, are denominated "tochars," or causeways, in contra-distinction to the more regular structure which is termed "droichet" or bridge.

Droichead-cleithe, or hurdle bridges, in Ireland.

But even in more regular structures, hurdles appear to have been used, as Irish writers distinguish as "droichet," a bridge of timber or stone, and a "droichead cleithe," or bridge of hurdles[1], and there are circumstances which justify

[1] A.D. 1116 this year (the Four Masters say 1120), three principal bridges were built by Toirlheach Ua Conchobair (Turlough O'Connor), viz.:—the bridge of Athluain (Athlone), and the bridge of Ath Crocha (near Shannon Harbour), and the bridge of Dunleodha (Dunlo). Chronicum Scotorum: A Chronicle of Irish Affairs from the earliest times to 1135, with a Supplement from 1141 to 1150. Edited with a Translation by William Maunsell Hennessy, M.R.I.A., 8vo., Dublin, 1866 (Master of the Roll's Series). A.D. 1125: The bridge of Athluain and the bridge of AthCroich were destroyed by the men of Meath. Annals of the Four Masters, by John O'Donovan, LL.D., 7 vols., 4to Dublin, 1851. A.D. 1129: The Castle of Athluain and the bridge were erected by Toirdhelb Ua Conchobhair in the summer of this year "in the summer of the drought." Ibid. A.D. 1133: The wicker bridge of Athluain and its Castle were destroyed by Murchadh Ua Maelseachlainn and Tighearnan Ua Ruairc. A.D. 1155: The bridge of Athluain was destroyed, and its fortress burned by Donnchadh, son of Domhnal Ua Maelseachlainn. Ibid. A.D. 1159: A wicker bridge (Cliath Droichet) was made at Athluain by Ruaidhir Ua Conchobhair for the purpose of making incursions into Meath. The forces of Meath and Teathba. . . . went to prevent the erection of the bridge, and a battle was fought between both parties at Athluain. Ibid. A.D. 1170: The Ua Maine plundered Ormond on this occasion, and destroyed the wooden bridge of Cille Dalua (Killaloe) Ibid. A.D. 1140: A wicker bridge was made by Turlough O'Connor across Athliag (Ballyliag, near Lanesboro').

the suggestion that our hurdle bridges were somewhat similar to those which are still used in the East, wherein the words of Dr. Layard in the "Nineveh Researches"—"Stakes are firmly fastened together with twigs, forming a long hurdle reaching from one side of the river to the other, the two ends are laid upon beams resting upon piers on the opposite banks. Both beams and basket-work are kept in their places by heavy stones heaped upon them." And he adds—"Animals, as well as men, are able to pass over this frail structure, which swings to and fro, and seems ready to give way at every step."[1] Apparently it was a structure of this kind to which the Four Masters refer, when recording that "O'Donnell ordered his army to construct a strong hurdle bridge [across the Mourne], which being done, his whole army, both infantry and cavalry, crossed over," and, "They then let the bridge float down the stream, so that their enemies could only view them from the opposite side.[2]

<sub>Appendix.</sub>

<sub>Hurdle bridges in Asia.</sub>

Assuming, therefore, that the "Ath Cliath," or Ford of Hurdles, mentioned in the "Dinn Seanchus," was a species of bridge, I will proceed to show that the received opinions respecting the first bridge at Dublin are wholly incorrect.

In our published histories it is almost invariably stated that the first bridge at Dublin was built by King John; and his charter of the 3rd July, 1215, is considered to afford proof of the fact. By that charter (which greatly increased the privileges conferred by Henry II., and also those given in 1192 by John, when Earl of Morton), the King grants to his citizens of Dublin that they "may make a bridge over the water of the Avenlithe wherever it may appear most expedient for them."[3] The inference deduced being, that as there was no similar grant in any preceding charter, there had

<sub>Bridge at Dublin before King John's reign.</sub>

---

[1] "Nineveh, its Remains," By Austin H. Layard, 2 vols., 8vo., London. 2d Edit., 1849, p. 192.

[2] A D. 1483. Annals of the Four Masters.

[3] Rotuli Litterarum Clausarum in Turri Londinensi, asservati, 2 vols., folio (1833–1844). Edited by Thos. Duffus Hardy, vol. 1., p. 219.

not been previously any bridge at Dublin; and, as William of Worcester states, that in the same year King John built the first bridge at Bristol (having shortly before sent to France for Isenbert, the Architect, to complete the first stone[1] bridge at London),[2] his desire for bridge-building had led to the building of the bridge at Dublin, the Chief City of his lordship of Ireland, and the seat of his Bristol colony.

This assumption is, however, negatived; in fact, if there had been any reference to records in the Tower of London which relate to this charter, it never could have been urged.

*King John grants the city his half of the Liffey.*

Amongst the "Close rolls" of King John, are his instructions to the archbishop of Dublin, dated 1st February, 1215, in which he says:—"The burgesses of Dublin have offered us 200 marks to have their town to farm in fee by charter, with the part of the river which belongs to us. You may take that fine, or a greater, as shall seem to you most expedient for us, and then they may send for our charter, which we will make as you may devise."[3] A subsequent letter, dated Devizes, the 5th July, shows that the archbishop was an able negotiator, as he extracted from the citizens 100 marks more than they had offered to the King,[4] the important document relating to the bridge being dated the 23rd August, 1214, that is in the year before the charter was granted or negotiated for. Here the king informs the archbishop that he has authorized his citizens of Dublin to build a bridge

---

[1] London Bridge (then of wood), was destroyed by fire A.D. 1136. It is supposed to have been erected between A.D. 993 and A.D. 1016. History of London by William Maitland, F.R.S., folio, London, 1739, p. 33.

[2] "John, by the grace of God, &c., to the Mayor and Citizens of London, greeting. Considering in how short a time the bridges of Saintes and Rochelle. . . . . by the diligence of our faithful clerk, Isenbert, master of the schools of Saintes. . . . . . have been constructed. We have urged him. . . to come. . . and use the same diligence in building your bridge. . . Witness, &c.. 18th day of April, in the 3rd of our reign (A.D. 1202).

[3] Rot. Litt. Claus., 16 Johan, p. 186.

[4] *Ibid.*, 17 Johan, p. 129.

over the water of the Avenlithe, where it shall seem most expedient for the use of the city, and that "they may cause the other bridge over that water, formerly made, to be destroyed if it shall be expedient for their indemnity (indempnitati),"[1] thus incontestably proving that there was a bridge at Dublin prior to the charter of 1215. Nor is the evidence of this fact confined to a single document. There is in the Tower another charter of King John confirming a grant to Hugo Hosee of land "at the stone gate near the bridge," a document which through the kindness of Thomas Duffus Hardy, esq., Keeper of the Tower Records, I had also an opportunity to examine, leaving no doubt respecting the date, which is the 4th June, 1200;[2] and further, if it were necessary to add to such instances, we might refer to the transcript of Urban the Third's bull in Alan's Register (in the Archiepiscopal Library, Dublin) to show that the bridge existed in 1186, or to the chartulary of St. Thomas's Abbey, known as Coppinger's Register (which is now in my possession), to show from a grant by Thomas La Martre that the bridge existed in 1177,[3] and to other ecclesiastical documents which refer to this bridge at an earlier date. Nor is it devoid of probability that the bridge thus referred to was one which had been erected by the Danish possessors of Dublin. It must be recollected that although John permitted the citizens to build a bridge in 1215, we have no evidence that in 1215 the citizens destroyed "the bridge formerly made," or that they built

*The citizens may make a new bridge or keep the old.*

---

[1] *Ibid.*, 16 Johan, p. 172.

[2] Datum Apud Falesiam, 4to die Junii, regni nostri anno secundo. *Ibid.*, p. 69.

[3] Thomas La Martre gave to the Abbey of St. Thomas (Thomascourt, Dublin), a plot of ground *at Dublin Bridge*, situate between the ground which he had given to his wife, Margaret, and that which he had granted to the Hospital of Kilmainham. Witnessed by Godfrey of Winchester in the latter end of K. Hen. II. Coppinger's Register of St. Thomas's Abbey, p. 88. Haliday MSS., Roy. Irish Academy, Monasticon Hibernicum, by Mervyn Archdall, p. 182, 4to, Dublin, 1786.

APPENDIX.

Bridge of the Ostmen.

another bridge at that period, although permitted to do so. As yet the assumption that any bridge was built at Dublin during King John's reign rests solely on the fact that permission was then given to destroy one bridge and to build another, whilst we have records to prove that both before and considerably after that period there was a bridge at Dublin called "the Bridge of the Ostmen." In a grant to Ralph la Hore in 1236, the land is described "in capite pontis Ostmannorum."[1] The name is repeated in a grant to William de Nottingham so late as 1284, which describes a stone tower as being "juxta pontem Ostmannorum," and as these records also refer to "the gate of the Ostmen,"[2] to "the old quarry of the Ostmen" ("a veteri quadrivio Ostmanorum"), &c.,[3] there are grounds for supposing that the works so denominated had been executed by the Ostmen, and were not works thus called from proximity to the suburb of Ostmantown. However, having proved from Anglo-Norman documents that there was a bridge at Dublin prior to the year 1200, I will now trace it through native records, and establish for it a much higher antiquity. And here I may observe that whatever may have been the name

[1] "Know all men that we, the citizens of Dublin, have by this our charter granted and confirmed to Ralph Hore, our fellow-citizen, a tower of ours with its appurtenances, situated at the head of Ostmen's bridge on the south, to be held of us by him and his heirs for ever."—Historic and Municipal Documents of Ireland, A.D. 1172-1320. From the Archives of the city of Dublin, by J. T. Gilbert, 8vo, London, 1870, p. 488 (Master of the Rolls' Series).

[2] "Know ye that we, the Mayor and Commonalty of Dublin, have given by this our charter to William Nottingham, our fellow citizen, a certain stone tower near the Ostmen's bridge, and joined to the tower beyond the Ostmen's gate, &c. Dated Sunday next after the Feast of St. Bartholomew, 12th Edward I. (A.D. 1285)."—White Book of Dublin, p. 54.

[3] "Know all men that we, the citizens of Dublin, have by this our charter granted and confirmed to Ralph Hore and William Russell, our fellow-citizens, a meadow of ours extending in length from the Old Quarry of the Ostmen to Kylmehanok," &c.—White Book of Dublin, J. T. Gilbert, *ibid.*, p. 486.

of this bridge after the Danes were expelled from Dublin, unquestionably it was previously called "Droichet Dubhghall," Dubhghall being the name of a man, probably that given by the Irish to the Danish founder of the bridge, as Dubhghall (literally the black foreigner) was a name which they frequently gave to their Danish invaders. They so called one of the Danish Chieftains killed at the battle of Clontarf,[1] who is mentioned in the Annals as "Dubhghall son of Amahlaeibh,"[2] the brother of Sitric, Danish King of Dublin in 1014.[3] We find that the bridge is thus called in the "Four Masters," where it is stated that "A.D. 1112, a predatory excursion was made by Domhnall, grandson Lochlan across Fine-Gall, that is to say, as far as Droichet Dubhghall." And that eminent Irish scholar, Mr. Eugene Curry, has furnished me with extracts from Irish manuscripts in the Library of Trinity College, Dublin, and in the Royal Library of Brussels, from which we can trace this bridge under the name of "Droichet Dubhghall" to the commencement of the eleventh century.

*APPENDIX.*

*Dubhgall's bridge and the battle of Clontarf.*

In Brussels there is a copy of the "Book of the Danish Wars,"[4] containing an account of battles in which the Danes had been engaged. Relating incidents of the celebrated battle of Clontarf in 1014, it states that the confederate army of the Danes having been routed, some of the fugitives were driven into the sea; whilst of the Danes of Dublin who were in the engagement only nine escaped from it, and "the household of Tiege O'Kelly followed these and slew them at the head of the bridge of Ath Cliath, that is Dubhghall's bridge." The older fragment of the manuscript of the same tract, in Trinity College library, merely states,

[1] War of the Gaedhil with the Gaill, p. 207.
[2] Ib., p. 165.  [3] Ib., p. 35.
[4] Since published under the title of "The War of the Gaedhil with the Gaill or the Invasions of Ireland by the Danes and other Norsemen. The original Irish text edited by James Henthorn Todd, D.D., M.R.I.A., F.S.A. Published by the authority of the Lords of the Treasury under the direction of the Master of the Rolls, 8vo, London, 1867."

APPENDIX.

"they were overtaken and slain at the head of the bridge of Ath Cliath;" but "The Book of Leinster" recording the death of Maelmordha, on his retreat from the battle, expressly states that he was drowned at "Dubhghall's bridge."[1]

Irish Bridges before the time of the Ostmen.

Beyond this period, that is, 150 years prior to the Anglo-Norman invasion we cannot produce distinct evidence of "a droichet" or bridge at Dublin, although it is highly probable that there was, previously, a regular structure of that kind across the Liffey. We know that these Northmen, who had only established their sovereignty on the sea-coasts of Ireland, had subjugated all England, and held frequent intercourse with it. Godfred II., who was King of Dublin in 922, was also King of Northumberland; and the "Saxon Chronicle" states that Anlaf (the Danish King of Dublin), after his defeat at Brunanburg, by Athelstan in 937, fled with his Northmen in "their nailed barks over the deep waters, Dublin to seek."[2] We might, therefore, infer that these Danish or Norwegian Kings having territory on both sides of the Liffey, did not omit to establish at Dublin the mode of crossing rivers which they must have seen in England. For although it may be doubtful if the Romans ever erected a stone bridge in Britain, it is certain that they erected many of wood,[3] the material most commonly used until the close of the twelfth century, when St. Benedict founded his order of "Pontifices" or stone bridge builders.[4] Yet if we cannot find the term "bridge" applied to any

[1] Ibid., Appendix C, p 251, chap. cv. Ibid., Introd., p. clxxxii.

[2] The Anglo-Saxon Chronicle in Monumenta Historica Britannica. Prepared by Henry Petrie, F.S A., and the Rev. John Sharpe. Published by command of Her Majesty. Folio, London, 1848, p. 385.

[3] Archæologia, vol. x., p. 34. Also ibid., vol. vii., p. 395, Eboracum or the History of the Antiquities of York, by Francis Drake, Folio, London, 1736, p. 53. History and Antiquities of New Castle upon Tyne, by John Brand, F.S.A., 4to, London, 2 vols., 1789.

[4] A secular order of Hospitalers was founded by S. Benezet towards the close of the twelfth century under the denomination of Pontifices or Bridge builders. Rees's Encyclopædia. Article 'Bridges.'

structure at Dublin prior to the year 1014, we have no difficulty in finding evidence that a roadway had been formed across the river before that period. Again referring to the "Annals of the Four Masters" we find that in the year 1000, "the Tochar," or Causeway of Athluain (Athlone) was made by Maelseachlainn, son of Domhnall, King of Ireland, and Cathal Ua Conchobhair, King of Connaught, and that they made the Tochar or Causeway of Athliag (Ballyliag near Lanesboro') in the same year, each carrying his portion to the middle of the Shannon.[1] This is referred to as illustrating the statement of the "Chronicon Scotorum" that in the year 999 King Malachy made a tochar at Ath Cliath (Dublin), until it reached "one half of the river,"[2] apparently the custom being that when a tidal or non-tidal river divided the territories of Irish kings, each claimed one-half of it and only built to the middle of the stream, and to this (irrespective of the division of land made by Mogh Naudhat and Conn) we may attribute that the earliest charters of Dublin only granted to the citizens the southern half of the Liffey being that within the kingdom of Leinster (Strongbow's portion with M'Morrough's daughter), the other half of the river being in the territory of Meath.

APPENDIX.

Site of the Causeway across the Liffey.

It is not necessary to the present inquiry to ascertain the precise position of this tocher (A.D. 1001.) Whether it had been made at the ford opposite St. Mary's Abbey, and was the origin of the well known tradition of an ancient communication between the Abbey and Christ Church. (St.

---

[1] Annals of the Four Masters, vol. ii., p. 744, and note *ibid*.

[2] ["The causeway of Ath Cliath was made by Maelseachlainn as far as the middle of the river." Chronicon Scotorum, p. 239. But the editor says in a note that the Annals of Clonmacnois and the Four Masters specify Athliag and are probably correct as Dublin was at this time subject to O'Brien, and neither that monarch nor his Danish subjects of Dublin would tolerate such an assumption of authority on the part of Maelseachlainn who had recently been forced to resign the supremacy in his favour. Note *ibid*. This work was not published till after Mr. Haliday's death.]

APPENDIX.

Stonybatter.

Mary's, on the north bank of the Liffey, alleged to have been built in 948, and the arches under Christ Church built on the south bank at as early a date)—or whether this tocher led to the old "bothyr," or road, now anglicised into "Stonybatter;"[1] or had occupied the site of that which long continued to be called the "old bridge"[2]—although

[1] ["A remarkable instance of this hardening process occurs in some of the Leinster counties, where the Irish word *bóthar* [boher] a road is converted into *batter*. This word "batter," is, or was well understood in these counties to mean an ancient road; and it was used as a general term in this sense in the patents of James I. It signifies in Wexford a lane or narrow road. "Bater, a lane leading to a high road." ("Glossary of the dialect of Forth and Bargy," by Jacob Poole; edited by William Barnes, B.D.") "As for the word Bater, that in English purpozeth a lane bearing to an highway. I take it for a meere Irish word that crept unawares into the English through the daily intercourse of the English and Irish inhabitants." (Stanyhurst, quoted in same.) "The word occurs in early Anglo-Irish documents, in the form of *bothir* or *bothyr*, which was easily converted into *botter* or *batter*. It forms part of the following names:—Batterstown, the name of four townlands in Meath, which were always called in Irish, Baile-an-bhothair, *i.e.*, the town of the road . . . Near Drogheda, there is a townland called Green Batter, and another Yellow Batter, which are called in Irish, *Boherglas* and *Boherboy*, having the same meanings as the present names, viz., *green road* and *yellow road*. We have also some examples, one of which is the well known name of Stonybatter. Long before the city had extended so far, and while Stonybatter was nothing more than a country road it was—as it still continues to be—the great thoroughfare to Dublin from the districts lying west and north-west of the city, and it was known by the name of *Bothar-na-gcloch* [Bohernaglogh], *i.e.*, the road of the stones, which was changed to the modern equivalent, Stoney-batter, or Stony-road."—The origin and history of Irish Names of Places, by P. W. Joyce, LL.D., M.R.I.A., pp. 43-45. 12mo. Dublin, M'Glashan & Gill, 1871.]

[2] "In the year 1428, the Friars Preachers of this convent of St. Saviour's had a school in an old suburb of Dublin, now called Usher's Island, with a large recourse of scholars of philosophy and theology. As the professors and students from Ostmantown could not conveniently come and go because of the river Liffey, a bridge of four arches, still standing, was built at the cost of the Friars' Preachers, being the first of the six bridges of Dublin, called everywhere to this day, the Old Bridge. To repay the cost, a lay Domini-

the old bridge had been destroyed in 1314,[1] its substitute swept away in 1385,[2] and at least twice subsequently rebuilt—it is sufficient to have traced so far the existence of an artificial passage across the Liffey at Dublin; but between this link and the next, by which we should form our chain of corroborative evidence, there is a long interval. We have records of bridges over small rivers in Ireland, in 924, and are told that a king of Ulster was celebrated for bridge-building in 739; but we cannot refer to any incident connected with the existence of a bridge or tochar at Dublin, between the commencement of the fifth century and the close of the tenth. This, however, is an interval in which we may safely rely on circumstantial evidence. It was within this period that Ireland was celebrated as the school of ecclesiastical learning. It was the Island of Saints, and from it ecclesiastics travelled throughout Europe to teach; and to it European scholars journeyed to learn. We may therefore rest assured that whatever of art or science was then known elsewhere, was not unknown in Ireland, and that when there was sufficient art to build churches and round towers, to construct "nailed barks," and to supply all that ships required for long voyages,

APPENDIX.

Old bridges of Dublin.

[1] "In the year 1315, Edward Bruce, with his army advanced to Castleknock, only three miles from Dublin northwards. Whereat the citizens being alarmed broke the bridge of Dublin, and burned the suburbs, and also demolished the monastery of the Dominican Friars in Oxmantown Green, and with the stones built Winetavern can, by leave of the City Council, took a toll, and I myself, when a boy, have seen the holy water vessel (as tradition had it) for sprinkling the passengers."—Hibernia Dominicana, by Thomas De Burgo. 4to, 1762, p. 189.

Gate and Audöen's Arch, with a wall running from one to the other."—Annales Hibernica, MSS. in Marsh's (St. Patrick's) Library. Class 3, Tab. 2, No. 7.

[2] "A.D. 1386. The king considering the losses of the citizens of Dublin through the late breaking down of Dublin bridge, has granted them a ferry over the Liffey, there for four years. (Table of tolls annexed.) 9th of January, in 9th year of King Richard II." Calendar of Patent Rolls of Chancery, Ireland. Folio. Dublin. (Record Publications) Art. 93, p. 124.

there was mechanical art sufficient to make any needful passage across such a river as the Liffey. It was at the close of this period, that an Irish saint (Mowena) had visited Croyland, celebrated for the most curiously constructed bridge in England,[1] and at the commencement of it, that Irish traders, in Irish ships had carried St. Patrick and others as slaves into Ireland out of Gaul, then covered with remains of Roman art. Passing, therefore, over this interval, and again taking up our chain of evidence at the fifth century, we find that between this period and the first century there must have been a roadway across the Liffey. For this highly interesting evidence I am indebted to the research of my friend Dr. Petrie for his "History and Antiquities of Tara."[2]

<small>Causeway over the Liffey in fifth century.</small>

The Ordnance Survey of Ireland having presented the long-desired opportunity for making a correct plan of the remains of Tara the existing vestiges were laid down, according to accurate measurement on a map by Captain Bordes of the Royal Engineers, who had charge of the Survey. While this was in progress Dr. Petrie and Dr. O'Donovan who were then attached to the Survey, made a careful search in all ancient Irish manuscripts accessible, for such documents of a descriptive or historical character as would tend to identify or illustrate the existing vestiges. The result was eminently successful in corroborating the statements of our early writers; works, the description of which had been previously regarded as mere bardic fictions, were traced with a degree of accuracy, which, so far, placed beyond doubt the truthfulness of these ancient authorities.

---

[1] Saint "Modwena expelled from his monastery in Ireland in the ninth century, obtained an asylum from King Ethelwulf, and erected a chapel (at Burton-on-Trent). Over the river is a noble bridge of freestone, 512 yards long, of 37 arches, built prior to the Conquest, and substantially repaired in the reign of King Henry the Second." Lewis's Topographical Dictionary of England.

[2] Read May, 1837, and published in the Transactions of the Royal Irish Academy, vol. xviii., A.D. 1839.

There is, however, only one of these identifications to which APPENDIX. it will be necessary, for the present inquiry, that I should refer.

In our oldest manuscripts it is stated that, in the first century, Ireland was intersected by five great roads, leading from different provinces, or petty Kingdoms, to the seat of supreme royalty at Tara.[1] Of these "slighes," or roads, the "Slighe Cualaun" was one traced with the greatest apparent certainty by the Ordnance Survey. It struck off from the Fan-na-g-carbad, or "Slope of the chariots," and led *via* Ratoath and Dublin into Cualaun; a district extending from Dalkey, southwards and westwards, and part of which, including Powerscourt, is designated in Anglo-Norman records, as Fercullen, or "the territory of the men of Cualaun." This road, consequently, must have crossed the Liffey, and that it did so near Dublin is confirmed by the fact, that the passage across the river there is frequently termed "Ath Cliath Cualaun."[2] Now it is impossible that a roadway for any general purpose could be carried across a river like the Liffey, subject to winter floods and the daily flow of the tide, unless that roadway was formed by a bridge, tochar, or structure of some kind raised above the ordinary high water mark. Such a structure, formed of timber or hurdles, the only material then used for that purpose, was doubtless that which, in the figurative language of the time, was termed an "Ath Cliath" or Ford of hurdles.[3]

*The five slighes or roads to Tara.*

*Slighe Cualaun crossed the Liffey at Dublin.*

---

[1] See Map of the Monuments of Tara Hill, restored from Ancient Documents, *Ibid*, plate 7, p. 152.

[2] *Ibid*, p. 229.

[3] Mr. Joyce in continuation of his remarks on the name of Stony-batter (*supra*, p. 222, and note *ibid.*), says "One of the five great roads leading from Tara which were constructed in the second century, viz., that called *Slighe-Cualaun* passed through Dublin by Ratoath and on towards Bray, under the name of *Bealach Duibhlinne*. Duibhlinn was originally the name of that part of the Liffey on which the city now stands (the road or pass of the [river] Duibhlinn), it is mentioned in the following quotation from "the Book of Rights"—

APPENDIX.

From the Slighe-Cualann crossing the Liffey at Dublin became the *re Bally-Ath-Cliath.*

Adding this evidence of a passage across the river to the distinct statements of the Diun Seanchus, I hope I may appear justified in the opinion I now venture to express, that those great authorities on Irish history, Stanihurst, Camden, and Ware, are incorrect in asserting that Dublin was called " Bally Ath Cliath," because the ancient city was built on a marshy soil, where hurdles were necessary to secure the foundations of houses ; and that in this, as in other cases, we may more safely rely on Irish annalists than on modern historians, and assert that the name " Ath Cliath " originated from a passage across the Liffey, that passage being made by hurdles, so laid as to form an artificial ford or bridge. I am aware that there was a ford on the Shannon, which also was called " Ath Cliath " ; but I am likewise aware that Irish manuscripts expressly state that it was so called, not from hurdles being placed (as they were at Dublin), in order to form a passage, but because stakes were driven in the river, and hurdles placed as a barrier to prevent an enemy from crossing.[1] Thus

" It is prohibited to him (the King of Erin), to go with a host, on Monday over the *Bealach Duibhlinne.*" "There can be, I think, no doubt (continues Mr. Joyce), that the present Stonybatter formed a portion of this ancient road, a statement that is borne out by two independent circumstances. First, Stonybatter lies straight on the line and would, if continued, meet the Liffey exactly at Whitworth bridge. Secondly, the name of Stonybatter, or *Bothar-na-gcloch,* affords even a stronger confirmation. The most important of the ancient Irish roads were generally paved with large blocks of stone, somewhat like the old Roman roads, a fact that is proved by the remains of those that can now be traced. It is exactly this kind of road that would be called by the Irish even at the present day, Behernaglogh ; and the existence of this name, on the very line leading to the ancient ford over the Liffey leaves scarcely any doubt that this was a part of the ancient *Slighe Cualann.* It must be regarded as a fact of great interest that the modern-looking name of Stonybatter, changed as it has been in the course of ages, descends to us with a history seventeen hundred years old written on its front." Joyce's Origin and History of Irish Names of Places, part i., chapt. 2, p. 45.

[1] Ath Cliath Meadrighe, now Clarensbridge in the county of Galway. " When the Seven Maines carried off the cattle of

disclosing a remarkable coincidence in the mode of defensive warfare practised by the ancient inhabitants of Ireland and of Britain, Cæsar informing us that the Britons, in a similar manner, had endeavoured to prevent his Army from crossing the Thames, by driving stakes in the river and on its banks and thereby obstructing the ford.[1] And it is further suggestive of similarity of habit with a considerable amount of mechanical art (also apparent in our huge monuments of stone), that in the first century, when the Fan-na-g-carbad, or "Slope of the chariots" existed at Tara, Cæsar was describing his contests with the Britons in their chariots constructed for war.

If this attempt to correct erroneous opinions respecting the origin of the ancient Irish name of Dublin should lead to further investigation by others more competent for the task and having more leisure for it, much of my object will be attained. I know that there are in various depositories and libraries in the United Kingdom and on the Continent, unpublished and almost unnoticed records and manuscripts relating to Ireland. And I feel confident that an examination of their contents would tend to remove many obscurities in the early history of our country; might correct many opinions respecting its aboriginal inhabitants and their connexion with other nations; and conjointly with the discoveries daily made, of long buried monuments, might enable us to verify many of these statements, which continue to be viewed with suspicion because as yet they rest solely on the authority of Irish annalists and bards.

Dartaidha, &c., they were overtaken by Eochaid Beag, &c., whereupon the Maines placed a barricade of hurdles of whitethorn and black in the ford until relief should come to them from Aitill and Meane." Information of Eugene O'Curry.

[1] Cæsar, Commentaries, book v. xiv.

APPENDIX.

## II.

### OBSERVATIONS EXPLANATORY OF SIR BERNARD DE GOMME'S MAP, MADE A.D. 1673.[1]

Alarm produced by the entry of the Dutch fleet into the Thames in 1667—Sir Bernard de Gomme's plan for the defence of the Harbour of Dublin in 1673—His project for a fort near Merrion-square—Ringsend then the chief landing place—Meaning of 'Ringsend'—The Pigeon House—Its history—Extent of ground overflown by the sea in 1673—The making of the North and South walls—Sir John Rogerson's wall — Double wall and road from Ringsend to the Pigeon House—Piles in the sand thence to Poolbeg—The building of the Long wall—The lotting for the North Lots—The erecting of the Ballast Board—Early history of the Bar at the Harbour Mouth—The deepening of the River and reducing the Bar the work of the Ballast Board.

*Sir Bernard de Gomme's map, A.D. 1673.* THE map, it will be observed, is entitled "An Exact Survey of the Citty of Dublin, and Part of the Harbour belowe Ringsend," and seems to have been formed by Sir Bernard de Gomme to exhibit the position of the citadel projected by him for the protection of the city and river.

This map, plan, and estimate, never published, and wholly overlooked by local historians,[2] is historically interesting, as showing the earliest design probably for the defence of

[1] "Observations explanatory of a plan and estimate for a Citadel at Dublin, designed by Sir Bernard de Gomme, Engineer-General, in the year 1673, with his map, showing the state of the harbour and river at that time, exhibited to the Royal Irish Academy, at their meeting on Friday the 15th of March, 1861," now first printed.

[2] [The original of this map and estimate for the projected citadel is to be found in the King's Library, British Museum. The map is marked "A crown," liii., 9. The estimate for the citadel at Dublin is indorsed:—"An estimate made by Sir Bernard de Gomme, His Majesty's Chief Engineer, for building of a Royall Citadell at Ringsend, near the citty of Dublin, in His Majesty's kingdom of Ireland, 1673," and is signed by him. This Map being four feet long by two and a half wide, could not be printed in this work; but a fac-simile is given of part. There will be observed a fort depicted on this map as standing on the neck of land at Ringsend near the point. It does not appear when this fort was first built or finally destroyed. In 1655, Colonel Oliver Fitzwilliam

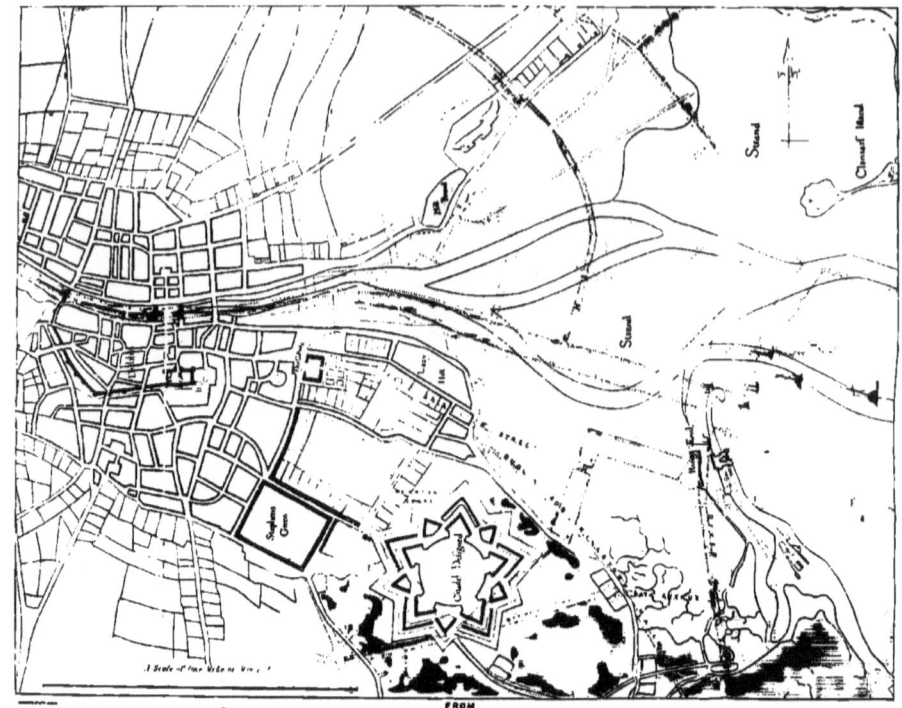

FROM
"An Exact Survey of the Citty of Dublin, and part of the Harbour belowe Rings End."
(Made by Sir Bernard de Gomme in the Year 1673.)

Dublin against an enemy approaching from the sea, and derives a further local interest from the means which it affords for contrasting the then state of the harbour of Dublin with its present condition.

And first as to the causes prompting the design of fortifying Dublin from an attack by sea at this particular period.

The defenceless state of the chief ports of England and Ireland had been forced upon the attention of Government shortly before, in consequence of the success of the Dutch fleet, which entered the Thames in 1667; and after breaking a chain drawn across the mouth of the Medway, took Sheerness and Chatham, and having burned the English ships of war stationed there, sailed out again with scarcely any loss. This successful invasion spread alarm throughout the kingdom, and the consternation was so great in London that nine ships were sunk at Woolwich, and four at Blackwall, to prevent the Dutch from sailing up to London-bridge and destroying the city.

In these circumstances Sir Martin Beckman and Sir

APPENDIX.

Alarm at the Dutch raid in the Thames, A.D. 1667.

of Merrion, second viscount, having won the favour of Cromwell, was ordered a restoration of his estates though a devoted Catholic and Royalist; and the Ringsend fort being found, on 11th October, 1655, on a reference to Attorney-General Basil (A. 8. 224), to be built on part of his estate of Merrion and Thorncastle, and not necessary to be continued as a fort (A. 9, 167), he had liberty on 19th February, 1656, to demolish the four bulwarks of the fort, undertaking to bring into the stores all the iron work belonging to the drawbridge upon demolishing the fort, and for his charges therein the [other] materials to be at his disposal as was desired (A. 86, p. 143). Books of the Commissioners of the Parliament of England for Ireland; Record Tower, Dublin Castle. But such hindrances were given to his getting back his lands, first by the Cromwellians (27th October, 1658, A. 30, p. 328), and after the King's Restoration by the Forty-nine Officers (Protestants), that it was not until the passing of the Act of Explanation 23rd December, 1655, containing a special enactment in his favour (sec. 67), that he could have got a secure possession; and thus had no opportunity probably to demolish the fort.]

Bernard de Gomme,[1] the Royal Engineers, were ordered to construct works for the defence of the Thames. These officers prepared plans for strengthening the fortifications at Sheerness and Tilbury; the works at Tilbury fort being entrusted to Sir Bernard de Gomme, who had previously been employed on the fortifications at Dunkirk; and his plans, with specifications, are now among the manuscripts in the British Museum.

Peace with the Dutch was shortly afterwards concluded, but did not last long; and at the commencement of another war, in 1672, Sir Bernard de Gomme was sent to Ireland to ascertain what works were necessary for the defence of ports in that Kingdom; and after a survey of Dublin and Kinsale, the plan and estimates now exhibited were presented to His Majesty King Charles the Second, on the 15th of November, 1673.

*Citadel to protect the mouth of the Liffey.*

The citadel at Dublin was designed to be a pentagon, occupying a space of 1,946 yards, with ramparts, ravelins, curtain, and bastions, the walls being intended of brick, faced with stone, and built on a frame of timber, and piles. It was to contain barracks for 700 men and officers, with a governor's house, and store houses for munitions of war, a chapel, a prison, a clock-tower, and gateway and drawbridges similar to those at Tilbury fort and Portsmouth, the estimated cost being, £131,227 5s. 9d.; the estimate for constructing a fort at Rincurran, to defend Kinsale, being £10,350.

*To be placed near Merrion-square.*

The site chosen for the Dublin citadel was near the space now occupied by Merrion-square, and it would be difficult to understand the grounds assigned for this choice, viz., its being capable of being relieved by sea without realizing to

---

[1] [Sir Bernard de Gomme, was Engineer General to Prince Rupert at the Prince's siege and capture of Bristol in 1643, and wrote a journal of the siege intended to form a chapter in an account of Prince Rupert's life and actions. Memoirs of Prince Rupert and the Cavaliers, by Elliot Warburton, vol. ii., pp. 236–267, 3 vols., 8vo. London, 1849.]

the mind the fact, that at that day the sea flowed almost to the foot of Merrion-square.[1] That such however were the grounds for the selection, appears in the letters of the Earl of Essex, Lord Lieutenant of Ireland, the report of Mr. Jonas Moore, in the year 1675, stating, "that if his Majesty should think fit to proceed in the design of building a fort royal on the strand, near Ringsend, as was designed by Sir Bernard de Gomme, it is doubtless the only proper piece of ground where a fort can be built so as to be relieved by sea, although for arms the sea air will be very prejudicial"[2] an objection, however, which did not prevent a fort being subsequently erected at the Pigeon House, nearly a mile seaward of the site selected by the royal engineer.[3]

In considering the grounds for selecting this site, it must

[1] ["26th January, 1792: A part of the South-wall suddenly gave way and a dreadful torrent broke into the lower grounds inundating every quarter on the same level as far as Artichoke-road. The communication to Ringsend and Irishtown is entirely cut off and the inhabitants are obliged to go to and fro in boats." Dublin Chronicle, 26th January, 1792: "Yesterday his Grace the Duke of Leinster went on a sea party and after shooting the breach in the South-wall sailed over the low ground in the South Lots and landed safely at Merrion-square." *Ibid.*, 28th January, 1792, W. M. G.]

[2] "Letters of the Earl of Essex, Lord Lieutenant of Ireland in the year 1675," 8vo, Dublin, 1723, p. 132.

[3] [The Pigeon House, first as an hotel, and then as a fort or magazine was preceded, by a block house for storing wreck. The Dublin newspapers of 1766 mention that a vessel being wrecked, a number of 'rockers' who always came down for plunder, were by this means disappointed. It got perhaps the name of Pigeonhouse from John Pigeon employed there. "8th June, 1786, ordered that John Mullarky and *John Pigeon* do attend on Saturday next." Journal of Ballast Office. "25th August, 1787: Your committee have provided a ground plan of the blockhouse which accompanies this report," and thereby allot one portion to Mr. Francis Tunstall, the inspector of the works of the Ballast Board, and other part of, O'Brien and his wife during pleasure as housekeeper" without salary but with liberty to retail spirits, they undertaking to keep the Corporation rooms clean and in good order and provide breakfast when directed for any members of the Board." *Ibid.* In 1790, was built an hotel, and in 1793, arose

APPENDIX.

North side of the harbour.

be borne in mind that any landing by an enemy on the north bank of the River, was nearly impossible by reason of the shoals of slob or sand extending to a great distance, and preventing access to the shore; but had an enemy been ever able to disembark, they would have the river between them and the object of their attack, as the city then lay althogether on the south side of the river, except the district called Ostmantown (the ancient settlement of the Danes or Ostmen), adjoining St. Michan's Church and Smithfield, the latter being long familiarly known under the corrupted name of Oxmantown-green.

South side of the harbour. Its state.

Upon the South side of the river, Ringsend was the chief landing place at the period of Sir Bernard de Gomme's design. The river not being yet quayed and deepened, as it has since been, flowed at low water in streams, winding in devious courses through a labyrinth of sands, as may be seen on Sir Bernard's map.[1]

beside the hotel a magazine of arms. 3rd August, 1790: "A house is intended shortly to be built on the present site of the Pigeon House, and is to be fitted up for the accommodation of persons having occasion to pass and repass between this city and England." Dublin Chronicle 3rd August, 1790. A.D., 1798: "An unexpected event has taken place in this city, namely a cession made by the Corporation for the Improvement of Dublin Harbour of their property in the Pigeon House dock, and newly constructed hotel, to Government, for the purpose of a place of arms and military port, if not for ever at least during this present war." Gentleman's Magazine, part i., p. 435. In 1814 the Board received from Government £100,183 as purchase-money of the Pigeon House basin and premises. Tidal Harbours Commission Report, vol. 1, p. 39a. Mrs. Tunstall's hotel was thought inconvenient and unsafe and she was obliged to retire about thirty years ago. W. M. G.] In the Dublin Penny Journal for September, 28th 1832, is to be found a legend entitled "The Pidgeon House, a tale of the last century." It is stated that there was then living at Ringsend one who had resided there near a century, and is vouched as the author of the story, of which it is enough for the present to say that from Ned Pidgeon, living in the house built "at the pile ends," the Pigeon House is alleged to have got its name. Dublin Penny Journal, vol. ii., No. 65, p. 99.

[1] Boate writes A.D. 1645, "Of dangerous brooks there are two

Above Ringsend the navigation became still more intricate and difficult. The long line of South Wall, nearly three miles and a quarter in length, from Ringsend to Poolbeg,

APPENDIX.

hard by Dublin, both running into the haven . . . the one at the north side a little below Drumconran [the Tolka] . . . the other at the south side close by the Ringsend. This called Rafernam water from the village by which it passeth [the Dodder.] . . . is far the worst of the two, as rising out of those great mountains southwards from Dublin, from whence after any great rain . . . it groweth so deep and violent that many persons have lost their lives therein; amongst others Mr. John Usher, father to Sir William Usher that now is, who was carried away by the current, nobody being able to succour him although many persons and of his neerest friends, both a foot and horseback, were by on both the sides. Since that time a stone bridge hath been built over that brook upon the way betwixt Dublin and Ringsend." Ireland's Naturall History, written [A.D. 1645], by Gerard Boate, late Doctor of Physick to the State in Ireland, and now published by Samuel Hartlib, Esq., and more especially for the benefit of the Adventurers and Planters therein, London, 1652; chapt. vii., sec. 7. " Of the Brooks of Drumconran and Rafernam by Dublin." Reprinted in a collection of Tracts illustrative of Ireland, by Alexander Thom, 2 vols., 8vo. Dublin, 1850. Mr. Usher was drowned in the beginning of the year 1629. For letters of administrations "of the goods of Mr. John Usher, Alderman of Dublin," were granted forth of the Prerogative Court, Dublin, 16th of March, 1629, to " Sir William Usher, son of the deceased." Grant Book, Public Record Office, Four Courts, Dublin. It must be remembered that the only way to Ringsend on those days when the tide was in was to cross the ford of the Dodder where Ball's Bridge now stands (for the sea then flowed to the foot of Holles-street). And at this ford, without doubt, Alderman Usher was drowned. The Dodder, it may be observed here, divides the lands of Baggotrath on the Dublin side, from Simmons-court on the other. The stone bridge mentioned by Boate occupied the site of Ball's Bridge, and must have been built between 1629 and 1637. It was suggested in 1623. " Easter 1623. To the petition of Richard Morgan praying an allowance for erecting of a bridge going to Ringsend, Ordered that as private men have a lease upon the land it therefore convenienceth themselves to build the said bridge." Assembly Rolls. " Midsummer 1640. Certain of the Commons petitioned, that in the year of Mr. Watson's mayoralty [A.D. 1637], there were some charges expended in the repairing of the bridge of Symons-court alias Smoothescourt, since which time the same has fallen to much decay, ordered that ten pounds be expended." C. Haliday's abstracts of City Assembly Rolls. Haliday

APPENDIX. carried over the South Bull,[1] through the water towards the bar, and terminated by the Poolbeg lighthouse, marking the entrance of the river, was not then thought of,[2] the sea

MSS., Royal Irish Academy.) Even at low water there was no passing on foot between Ringsend and Dublin. Dunton writes as follows in 1698 : "The first ramble I took this morning was to take my farewell of Ringsend . . . T'is about a mile from Dublin. . . . . After an hour's stay in this dear place (as all seaport towns generally are.) I took my leave of Trench, Welstead, and three or more friends and now looked towards Dublin; but how to come at it we no more knew how than the fox at the grapes; for, though we saw a large strand yet t'was not to be walked over because of a pretty rapid stream which must be crossed. We inquired for a coach and found that no such thing was to be had there but were informed we could have a Ringsend carr, which upon my desire was called and we got upon it, not into it. It is a perfect carr with two wheels and towards the back of it a seat is raised crossways long enought to hold three people . . . . The fare to Lazy Hill is four pence . . . . we were told that there were a hundred and more plying . . . . " Some account of my conversations in Ireland," p. 419. The Dublin Scuffle, by John Dunton, 12mo. London, 1699.

[1] [There are two great wastes of sand on the north and south sides of Dublin bay called Bulls, from the roaring of the surf against them when uncovered at low water. They were so called by the Irish. In Irish ' *tarbh* ' (pronounced *tarf*) means a bull. Hence Clontarf, the bull's meadow or pasture. See the Origin and History of Irish names of places by P. W. Joyce, M.R.I.A., 12mo., Dublin, 1871.]

[2] The following particulars concerning the forming of a new channel for the river Liffey, from near the site of the present Carlisle bridge to the Poolbeg Light House, a distance of nearly four miles, are derived from Mr. Haliday's collections. 16th January, 1707-8: Three Aldermen and Six of the Commons appointed by the Corporation to be a Quorum [Committee of Directors of the Ballast Office] to give directions to Ballast Master. (Ballast Office Journal). 26th January, 1707-8: That two iron Tormentors be made, and that the first fair day it be tried what depth of sand or gravel there is in places (to be pointed out) in the Channel. (*Ib.*) 29th January, 1707-8: Committee went to Cock [Cockle] lake and found that the water which was there when the tide is out may be prevented that course. The manner how not decided. River tried from Mr. Vanhomrigh's house to Ringsend point; found 5 feet depth of sand and gravel. Thence to Clontarf bar, 4 feet deep; No rocks (*Ib.*) 13th February, 1707-8: Mr. Morland, City Surveyor, to draw a map of the channel of the river from Essex bridge to the bar;

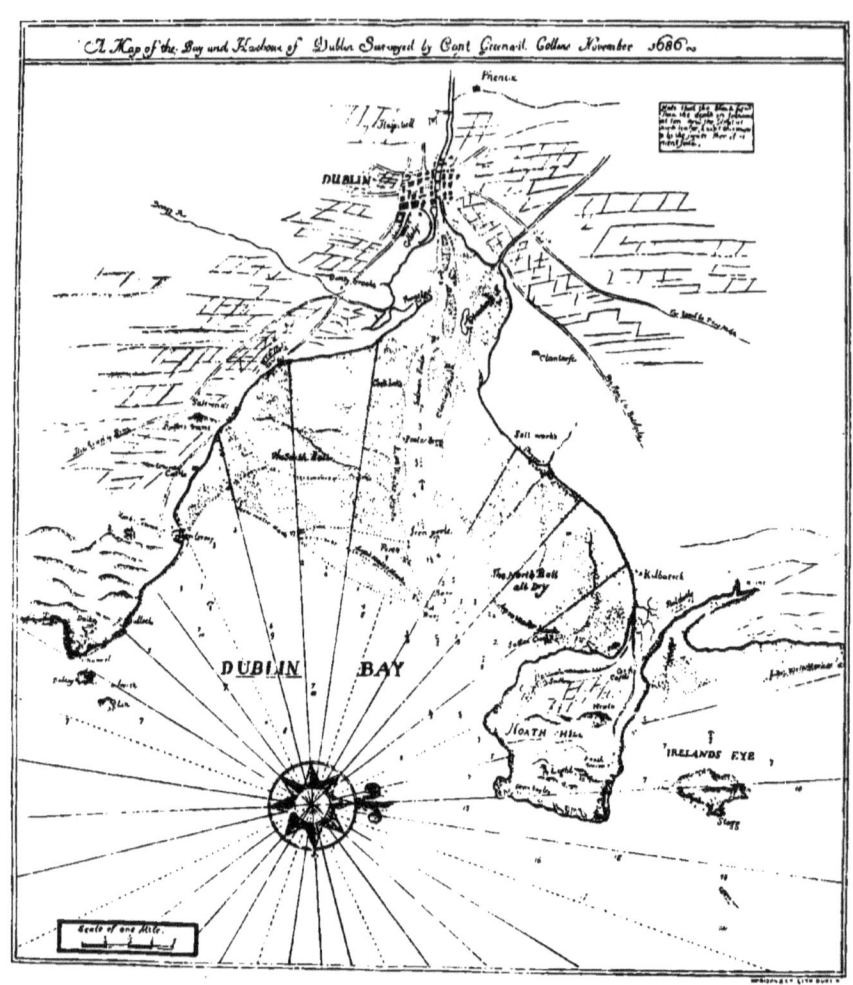

Dublin Bay and Harbour,
A.D. 1686.

## SCANDINAVIAN ANTIQUITIES OF DUBLIN. 233

NOTE—*continued*.

APPENDIX.

Mr. Morney, and two or three others best experienced in the channel from Vanhomrigh's house to the bar, to give their opinions in writing. (*Ib.*) 20th February, 1707–8: Mr. Holt brought the opinions (as ordered), that the Channel should run from Mr. Mercer's (formerly Vanhomrigh's) house directly with Green Patch, a little without Ringsend point. (*Ib.*) 21st July, 1710: Report of Committee of Ballast Office: Had conferred with persons interested in the ground on the north side of the Channel relative to piling there, who would not contribute to the expense. Directions for dredging the channel and to make a bank on the north side. (City Assembly Rolls). 20th October, 1710: The Committee appointed to stake out the mears and bounds [of the Channel] between Ringsend and Lazy Hill have not done so: The old channel will soon be filled up. The mears and bounds to be staked out, (City Assembly Rolls). 13th April, 1711: Instructions given for bringing great quantities of stone and faggots which will make good that part of the banks not already secured on both sides of the channel, and fill up the mouth of the old, and will keep the freshets within the bounds of the new channel, and will make the new channel deeper (*Ib.*) 2nd May, 1712: It is necessary to enclose the channel to carry it directly to Salmon Pool. Had consulted many who are of opinion that the best way will be by laying kishes filled with stones and backing them with sand and gravel, which is found by the experience of some years past to withstand all the force of the floods that come down the river (*Ib.*) 22nd July, 1715: Are laying down kishes to secure the north side of the channel and when a sufficient number of kishes are made will go on with the piling below Ringsend as formerly proposed: are now raising stones at Clontarf (*Ib.*) 14th October, 1715: Are laying down a quantity of kishes on the north side which has made good the bank as far as opposite Mabbot's mill. The remainder will be completed next summer, (*Ibid*). 4th Friday after Christmas, 1715: It is the opinion of merchants that the south side of the channel below Ringsend should be filled in, which will raise the south bank so high as to be a great shelter to shipping in the harbour, (*Ibid*). Same day: Petition that the strand between that taken in by Mercer and that granted to Sir John Rogerson be taken in, being now overflowed: that a wall be built to the east: sand and rubbish would fix it: length of wall 606 feet: Sir J. Rogerson would then be encouraged to take in his strand: Ordered that the work do proceed, and that the Ballast Office do back said wall (*Ibid*). 20th January, 1715-16: Have not been able to go on with the piling below Ringsend for want of oak timber: propose to carry the kishes up to Morney's dock (*Ib.*) 19th October, 1716: Have made some progress in piling below Ringsend with an Engine made here, and intend

APPENDIX.

NOTE—*continued.*

going on the South Bull next year. Find a difficulty in being supplied with oak timber for piles: Suggest fir for two or three rows. The engine from Holland is shipped, (*Ib.*) 19th January, 1716-17: Have continued piling below Ringsend with an engine as far as the sea would permit: Propose going on the South Bull: Have oak timber for one set of piles; but four rows of piles required, (*Ib.*) 19th July, 1717: Three hundred piles driven on South Bull: On North side have laid 258 kishes since last report of 18th January, 1717. Have filled the spaces between these with hurdles and stones, (*Ib.*) 18th October, 1717: On South Bull have driven 567 piles in three rows, since last report: the intervals filled with stones. On the North side have laid and filled 400 kishes this summer (*Ib.*) 17 January, 1717-18: Have laid 348 kishes on north side since last report (*Ib.*) 25th April, 1718: Have filled up the breaches made in the South Bull by last winter's storms with furze and stones, (*Ib.*), 13th July, 1718: Are proceeding with the wall on the South Bull. On the north side have laid kishes as far as opposite Ringsend; and are laying down kishes in a line from the east end of the aforesaid kishes towards the Island, (*Ib.*) 16th January, 1718-19: The piling of the South Bull is proceeding. Have agreed for one hundred tons of long piles from Wales, (*Ib.*) 20th July, 1720: The sea scarcely leaves the East End of the piles which makes the work slow: Are wattling between the piles which they hope will in time raise a bank (*Ib.*), 21st April, 1721: Instead of piling by the Engine which is found impracticable so far at sea, have used frames made of piles about twenty-two feet in length and ten feet in breadth twenty-four piles in each frame. These are floated out from Blackrock accompanied by two gabbards filled with stones quarried there, and the frames are then filled with stones and sunk, (*Ib.*) 23rd April, 1723: Have not proceeded as yet with the piling on the South Bull; but the season being proper, propose now to proceed, having 1225 pieces of timber for that purpose, (*Ib.*) 20th January, 1726: The thirteen frames mentioned in the last report have withstood all the storms, except one frame sent a drift (*Ib.*) 19th January, 1727-8: Have set down four more frames, (*Ib.*) 19th July, 1728: Have set down eight frames more; about 300 feet in length, (*Ib.*) 13th October, 1728: To protect the float men raising stones at Blackrock, suggest that two frames be set down at Blackrock. 14th October, 1726: Four more frames made since the last report which together with the former nine are set down on the South Bull extending in length eighteen perches. The floats are now securing the same with stones from Blackrock, (*Ib.*) 20th October, 1727: Have this season made seven frames all of the new model, containing 400 feet in length, (*Ib.*) 17th January, 1728-9: One frame of piles for piling the channel of

NOTE—*continued.*

the Liffey went adrift. Some of the piles which composed it are in possession of Lord Howth, and some of Mr. Vernon who refuse to deliver them: Mr. Recorder to advise, (*Ib.*) [They were afterwards given up], 10th April, 1729: Could not proceed with the work at Blackrock by reason of the stormy weather, nor with the new frames at Cock [Cockle] Lake, (*Ib.*), 8th July, 1729: The work having been left incomplete a deep gut has been formed between this summer and last winter at the east end of the frames which has carried a spit a great way into the Channel and is dangerous for shipping; and will be worse if the carrying on of the frames be longer delayed: Suggest an Act of Parliament giving power to borrow, (*Ib.*), 17th October, 1729: Find the old frames very much decayed by worms and will require repair: Have no other dependance for stones, but Blackrock. The gut at the frames, and spit north-eastwards increasing. The bank above the west end of the frames is much carried away through Cock (Cockle) Lake. Propose a work across the same, (*Ib.*), 16th October, 1730: Have finished twenty-five frames: in length about thirty-seven perches. The work across Cock (or Cockle) Lake is proceeding (*Ib.*), 15th April, 1731: Have paid £38 12s. 4d., for repairs of the west end of the north wall, (*Ib.*), 17th July, 1731: The bank at the west end of Cock (or Cockle), Lake called Salmon Pool bank, running southwards to the Brickfields is very high, and is not under water above two feet with common tides, whereas on the line leading to Ringsend there is above six feet on the same sands so that the work cannot be continued thither without frames. Are of opinion that if the work from Cock (or Cockle) Lake be carried towards the Brickfields with only a double dry stone wall filled in between with gravel it would not only be more lasting and cheaper, but also make the bank in said angle rise faster, but chiefly make the basin within the bar the larger and able to contain more water, and consequently by the flux and reflux of the tide will deepen the bar which they fear is already prejudiced by shutting the water out of the harbour by the taking in of Sir John Rogerson's-quay ground, and the North Wall; Ordered that the said wall be carried on towards the Brickfields as proposed by the Commissioners, (*Ib.*), 19th October, 1733: Find deeper water by a new channel at the east end of the frames since the stopping up of Cock (or Cockle) Lake which, as it becomes broader, carries the spit further northwards, (*Ib.*) (From C. Haliday's Abstracts of the City Assembly Rolls. Haliday, MSS. Royal Irish Academy.) The double dry stone wall filled between with gravel (which now forms the road from Ringsend to the Pigeonhouse fort) was completed in 1735, (Tidal Harbour Commissioners second report. Captain Washington's report and evidence to the report annexed,

APPENDIX. not banked out from the south side of the city by Sir John Rogerson's-quay,[1] spread itself over ground now laid out in

Parliamentary Papers, vol., xviii., Part I.) In October, 1735, a Floating Light was placed at the east end of the Piles. In June, 1761, the long wall of cut stone from the present Pigeonhouse was begun by erecting the present Poolbeg Lighthouse (*Ibid.*) This wall was completed in 1790. "28th August, 1788: So great is the progress already made in the Mole or Jettie in our harbour, commonly called the South Wall or Ballast Office Wall that besides the mile and a quarter from Ringsend to the Block house, there are upwards of 3,000 feet in length of it completed from the new work from the Lighthouse westwards" (Dublin Chronicle), "10th January, 1789: The work is in such forwardness that it will be completed in about eighteen months." (*Ibid.*.) W. M. G.] I am further indebted to my friend William Monk Gibbon, LL.D., for the following curious notices connected with the Piles on the South Bull. "25th February, 1744: On Wednesday last were tried in the King's Bench (amongst others), Peter Fagan and James Flanagan and were (as sentenced), whipped on Thursday from Irishtown to Merrion for digging up piles at the Strand, Dublin News Letter," "17th May, 1766: The two murderers who were hung in gibbetts at a little distance from the new wall were put up in so scandalous a manner that they fell down on Tuesday, and now lie on the piles, a most shocking spectacle." Pue's Occurrences, vol., lxiii., No. 6488, W. M. G.]

[1] Lease in fee farm by the Corporation of Dublin to John Rogerson, Esq., A.D. 1713. (Printed Rental of the Estates of the Corporation of Dublin, by Francis Morgan, Law Agent, Folio, Dublin 1867.) Acts of Assembly 17th July, 1713: John Rogerson, Esq., informs the City Assembly that he intends to speedily take in the Strand between Lazy Hill and Ringsend which the Assembly hope will improve the new channel, and Mr. Rogerson desires to be furnished with sand and gravel by the gabbards when they have not work with shipping, he paying three pence per ton. City Records. [23rd August, 1741: Died at his house in Mary-street of a fever the Right Hon. John Rogerson, Esq., Chief Justice of the King's Bench. He came to the Bar in 1702. Was made Recorder of Dublin, 3rd November, 1714. Same year became Solicitor-General; and Attorney-General May, 1720, and Lord Chief Justice May, 1727. (Dublin News Letter, Richard Reilly's No. 485, 23rd March, 1744.) To be sold that part of the South Strand in the city of Dublin which lies eastward of the arch on the High road from Dublin to Ringsend, containing 133 acres plantation measure the estate of the late Right Hon. Chief Justice Robinson whereof 2A. 2R. are bounded by Rogerson's-quay, and laid out for building, Dublin Journal, No. 1883, W. M. G.]

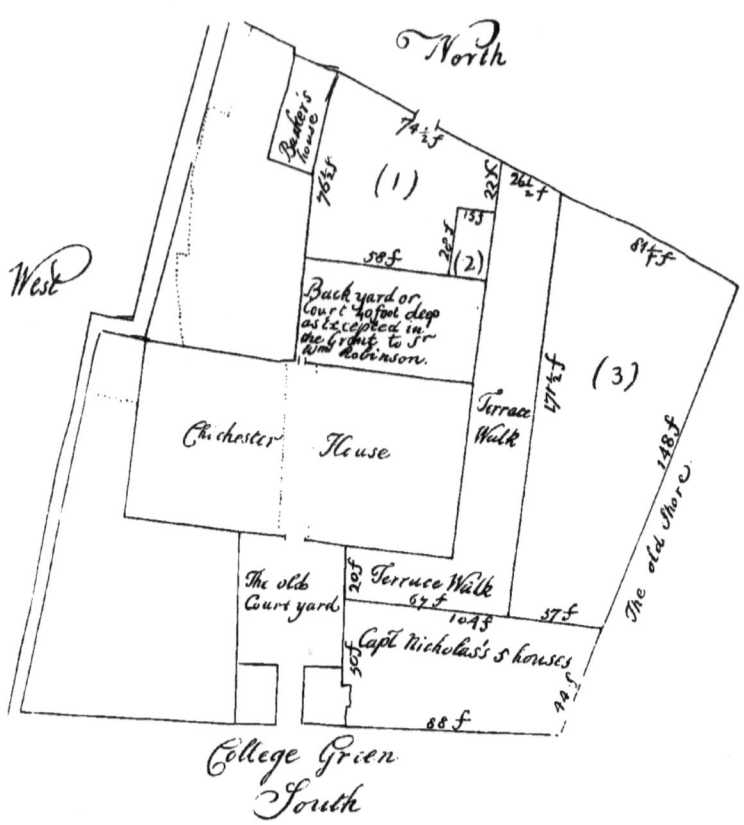

Refference.

1. Is the residue of the back yard and stable yard exclusive of a back yard or Court as was excepted in the Grant to Sir W. Robinson, Knight.

2. The old range in the stable yard which was said to contain 5 rooms

3. Is the gardens belonging to Chichester House, exclusive of the Terrace Walk which was excepted in the grant to Sir Will.m Robinson and exclusive of Nicholas's five houses and all other interests already purchased by or for His Majesty.

All the rest of the premises we conceive to be unquestionable and in a settled state.

Given under our hands this 11th day of September 1734.

per { Tho.s Cave and Gabriel Stokes } Surveyors.

## SCANDINAVIAN ANTIQUITIES OF DUBLIN. 239

streets,[1] so that Ringsend true to its name Rin or Reen meaning a spit or point presents itself in Sir Bernard de Gomme's map as a long and narrow tongue or spit of land running out into the sea, the water on its western side spreading over all the low ground between Irishtown and the slightly rising ground on which stand the barracks at Beggar's Bush, and under Sir Patrick Dunne's hospital, along the line of Denzille-street and Great Brunswick-street, to Townsend-street, called Lazey, otherwise Lazar's Hill, and flowing even to that front of the Parliament House called the Lord's entrance, facing College-street, as may be seen on the ground plan of Chichester House (the site of which the Parliament House occupies), where ground under this face is described as "the Old Shore."[2] At Lazar's hill

APPENDIX.
Ringsend.

Frigate launched at Lazar's Hill.

---

[1] Sir Bernard de Gomme's Map of 1673.

[2] [Attached to the plan is the following return: "To the Right Honourable and honourable the Commissioners appointed by Commission under the Great Seal of Ireland in pursuance of an Act of Parliament made in the third year of His present Majesty intitled an Act to enable His Majesty to purchase the respective interests of the several persons entitled to the houses and grounds adjoining to the New Parliament House. May it please your honours, in obedience to your honours' order to us directed dated 28th of May last, whereby we were required jointly to survey all and singular the out-grounds and gardens belonging to a certain house demised to Sir William Robinson, Knt., by His late Majesty King Charles the Second excepting such parts of the premises thereby demised as hath been purchased by His Majesty in pursuance of the before recited Act. And having given due notice in writing to Mr. John Williams, Agent to your honours and to the other parties concerned in interest to attend said survey, and having heard what was offered by said John Williams in behalf of His Majesty and what was offered by Mr. Hutchinson on behalf of himself and of Richard Gering, Esq., did proceed to survey the same and having then and at sundry times informed ourselves by divers witnesses, persons capable to give us true information of the mears and bounds thereof. We have made a true survey ; a Map whereof we have hereunto annexed, and do find that of all and singular the premises in the said Letters Patent contained and demised as aforesaid nothing now remains to be purchased by His Majesty in pursuance of the said Act, except the following parcels, viz., No. 1, No. 2, and No. 3, whose boundaries and

APPENDIX. in the year 1657, we find a frigate built and launched. Among the Treasury warrants issued by the Commissioners of England for the affairs of Ireland, is an order dated the 24th March, 1657 : "That James Standish, Receiver-General, do issue forth and pay unto Mr. Timothy Avery the sum of £100, on account, the same being to be by him issued out towards the finishing and speedy fitting to sea the new ffrigatt, called the Lambay Catch, now rebuilt and lately launched, att Lazey Hill, Dublin, according to such orders as he shall receive in writing under the hand of Captain Edward Tomlins, and Joseph Glover, who is to command the said shipp, for payment whereof this is a

dimentions are described in the said Map and Table of Reference thereto belonging. All which is most humbly submitted to your honours, this Eleventh day of September, 1734, by

Your Honours Most dutyfull and Most Obedient Servants.

THOMAS CAVE.
GABRIEL STOKES.

From the Original, Public Record Office, Four Courts.

Lord Mountmorres says, "I remember to have heard from a clerk of the House of Lords, Mr. Hawker, that Chichester House was very inconvenient; and so it was reported by a Committee in Queen Anne's reign. I cannot help lamenting (he continues), that a Map of the disposition of the apartments and grounds of Chichester House which about twenty years ago was hung up in the House of Commons Coffeehouse was unaccountably lost." History of the Irish Parliament from A.D. 1634 to 1666, by Lord Mountmorres, Vol. 2, p. 100, 2 vols. 8vo., London, 1792.]

[In 1784, when making the present portico in Westmoreland-street for a separate entrance to the House of Peers it was found that the buildings on this east side of the Parliament House stood on ground with declivities so sudden and so great as to make it difficult to bring the line of cornices, windows and rustic basement of the new portico into harmony with the lines of the original building; for here on the east the foundation was the 'Old Shore' line marked on the plan of Chichester House. It was only overcome by James Gandon the architect employing Corinthian Columns which are taller than the Ionic Order used in the main building, and even then the portico was ascended by steps. Life of James Gandon, architect by his son. Edited by Mulvany, pp. 83-85. Hodges and Smith, Dublin, 8vo., 1846. In Speed's map of 1610, there is a pill or narrow inlet from the Liffey running up to this eastern front. The regular course of the shore line seems to have been Fleet-street by the same map.]

warrant," &c.[1] Ringsend was then a place of arrival, and departure for Lord Deputies with their attendant trains;[2] and here, it may be remembered, Oliver Cromwell, as Lord Lieutenant, landed in the month of August, 1649, with an army of 13,000 men, to commence his memorable nine months' campaign in Ireland.

*Way from Ringsend to Dublin in 1673.*

From Ringsend the direct approach to Dublin lay across ground overflowed by the tide, but passable at low water for man or horse about the place where the Ringsend bridge now stands. At full tide the way lay more inland, through the fields of Baggot Rath, the line of approach

---

[1] Book of Treasury Warrants, A.D. 1656-1657. Record Tower, Dublin Castle. [As late as 1744 there was another launch. "Last Thursday, 'the Boyne' privateer was launched at George's-quay, at which vast numbers of spectators were present who wished her a good voyage and to take her enemies," 29th September, 1744. The Dublin Journal, W. M. G.] [In A.D. 1663 in Hic et Ubique, a Comedy "Trust All" addresses "Bankrupt."—"That's strange! There's not a Frigott hardly that lies moored up at Lazy Hill, Kilmainham, or the rest of the docks, that properly belong to that fleet, but they're all foul in the gun-room." 'Hic et Ubique' a Comedy 'by Richard Head, Dublin 1663.' Among the First Earl of Charlemont's collection of Old Plays, lately in Charlemont House, Dublin. These expressions are allegorical, and mean ladies of a certain class satirised in this Comedy.]

[2] Be it remembered that on Saturday the 12th of March, 1614, the Honorable Sir Arthur Chichester, Lord Chichester of Belfast, Deputy General of Ireland, after holding the sceptre of that Kingdom for nine years, five weeks and upwards, embarked in the King's Sloop called 'the Moon,' Beverley Newcomen, son and heir of Sir Robert Newcomen, Commander, on his voyage to England, being escorted from his house called Chichester House to the place called 'the Ringe's Ende' where the Sloop's boat awaited him, by the Lords Justices, Privy Council and others, Officers of the Army, Pensioners, and Members of Parliament, and the Mayor and Sheriffs, and the greater part of the Citizens of Dublin, all anxious to show their love, &c., &c. Exchequer Roll, 11th James I., (translation). Lord Berkely landed here, 1679, De Ginkle sailed hence, 1691. (Story's War of Ireland, p. 285). Earl Wharton landed here, 1709. [The great guns were sent down to Ringsend to wait the arrival of the Duke of Devonshire our Lord Lieutenant, who is hourly expected here, Dublin News Letter, 29th September, 1741. W. M. G.]

R

being through Irishtown, nearly along the course of Bath-avenue, and by the line of Mount-street and Merrion-square to the castle.[1]

*Plan for a Harbour at Ringsend in 1674.*

In the year 1674—that following the visit of Sir Bernard de Gomme—Andrew Yarranton,[2] the publisher of some plans for the improvement of harbours in England, came to Dublin, and was, as he states, "importuned by Lord Mayor Browster to bestow some time on a survey of the port," the result of which was, that considering it impossible to deepen the water on the bar, he offered suggestions for an artificial harbour and fort for its defence on the strand (then covered by the tide) between Ringsend and "the Town's End street;" the want of some protection for the trade of Dublin being then a subject which engaged public

---

[1] The ground for Bath-avenue was only recovered from the sea about 1792. ["31st May, 1792: The marsh between Beggar's-bush and Ringsend, through which runs the Dodder on its way to Ringsend-bridge, is, we hear, taken by Mr. [Counsellor] Vavasour from Lord Fitzwilliam, for 150 years, at £190 per annum. This tract, which is inundated every tide, Mr. Vavasour will (it is said) reclaim by a complete double embankment of the Dodder . . . The river is to be turned to its own channel, which is the centre of the piece of ground south of Ringsend-bridge . . ." Dublin Chronicle. W. M. G.]

[1796. The branch of the Dodder which ran out between Tritonville and Irishtown was diverted by the Ballast Board into the New Channel. Ballast Board Books. W. M. G.]

[2] "I being at Dublin in the month of November, 1674, there happened a great storm which blew one [ship] to sea, where ship and men perished, and blew another upon the rocks near the point of Howth . . . I also found from Lord Mayor Brewster and others that the badness of the harbour did occasion the decay of trade. I then acquainted him with my thoughts as to a good harbour at Ringsend. Upon which he did importune me to bestow some time in a survey . . . If there were a harbour at Ringsend, as in the map described, this advantage would be gained. At present there is at least £500 *per annum* paid to persons that carry and recarry people in the Ringsend coaches to and from the ships; all this would be saved . . and, by the ships coming up boldly to Lazy-hill, trade will be made easy." England's Improvement by Land and Sea to outdo the Dutch without fighting, to set at work all the poor of England . . . pp. 150. By Andrew Yarronton, gent., small 4to, London, 1677.

attention, in consequence of a French privateer having entered the bay, and captured and carried off a Spanish ship from near the bar of the river.[1]

Yarranton's plan appeared in a treatise entitled "England's Improvement by Sea and Land, to outdo the Dutch without Fighting," published in 1677.

The plan of a citadel, as projected by Sir Bernard de Gomme, though not executed, seems not to have been wholly laid aside, for in a fine collection, in folio, of plans of all the forts existing in Ireland, in the year 1684, with their elevations beautifully executed in water colours, together with projects for additional defences, preserved at Kilkenny Castle, the same design reappears. This volume of plans is entitled "A Report drawn up by direction of His Majesty King Charles the Second, and General Right Hon. George [Legge] Lord Dartmouth, Master-General of His Majesty's Ordnance in England, and performed by Thomas Phillips, anno 1685;"[2] and it contains several plans and details "for a citadel to be built over Dublin," the site being apparently the same as that chosen by Sir Bernard de Gomme, and the form similar.

The plans of Yarranton and De Gomme directed attention to the improvement of the port of Dublin, the trade of which was then carried on by vessels of from fifty to one hundred tons burden.

As there was no corporate or other body in Dublin

*Fort at Merrion Square still intended in 1685.*

*History of the Ballast Board*

---

[1] May 29th, 1675. "One matter of some moment I have to acquaint you with . . . A Spanish ship was taken by a French privateer close to the bar of this harbour, and carried away on Thursday, in the evening . . . This accident has much disturbed the merchants of this town." Earl of Essex's State Letters. Lord Lieutenant of Ireland. 8vo, Dublin, 1773, 2nd edition, p. 242.

[2] See the print of a very fine map by this artist, entitled "The Ground Plan of Belfast, per Tho. Phillips, Anno. 1685," giving elevations of the Castle, Churches and principal Houses, in the "History of Belfast," by George Benn, 8vo, Marcus Ward and Co., London and Belfast, 1877.

APPENDIX.

entrusted with the conservancy of the river, and especially empowered to raise ballast, Henry Howard petitioned the Lord Lieutenant in 1676 that a patent might be granted to him, pursuant to the king's letter, which he had obtained, for establishing a ballast office.[1] This, however, was opposed by the Lord Mayor and citizens, on the ground that the charter of King John gave to them the strand of the river,[2] where ballast should be raised,[2] and they, therefore, prayed that permission to establish a ballast office might be granted to them, they applying the profits thereof to the maintenance of the intended "King's Hospital" (since better known as the Blue Coat School).[3] The Lord Lieutenant neither granted the prayer of the one petition or the other, nor did Howard execute a lease which he had proposed to take from the city.

[1] Acts of Assembly, 1676. Henry Howard petitioned the Lord Lieutenant for order to pass Letters Patent for a Ballast Office in all the ports of Ireland pursuant to Letters under the King's Privy Seal granted him five years since. The Corporation answer that by the Charter of King John they own the Liffey and the strand within the franchises of the city; that they have, by acts of Assembly, laid down rules for ballasting; and by a late Assembly, in July last, have revived their ancient right to said ballast, and hope to have a Ballast Office, the profits whereof are intended for the King's Hospital. City Assembly Roll.

[2] A.D. 1200. King John confirms former charters, and grants to the citizens the fishery of one half of the Liffey, with liberty to build on the banks at their will. Dated at Upton, 6th of November, in the 2nd year of his reign. Historic and Municipal Documents from the Archives of the City of Dublin, &c., 1172–1320. Edited by J. T. Gilbert, F.S.A., 8vo, Dublin, 1870. A.D. 1215. Confirms to them the city in fee-farm with that part of the Liffey which belongs to them together with one part of the said river, except such fishings as we have granted in free alms [to St. Mary's Abbey, &c.], and such others as are held by ancient tenure. Dated at Marlbrege, 3rd of July, in the 17th year of his reign.

[3] Acts of Assembly. Nativity of St. John, 1682: Thos. and Henry Howard petition to the city: that the king had granted them his Letters for a Patent for erecting a Ballast Office in Ireland; that they are willing to take a lease of the Port of Dublin from the city at fifty pounds a year, and to surrender their title.

The Corporation of Dublin, still anxious to improve the port, petitioned the House of Commons in 1698, stating that "the river had become so shallow, and the channel so uncertain, that neither barques nor lighters of any burden could get up except at spring tides, much merchandise being unloaded at Ringsend, and thence carted up to Dublin;" and, therefore, prayed that they might be permitted to establish a Ballast Office.[1]

<small>APPENDIX. Corporation pray Parliament for a Ballast Board in 1698.</small>

On this petition the "Heads of a Bill," were prepared and transmitted to England, conformable with Poyning's law,[2] but the Bill was stopped in England by some persons there (as was alleged), who endeavoured to get a grant from the Admiralty for the benefit of the chest at Chatham."[2]

---

Ordered a lease for thirty-one years, at £50, covenanting to take such rates only as the Corporation shall think fit. City Assembly Roll. Christmas, 1685. The Howards, having neglected to perfect their lease, order for lease therefore declared void, and petition to the Lord Lieutenant that H.M. may direct Letters Patent to pass to the city for a Ballast Office. City Records.

[1] 23rd Nov., 1698. Petition of Lord Mayor, &c., to the Commons in Parliament that the river is choked up . . . by gravel and sand brought by the fresh-water floods and ashes thrown in . . . and, by taking ballast from the banks below Ringsend, which so breaks the banks that the river has carried great quantities of the loose sands thereof into Poolbeg, Salmon Pool, Clontarf Pool, and Green Patch, which were the usual anchoring places, but are now become so shallow that no number of ships can with safety bide there, and the river, also between Rings End and the Custom House, by this means, and by the building of several bridges which has shifted the sands, has become so shallow that the channel is of little use, and barks of any burden must unload, and the citizens bring up their coals, &c., by land; they, therefore, pray for a Ballast Board, to be governed by petitioners, to whom the river and the strand belongs. Commons Journals, vol. ii., p. 274.

[2] 22nd July, 1707. Petition of John Eccles, Nathaniel Whitwell, and Robert Chetham, merchants, on behalf of themselves and others, showing that the port and channel in the harbour of Dublin are almost destroyed by the irregular taking in and throwing out of ballast, &c., insomuch that Clontarf pool and Salmon pool have lost, within a few years, above two feet of their former depth of water, &c. For remedy whereof several merchants of Dublin formerly

APPENDIX.

It is more likely, however, that the opposition originated in some jealousy respecting the Admiralty jurisdiction of the Port, the Lord Mayor being "Admiral of Dublin,"[1] over

applied to Parliament for a Ballast Office, &c., and heads of a Bill passed the House, but same was stopped in England by some persons who endeavoured to get a grant thereof from the Admiralty Office there for the benefit of the Chest at Chatham. Ordered, That leave be given to bring in Heads of a Bill, &c., and that it be recommended to the Lord Mayor, Mr. Recorder of Dublin, Mr. Connolly, and Mr. Serjeant Neave, to prepare and bring in same. Common's Journals, vol. ii., pp. 503, 504.

[1] 21st March, 1372. Upon an inquisition *ad quod damnum* the jury find that it would be of no damage to the king or others to grant to the Mayor and citizens of Dublin, the customs of all merchandise brought for sale, either by land or sea, between Skerries and Alercornshed, otherwise Arclo. 46 Edward III. "White Book of City of Dublin."

A.D. 1582, 25 January, (24 Elizabeth) the Queen, by her charter, granted the office of Admiralty to the Mayor, &c., of Dublin, wherever the sheriffs of the said city may lawfully receive customs, namely—between Arclo and the Nannywater. Exchequer Mem. Roll 24th, 25th, 26th of Elizabeth, membrane 11th. [Three years later the Corporation obtained an amended charter; but in 1615 the city lost this jurisdiction by a judgment of the Court of King's Bench. In that year Sir John Davys, Attorney-General, filed an information against the city of Dublin for (amongst other things) usurping Admiralty jurisdiction. The city pleaded a Charter of Edward VI., and a grant by Queen Elizabeth, dated at Weald Hall [in Essex], the 13th of August, in the 27th year of her reign (A.D. 1585), confirming the charter of Edward VI., and giving the city the office of Admiralty, with a court of Admiralty, water bailiffs, &c., between Arclo and Nannywater, "in order that they may the better apply themselves to the defence of the city." Judgment for the crown. King's Bench Roll, 4th to 19th Jas. I., Exchequer. But the Corporation still claimed anchorage fees. In 1708, Easter Assembly—That water bailiffs of the Lord High Admiral of England exact fees for anchorage in the port of Dublin. Ordered that the Lord Mayor prevent such exactions in future by prosecuting such as pretend to exact anchorage fees. City Records.

15th February, 1727-8.—The Corporation addressed Lord Carteret, Lord Lieutenant, alleging that Queen Elizabeth, by charter dated 26th of June, in the 24th year of her reign, granted them the office of Admiralty, which they always exercised until the reign of King James II., "and the government of the city being then in the hands of Papists, the Protestants who suc-

which the Lord High Admiral of England claimed to be supreme. This obstacle was removed in 1708, when the Ballast Office was created by an Act of the 6th of Queen Anne : for the city had privately promised the Queen's Consort, Prince George of Denmark, then Lord High Admiral of England, an annual tribute " of one hundred yards of the best Holland duck sail cloth, which shall be made in the realm of Ireland," although there was no clause to that effect inserted in the bill; and this tribute was for a time regularly sent to London, and on one occasion when it was omitted it was formally demanded by the Admiralty, and then forwarded by the Corporation.[1]  *APPENDIX.*

*Ballast Board created by 6th of Q. Anne, A.D. 1708.*

To the establishment of this Ballast Office in 1708, and the remodelling of it in 1787, under the name of "The Corporation for Preserving and Improving the Port of Dublin," we owe the extraordinary improvement manifested by an inspection of the map.

It will be observed that the high water mark was "the Towns-end-street" on the one side, and what yet retains the name of "the North Strand" on the other; and a curious illustration of the state of the harbour is found in the fact  *Improvements by Ballast Board.*

ceded were unacquainted with their privileges, and have but lately discovered that the said power was vested in them. Haliday's Abstracts of City Assembly rolls. Haliday MSS., Royal Irish Academy.

28th October, 1761.—Petition to Parliament of the Corporation of Dublin, stating that from time immemorial the harbour of Dublin was the petitioners' inheritance: that Queen Elizabeth, by her charter in the 24th year of her reign, granted them the Admiralty of the ports and harbours from Ardo to Nannywater, and prayed additional powers. Common's Journals, VII., 22.

[1] 24th May, 1708.—Acts of Assembly. — Committee of Ballast Office petition the General Assembly for liberty to render to the Lord High Admiral, Prince George of Denmark, the Prince Consort, according to promise 100 yards of the best Holland duck sailcloth that should be made in Ireland. Ordered that it be paid for out of the Ballast Office fund, and delivered at the Admiralty at London. City Assembly Roll.

Acts of Assembly--17 July, 1731.—The Admiralty demand the 100 yards. There being no clause in the Act ordering it; Ordered— To be furnished and sent regularly in future.—*Ibid.*

APPENDIX.

New land made.

that, during a storm in 1670, the tide flowed up to the College,[1] and at a later period, that a collier was wrecked where Sir Patrick Dunne's Hospital now stands.

The soil raised by dredging the river during 130 years has contributed to fill up the space now occupied by the Custom House, Commons-street, Mayor-street, &c., to the north; and Great Brunswick-street, &c., to the south; and so late as 1728, when "Brooking's map of Dublin" was published, the whole ground known as the "North and South Lotts" was still covered by the tide, the name of "Lotts" originating in the resolution of the Lord Mayor and citizens to apportion them out, "and draw lots for them,"[2] with the stipulation that they should be enclosed from the river by a wall, and filled up.

---

[1] "March, 1670. A great storm; wind at S.E. The water overflowed the bank at Ringsend, Lazar's hill, and over Mr. Hawkins's new wall, and up to the College." Hist. of the City of Dublin, by Walter Harris. Annals, p. 353. 8vo, Dublin, 1766.

[2] This was done in the year 1717. The following is a title of a printed map: "A map of ye strand of ye north side of ye channel of ye River Life, as it was granted and set out in Easter Assembly, 1717, by the Right Hon. John Bolton, esq., Lord Mayor of ye City of Dublin, W. Empson and David King, sheriffs; and the deeds and this map perfected in the mayoralty of Anthony Barker, esq., Lord Mayor [A.D 1718] John Reyson and Valentine Kidde, sheriffs.

[The corporation adopted this system of lotting when taking in portions of Stephen's-green and Oxmantown-green: thus, Michaelmas Assembly, 1663. "The Committee of City Revenue report that seventeen acres plantation measure of Stephen's-green may be set to the advantage of the city." Bergin's Index to the Assembly Rolls, p. 180.

August, 1664. "Memorandum of the several lotts of land set out in Stephen's-green, and the respective tenants of each." On the west and east sides are shown eighteen and fifteen lots respectively; on the north and south sides thirty-three and twenty-four lots. "The fines for each lease to be applied in walling in and paving the Green for the ornament and pleasure of the city."--*Ibid.*

Christmas Assembly, 1664-- "Order that part of Oxmantown-green be taken and set by lots in feefarm, reserving a highway and large market place [Smithfield]. Order for staking out the lots to be disposed of by lottery." The lots, ninety-seven in number, here follow. --*Ibid.*]

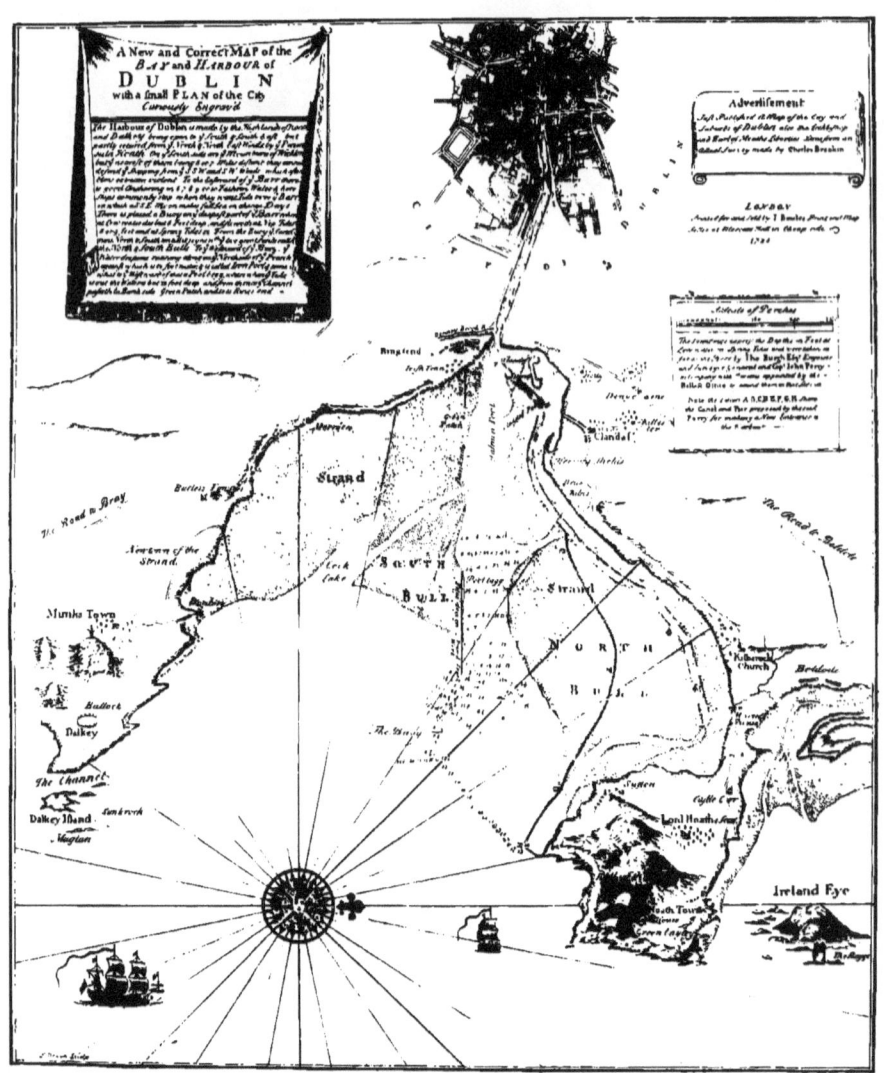

Bay and Harbour of Dublin.
A.D. 1728.

But the greatest improvement as regards the trade of the Port has been the partial removal of the bar at the mouth of the river. For the removal of this bar the most eminent engineers had been consulted. In 1713 the Ballast Office procured the services of Captain John Perry,[1] who had been employed at Dover harbour, and at the Daggenham breach in the Thames; but, although he suggested plans by which it was conceived that the depth of water might be increased, the task was considered as hopeless, that to render the port fit for vessels drawing even twelve feet of water, it was proposed that an artificial harbour should be constructed near Ringsend, one engineer suggesting that this harbour should be accessible by a ship canal, along the Sutton shore;[2] and another, that the canal should be

APPENDIX.
Bar lowered.

---

[1] "Proposals for rendering the Port of Dublin Commodious." By Captain John Perry. 8vo, London, 1720.

[2] This would seem to have been a plan of Perry's. For the rare and finely engraved map of Captain John Perry's scheme, here photographed and lithographed, I am indebted to my friend Richard Bergoin Bennett, esq., of Eblana Castle, Kingstown. The original engraving measures 2 feet 2 inches by 1 foot 9½ inches. In the Appendix to the Second Report of the Tidal Harbours Commissioners will be found a full account of this project. In July, 1725, the Lord Lieutenant and Council ordered a map and soundings to be made of the harbour, and that Captain Burgh, Engineer and Surveyor-General, and Captain John Perry, should assist those appointed by the Ballast Board to examine the har-

bour. On 31st August, 1725, the survey was made, and on 29th September, 1725, Perry published his account of a new approach with a plan. On 29th November, 1725, the plan was referred by the Lord Lieutenant and Council to the Ballast Board; and they, on 3rd February, 1726, reported against it. Their objections are given in the Tidal Harbours Commissioners' Second Report. *Ibid.* Parliamentary Papers, vol. xviii., part i., pp. 13, 14. Perry anxious, probably, to enlist the favour of the public towards his scheme, may have published this map at his own expense in 1728. Mr. Haliday sought in vain for a sight of this map as appears by the following:—

"In Gough's Topographical Antiquities of Great Britain and Ireland, p. 689, it is stated there is a map of the city and suburbs of Dublin, by Chas. Brookin, 1728, and

APPENDIX.

from Dalkey or Kingstown, so as altogether to avoid the bar.¹

Large Ships accommodated.

The works executed by the Ballast Office have, however, so far removed the bar, that at the spot where Nicholas Ball proposed, in 1582, "to build a tower like the Maiden tower at Drogheda,"² there is now twenty-five feet of water at spring tides; and the river, which in 1713, could only be used by vessels of 50 to 100 tons burden, is now used by vessels of 1,000 to 1,100 tons register, and drawing twenty-one feet of water; the effect of the improvement being such that the Ballast Office must construct new docks for the large vessels now frequenting the port, as the Custom-house docks, planned by Sir John Rennie so late

* a map of the bay and harbour of Dublin with a small plan of the city, 1728. I have Brookin's map, but I have never seen or heard of any person who had seen the map of the bay and harbour of 1728. Possibly some of your correspondents could give information on the subject, and also if there be any map of the city, either printed or manuscript, between Speed's map of 1610 and Brookin's of 1728, and where? 25 February, 1854. (Signed) C. H." Notes and Queries, vol. ix., 174.

¹ In a "Plan for Advancing the Trade of Dublin," printed by William Watson & Son, Capel-street in 1800, it was proposed to avoid the Bar, at a cost of £102,144, by enclosing Dalkey Sound, and to come thence by a canal direct to Dublin. Parliamentary Records of Ireland, vol. i., p. 188.

² Midsummer, 1566, Acts of Assembly. Agreed, that Gerald Plunket, for his great charges in maintaining bowyes (buoys) or marks at the bar of the haven, shall have of every boat of 6 tons to 20 tons four pence per ton, of 20 to 30 six pence, of every ship twelve pence. City Assembly Roll, 8th Elizabeth.

Midsummer, 1582 Nicholas Duff and Nicholas Ball, who had undertaken to keep a perch at the bar, are to build a tower at Ringsend. *Ibid.*, 24th Elizabeth.

A.D. 1588. Forasmuch as Nicholas Ball hath surrendered, &c., in respect of a tower which by him should be builded on the bar, and, the perches having fallen, Captain George Thornyn to have [      ] years' interest on the perquisites, he building up a tower on the bar at Michaelmas next. The water bailiffs to put up a perch or buoy at their own charge. *Ibid.*

as 1821, are incapable of receiving steam or other large vessels, the sill of the lock gates being now four feet above the deepened bed of the river in front.

CHARLES HALIDAY, M.R.I.A.

Monkstown Park, county Dublin,
15th March, 1861.

# TABLE OF CHAPTERS.

## BOOK I.

### CHAPTER I.

No cities among the early Irish.—The site of Dublin a place of no distinction amongst them.—Dublin founded by Scandinavians, and made their capital.—Thence became the capital of the English.—Denmark filled by Saxons who escaped thither to avoid forced baptism by Charlemagne.—The Norsemen, infected by these exiles with their hatred, ravage the coasts of France.—Their ravages of England.—They plunder the islands and coasts of Ireland.—Their ravages on the mainland of Ireland.—The Dubhgoill and the Finnghoill.—Aulaff of the Dubhgoill settles at *Dubhlinn of Ath Cliath*, A.D. 852, . . . . . 1

### CHAPTER II.

The founding of Dublin.—The story of Turgesius discussed.—Aulaff, descended of Regnar Lodbrog, founds Dublin, A.D. 852.—Legend of Aulaff, Sitric, and Ivar, three brothers, founding, respectively, Dublin, Waterford, and Limerick, disproved.—Irish and Danish names of the site of Dublin.—Dublin and Northumbria for a century under the same Danish kings.—Legend of Regnar's death in Northumbria.—Regnar put to death in Ireland by the Irish.—Regnar Lodbrog, the Thurgils, or Turgesius of Irish annals.—Account of Turgesius from Dr. Todd's "War of the Gaedhill with the Gaill," . . . . . . . . . 19

### CHAPTER III.

Ivar, conqueror and King of Northumbria, identified with Ivar, King of Dublin.—Of the joint career of Aulaf and Ivar.—Ivar's successors in East Anglia and Northumbria, . . . . 36

### CHAPTER IV.

At Ivar's death, his sons, Godfrey and Sitric, were in France.—Cearbhall (Carrol) ruled at Dublin.—Sitric slays his brother Godfrey, and embarks for Dublin.—Recovers Dublin.—His attempt on Northumberland defeated.—Dies, and his son Aulaf, succeeds.—Aulaf recovers Northumberland.—Dies at York.—Famine in Ireland through locusts.—Emigration of Danes to Iceland.—The Irish expel the Danes from Dublin, . . . 44

## CHAPTER V.

Gormo, King of Denmark, rules East Anglia.—Reginald and Sitric, sons of King Aulaf, rule in Northumberland.—On the settlement of Normandy fresh fleets of Danes come to England from France.—Part settle at Waterford. - Sitric of Northumberland recovers Dublin.—His brother Reginald sails to Waterford, and rules there and at Limerick.—Defeats of the Irish by Reginald and Sitric, . . . . . . . . . . 50

## CHAPTER VI.

Reginald and Sitric, sons of Godfrey, King of Dublin, return to Northumberland.—In their absence the Irish attempt to recover Dublin.—Reginald and Sitric made Kings of different divisions of Northumbria.—Death of Reginald, . . . . . 57

## CHAPTER VII.

Godfrey, son of Reginald, through Sitric's absence, assumes the rule at Dublin.—His conflicts with the Danes of Limerick and their allies Canute and Harold, sons of Gormo, King of Denmark.—Sitric dies, and Athelstan annexes Northumberland.—Sitric's sons come to Ireland.—Godfrey vainly attempts to recover Northumberland.—His renewed conflicts with the Danes of Limerick aided by the sons of Sitric.—Death of Godfrey.—Athelstan makes Eric Blod-Ax, Viceroy of Northumberland, . . . 61

## CHAPTER VIII.

Aulaf, King of Dublin, attempts to recover Northumberland.—Is defeated by Athelstan at Brunanburg.—Returns to Dublin.—The Irish besiege Dublin, . . . . . . . 69

## CHAPTER IX.

King Edmund dies A.D. 946,—Aulaf Cuaran, King of Dublin, contests Northumberland with King Eadred, Edmund's successor.—Aulaf, after four years' possession of Northumberland, is expelled.—He returns to Ireland.—His extensive Irish connexions.—His throne at Dublin disputed by his nephew.—Aulaf recovers it.—Goes a pilgrimage to Iona.—Abdicates.—Maelsechlain overthrows Reginald, Aulaf's son.—Maelsechlain proclaims the freedom of Ireland, . . . . . . . . 73

## BOOK II.

OF THE SCANDINAVIANS OF DUBLIN AND THEIR RELATIONS WITH NEIGHBOURING KINGDOMS.

### CHAPTER I.

#### DUBLIN AND THE ISLE OF MAN.

Page

Man for the Romans an Irish island.—Man yields tribute to Baedan, King of Ulster, A.D. 580.—Thenceforth said to *belong* to Ulster.—Conflicts between the Norwegians of Ulster and Danes of Northumbria about Man.—Claimed by Reginald, brother of Sitric, King of Dublin, from Barid of Ulster.—Magnus, King of Man, grandson of Sitric, with the Lagmen, sails round Ireland doing justice.—Magnus, one of the eight kings who rowed King Edgar's barge on the Dee.—The ground probably of the forged charter of King Edgar pretending dominion in Ireland.—In the eleventh century intermarriages make it hard to say whether the kings of Dublin are to be called Danish or Irish.—De Courcy's claim to Ulster through his wife, daughter of the King of Man.—King Henry Second's jealousy.—De Courcy's fall, . . . . . . . . . . . 82

### CHAPTER II.

#### DUBLIN AND NORWAY.

Notices of Dublin frequent in Norwegian and Icelandic history.—Constant intercourse between Dublin and Norway.—Ostmen from Dublin fight for Norwegian liberty at the battle of Hafursfiord.—Led by Cearbhall, King of Dublin, or his son-in-law, Eyvind Austman.—Every King of Norway (almost) visits Dublin.—Biorn, son of Harold, King of Norway, visits Dublin as a merchant; also King Hacon.—Dublin the port for sale of Scandinavian prizes, or cargos of merchandize, . . . . 94

### CHAPTER III.

#### DUBLIN AND ICELAND.

Iceland visited by Irish previous to its discovery in A.D. 870 by Lief and Ingolf, Norwegians.—Lief bringing captives from Ireland is saved by their device from perishing of thirst.—Many descendants of Cearbhall, an Irishman, King of Dublin, follow his son-in-law, Eyvind Ostman, and settle in Iceland.—Auda, widow of King Aulaf founder of Dublin, retires thither.—Auda becomes a Christian like her brother-in-law, an emigrant from Ireland.—Descendants of Aulaf and Auda settlers in Iceland.—Other emigrants from Ireland.—America discovered long before

Columbus by Norsemen connected with Dublin.—Ari, a descendant of Cearbhall's wrecked on the coast of Florida A.D. 983.—Gudlief from Dublin driven by storms to America A.D. 936.—Is addressed in Irish.—Finds it is Biorn, long banished from Iceland, . . . . . . . . . 98

## CHAPTER IV.

### DUBLIN AND THE SCOTTISH ISLES.

The Hebrides and Orkneys visited by Irish ecclesiastics long before their occupation by the Scandinavians.—Saint Columba retired from Ireland to Hy (one of the Hebrides), A.D. 563.—Founded a monastery there.—The Scandinavians plunder Hy-Colum-Cille, A.D. 802.—From the Orkneys and Hebrides they plunder in Ireland, Scotland, and Norway.—Harald Haarfagr, King of Norway, sends Ketill Flatnef against them.—Ketill becomes their leader.—Allies himself with Aulaf, the White, King of Dublin.—Marries his daughter.—Scandinavian ravages in Spain and Africa.—They land their Moorish captives in Ireland.—Spanish, Irish, and Scandinavian histories confirm this account, 113

## CHAPTER V.

### DUBLIN AND THE MAINLAND OF SCOTLAND.

Difference between the Scandinavian invasions of Scoland and Ireland.—In Scotland they were as conquerors.—The Scandinavians at Dublin, colonists.—Aulaf, King of Dublin, intermarries into the families of Irish Kings.—Enumeration of Aulaf's connexions with Irish royalty.—His connexions with the Scandinavian Lords of the Isles.—Marries Auda, daughter of Ketill, Lord of the Hebrides.—Keneth M'Alpin, King of Scots, calls to his aid, Godfrey, Chief of Ulster.—Godfrey becomes Lord of the Isles.—Aulaf's expedition with his son Ivar, against the men of Fortrenn.—Aulaf slain there, A.D. 869.—His son, Ivar, returns, and reigns at Dublin.—Ivar dies, A.D. 872.—Ivar's grandson driven out of Dublin by the Irish, A.D. 962.—Invades Pictland, and is slain at Fortrenn, A.D. 904, . . 118

## CHAPTER VI.

### RELIGION OF THE OSTMEN OF IRELAND.

Few details in Irish Annals concerning the form of Paganism of the Ostmen of Ireland.—Date of their conversion to Christianity.—The conversion of King Aulaf Cuaran in England.—The first Ostman bishop of Dublin consecrated there.—King Aulaf Cuaran's conversion in England decides the religion of many of his subjects in Ireland.—The rest remain worshippers of Thor.—Proofs of this worship in Irish Annals.—Whether the prefix Gille be Scandinavian or Irish discussed.—Deductions drawn from its use in Scandinavian and Irish names.—The division of Ireland into four provinces, not Scandinavian, but of ecclesiastical origin. —The Dyfflinarskiri or Scandinavian territory around Dublin.— Its bounds co-extensive with the early Admiralty jurisdiction of the Mayor and citizens of Dublin, . . . . . . 122

# BOOK III.

## THE SCANDINAVIAN ANTIQUITIES OF DUBLIN.

### CHAPTER I.

#### OF THE STEIN OF DUBLIN.

Bounds of the Stein.—Priory of All Hallowes, founded on the Stein.— Neck of land at the Stein formed by the confluence of the Liffey and the Dodder.—The favourite landing place of the Northmen of Dublin.—Bridge and mill of the Stein.—Long Stone of the Stein.—Site of the Long Stone.—The Stein (or Stain) named from this Stone.—References to the Long Stone in city leases.—Scandinavian tombs on the Stein, . . . . 143

### CHAPTER II.

#### OF THE THINGMOUNT OF DUBLIN.

The monuments of the Stein shown to be Scandinavian.—Custom of the Northmen to set up a Stone at their first landing place.— And to erect temples to Thor and Freija adjacent.—Also a Thingmount or place of public meeting and judicature.—The Thingmount of Dublin erected on the Stein.—Remained till A.D. 1682.—Account of its removal.—Church of St. Andrew Thengmotha.—Built probably on the site of a Temple of Thor or Freija.—Meeting of King Henry the 2nd with Irish princes on the Stein near the Church of St. Andrew.—Understood probably by the Irish as either a Thing-mote or a Festival meeting.— Not as a submission or surrender of independence.—Hoges.— Hoge-Tings. — "Hoggen Green," "Hogen butts," and "St. Mary del Hogges," all called from this adjacent Hoge or Tingmount, . . . . . . . . . . 156

S

# APPENDIX.

## I.

### ON THE ANCIENT NAME OF DUBLIN.

Shallowness of the navigable channel of the Liffey in early times.—Fords at Dublin.—Bally-Ath-Cliath, the Town of the Hurdleford, the original name of Dublin.—Mistakes of Stanihurst, Ware, and others as to the origin and meaning of the name.—Circumstances misleading them.—The true meaning of Bally-Ath-Cliath stated in the Dinn Seanchus.—Nature of the structure of the Hurdleford.—Tochers or wooden causeways distinguished from Droichets or bridges.—Droichets or regular bridges distinguished from Droichet-Cliaths —A regular bridge at Dublin before the English Invasion.—Bridge of the Ostmen or Dubhgall's bridge.—Early bridges in England.—Rebuilding of London Bridge in stone in King John's reign.—Site of the Hurdleford of Dublin discussed.—Dr. Petrie's identification of the five great Slighs or roads leading from Tara in the first century of the Christian era.—The Hurdleford at Bally-Ath-Cliath shown to be in the line of the Sligh Cualan, . . . . . . . . . . 202

## II.

### OBSERVATIONS EXPLANATORY OF SIR BERNARD DE GOMME'S MAP,
### MADE A.D. 1673.

Alarm produced by the entry of the Dutch fleet into the Thames in 1667.—Sir Bernard de Gomme's plan for the defence of the Harbour of Dublin in 1673.—His project for a fort near Merrion-square.—Ringsend then the chief landing place.—Meaning of 'Ringsend.'—The Pigeon House.—Its history. — Extent of ground overflown by the sea in 1673.—The making of the North and South walls.—Sir John Rogerson's wall.—Double wall and road from Ringsend to the Pigeon House.—Piles in the sand thence to Poolbeg.—The building of the Long wall.—The lotting for the North Lots.—The erecting of the Ballast Board.— Early history of the Bar at the Harbour Mouth.—The deepening of the River and reducing the Bar the work of the Ballast Board, . 228

# INDEX.

Aberfayle (Perthshire), 175, n.
Abrodites, 8.
Acquitaine, K. John, Duke of, 185.
Adam of Bremen, lx., 53, n.
Adam fitz Robert, murder of, lxxi., n.
Ad Quod Damnum (inquisition), 246, n.
Adamnan, iv., 113, n., 121, n., 172, n.
Addington, lxxxix.
Admiral, The Lord High, claims anchorage fees in Port of Dublin (1708), 246, n., 247.
Admiralty of Dublin.
—— jurisdiction of, granted to Mayor, &c., of Dublin, 140, 246.
—— between Arclo and Nanny water, n., ib.
—— customs between these limits granted to them (46 Ed. III., ib.
—— admiralty jurisdiction in (27 Elizabeth), ib.
—— annulled (12 James I.), by judgment of King's Bench, ib.
Aedh, 57, 63, n.
Aedh, son of Conchobar, King of Connaught, 47.
Aedh Finnlaith, King of Ireland, 47, n., 59, 77, 118, 119.
Africa, 115, 116.
Agar House, on Arran-quay, viii., n.
Aghaboe, 54.
Aighneach, or Snam Eidhneach (Carlingford),
Aileach, 2, 72, 111, 112.
Ailill, 28, 30.
Ailill, s. of Colgan, 16.
Ain, 88.
Ainge, river (Nanny), 24, n.
Airghialla, 86, n.
Aitill, 227, n.
Akranes promontory, 105.
Alan's register, 217.
Alba, 47, 57, 120.
Albain, 82, n.

Alban Alband, or Halfdan, 44, n.
Albanaich, 43.
Albanenses, 121.
Albdarn (Halfdan), 64.
Albene, or Delvin rivulet, 142, n.²
Alcluit, 38, 39, n.
Albdan, 115, see Halfdan.
Alder, Mr., vii., viii.
Alercronshead (Arklow), 139.
Alexander the Great, xi.
—— the Third (Pope), ib.
Alexandria, l., n.
Alfred, King, 42, 48, 50, 70, 100, 127.
Alfus, 101.
Alfwyn, daughter of Ethelflæd, 57.
All Hallows, Priory of, lxxv., cxviii., 145, 146, n., 149, 150, 178, and see All Saints.
—— Register of, 162.
Allen, Giles, 146, n.
—— John, Judge of Metropolitan Court, 146, n.
—— Colonel, John, xc., xcii.
Allman, Professor, 210.
Alloid, Manonnan, s. of, 82, n.
Alorekstad, 135, n.
Althing, 104, 160, 169, 197.
Alvdon, see Halfdan.
Amaccus, and see Maccus, son of Aulaf Cueran, 75, n.
Amhlaeibh Ceancairech (Aulaf Ceancairech), 66, n., 69.
America, 105, 107.
American map paper, cxxiii.
Amiens-street, cix.
Amory, Jonathan, 212, n.
Amrou, l., n.
Andalusia, 117.
Anglesey, Earl of, 152.
Anglesea, Isle of, xxxvii., 50, 87.
Anglo Saxons, 64.
Angus, s. of Erc, 82 n.
Anjou, King John, Count of,
Annagassan river, 19, n., 64, n.

s 2

Annals of Loch Cé, lxxxii.
Annesley, Sir Francis, cviii., n.
Annesley, Arthur, 165.
Annuth, 42, n.
Antony and Cæsar, l., n.
Antrim, coast of, 11, n.
Anwynd, 42, 43.
Arabia, l., n.
Aralt for Harald.
Archdale, Mervyn, 217, n., 146, n., 192, n.
Archery butts, 169, and see Hoggen butt.
Ard Macha (Armagh), 16.
Ari, lx.
Ari Frode, 100, n.
Aric mac Brith, 63, n., 71, n.
Arklow, lxvii., 138, 139, 140, 141, and see Arklow and Nanny water, the bounds of Admiralty jurisdiction of Dublin, 246, n., 247, n.
Armagh, 2, n., 16, 20, n., 33, 34, 35, 36, 38, 67, 123.
—— archbishop of, cviii., n., 177.
—— fosoirchinneach of, 132, n.
Arnulf, Emperor, 45, n.
Arran-quay, lxxix., viii., xxi., lxix.
Arran-street, East, 212, n.
Artichoke-road, 231, n
Artists' Warehouse, Fishamble-street, 209.
Asolfus Alskek, 105.
Asdisa Bareysku, lviii., 103.
Askel Hnokkan, 101.
Askellshofda, 101, n.
Assembly Rolls of City of Dublin, xv., xxv.
—— Acts of (and Corporation of Dublin), 203, n.
Asser, 25, 37, n., 41, n., 42, n., 44, n.
Aston's-quay, cxviii., 147, n.
Astorga, xci.
Ath, 213.
Athairne Ailgeasenh, 213.
Ath-crocha (Shannon harbour), bridge of, A.D, 1116, 214, n.
Ath-Cliath, 3, 23, 47, 56, 58, 61, 69, 85, 142.

Ath-Cliath of ships, 23, n.
—— of swords, ib.
—— bridge of (A.D. 1014), 219, 220.
—— fortress of, 49, 58, 69.
—— fortress of, the foreigners at, lxv.
—— the foreigners of, 39, 56, 66, 69, 72, 74, 79.
—— green of, 152, 184.
—— battle of (Kilmashogc), 59, 60, 64, 65.
—— plain of, 152, n.
—— the orator of, 132.
—— mistakes concerning origin of name, 207, 209, 210, 212.
—— true meaning, 213, 215, 226.
—— tochar or causeway at, 221.
—— meaning of, 23. Ostmen fortress at Dubhlinn of Ath-Cliath, A.D. 840, 23. Site of fortress, ib. Foreigners of, 39, plunder Munster and Connaught, ib.; Flanns defeat by, 47; foreigners of, expelled by Cearbhall, s. of Muirigen, 49; the foreigners under Sitric, s. of Godfrey, recover Dubhlinn of Ath-Cliath, 54; battle of Kilmashoge, called battle of Ath-Cliagh, (A.D. 919), 59; defeat of the Irish under Niall Glundubh, ib.; Reginald, s. of Godfrey, rules at, A.D. 921, 61; Irish attack in his absence, 64; failure of, ib.; return of Godfrey, 66; the Mac Elghi (sons of Sitric) take Dublin, 67; Muircheartagh and his Leather Cloaks besiege Ath-Cliath, 71, 72; fail, 72.
Ath-Cliath-Cualann, lii., 225.
Ath-Cliath Meadrighe, 226, n. (now Clarensbridge, co. Galway).
Ath-Cliath on the Shannon, 226.
Ath-Cruithne, 64.
Athelstan, 64, 65, 66, 68, 69, 70, 71, 124; illegitimate brother of Edward, K. of Anglo-Saxons, 64; drowns his legitimate brother Edwin, ib.; by the aid of the Northumbrian Danes usurps the

## INDEX. 261

Athelstan—*con.*
 rule of the Anglo-Saxons, *ib.*;
 usurps the kingship of the Northumbrian Danes, 65; Godfrey, K.
 of Dublin, recovers this kingship
 for a short time, 66; is expelled
 by Athelstan, *ib.*; who appoints
 Eric-Blodax, a Dane, viceroy, 68.
Athelstan, K. of Anglo-Saxons, conquers Aulaf at Brunanburg, A.D.
 937, 220.
Athgus, Manannan, s. of, King of
 Man, 82, *n.*
Athliag, tochar or causeway at, 221,
 see Ballyliag.
Athlone, 34.
—— tochar or causeway, 221.
—— bridge of (A.D. 1116), 244, *n.*
—— the wicker bridge of (A.D.
 1133), 214, *n.*
—— castle of, A.D. 1120, 214, *n.*
Ath Truisten, 72, 142.
Atkinson, Edward, xli.
Attar, 53.
Auda, Queen, lvii., lviii., lx.
—— d. of Ketill Flatnef, 101, *n.*,
 102, 103, 114, 120.
—— wife of Aulaf the White, 101, *n.*
Audöen's arch, 223, *n.*
Augustus Cæsar, 2, *n.*
Auisle, 22, *n.*
Aulaiv, K. of Lochlann, 19, *n.*
Aulaff, s. of the K. of Lochlann, 19.
Aulaf, Aulaiv, Amhlaeibh, Amaleff,
 and Amlevus, or Olaf, 20.
Aulaf K., the White, lvii., lviii., lx.
—— 37, 38, 39, 40, 41, 43, 47, 53,
 54, 61, 85, *n.*, 98, 101, 102, 104,
 107, 108, 114, 118, 120, 121, 126,
 142.
—— his arrival, 19; his name in
 Irish, 20; takes Dublin, *ib.*,; is
 made king of it, *ib.*; story of
 Aulaf, Sitric, and Ivar, being
 Kings of Dublin, Waterford, and
 Limerick respectively, false, 20,
 22; he conquers the Picts and
 destroys Fortren, their capital,
 36 and *n*³; accompanies Ivar,

Aulaf—*con.*
 King of Dublin, to East Anglia,
 37; they conquer it and Northumbria, *ib.*; Ivar made King of
 Northumbria, *ib.*; their second invasion of Scotland from Dublin, 30;
 they besiege Dunbarton the capital
 of the Britons of Strath Clyde, *ib.*;
 the ravages of Ivar and Aulaf in
 Munster and Connaught, 39;
 Aulaf dies, A.D. 871, 40; Ivar dies
 A.D. 872 *ib.*; Eystein (or Ostin),
 Aulaf's son, slain by a stratagem
 of the Albanaich (or Scots), 43.
Aulaf Cuaran, 73, 75, 76, 77, 79,
 80, 91, 92, 96, 126, 181, *n.*
—— rules at Dublin, 73; lands in
 Northumbria (A.D. 949), 74; after
 four years is expelled, 75; returns
 to Ireland, 76; marries Dunlaith,
 daughter of Maelmhuire, 77;
 marries Gormflaith, daughter of
 Murchadh, K. of Leinster, 78;
 Aulaf's Irish connexions, 77, 78;
 Aulaf, son of his brother Godfrey,
 K. of Dublin, succeeds his father,
 79; Aulaf Cuaran claims the
 throne, Aulaf his nephew defeats
 him, *ib.*; Aulaf Cuaran goes a
 pilgrimage to Iona, *ib.*; called in
 Irish Aulaf son of Sitric, *ib.*;
 abdicates, 80; Maelseachlainn, his
 stepson, succeeds him, *ib.*
—— son of Godfrey, 67, 68, 69, 70,
 71, 72, 79, 124.
—— son of Godfrey (s. of Reginald),
 succeeds his father as K. of Dublin (A.D. 932), 68: by right K.
 of Northumbria, *ib.*; Athelstan
 opposes, sends to Denmark for
 Eric-Blodax, son of Harald Harfagre, *ib.*; appoints him viceroy,
 *ib.*; he is baptized, *ib.*; resides at
 York, *ib.*; Aulaf attempts to recover Northumbria, 69; sails from
 Dublin, and with a fleet of 615
 ships lands at the Humber (A.D.
 927), 70; is defeated by Athelstan
 at Brunanburg, *ib.*; returns to

Aulaf—*con*
  Dublin, 71; the Irish besiege Dublin under Donnchadh, K. of Ireland, and Muircheartach of the Leather Cloaks, *ib.*; they fail, 72; ravage the country, *ib.*; Muircheartach marches from Aileach (Elagh, co. Donegal) round Ireland, *ib.*
—— son of Sitric, 48, 65.
—— s. of Sitric, s. of Aulaf Cauran, 91, 124, 125, 128, *n.*
—— Ceanncairech (and see Amhlaeibh Ceancairech), 66.
—— K. of Dublin, his retreat thither from Brunanburg (A.D. 937), 220.
—— the Red King of Scotland, 69, *n.*
—— Tryggevesson, King, 181, 182.
—— and the Irish sheep dog, lxiv.
Aufer, 64.
Austfirdinga fiordung, 134, *n.*
Avangus, 105.
Avenlithe, see Liffey.
Avery, Timothy (1657), 240.
Awley, Fivit, 71, *n.*
Awley, mac Godfrey, 71, *n.*
Agmund, 52.

Babylon (Old Cairo), 1., *n.*
Babylonian, Captivity, The, 80.
—— the rule of the Ostmen likened to, 80.
—— next to the captivity of Hell, *ib.*
—— Maelsachlainn defeats the foreigners of Dublin (A.D. 980), *ib.*
—— his famous proclamation of freedom for the Ui Neill, *ib.*
Bacon, J. C., xli.
—— Sir Francis, xxii.
Baden, Duchy of, xxviii.
Baden, 110, *n.*
Baedan, K. of Uladh, 84.
Bœgsec, 41.
Baidr, 85.
Bagot Rath, 145, *n.*, 241.
  —— street, Lower, 170, *n.*
Baile-an-bhothair, 222, *n.*

Balbriggan, xxxvii., *n.*
Baldur, s. of Odin, 172.
Baldoyle, 142.
Ballast, irregular taking of, destroys the harbour (1698), 245, *n.*
Ballast Board, cvi., cx., cxi., cxii., cxv., cxvi., cxix.
—— origin of, cxi.
—— their management of Irish Lighthouses, xliii., xliv., xlv., 202, 231, *n.*³, 242, *n.*
—— history of, 243–247.
—— renamed (1787) Corporation for Preserving and Improving the Port of Dublin, 247.
Ballast Office Wall (see South Wall).
Balliowen in Isle of Man, 176.
Ball, Nicholas (1582), 250, *n.*
Ball's Bridge, cxxi., 170, *n.*, 232, *n.*, 1.
—— bridge first built here, A.D., 1629–1637, 232, *n.*¹
Bally-ath-Cliath., xlviii., see Ath-Cliath.
Ballygunner, lxvii., and *n.*, *ib.*
—— Temple, *ib.*
—— more, *ib.*
Bally-lean cliath, 207.
Ballyliag (now Lanesboro'), 214, *n.*, 221.
Balrothery, inhabitants of, barony of, 205.
Baltic, The, 8, 11–14.
—— Coffee House, xcvi.
Baltinglas, xcv.
Bangor, N. Wales, 1716, *n.*²
Banks, Commissioners of Inquiry as to Joint Stock, xii.
Bank Acts, of Scotland and Ireland, xlii.
—— of Ireland, xxxvii., xlii.
Bann, river, 85, *n.*
Bar, The lowering of, xlv.
—— Captain John Perry's plans (1720), for avoiding, 249.
—— Proposals for rendering the port commodious (1720), 26, *n.*
—— appointed by Ballast Board to survey the harbour with Captain

# INDEX. 263

Bar—*con.*
J. Burgh, Engineer and Surveyor-General (1725), 249, *n.*
—— their plans of improvement rejected by Ballast Board, *ib.*
—— account of, in second report of Tidal Harbours Commissioners, *ib.*
—— A.D. 1582, a tower (like Maiden tower at Drogheda), projected at, 250, *n.*
—— in 1861, twenty-five feet over the bar at spring tides, *ib.*
Bargy, barony of, 222, *n.*
Barid, 85.
Barid Mac-n-Oitir, 54, 85, *n.*[1]
—— O'Hivar, 85, *n.*
Barith, 47, *n.*, 63, 85, *n.*, 86.
Barnes, William, 222, *n.*
Barnewall of Turvey, Viscount Kingsland, see Lord Kingsland.
Barker, Antony, Lord Mayor (1718), 248, *n.*
Barr, Richard, Alderman, 169, *n.*[1]
Barrington, Daines, 167.
—— Sir Jonah, lxxxviii.
Barrow river, 53, *n.*, 55, *n.*
Barry, Rev. George, 157, *n.*, 159, *n.*
—— Sir James, afterwards Lord Santry, 212, *n.*
Bartholinus, lx., 42, *n.*, 45, *n.*, 62, *n.*, 69, *n.*, 127, *n.*
Basil, Attorney-General (A.D. 1655), 228, *n.*
Bath, Earl of, lxvii., *n.*
—— avenue, cxxi., 242.
Batter, see Bothyr.
—— Green, 222, *n.*
—— Yellow, do., *ib.*
Batterstown, 222, *n.*
Baugus, 101, and *n. ib.*
Beechy, Captain, R.N., xlv.
Bealach Duibhlinne, 225, *n.*
Beckman, Sir Martin, 229.
Bede, The Venerable, 171, 213.
Beggar's-bush, cx., 239, 242, *n.*
Belfast, history of by George Benn (1877), 243, *n.*
—— Belfast, Sir Arthur Chichester, Lord, 241, *n.*

Belfast, Lord, departure of, from the Ring's-end, *ib.*
Bellew, Mr. 168, *n.*[4]
Bennchoir (Bangor, co. Down), 16.
Benn, George, history of Belfast, by, 243, *n.*
Bennet, Richard Bergoin.
—— has copy of Captain John Perry's rare map of the Harbour, cvii., 249, *n.*
—— with ship canal along Sutton shore to avoid the bar.
Bentham, Jeremy, xii.
Beorgo, d. of Eyvind Austman, 102, 105, *n.*
Berkely, the Lord Deputy (1679), 241, *n.*
Bernicia, 41.
Bertiniani, 8, *n.*[3]
Berwick on Firth of Forth, 38.
—— on Tweed, 38.
Betham, Sir William, 150, *n.*[1]
Bewley, Thomas, xli.
Biadmyna, lxv.
Biolan, King, 53.
Biorn Asbrand, 106, 107.
—— Austman, lvii.
—— Ironsides, s. of Regnar Ladbrog, 22, 45.
—— s. of K. Harold, 97.
Birsa isle, 174.
Blacaire, 73.
Black Book of Christ Church.
—— men, 115.
—— Monday, 179, *n.*
—— pagans, 85, *n.*[1]
—— rock, cxiv.
—— frames of piles for channel of Liffey, made at, 236, 237.
Bladen, Alderman, 197, *n.*
Blaeja, d. of Ella, 32, *n.*
Blaemenn, Africans, 116, x., *n.*, *ib.*
Block house, The, 238, *n.* (see Pigeon House).
Bloomfield, Rev. Francis, 174, *n.*[3]
Blowick (Bullock), 138.
Blue land, 116.
—— men, 115, 116.
Boate Gerard, cxiii., cxxi., 232, *n.*[1]

Boden see, xxviii., *n.*
Bodleian Library, c.
Bohar-na-gloch, 222, *n.*
Bolton, John, Lord Mayor (1717), 248, *n.*
—— Richard, 169, *n.*[1]
—— street, 212, *n.*
Boot lane, 212, *n.*
Booths for dwellings, 210, *n.*
Bordes, Captain, R.E., 224.
Bork, the Fat, 105.
Bornholm, 175.
Borrishool, barony of, 15, *n.*
Bosworth, 52, *n.*[2]
Bothar-na-gloch (Stonybatter), 222, *n.*, 226, *n.*
Bothyr, *n.*, batter (a road), 222.
Bottiler, James, Earl of Ormond, 146.
Boulogne, 46.
Bowles, W., cvii.
Bowling green, The, 169.
Boyce, Joseph, xli.
Boyce *v.* Jones, decides the illegality of the Skerries Light Dues, xxxix.
Boyle, Alex., xli.
Boyne, The privateer, 241, *n.*
Bradogue, river, 212.
Brady, Maziere, ix., x.
Bran, 120.
Brand, John, 157 and *n.*, *ib.*, 157, *n.*, 220, *n.*
Brandon Hill, 55, *n.*
Bray, 164, *n.*
Breagh, Lord of, 119.
—— The King of, 59.
Breagha, 74.
Breakspeare, Nicholas, see Pope.
Brehon laws, 185, *n.*, 186.
Breidvikinga Kappi, 106, *n.*[6]
Breifne, 69.
Bromegham's tower, 204, *n.*
Bretland, see Wales.
Brewster, Lord Mayor, (1674), 242.
Brian Borumha, 78, 79, 88, 91.
Brickfield (The Merrion), 237.
Bridewell on Hogs Green, 196, *n.*

Bridge of the Ostmen, xlvi., xlvii., xlviii., (see also Droichet Dubhgall).
Bridges of Iceland, lxv.
—— early, in Ireland, xlviii., 223.
Bristol, 3, *n.*, 185.
—— first bridge at, xlvi.
—— — bridge built at, A.D. 1202, 216.
—— — Sir Bernard de Gomme, at capture of, by Prince Rupert, 1643, 230, *n.*
Brittany, 53.
Britain, inhabitants of ancient, 227.
Britons of Strathclyde, 38, 43.
British and Irish Steam Packet Company, xxxix.
British Museum, 228, *n.*, 230.
Borlase, 158, *n.*
Brooking's map of Dublin, A.D.1728, cvi., cxix., cxx., 196, *n.*, 203, *n.*, 248, 249, *n.*
Brophy, Peter, xli.
Brow of the Hazelwood, 209, 210, see Drom Choll Coill.
Bruce, K. Edward, 223, *n.*
Brunalban, 82, *n.*
Brunanburg, 63, *n.*, 69, *n.*, 70, 71, *n.*, 94.
Brussels, Royal Library at, 219.
Buerno, 26.
Buhred, K, 13, *n.*
Bulls, the South and North, 234, and *n.*, *ib.*
Bullring, Mayor of the, 179.
Bullock, 138.
Burdett, Sir Francis, vi., *n.*
Burgess roll, earliest of Dublin, lxviii.
Burgh, Captain, Engineer, Surveyor General, (1725), 249, *n.*
—— appointed to examine the harbour with Captain John Perry, *ib.*
—— their plans, *ib.*
—— rejected by Ballast Board, *ib.*
Burgh quay, cxvii., cxviii.
Burials, Scandinavian, mounds for great, standing stones for brave men, 154, *n.*
Burke, Edmund, lxxxi.

INDEX. 265

Burke, Edmund, his father's house on Arran-quay, next to that afterwards C. Haliday's, viii., *n*.
—— Sir Bernard, xxvi., 136, *n*.
Burnt Nial, lv., *n*.
Burton-on-Trent, 224, *n*.
Bury St. Edmunds, lxvii., *n*.
Bush river, 84, *n*.
Butlers of Ormond, The, 145.
Butler, Rev. Richard, 145, *n*., 146, *n*., 162, *n*.
Butts, 167, and see Butt.
Byrne, Colonel Miles, xci.

Cadiz, 117.
—— ancient Gades, 115, $n^3$.
Caen, in Normandy, 130.
Cæsar Augustus, 2, $n^1$.
—— Julius, 227.
—— Commentaries of, *n*., *ibid.*
Cagework houses, 211.
Cairbre Riada, 84.
Cairo, old, l., *n*.
Caithness, liii. 81, *n*., 102, 157, *n*.
Calendar of State Papers of Queen Elizabeth, 204, *n*.
—— James First's reign, 203, *n*.
Callwell, Robert, xli.
Cambridge University, xlv.
Camden, 90, *n*., 92, *n*., 206, 226.
—— Society, 210, *n*.
—— Earl, lxxvii.
Canary Isles, cxxii., *n*.
Cantabrian Sea, 115.
Canterbury, 123, 177.
Cantok, Master Thomas, lxxii.
Canute, 67, 71, *n*., 123, 181, 195, 199.
—— son of Gormo-hin-Gamle, 62, 63.
Canutus Hördaknutus, 33, *n*.
Cape Clear, liv.
Capper, Samuel James, M.P., xxviii., *n*.
Caradoc, 87, *n*., 24, *n*., 50, *n*., 52, *n*., 53, *n*., 58, *n*.
Carey, Sir George, see Cary.

Carlingford, lxvii., 15, 35, 94, 137, see also Snam Edneigh.
Carlisle Bridge, xciii, 234, *n*.
Carlow county, 55, *n*.
Carlus, 38.
—— s. of Aulaf, K. of Dublin, 20, *n*., 128.
—— the sword of, 126, 123.
Carn Brammit, 23.
Carrick-on-Suir, lxxvii.
Carroll, Sir James, cxvii., cxviii.
—— 169, $n.^1$, 145, $n.^2$
Carteret, the Lord, L.l., 246, *n*.
Cary, Sir George, cvii., *n*.
Cary's Hospital, lxxiii., cvii., *n*.
Carey, Rev. Dr., Archbishop of Dublin, 190.
Cashel, Synod of, 136, 186.
—— Archbishop of, 177, *n*.
—— Archbishoprick, of, 135, *n*.
—— Maelgula Mac Dungail, K. of, 126, 136.
Cassel, 6, *n*.
Cassels, architect, xciv., *n*.
Castlereagh, Lord, lxxxix.
Castles, Danish, in Ireland, lxv.,lxvi.
—— Colonel, 165, $n.^1$
Castleknock, 223, *n*.
—— inhabitants of barony of, 205.
Castle-street, 208, 209, 210.
Castellis, The, xcvi.
Cat, 82, $n.^1$, and see Caithness.
Cave, Thomas, (1784), 240, *n*.
Ceallach, prince of Scotland, 71, *n*.
Ceann Maghair, 85, *n*.
Ceanannus, 74.
Cearbhall, 19, *n*., 22, 23, 39, 45, 47, 53, 54, 66.
—— lord of Ossory, 95, 100, 101, 102, 104, 105, 119, 120.
—— (Carroll), in alliance with Aulaf and Ivar, 39; reigns at Dublin, A.D. 872-885, 45; dies A.D. 885, 46. Flann, his sister's son claims rule, but is defeated by the foreigners at Ath Cliath, 47.
—— Aulaf, the White, his nephew, 54, Cearbhall, called King of Liffe of Ships. *ib.*, *n*.; slain, A.D.

## INDEX.

Cearbhall—*con.*
  909, *ib.*; Diarmid, his son, dies A.D. 927, *ib.*
—— son of Muirigen, 49, 77.
—— son of Muirigen, K. of Leinster, drives the foreigners out of Ath Cliath, 49; they take refuge at Ireland's Eye, *ib.*; land in Anglesey, 50; are defeated at the battle of Ros Meilor, *ib.*; are given lands in Mercia, near Chester, by Ethelflœd, *ib.*
—— s. of Dunghal, 23.
Ceile Des (Culdees), 61.
Cellach, K. of Leinster, 31.
Cellachan, K. of the Islands, 71, *n.*³
Cenn Fuait (Confey), 55; battle of, 56.
Cennedigh, 77, *n.*
—— Lord of Laighis, 119.
Census Commissioners, xxxiv.
Ceolwulf, 41.
Chain Book of City of Dublin, xxv.
Channel Islands, 195.
Chapel, Walter, lxxi., *n.*
Chapelizod, lxxx.
Charlemagne, iv., 5, 6, 7, 9, 10, 14, 119.
—— his conquests and forced conversions of the Saxons, 5; they fly into Denmark, 8; their hatred to clergy, *ib.*; forced by him out of Denmark, 9; Danes and Saxons revenge themselves on France, 9; infest England, 10, and Ireland, 11; their raids on the island hermitages, *ib.*; why and when they became pirates, 12–14; their ravages in Ireland, (A.D. 807–836), 16–18; called by the Irish Dubhghoill, 18; supposed to be Danes, *ib.*; A.D. 847, a fleet of Finnghoill, *ib.*; supposed to be Norwegians, *ib.*; the conflicts between them, *ib.* and 19.
Charlemont, Lord, xxii.
—— House, Library at, xxii., 241, *n.*
Charles, the Fat, King of France, 46.
—— the Simple, King of France, 52.
—— First King, 203, *n.*

Charleston, S. Carolina, xxvi.
Chase, The, a Fenian Tale, lxii., *n.*
Chatham "Chest, The," at, 245, 246, *n.*
—— Chatham and Sheerness, alarm at, by Dutch raid (1667), 229.
Cheevers, Walter, xiv.
Chester, 50, 52, 58, 87.
—— Ethelflœd, Lady of Chester, gives the Danes driven out of Dublin (A.D. 900) lands on which to erect stalls and houses, 50.
Chetham, Robert, 245, *n.*
Chichester, Sir Arthur, lxxiii., *n.*, cvii., *n.*
—— Lord Belfast, his departure from the Ring's End, 1614, 241, *n.*
—— Sir Edward, cvii., *n.*
—— House, cvii., 203, *n.*, 241, *n.*, 239, 240, *n.*; the old shore, 239, *ib.*; ground plan of, (A.D. 1734) 239, *n.*, site of New Parliament House, *ib.*
Cholera morbus, xxxvi.
Christ Church, Dublin, 221, and see Holy Trinity, 92, 148.
—— Christ Church-hill, xlvi.
—— place, 208.
—— seneschal of, lxxi., *n.*, lxxii.
Christian, William, 152.
Christiania, 12, *n.*
Christmas customs, 173.
Church of St. Andrew, 162; the old, 145, *n.*; of Delgany, 148; of the Holy Trinity (and see Christ Church), 148; of St. Patrick's, 148; the Round, 179; of St. Stephen, 149.
Church-lane, 162.
Churchtown (Dundrum), lxxxv.
Cianachta, 16.
—— Breagh (in Meath), 24.
Cicero, his name for a library, xv.
Ciarraighi, the, 55.
Cill-dara (Kildare), 17, 47, 65, *n.*
Cill-Maighnenn, 152, *n.*, or Kilmainham.
Cill-Martin (Wicklow), 139.

Cillmosamhog, battle of, 59.
Cille-Dalua, see Killaloe.
Cinaedh, s. of Alpin, K. of Scots, 120.
—— son of Conang, 24.
Circular Belfries, 174.
—— Semi-circular, 174.
—— churches, 174.
Circular-road, the, 212, *n.*
Citadel to defend Liffey mouth (1673), 228, *n.*²
City of Dublin Steampacket Company, xxxix.
City-quay, cxix.
Clachan, circle of stones, 175, *n.*, 176, *n.*
Clachan (for Church), 175.
Claims, Court of, lxvii., *n.*
—— book of, (1702), 203, *n.*
Cluain Dolcain (Clondalkin, county Dublin), 16.
Clane, 147.
Clare, the Lord Grattan's answer to, xiii.
—— county, gold ornaments found in, 127, *n.*
Clarensbridge, county Galway (Ath Cliath Meadrighe), 226, *n.*
Clear, Cape, 16.
Cleaseby and Vigfusson, 129, *n.*, 130, *n.*, 134, *n.*, 135, *n.*, 195, *n.*
Clifden, the Viscounts, xxi.
—— Henry, Viscount, viii., *n.*
Clondalkin, 16, *n.*, 20, 38, 142.
—— Aulaf's "Dun" at, 38.
Clonfert, 34, 35.
Clonlyffe, 132, *n.*
Clonmacnois, 34, 35, 36, 63.
—— annals of, 221.
Clonmel, lxxvii.
Clonmore (in Leinster), 17, *n.*
Clonmor, (Clonmore, county Louth), 16.
Clontarf, battle of, xlvii., xlviii., lii., 78, *n.*, 219.
—— bar, 234, *n.*²
—— the Island of, 205.
—— pool, cxii., cxiii., 245, *n.*
—— port of, lxxvi.

Cluan Ferta, of Brennan, 34.
Cluain Iraird, 126.
Cluain-mor-Maedhog (Clonmore in Leinster), 17.
Cluain-na-g Cruimhter, bridge of, 64.
Clut Radulph and Richard, 145.
Clysma (Suez), l., *n.*
Clyst, St. George, xxviii.
Cochran, Captain, cxxii., *n.*
Cock (cockle) lake, cx., 5, 234–238.
Codd, Francis, xli.
Coffee House, the House of Commons (1792), 240 *n.*
Cogan, Milo de, 149, *n.*
—— Rev. A., 136, *n.*
Colburn, Henry, lxxxix
Cole, Henry, lxx., *n.*
Colebrant, 71, *n.*
Colgan, 3, *n.*, 11, *n.*, 12, *n.*, 113, *n.*
Colla, Lord of Limerick, 85, *n.*
—— son of Barith, 63.
College, The, 147.
College-green, 203, *n.*
Collins, Captain Greenville, cvi.
Colton, Archbishop, 189, *n.*
Colton and Co., New York, cxxiii., *n.*
Columbanus (Rev. Charles O'Connor, D.D.), 172, *n.*
Colum Cille (Saint Columba), 43; his relics brought (A.D. 850) from Iona to Dunkeld, 43, *n.*; thence to Ireland on the invasion of Scotland, by the Danes, A.D. 874, *ib.*
Commerce, Chamber of, xxxvii., xxxix., xli., xlv.
Commission, Land Tenure, of 1843, xxxiv.
Commissioners of Parliament of England for Ireland (1657), 228, *n.*², (1657), *t.* 240; order of, *ib.*
Commissioners, see Record Commissioners.
Commons-street, 248.
Conang, 24.
Conaille, 16.
Conaing, Lord of Bregh, 119.

Coachobhar, 78.
—— King of Ulster, 82, n.
—— s. of Maelsachlainn, 91.
—— s. of Flann, King of Ireland, 59.
Confey, see Ceun Fuait.
Conghalach, King of Ireland, 74, 78, 79, 91.
Conn, 221.
Connaught, see Cunnakster.
—— lxv., 34, 35, 63, 82, n.
Connemara (A.D. 807), 15, 16, 63.
Connolly, Mr. (1707), 246, n.
Conemhail, s. of Gilla Arri, 132.
Conor Mac Dearmada, half King of Meath, 126.
Conquest, 186, n.
Constance, Lake of, xxvii., xxviii.
Constantine, s. of King Kenneth, 36, n., 37, n., 40, n.
—— s. of Aedh, King of Scots, 57.
—— King of Scots, 70, 121.
—— s. of Iago, 89.
Cooke, Samuel, of Sunderland, xxvi.
—— employed to establish the Lord Kingsland's advowsons, xxvii.; brings over James F. Ferguson, ib.; his household at Sandymount, ib.
Coolock, inhabitants of barony of, 205.
Cooper, Sir Astley, viii.
Copenhagen, xv., lii.
Coppinger's Register of St. Thomas's Abbey, xxxi.; 217; and see St. Thomas's Abbey Chartulary.
Cork, lxix., 16, 54, 137.
Coranna, 117.
Cormac, liv.
—— Mac Art, 83.
—— Cuilenuan, King and Bishop of Cashel, 77.
Cornwall, lxvii., n., 28, 95, n.
Corporation of Dublin, 203, n.
Corporations, The Eight (of Dublin), 212, n.
Corporation for Preserving and Improving the Port of Dublin (see

Corporation—con.
also Ballast Board, 202, 231, n.³, 247.
Cosgrach, s. of Flannabhrad, 15.
Cosgrave, Johannes, 193, n.
Cossawara, 71, n.
Cotgrave, Randle (A.D., 1610) xxiv., n.
Court Thing, 159.
Cox, Sir Richard, iii.
Crabbe, Rev. George, quotation from, iv.
Crampton Monument, The, cxviii.
Crane, The, 203, n.
Creaghting, practice of, 210, n.
Crofts, Philip, cxviii.
Croker, Crofton, 210, n.
Cromwell (Oliver), xiv., xcii., 212, 228, n., 241.
Cromwellians, 228, n.²
Cross, The (like Thor's hammer sign), 125, n.
Crosthwaite, Thomas, xli.
—— Leland, ib.
Croyland Abbey, 224.
Cruinden, 47.
Cruithne, 83.
—— Irish Picts (see Picts).
Crumlin (co. Dublin), 4, n.¹
Cualann (Cullen), li, 23.
—— (Fercullen), in co. Wicklow, 225.
Cuiges, or fifths of Ireland, 134, n.
Cuilen, son of Cearbhall, 46.
Culdees, 61; see Ceile Dees.
Cullenswood, 179, n.
Culpepper, The Lord, lxviii., n.
Cumberland, Malcolm, King of, 87.
Cumberland, 24, n.
Curran, J. Philpot, lxxx., cii., and n., ib., 196, n.
Currency Inquiry, xlii.
Curry Eugene, 219, 227, n. (see O'Curry).
Customs received to their own use by the several walled towns at accession of James I., 203, n.
Custom House in 1620, 211, n.
—— the new, 202, 203, n., 245, n.

Custom House, the present, building of, 248.
—— fire in 1833, xlii.
Cymry The, 176, n.²

Daggenham breach ; in the Thames, 249 ; Captain John Perry employed to repair (1713), ib.
Dagobert, King, xxviii., n.
Daimhling (Duleek), 16.
Dal Aradia, 85, and ib. n.
Dalby Point, Isle of Man, 156.
Dal Cais, 79, 152, n.
Dalkey, li., lxxvi., 139, n., 225.
—— ship canal from, to Dublin, projected (1800), 249, n.; to avoid the bar, ib.
—— pirates gibbeted at, cxxii., n.
Dal Kollus, 104.
Dal Riada, 84, 85, 89, 93, n.⁵, 113, 120.
—— Scottish kingdom of, founded by Fergus, s. of Erc (A.D., 503), 84.
Dalriads of Ulster, Fergus, s. of Erc, King of, 82, n.
Dam-street, 194, n.
Dam gate, The, 194.
Damass gate, 165, n.
Dames gate, 204, n., 205.
Damory Ricardus, 195, n.
Danes, see Dubhgoill.
—— of Dublin (A.D., 1014), 4, n., 9, 11, 15, 19, n., 51, 52, 219.
—— (or Ostmen), 232.
—— of Ireland (in Herts), 182.
—— of the north of Ireland, 69.
—— Prince of the New and Old, 65.
—— the conversion of, 125.
Danish Wars, Book of the, 219, see War of the Gaedhil with the Gaill, 219.
Darcy, John, xli.
Dartaidha, 226, n.
Dartmouth, Hon. George Legge, Lord, 243.
Dasent G. Webb, LL.D., lv., n., lx., lxv., 134, n.

Davys, Sir John, xxiv., lxx., n., 138, n., 186, n., 212, n.
Davis, Sir Paul, cviii., n.
—— Sir William, 166.
Dearbhforghaill, 92.
Dearc-Fearna (Cave of Dunmore, co. Kilkenny), 66, n.⁵
De Burgo, 136, n.
—— Thomas, 211, 222, n.
De Cogan, Milo, 164, n.
De Courcy, 93, 94.
—— Vivian, 132, n.
Dee, river, 19, n.
—— (at Chester), 87.
—— (co. Louth), 64, n.⁵
De Ginkle (1691), 241, n.
De Gomme, Sir Bernard, xliii., cv., cvi., cix., cx., cxi., cxxi., 228, 229, 230, 232, 245.
—— his map of river and harbour of Dublin (1673), 228-231, also 230, n.
Deira, 24, n., 41.
De La Boullaye le Gouz, 210, n.
De Lacy, lxvi., n.
Delacour, Mr., n.
Delaporte, Anne Marguerite, xxix.
Delgany, 148.
Del Hogges, abbey of, 193, n.
Delg-inis, or Dalkey, 139, n.
De Loundres, Archbishop, 148.
Delvin Rivulet, or Albene, 142, n.
—— River, 138.
De Mezerai, Histoire de France, 7, n.¹, 8, n.¹, 9.
Denmark, 6, 8, 9, 11, 24, 26, 38.
—— Prince George of, 247.
Denzille-street, cx., 239.
Depping, 9, n.
Derg-dheire, 34.
Derry city, 17, n.
—— diocese of, 189, n.
Doomsters, 170.
Desert-Martin, liv.
Desert Creat, liv.
—— Serges, ib.
Desiderata Curiosa Hibernica, 169, n.¹
Des Roches, Mons., 6, n.

Desterre, J. N., vii.
—— his duel with O'Connell, *ib.*, *n.*
—— his conduct at the Mutiny of the Nore, *ib.*
Davenport, 58.
Devizes, K. John's letter from, to build a new bridge at Dublin or keep the old, 216, 217.
Devonshire, Duke of (L.L. 1741), lands at Ringsend, 241, *n.*
Diarmid, son of Cearbhall, 66.
—— s. of Maelnambo, 92.
Dicuil, xlix., *n.*, l., *n.*, liii., liv.
—— 98, *n.*, 113, *n.*
Dinn Seanchus, 213, 215, 226.
Dachonna, Saint, 12, 22, *n.*, 46, *n.*
Dowcra, Lord, 147.
Dodder river, cx., cxxi., 145, 148, 149.
—— port of, lxxvi.
—— (Rafernam water), 232, *n.*¹, 242, *n.*
Doddridge, Life of Col. Gardiner, xiii.
Doire-Chalgaigh (Derry), 17.
Dolier-street, lxxiv., xciv.
Dollar Bay, cxxii., *n.*
Dam-street, 194, *n.*
Domhring, 126, *n*¹.
Dombrain, Sir Jas., R.N., xlv.
Domesday Book, 198, 180.
Domhnall, s. of Muircheartach, 85, *n.*³
—— Donn, 77.
—— brother of Donnchadh, 60.
—— Claen, King of Ireland, 80, and *n.*³ *ib.*
—— grandson of Lochlan, 219.
Dominicans, The, 222, *n.*, 223.
Dominic-street, new, 212, *n.*
Dominus Angliæ, K. Richard I., 189.
—— Hiberniæ, John Earl of Moreton, 189.
Domville Henry, lxxviii.
—— John, lxxviii.
Donnchadh, King of Ireland, 71, 119, 142.

Donnchadh, brother of Conchobar, 59, 60.
—— son of Flann, 69, *n.*
—— Donn, 77.
—— son of Brian Borumha, 78, 91, 92.
—— son of Domhnal Ua Maelseachlainn, 214, *n.*
—— Abbot of Cill-Dearga, 47.
Donegal, 63.
Dorsetshire, 89.
Dover Harbour, Capt. John Perry's survey of (1713), 249.
Downs, The, xli.
Down survey, map of harbour, cvi., lxxvi.
Downpatrick (Dun da Leathghlas), 16, 86.
Drake, F., 77, *n.*
—— Francis, 220, *n.*
Drafdritus, 99, *n.*
Drogheda, 222, *n.*
Droichet, 214.
Droichead Cleithe, 214, and *n.*, *ib.*
Droichet Dubhgall, xlvii.
Dubhgall's bridge, 219.
—— (perhaps Dubhgall, s. of Aulaff), *ib.*
Droichet at Dublin, 220.
Drom Choll Coill, 209.
Dromin, near Dunshaughlin, 17, *n.*
Dromod (South Wales), 53.
Drontheim, lxv., and *n.*, *ib.*
Druids, 32, *n.*
Druids, sorcery of, 172, *n.*
Drum-h-Ing (Dromin, Cilleath), 17.
Drumconran (Drumcondra), 232 *n.*¹
Dabhall River (Blackwater in Tyrone), 85, *n.*
Dubhchoblaig, 78.
Dubhgoill, 17, 19.
Dubhgalls and Finngalls, 61, *n.*, 65.
Dubhgall's bridge, 219, 220.
Dubgoill or Danes—the earlier of the northern invaders, 5, 9 ; cause of their greater fierceness, 5, 9 ; their attacks on France, 10 ; on

INDEX. 271

Dubgoill or Danes—*con.*
England, *ib.*; on Ireland, 11 ; on the coasts and island hermitages, *ib.*; in the interior, 14, 15 ; list of their raids, 16.
Dubhlinn, 3, 23, 24, 207, *n.*, 225, *n.*
—— of Athcliagh, 23, *n.*, 54.
Dubh Lochlannaigh, 18, *n.*
Dublin—no town there before the time of the Ostmen, 2 ; meaning of Dubhlinn, 3; Ostmen, Kingdom of, founded A.D. 852, 5 ; called Dyfflin by the Ostmen, 23 ; Duvelina by the Anglo-Normans, *ib.*; a Norwegian fortress there before Aulaff's arrival, *ib.*; governed by same king as Northumberland for near a century, 24 ; Ptolemy's supposed notice of in second century, 2 ; Jocelin's inflated account of, *ib.* ; Dubhlinn, meaning of, 3, 23; Colgan's list of supposed bishops of from the arrival of St. Patrick, *ib.*, *n.* ; founded by Ostmen, A.D. 852, 5, 19 ; plundered by Maclsachlain, A.D. 847, 24 ; supposed taking of by Regner Lodbrog, 28, 29; or Turgesius, 31 ; death of Ivar, K. of the Ostmen at Dublin, A.D. 872, 36, 40 ; Ivar, K. of Northumbria and Dublin, *ib.* ; Cearbhall (Carroll) reigns there, A.D. 871-885, 45 ; Sitric, s. of Ivar, from France, returns and reigns at Dublin, 46 ; Flann's conflict with the foreigners of Ath-Cliath, 47 ; Sitric slain at, 48 ; Godfrey, s. of Sitric, K. of Dublin and Northumbria, *ib.* ; Ostmen expelled from, 897, 49 ; Sitric, s. of Godfrey, recovers Dublin, A.D. 919, 54 ; in his absence in Northumberland Niall Glundubh tries to gain it, 58 ; is defeated at Kilmashoge, near Rathfarnham, 59 ; Godfrey, s. of Reginald, rules at (A.D. 921), 61 ; marches from, against the Danes of Limerick,

Dublin—*con.*
63 ; Dublin attacked in his absence by Irish, 64 ; his return, 66 ; loses Dublin to the sons of Sitric, 67 ; Godfrey, K. of Dublin and Northumbria (A.D. 932), 68 ; Aulaf, s. of Godfrey, K. of Dublin, 69—sails from Dublin to the Humber to recover Northumberland, 69—is defeated at the battle of Brunanburg, 70—sails back to Dublin, 70, 71 ; Muircheartagh and his Leather Cloaks besiege Dublin, 71, 72—fail 72.
—— The ancient name of, essay upon, xlvi.
—— Bally-ath-Cliath, ancient name of, 206.
—— foundation of boggy, 206, 209.
—— kingdom of, 5, 87, 90, 91.
—— Cearbhall, King of, 45.
—— Guthfrith, King of, 66.
—— Aulaf, King of, 68.
—— Aulaf, son of Godfrey, King of, 79.
—— the foreigners of, 74.
—— the Gentiles of, 74.
—— Archbishop of, cviii., *n.* in A.D. 1215, 216.
—— Archbishopric of, erected (A.D., 1148) 135, *n.*
—— and Glen-da lough, united diocese of, 140, 148.
—— Synod of, A D. (1175), 188, see Vivian Cardinal.
—— Roman Catholic Bishop of, Dr. Cary, 190.
—— the bridge of, 205.
—— Tochar at, 221, 223.
—— old bridge of, 222, *n.*
—— bridges, of, 215.
—— a bridge at, before King John's reign, 215.
—— licence to citizens (A.D., 1192), to make a bridge, *ib.*
—— Castle, 23, 204, *n.*, 205.
—— Castle, Record Tower at, 228, *n.*, 2.
—— capture of, by Strongbow, lxix.

## 272　INDEX.

Dublin, burgesses, 216.
—— Mayor of, and his jurats, 169.
—— Lord Mayor and citizens of, 244.
—— Corporation of, 146, $n^3$.
—— Assembly Rolls of, xv.
—— sole owners and managers in early times of, port and river, xxv.; their records, *ib.*
—— memoranda and freeman rolls of, xxxi.
—— printed rental of estates of, by Francis Morgan, solicitor, 238, *n.*
—— grant of customs from Arclo to Nanny-water (A.D., 1372), 246, *n.*
—— Harbour of, Corporation of Dublin claim it as their inheritance (1761), 247. *n.*
—— ship canal to, from Howth, projected (1728), 248.
—— ship canal from Kingstown or Dalkey to, projected (1800), 249, and *n.*, *ib.*
—— grant of Admiralty to (A.D., 1585), 246, *n.*
—— annulled in King's Bench, (1615), *ib.*
—— lease of, port of, at £50 a year offered (1605), 245, *n.*
—— the key of, 149.
—— Thingmote of, 162.
—— Thingmount of, 190.
—— Governor of, A.D., 1647, 165, $n^1$.
—— Recorder of, A.D., 1613, Richard Bolton, 169. $n^1$.
—— Recorder of (1707), 245, *n.*
—— defence of, against attack by sea, Sir Bernard de Gomme's plan for, 228, 230.
—— Corporation for preserving and improving Port of, 247.
—— the Dublin Scuflle (1699), 232, $n^1$.
—— Journal, 238, *n.*, 241, *n.*
—— News Letter, 241, *n.*
—— Penny Journal, 231, *n.*, 3.
—— and Kingstown Railway, xxxv.
Dubliter Odhar, 17.

Ducange, 193, 194.
Duchesne, 117, *n.*
—— 6, 13, *n.*, 44, *n.*, 48, *n.*, 52, *n.*, 60, *n.*
Dudo, 52, *n.*, 57.
Duff, Nicholas (1582), 250, *n.*
Dufthack, lvi., lvii., *n.*
Dufthach, 101, Icelandic for Dubh thach.
Dufthakster, 100, *n.*
Duleek (Daimhliag), 16.
—— Upper and Lower, 24, *n.*
Dumbarton (Strath Cluaide), 39, *n.*
Dunadhach, s. of Scannlan, 17.
—— 15.
Dunblane, 53.
Duncannon Fort, cxxii., *n.*
Dunchadh, Abbot, 13, *n.*
Dundalk, 34, 35.
Dun da-Leathghlas (Downpatrick), 16.
Dundrum (Churchtown), lxxxv., xcii.
Dun Edair, 213.
Dungan, Lord, 147.
Dunghal, Lord of Ossraighe, 47.
—— Lord of Ossory, 23.
Dunkeld, 43, *n.*
Dunlang, King of Leinster, 30.
—— 77, *n.*
Dunlaith, daughter of Maelmhuire's 77.
Dunleary, lxxxiv.
—— poor of, xxxv., deprived of their bathing place, *ib.*
Dunleer (Llannlere), 16.
Dunlo, bridge of, A.D., 1116, 214, *n.*
Dunmore, see Deare Fearna.
Dunne, Sir Patrick's, Hospital, 239, 248.
Dunseverick, 64.
Dun Sobhairce (Dunseverick), 64, *n.*
Dunton, John (The Dublin Scuffle, 1699), 232, *n.*, 1.
Durham co., xxvi.
Dutch raid in the Thames, A.D, 1667, 229.
—— peace with, 230.
—— renewed war with, 1672, *ib.*

INDEX.    273

Duvelina, 23.
Dyfflin, lxv., 23.
Dyfflinarskiri, lxiv, 20, 55, 138, 139, n.¹, 140.
Dyvelin, lxvi, n.
—— Kaye of, lxxvi.
Dyved, 89.

Eachmarch, 92.
Eadred, King of Northumberland, 74, 75, 76.
East Angles, 37.
East Anglia, 15, 25, 26, 33, 37, 39, 41, 42, 43, 44, 47, 62, 69, n.
—— invaded (A.D., 870), 37; Edmund, King of, defeated and slain, 40; Gormo, son of Frotho, King of Denmark reigns, 41; resigns Denmark, ib.; settles in E. Anglia, and divides it amongst his followers, ib.
East Indies, 210, n.
Easter, the goddess, 174.
Eblana, Ptolemy's supposed notice of, 2.
Eboracum, or antiquities of York, 220, n.
Ecgferth, K., his monastery at Wearmouth destroyed by the Northmen, 11.
Eccles, John (1707), 245, n.
Ecwils, King, 52.
Edgar, King, 86, 87, 143, 178, n.
Edinburg, lxvi., n., lxxxvii.
Editha, daughter of King Edward, and sister of Thyra, 65, n.
Edmund, K. of East Anglia, 26, 60, 71, n.
—— Saint and King, lvii., n., 40, 41, 60, 73, 124.
Edna, 105.
Edward, son of Alfred, King of England, 51, 52, 57, 58, 62, 64, 65, n.
Edward I., rolls and records of, lxxii.
—— II., Plea roll of, lxix, n.

Edward III., xxviii.
Edwin, 195.
—— son of King Edward, 64.
Egbert, 39.
Eghbricht, King, bishops fight in his armies against the Danes, 13, n.
Egils, 70.
Egibsly isle, 174.
Eginhard, 6.
Egypt, xlix., n.
Elagh, or Aileach, 2.
Elbe, The, 7.
'Elche,' or 'Elgi,' for the Danish, 'Enske,' i.e., English, 42, 43.
Elgar, Earl, 182.
Elir, s. of Barid, 85, n.
Elizabeth, Queen, 146, n.
Ella, K. of Northumberland, 25, 26, 27, 28, 30, 37.
Ellacombe, Rev. H. F., xxviii.
Ellis, Sir John and Sir William, xxi.
Ellis's-quay.
Eloir, son of Barith, 63, n.
Elphin, 172, n.
Ely Inquisition, 198.
Emania, 2, n.
Emmett, Robert, xci.
Empson, W. (sheriff, 1717), 248, n.
Ennis, Sir John, Bart., xli.
Enske, 42.
Eochard Beag, 226, n.
Eogannen, M'Ængus, K. of Picts, 120.
Eoghanachta, The, 55.
Eresbourg, 6.
Eric, 70.
—— s. of Harald Harfagr, 73, 75, 96.
—— s. of K. Harald, Grœfeld, 86, n.
—— Blodaxe, King, 68.
—— The Red, 107, n.
—— son of Barith, 63, n.
—— King of the East Angles, 51.
Erleng, son of King Eric, 75, n.
Erne river, 63.
Erps, 104.
Esker (co. Dublin), 4, n.
Essex, 51.

T

Essex-bridge, 203, 234, n., 2.
Essex, Earl of, cix., n.
—— Earl of, Lord Lieutenant, 231, 243, n.
—— Earl of (1644), lxvii., n.
Ethelflœd, Lady of the Mercians, 50, 52, n., 57, 58, n.
Ethelwald, 51.
—— s. of K. Alfred, rejected by the Saxons, is made by the Danes of Northumbria their king, 51 ; with Eric, K. of the East Angles, ravages Mercia, ib.; both slain returning, ib.
Ethelwerd, 25, 37, n., 40, n., 41, n., 42, n., 48, n., 53, n., 37, n., 40, 44, n.
Ethelwalf, K., 13, n., 224, n.
Eubonia (Isle of Man), 84, n.
Eugenius III., Pope, see Pope Eugenius.
Eva, d. of King Dermot M'Murrough, 4, n.
Everhard, The Count, 46.
Evinus, 172, n.
Exchequer, Record of Court of, xxv. ; sorted and catalogued by J. F. Ferguson in 1850, xxvi. ; occassion of, ib.
Explanation, Act of, 228, n., 2.
Eystein, s. of K. Aulaf, 40, n., 43.
Eyvind, lxv.
—— Austman, 95, 101, 102, 120.

Fagan, Christopher, 203, n.
—— James, xli.
Falesiam (Falaise), K. John's letter dated at, 217, n.
Falkland, Lord Deputy, cvii., n.
Fan-na-g-carbad (Slope of the Chariots) at Tara, 225, 227.
Farannan, Abbot of Ardmacha, 34.
Faroe Islands, xlix., n., liv., lvii., 102, 129.
Faversham (Kent), 182.
Feargus, Bishop of Kildare, 13.
Fearna, see Deare Fearna.
Fearna (Ferns), 17.
Fenian Tales, lxii., n.

Fennor, 17, n.
Fercullen, li.
—— co. Wicklow, bounds of, 225.
Fergus, s. of Erc, K. of the Dalriads of Ulster, 82, n., becomes K. of Scots, ib.
—— II., King. 83, n.
Ferguson, James Frederic, history of, xxv., xxxi., xcv., cvii.
Fermoy, Book of, xcviii., 82, n.
Ferns, 3, n., 17, n.
Fidelis, Brother, xlix., n.
Fingal, s. of Godfrey, K. of Man, 93.—20, 138, 142.
—— plunderers of, 205.
Fingala, d. of MacLauchlan, s. of Muircheard, K. of Ireland, 93, n.
Finn Gall, 142, n.
Finglas, Cross of, 205.
Fiannbhair (Fennor), 17.
Finn Lochlannaigh, 18, n.
Finngalls and Dubhgalls, 61, n., 65.
Finnghoill, 13, 19, 44.
—— first Norwegian invaders, 18.
—— their conflicts with the Dubhgoill or Danes, ib., and 19.
Fimtardom, 160.
Fiords, The Five, lxvii.
Fiordr, a frith, 137, n.
Fiordungar, or quarter of Iceland, 134, n.
Fishamble-street, 208, 209.
Fishing of the Liffey, 244.
Fitzgerald, Lord Thomas, xcvi., 205.
—— Lord Edward, xvii., lxxxvii.
Fitzsimon, Christopher O'Connell, 193, n.
Fitzwilliams, William, 150.
Fitzwilliam, Col. Oliver, second Viscount Merrion, 228. n., 2.
Flana, King of Iceland, 21, n., 47, 49.
—— s. of Maelsachlainn, 119.
Flann Sinna, 77, 78, 119.
Flanders, 8, 46.
Flannag Ua Cellaigh, K. of Bregha, 128.
Flauna, d. of Dulaing, 119.
Fleet-street, lxxiii., n., xciii.

## INDEX. 275

Fliotshild, 101.
Floating Light at Poolbeg, 238, *n.*
Floki of the Ravens, lix.
Florentine merchants, xxx.
Florida, 105.
Folkstone, 158.
Forth and Bargy, baronies of, 222, *n.*
Forthuatha (in co. Wicklow), 16.
Fortren, 36, 48, 120, 121, 122.
Forster, Alderman Charles, 212, *n.*
Forty-nine Officers (Protestant), the, 228, *n.*, 2.
Foster, Rt. Hon. John, lxxxviii.
Four Courts, The, xcvi.
Four Provinces, The, 137.
Foxall, James, xli.
France, 9, 10, 13, 22, 45, 50, 52.
—— K. of 187.
Franks, 5, 8, 46.
Frankfort, xxviii.
Freyja, 123, 157, 158, 172, 176, 178, 197.
French privateer captures a Spanish ship in bay of Dublin (1675), 243.
Friars, Preachers (A.D. 1428), 222, *n.*
Friday, or The Goddess Freyja's day, 174.
Fridgerda, daughter of Cearbhal, 102.
—— daughter of Thoris Hyrno, 102.
Friscobaldi, xxx.
Frisia, 46, *n.*
Frith of Forth, 15, 53.
Frizons, 9.
Frode, s. of Harald Harfager, 96.

Gades, Straits of, 115, *n.*, see Cadiz.
Gaditanian Straits, 115.
Gaiar, grandson of Uisnech, K. of Ulster, 83, *n.*
Gaimar, Geoffry, 26, 73, *n.*, 74, *n.*
Gaithen, 119, 77 *n.*
Galicia, 117.
Gall, Gaedhl, 131.
Galls, islands of the (Hebrides), 82, *n.*
'Galli, The,' 28.
Gallows Hill, 161, 170, and *n.*, *ib.*
Gamle, son of King Eric, 75, *n.*
Gamla, Upsala, 197.

Gandon, James (1792), 240, *n.*
Gardar's isle (Iceland), lv., lvi.
Gardar, 98, *n.*²
Gardiner, Colonel, Life of, xiii.
Gargantua, ix.
Garget, John, lxxi., *n.*
Garristown, xxvii.
Gascoigne, Henry, cix., *n.*
Ganga, Rolfr., 53, *n.*
Gaul, 224.
Geasa-Draoidecht, 172, *n.*
Gebennach, son of Aedh, 55.
Gellachan, King of the Islands, 71, *n.*
Gentiles, 18, 56, 120.
'Gentiles, White and Black,' The, 44.
George's-quay, xci., 241, *n.*
Gering, Richard (1734), 239, *n.*
Geva, 6, *n.*
Gibbon, William Monk, LL.D., xxix., cviii., *n.*, cix., cxvi., cxx., and *n.*, *ibid.*, 238, *n.*
Gidley, George, cxxii., *n.*
Gilbert, J. T., 145, *n.*,³ 194, *n.*, 218, *n.*, 244, *n.*, lxviii., *n.*, lxxxii., lxxxii.
Gilla, 129, 132, 133.
—— Arri, 132.
—— s. of Arrin, 132, *n.*²
—— Caeimglen, s. of Dunlaag, 132, *n.*²
—— Cele, s. of Cearbhall, heir of Leinster, 132, *n.*²
—— Chomghaill, 131, 132, 133.
—— Chommain, s. of the Lord of the Diarmada, 132, *n.*²
Gill-Colen, 132.
Gilla-Colm, 131.
Gilla Mocholmog, 131, 132, *n.*²
—— Phadraigh, s. of Dunchad, Lord of Ossraighe, 132, *n.*²
Gille, 108, 129, 131, 133.
—— Count of the Hebrides, 129.
—— the Lagman, 129.
—— the Russian Merchant, 130.
—— The back thief of Norway, 130.
Gillebert, Bishop of Limerick, first Apostolic Legate to Ireland, 124, *n.*¹

Gillebrighde, 133.
Gille-Christ, Harald, K., 132.
Gill-Colom, Chief of Clonlyffe, &c., 132, *n.*
Gille Phadraigh, s. of Imhar of Port Largi, 131, *n.*,² 133, *n.*²
Gille, 129.
Gilmcholmoc, lxxiv., 164, *n.*²
Giolla, 129.
Giselda, daughter of Emperor Lothair, 46.
Gisle, daughter of King Charles the Simple, 52, *n.*
Gizeh, The pyramids of, l., *n.*
Glas, Captain, cxxii., *n.*
Glasgow, Steam Packet Company, xxxix.
Gleann-da-Locha (Glendalough), 17.
Glencree, 150.
Glendalough, 17, *n.*
Glen-da-lough and Dublin, diocese of, 140, 148.
—— Bishop of, 141.
Glen-finnaght, 84, *n.*
Glen, Southwell, co. Dublin, 59, *n.*
Gliomal for Gluniaran.
Glover, Joseph (1657), 240.
Gluniaran, 48, 77, 78.
—— s. of Diarmid, 92.
—— K. of Dublin, 104, *n.*⁴
Gluntradhna, 48.
—— s. of Gluniaran, 104, *n.*⁴
Glyde river, co. Louth, 64, *n.*,⁵ 19, *n.*
Godfrey, K. of Denmark, 9, 68.
—— son of Ivar, 44, 45, *n.*, 46; with his brother Sitric ravages France, 46; is paid 12,000 lbs. of silver by Charles the Fat to quit France, *ib.*; agrees to renounce paganism and marry Giselda, daughter of the Emperor Lothair, *ib.*; treacherously slain by his brother Sitric, *ib.*; called in Irish "Jeffrey Mac Ivar, King of the Normans," *ib.*; a plague of locusts the year of his death, 49; Reginald and Sitric his sons, 51, 54.
Godfred II., King of Dublin, xlviii.

Godfred II., A.D. 992, 220.
Godfrey, s. of Ragnall, 93.
Godfrey, son of Reginald, 61, 62, 63, 65, 66, 67, son of Godfrey, K. of Dublin; becomes King of the Ostmen of Dublin, A.D. 921, 61; plunders Armagh, *ib.*; overtaken by Muircheartach, son of Niall Glundubh and defeated, *ib.*; marches from Dublin to oppose Gormo Enske's attack on Limerick 63; forced to return to Dublin, 64, which is besieged by Muireadach, K. of Leinster, *ib.*; who is defeated, and he and his son Lorcan taken prisoners, *ib.*; Godfrey's sons and a Danish fleet defeated on the coast of Ulster, *ib.*; rescued by their father, *ib.*; Godfrey regains Northumbria, 65, but is soon driven out by Athelstan, 66; returns to Dublin, *ib.*; plunders Saint Bridget's shrine at Kildare, *ib.*; massacres 1,000 in a battle at Dearc Fearna (cave of Dunmore, co. Kilkenny), *ib.*; defeats the Danes from Limerick, led by Aulaf Ceanncairch in Ossory, *ib.*; dies, A.D., 932, 68.
Godfrey O'Hivar (son of Reginald), 57, *n.*
—— son of Sitric, 71, *n.*, 74, 125, *n.*; succeeds his father as K. of Dublin, 48; is King also of Northumbria, *ib.*; dies A.D. 896, *ib.*; buried at York, *ib.*; leaves three sons, Niall, Sitric, Reginald, *ib.*
—— s. of Harald, Lord of Limerick, 88, 89.
Godfraidh, s. of Fearghus, Lord of Ulster, 120.
Godfrey, K. of Man, and of Dublin, 92.
—— brother of Eachmarcach, K. of Man, 92.
—— K. of Leinster, Wales, and Dublin, 92, *n.*
—— of Winchester, 217, *n.*
Godefrid (see Sitric), 46, *n.*

INDEX. 277

Godred or Godfrey, K. of the Ostmen of Ireland, 96.
—— s. of Sitric, K. of Man, 90.
—— Crovan, 90, 93.
Godrim, Godrum, or Guthrum, 41, 42, 47.
Godwin, Earl, 92.
Gomme, Sir Bernard, see De Gomme, 228, 229, 230, 232.
—— his map of river and harbour of Dublin (1673), 228, 231.
—— who, 230, $n$.
Gormo, 33, $n$.
—— Danus, King of Denmark, 51; succeeds Eric as K. of the E. Angles, 51; his pedigree, $ib.$, $n.^6$; treaty between him and K. Edward, s. of K. Alfred, $ib.$, $n.^7$
—— Enske (or English), 32, 42, 43, 46, 47, 51, $n.$, 62; King of E. Anglia, 51; son of Frotho, K. of Denmark, $ib.$; invades Wessex, 42; Alfred's treaty with him, $ib.$; he is baptized and called Athelstan, $ib.$; resigns Denmark to his son, 43; settles in E. Anglia, $ib.$; and divides it amongst his followers, $ib.$
—— s. of Frotho, 41, 42, 43.
—— Gamle, 51, $n$.
—— grandson of Gormo Enske, 62.
—— K. of Denmark and E. Anglia, 62; marries Thyra, daughter of K. Edward, $ib.$; the Danes of E. Anglia accept Edward as king, $ib.$
—— Grandœvus, 62, $n.^2$, 69, $n$.
—— Mac Elchi, 67.
Gormflaith, 91, $n.^5$, 101.
Gough, Topographical antiquities of Great Britain and Ireland, cvi., 249, $n$.
Grafton-street, 150.
Gragava, 53, $n.$, 57, $n$.
Grágás Lögbok, Islendinga, 199, $n$.
Grange Con, xcv., $n$.
Grangegorman lane, 212, $n$.
Granta bridge, 42.
Granville, Dr., xv.

Grattan, Rt. Hon. Henry, xii.
Graves, Rev. James, xcvii.
—— Dr. Robert James, M.D., ix., x.
Gray's Inn, v.
Great Brunswick-street, 239, 248.
—— Council, ordinance of, A.D. 1455, 205.
—— Northern Railway terminus, cx.
Greece, 210, $n$.
—— river, 72, $n.^1$, 142, $n$.
Green Batter, 222, $n$.
Greenoge, 195.
Green Patch, cxii., cxv., 245, $n.$, 235, $n$.
Grenehoga, 195.
Gregory of Tours, 1., $n$.
Griece river, 72, $n.$, 142, $n.^1$
Grimolf, 101.
Grufudd, K. of Wales, 123.
Gruffyth ap Madoc, 58.
Grynhoe, 174, $n.^3$
Guadaliquiver river, 117.
Gudlief, 105, 106, 107.
Gudrord, son of King Eric, 75, $n$.
—— s. of Halfdan the Mild, 116.
Guernsey, 195.
Guinness, Arthur, xli.
—— Benj. Lee, xli.
Gulathingenses laus, 199.
Gunnar, iii., lxvii., lxviii., 101, $n.$, 108, $n$.
Gunnar's holt, lxviii., 101, $n.^8$
—— Stadr, lxviii.
Gunhild, Queen of Norway, 109.
Gurmundus, 32.
Guthferth, 42.
Guthfrith, King, 66.
Guthrum (see Godrim).
Guttorm, son of King Eric, 75, and $n.$, $ibid$, 96, 97.
Gyda, sister of Aulaf Cuaran, 124.


Hadrian (Emperor), 1., $n$.
Hæretha, 10.
Hafursfiord, 95, 98, $n.^2$
—— battle of, lv.
Hoga, Hoge, or Oga, 196.

Hakon, K. of Norway, 155, n.[1]
—— Guda, K., 125, n.[6]
—— son of Harald Harfagre, 68.
—— K. (Athelastan's foster son), 68, 125.
—— King, his warriors buried in their ships drawn to the battlefield, 103, n.
Halfdan, 41, 43, 44, 45, 46, 52, 66, (and see Albdarn).
—— K. of Lochlann, 114, 116.
—— the Mild, s. of King Eysteinn, 116.
—— Whitefoot, K. of Uplands, 20, n.
—— brother of Ivar, 41; becomes King of Northumbria, ib.; conquers the Picts and Strathclyde Britons, ib.; apportions Northumbria amongst his men, 44; returns to Ireland, ib.; claims the rule over the Finnghoill, ib.; slain in a battle between Danes and Norwegians at Lough Strangford, ib.
Haliday, Esther, lxxvii.
—— Charles, sent to London to learn business, v.; declines Mr. Delacour's civilities, ib.; becomes clerk at Lubbock's bank, ib.; studies hard in London, vi.; his literary friends there, ib.; returns to Dublin and embarks in the bank trade, viii.; his residence on Arran-quay, ib.; his overwork produces a vision, ib.; his poetical answer to Mrs. Hetherington, ix.; hires Fairy Land, near Monkstown, ib.; his mode of life there, ib.; resolves to apply himself for a time exclusively to business, x., xi.; journal of his reading, xi.; his villa at Monkstown park, xiv.; his study at, xv.; loses the sight of one eye, xvi.; supposed cause of, ib.; his fears for the other, ib.; book collecting, ib.; the Secret Service Money Book, xvii., xviii.; its history, ib.; Dr. R. R. Madden's account of the Secret Service Money Book, ib.; Hali-

Haliday—con.
day's library, extent of, xviii.; given by his widow to the Royal Irish Academy, xix.; anecdote of Dr. Willis, ib.; of Reginald Heber, ib.; his humanity to his servants, ib.; his 'Lucullan Villa,' xx., xxi.; undertakes a history of the port of Dublin, ib.; his morning studies, xxiii., xxiv.; his commonplace books, ib.; studies ancient records, xxv.; made acquainted with James Frederic Ferguson, ib.; works executed by him for Mr. Haliday, xxx.; Haliday's contributions to the daily Press, xxxi.; pamphlets written by him, xxxii.-xxxvi.; his courage during the cholera at the Mendicity Society, xxxii.; urges sanitary legislation for towns, xxxiv.; obtains bathing-places for poor of Dunleary and Kingstown, xxxv.; public offices filled by Haliday, xxxvi.; Honorary Secretary of Chamber of Commerce, xxxvii.; frees Dublin shipping of the Skerries and Ramsgate Light dues, xxxvii.-xxxi.; recognition of his services by shipowners of Dublin, xxxix., by merchants of his conduct as Honorary Secretary of the Chamber of Commerce, xli.; his defence of the Ballast Board, xliii.-xlv.; his essay upon the ancient name of Dublin, xlvi.; letter to his father about Henry Domville, lxxviii.; proposes to his father a partnership, ib.; letter to his brother William on his marriage, lxxxiv., on his sickness, ib.; opposes a scheme for a viaduct across Westmoreland-street, xciii.; supports De Lessops' views of the canal at Suez, ib.; protects the bathing-place of the poor at Irishtown, xcviii.; begins a voyage round the coasts of Ireland, xcix.; its results on his

INDEX. 279

Haliday—*con.*
health, c.; his visit to the Bodleian Library, *ib.*; his grave, *ib.*; his wife gives his library to R. I. Academy, cii., ciii.; his portrait placed in the Academy, ciii.; letter of Richard Welch, his executor, to the Academy, ciii.; characteristics of Charles Haliday, ciii., civ.
—— Daniel, M.D., ix., lxxviii., lxxxvii.–xcii.; a younger brother of Charles, lxxxvii.; practises at Paris, *ib.*; his national feelings, *ib.*; his treatment of Thomas Nugent Reynolds, *ib.*; his friendship with Sir Jonah Barrington, lxxxviii.; account of Sir Jonah's History of the Union, *ib.*; his friendship with Colonel John Allen, xc.; trial of Allen with Arthur O'Connor and Quigley for High Treason, *ib.*; Allen's conduct in the Rebellion of '98, xci.—in Robert Emmet's Rebellion, *ib.*; his escape to France, and military services there, *ib.*; C. Haliday's kindness to Col. Allen's sisters, xcii.; Daniel's death, grave, and epitaph, *ib.*
—— William, the elder, lxxvii.–lxxx.
—— William, junior, vii., viii., lxxviii.–lxxv.; made Deputy Filacer of Common Pleas, lxxx.; his knowledge of languages, lxxxi., *ib.*; publishes a translation of Jeffrey Keatinge's History of Ireland, *ib.*; originates the printing of the Irish on one page, the English on the opposite, lxxxii.; publishes an Irish grammar, lxxxiii.; prepares an English-Irish dictionary, *ib.*; his labours appropriated by another, *ib.*; his marriage, lxxxiv.; his brother Charles's letter, *ib.*; his sickness and death, lxxxv.; his death, grave, and epitaph, lxxxvi.
—— Mrs., otherwise Mary Hayes,

Haliday—*con.*
ci.; gift of her husband's library to the Royal Irish Academy, cii., ciii.; her death, ciii.
—— Margaret, lxxx.
Hallthor, 99, $n.^3$
Halsteinn, 104.
Hanger-Hoeg, 161, 170.
Harold, see Roilt.
—— 53,
—— Blaataud, 69.
—— the black, 90.
—— Gille, King, 96.
—— Gille-Christ, K., 132.
—— Grœfeld, K. of Norway, 109.
—— Fair hair, lv., lvii., *n.*
—— Harfœgr, King, 96, 114, 39, *n.*, 68, 73, *n.*, 76.
—— s. of Gormo Enske, 32, *n.*, 43, 47, *n.*, 51, *n.*
—— s. of Gormo-hin-Gamle, 62, 63.
—— Hardraad, K., 90.
—— (King of England), 71, *n.*
—— son of King Eric, 75, *n.*
—— Lord of Limerick, 87.
—— Harold, K., 108, *n.*
Harbour Department of Admiralty, xliii.
Hardwicke, Lord, lxxxix.
Hardy, Sir Thomas Duffus, xcvi., 217.
Harekr, son of Eadred, 75.
—— son of Guttorm, 75.
Harrington, Henry, xcv.
—— Sir Henry, xcv., *n.*
Harris, Isle of, lxvi., *n.*
Hasculf, lxix., lxxvi.
Haskields-stadr, 135, *n.*
Ifaslou, 44, *n.*, 46.
Hastings, 47, 50.
Haughton, James, xxxii.
Haugr, or Hogue, 155, $n.^2$
—— a hou, a mound or cairn over one dead, 195, *n.*, 197.
Hawker, Mr. (1792), 240, *n.*,
Hawkins, Mr., 147.
—— street, cxviii.
—— wall, cxviii., lxxiv., and *n.*, *ib.*, lxxvi., 146, $n.^3$, 248, *n.*

Hayes, Major-General Thomas, ci.
—— Mary, otherwise Haliday, ci., cii., ciii.
Hazlewood, Brow of the, 209, see Drom Choll Coil.
Head, Richard (1663), 241, n.
Heahmund, Bishop, 13, n.
Hearn, 71, n.
Heber, Reginald, xix.
Hebrides, The, see also Sudreyar, lv., lvi., 11, 15, 82, 89, 112, 114, 120.
—— Danish place, names in, lxvi., and n., ib.
Hecla, iv.
Helgi, 53.
—— Beola, lvii., 103.
—— Magri, lviii., 101, 103.
—— son of Olaf, 20, n.
—— marries Thorunna Hyrna, 101, n.$^2$
Hella (Ailill), 28, 29.
Hennessy, W. M., lxxxii., 214, n.
Henry, fitz Empress, lxix, n.
Henry II., King, 3, 4, n., 14, n., 23, 71, n.$^1$, 94, 136, 145, n.$^3$, 183, 184, 185, 186, 187, 191.
—— III., King, 189.
—— IV., King, 146, n., 149.
—— VIII., King, 146, n., 164, n., 190.
Herbert, auctioneer, xcv.
Hereford (burnt by Danes of Ireland), 182.
Hereferth, 13, n.
Herjolf, 104.
Hermits, Irish island, 98, n.
Herodotus, lx.
Hesculf (Hasculf), lxxvi.
—— for Hasculf Mac Torkil, 149, n.
Hetherington, Richard, cii.
—— Mrs., ix.
—— Miss, cii.
Heydan, Richard, 203, n.$^2$
Hibbotts (Hybbotts).
'Hic et Ubique,' a Comedy' (1663), 241, n.
Hicks, Thos., cviii, n.
Hi Cholium-Chille for Iona.
Higden, 21, n.$^1$, 50, n.$^6$

High-street, 208, 209.
Hill of Pleas, 170.
Hingamond, 50.
Hingnar, s. of Regnar Ladbrog, 26, 37, n., 38, 39, 41.
—— and Hubba, 181.
Hjörleif, lvi., lvii., and n., ib.
Hoa, 71. n.$^3$
Hoey's-court, xcii.
Hofdastrondam, 102.
Hofud (Howth), 138.
Hoga, Hoghia, and Haghia, 195.
Hogan's Green (for Hoggen Green), lxxv., 196, n.
Hog and butts, lxxv., 197, n.
Hoggen but, 191.
Hog hill, 196, n.
—— lane, 196, n.
Hoggen but, 196, lxxv., 166, 167, 168, 169, n.$^1$
—— Green, 162, 163, n.$^2$, 166, 168, 191, 196, lxxiii., lxxv.
'Hogges,' general in Scandinavian places, 195.
—— (or Oghs), 191.
—— butts, 168.
—— King's, 197.
—— Le, 164, n.$^2$
—— (nunnery of Saint Mary del.).
—— wrong derivations of Hogges, 192.
Hog's Green (for Hoggen Green), lxxv., 195, n.
Hogs hill, 191, 196.
Hogue, 196.
Hoighold, age of mounds for dead, 195.
Holland duck sail-cloth, 247.
—— pile driver from (1721), 236.
Holles-street, the sea at foot of, 232, n.$^1$
Holmpatrick, lxvii., 138.
Holt, Mr., 235, n.
Holyhead, xxxvii.
Holy Land, The, l., n.
—— Trinity, the Chapter of, 148.
Homer, lix.
Homerton, vi.
Hook, The, cxxii., n.

Hore, Ralph, 218, *n.*
Horham, Ricardus de, 194.
Hoskulld, 107.
Hosee, Hugh, 217.
Hospital of Lepers, Dublin, 148.
Hougue, La., Hattenas, 195.
—— La, Fongue, 195.
House Thing (Hustings), 160.
Hoved (Howth), lxvii.
Hou, or Hogue, 155, *n.*²
Howard, Henry, cxi., 244.
—— Thomas and Henry, 244, *n.*
Howel Dha, 69, 89.
—— s. of Edwin, 97, *n.*¹
Howth, 16, 138.
—— Head, fortress of, 213.
—— point of, 242, *n.*
—— Earl of, 237.
Hrut, 104.
Hryngr (Eric), son of Harald Blaatand, 69.
Huammsfiord, 103.
Hubba, 38, 39, 41.
—— s. of Regnar Lodbrog, 26.
Hudibras, c.
Hvitra Manna Land (America), 105.
Humber river, 24, 37, 70.
—— stane, 181.
Hurdles, for foundations, 206, 207.
—— ford of, what, 214.
Hurdle bridge by O'Donnell, for escape over Shannon, A.D. 1483, 215.
—— bridges in Asia, 215.
Hutcheson, Mr. (1734), 239, *n.*
Hutchinson, Daniel, 203, *n.*²
Hutton, Thomas, xli.
Hybbotts, Sir Thos., cvii., *n.*
Hy-Cohun-Cille, 113.
Hymns, Book of, 2, *n.*
Hyrna, Thoranna, sister of Auda, wife of Aulaf the White, K. of Dublin, 101, *n.*³

Iceland, liii., liv., lvii., lx., lxi., 49, 98, *n.*², 98, 99, 100, 102, 113, 125.
Icelandic bards, lviii.

Iceland, bridges of, lxv.
Icelandic Saga makers, lviii.
Igmund, 50, 52.
Igwares, 37.
Imhar (see Ivar), 21, *n.*
—— 54, *n.*, 58.
—— Tanist of the foreigners, 74.
Inbher Ainge, or Nannie Water, 140, *n.*²
—— mor, Arklow, 139, *n.*¹
Ingolf, lv., lvi., lvii., 98.
Inguald, 60, *n.*
—— son of Thora, 20, *n.*
Ingulphus, 13, *n.*¹, 43, *n.*⁴, 50, *n.*⁶, 52, *n.*², 70, *n.*⁴
Inguares, 37, *n.*
Inis-Caltra, 34, 35.
Inis Cathaigh, 88.
—— Doimhle, 79.
—— Erin, Ireland's Eye, 139, *n.*¹
Innisfallen, Annals of, 11.
Innishowen, barony of, 2, *n.*³
Inish murry, liv.
Inish murry isle (co. Sligo), 12.
Innsi Orc, 115.
Inis Rechru, Lambay Isle, 139, *n.*¹
—— Slibhtown (island in Limerick harbour), 63, *n.*¹
—— Ulad, 79.
Innse Gall, 82, *n.*¹
Innes, 84, *n.**
Innocent, see Pope.
Innocence, Decree of, lxvii.
Iona, 43, *n.*⁹, 39, 91.
Ireland's Eye, 49.
—— Eye, island, 139, *n.*¹
Ireland, originally divided into fifths, 134, *n.*³
—— originally into two Archbishoprics, 135; made into four, A.D. 1148, 135, *n.*⁵
—— travels in, in 1603, and in 1644, 210, *n.*
Irish ancient roads, 226, *n.*
—— booths, 210, *n.*
—— ecclesiastics in Iceland, 113.
—— houses in towns in 1644, 210, *n.*
—— island hermits, 98, *n.*

## 282　　　　INDEX.

Irish houses in the wilds in 1603 and 1644, 210, n.
—— Light Houses, Board of, xliii., xliv.
Irishmen's islands (in Iceland), 100.
Irish sheep-dog, 111.
Irishtown, xcviii., 239, 242, n.
—— and Ringsend, 231, n.
Irish Woollen Warehouse, Castle-street, 209.
Irland Mikla, Great Ireland (or Florida), 105.
Irminsul, 6.
Isenbert, the French bridge architect, xlvi., 216; builds the first stone bridge at London (A.D. 1202), ib.
Isidore of Seville, xlix., n.
Isla, terraced mount at, 162.
Isle of Man, 54.
Isles, the kingdoms of (and see Hebrides), 82, 93.
Islendinga Saga, lvii., n.
Islip, Walter de, 194, n.
Israelites, 158.
Italy, 210, n.
Ivar, 38, 39, 40, 41, 44, 45, 47, 48, 54.
—— K. of Dublin, lxxvi.
—— K. of Denmark, s. of Regnar Lodbrok, 22, 24, 28, 32, 33.
—— s. of Regnar Lodbrog, K. of Dublin, 100, 102, 154; son of Regnar Lodbrog, 36; he and Aulaf land in East Anglia, 37; invade and conquer Northumbria, ib.; Ivar made King of Northumbria, ib.; succeeds Aulaf as King of Dublin, A.D. 871, 40; dies A.D. 872, ib.; Halfdan, brother of Ivar, and Bægsec, became Kings of Northumbria, ib.; Halfdan spoils the Picts and the Strathclyde Britons, 43; Godfrey and Sitric, sons of Ivar, 45; plunder France A.D. 881, ib.; are paid 12,000 lbs. of silver by Charles the Fat to leave France; 46.

Ivar, grandson of Ivar, K. of Dublin, 122.
—— son of Guttorm, 75.
—— s. of Sitric, s. of Aulaf Cuaran, 126.
—— (of Limerick), 20, 21, 22.
—— Lord of Limerick, 88.
—— O'Hegan, 135, n.[3]

Jefferson, President, xvi.
Jeffry MacIvar (Godfrey, son of Ivar), see Godfrey.
Jenkins, Sir Lionel, lxvii., n.
Jerusalem, 1., n.
Jocelin, 2, n.[1]
Johan le Devé, 149, n.
Johnstone, 93, n.[6], 29, n.[2]
Jones, Dr. Henry, Bishop of Meath, 164.
Jones, Col. Michael, lxxv., 165, n.[1]
—— Mr., owner of Skerries Light Dues, xxxviii.
Jordan river, 158.
Joyce, P. W., 222, n., 225, n., 226, n., 232, n.[1]
Joymount, cviii., n.
Junot, General, xci.
Juries of Ostmen at Dublin, lxxii.
—— separate, of English, Irish, and Ostmen at Limerick, lxxii, n.
Jutes, 15.
Jutland, 11, 175.

Kadlina, daughter of Ganga Rolf, 53, n.[2]
Kiarval (or Cearbhall), of Dublin, 100.
Keatinge, Geoffry, D.D., lxxxi., 21, n., 134, n.[2]
Kells, 79.
Kelly, J. L., xli.
Kenneth, King of Scots, 36, n.,[3] 43, n.[9], 47, n., 87.
Kerry, the men of, see Ciarrighi.
Ketell, Flatnef, 53, n.[2]
Ketill, Flatnef, 101, n.,[2] 102, 114, 120.

INDEX. 283

Ketel Heugs, 101, n.⁸
Ketell (or Oscytel), 43, 53.
Kettleby, Yorkshire, 130, n.⁴
Kevin-street, 207, n.⁴
Kiaran, 105.
Kiartan, 106, 107.
Kiarval (and see Cearbhall), 45, n.¹
Kidd, Valentine (Sheriff), 1718, 248, n.
Kilbarrack, cvii., 132, n.²
Kildare, Thomas, Earl of, A.D. 1455, 205.
—— 17, n., 56, 66.
—— street, 193, n.
Kilkenny, 66.
—— Castle, 243.
Kill-Aracht, 172, n.³
Killaloe, Bishop of, cviii., n.
—— plank bridge of (A.D. 1140), 214, n.
Kilmainham, see Cill-Maighnenn, 152, n.⁴
—— Hospital (of Knights of St. John), at, 217, n.
Kilmehanock, 218, n.
Kilmallock, lxxi., n.
Kilmashoge (and see Cill-Moshamhog), 58, n.
Killmohghenoe, 148.
Kilruddery, 164, n.²
Kinaston, Colonel, 165, n.¹
Kings of the Irish, 3, n.; chief kings dwelt at Tara, ib.; kings of Leinster at Naas and Ferns, ib.
Kinshelas (Ui Ceinnsalaigh), 16.
King's Hogges, 197.
—— Bench, lost rolls of, xxviii.
—— Hospital, cxi.
—— Hospital (Blue Coat School), 244.
Kinsale, Sir Bernard de Gomme to plan defence of, A.D. 1672, 230.
Kingsland of Turvey, Matthew Barnewall, lord; his low degree, xxvi.; his recovery of the title, ib.
Kishes filled with stones to form Liffey channel, 235, 238.

Kishing of the Liffey, cxviii., cxix.
Knatchbull, Edward, 193, n.
Konal, lviii.
Korna-baugr, 195, n.
Krossholar, 103.
Kuda, the ship, 101, n.⁶
Kudafliotsos, 101, n.⁶
Kunnakster (Connaught), lxvii., 135.
Kylan, 105.
Kynaston, see Kinaston.

Lade, 127.
Lagmanns, The, 88, 160.
La Hore, Ralph, 218.
Lamb, Charles, vi.
Lambard, 42, n.⁴
Lambay, lxvii.
—— Isle, Inis Rechra, 139, n.¹
—— Catch, The (1657) 240.
Lancashire, 24, n.
Lanfranc, Archbishop, 93.
Lanesboro', 214, n.
Lanfranc, Archbishop, 76.
Langtoft, Peter, 71, n.¹
Langue, d'Oc, lxxiv., n.
—— d'Oil, ib.
Languedoc, 10.
Larne Lough (Ulfricksfiord), 15, 137, n.²
Lassberg, Joseph von, xxviii.
Latiniers, 184.
La Touche, Wm. Digges, xli.
Laun, 47, n.
Lawhill of Iceland, 159.
Law of Saint Patrick, 189.
Lawmen, 170.
Law Mount, or Logbergit, 161.
Laxa, 102.
Lax-lep, 55, n.
Lazar's Hill, cx., cxii., cxviii.
—— frigate launched at, 240, 148, 152.
Lazy (or Lazar's) Hill, 232, n.¹, 235, 238, n., 239, 241, n., 242, n., 248, n.
Lea river (Herts), 182.

Leaps, Gormflaith's three leaps or jumps that a woman should never jump, 78, *n*.⁸
Lecan, Yellow Book of, 82, *n*.¹
Lee, the river, see Lin.
Leeson, Joseph, 193, *n*.
Leges, Gula Thingenses, 199.
Leghorn, cxxi., 4.
Legge, Hon. George, Lord Dartmouth (1685), 243.
Le Hogges, lxxiv.
Leibnitz, lxxxi.
Leif, lv., lvi.
Leighin-ster (Leinster), 134.
Lughteburg, Robert, 146.
Leinster, lxvii., 23, 29, 64, 79, 80, *n*.
—— King of, 3, *n*, 4, *n*.
—— Kingdom of, 221.
—— men, 56.
—— southern parts of, 204.
—— book of, 4, *n*.
—— Duke of, cxxi.; in his yacht shoots breach in south wall, and lands at Merrion-square, 231, *n*.
—— House, 193, *n*.
Leixlip, 55, 138, 141.
Le Martre, Thomas, 186, *n*.², 217.
Lentaigne, Benjamin, lxxix., lxxx.
—— Sir John, lxxix.
Leofrid, 58.
Leogaire, King, lxii.
Leoris, Peter de, 14, *n*.
Lepers, 61.
—— Hospital, 148.
Le Poer, John fitz John fitz Robert, lxix., *n*.
Leprosy, 74.
Lesseps, M. Ferdinand, xcvii.
Leslendle, Castle of, lxvii., *n*.
Leth, Chuinn, 33, 34.
Letronne, xlix, *n*.,1, *n*., 98, *n*.², 113, *n*.
Lewis, King of France, 71, *n*.
—— isle of, lxvi., *n*.
Lichfield, 194, *n*.
Lidwiceas, the, 53.
Lief, s. of Eric, 107, *n*.³
Liffey, the, cx.

Liffey, the river, 23, 138, 141, 55.
Liffe of ships, Cearbhall, King of, 54, *n*.
Liffey, early passage and bridges across, 207, *n*., 211, 212, 213, 220, 222, *n*., 224, 203, *n*.
—— crossed by Slighe Cualann near Dublin, 225.
—— fort planned on south side to protect, A.D. 1673, 228, 229, 230.
—— on north side not required, 232.
—— King John's half of, 216.
—— gives liberty, A.D. 1214, to citizens to build a new bridge over, or to keep the old, 216, 217.
—— southern half of, 221.
—— shallowness of, A.D. 1590, 204.
—— fords of, between Dublin and Lucan, 205.
—— piling of, cxviii., cxv.; walling of, cxvii.; kishing of, cxviii., cxix.
—— the forming of a new channel for, 234, 238.
—— straightening of bed of, xlv.
Lighthouse, the Poolbeg, cxiv., cxv., 238 *n*.; begun 1761, *ib*.
—— wall, cxv., cxvi., 238, *n*.; begun 1761, *ib*. (See south wall.)
Light floating at Poolbeg, placed A.D. 1735, 238, *n*.
Lighthouses, Irish, xliii.
Limerick, lxix., 3, *n*., 20, 21, 35, 55, 62, 63, 85 and *n*.², *ib*., 87, 88, 95, 117, *n*.², 186, 137.
—— harbour, island in (Inis Slibhton), 63, *n*.¹
—— separate juries of Englishmen, Irishmen, and Ostmen at, lxxii., *n*.
—— and Foynes railway, xcvii.
Lin river (the Lee), 55.
Linn Duachaill (near Annagassan, county Louth), 19.
—— Duachaill (Magheralin), 64, *n*.⁵, 66.
Lindesey, 29, *n*.
Lindesness, 29, *n*.

Lindiseyri (Leinster), 29, *n.*
Lindisfarne, 10, 11.
Lir, Manannan, s. of, 82, *n.*[1]
Lismore, 54.
—— Ostman, bishop of, Pope's legate, 188.
Littleton, 136, *n.*[2], 138, *n.*[2]
Liverpool, cxx., *n.*
Loarn, s. of Erc, 82, *n.*[1]
Loch Bricrenn (Loughbrickland), 17.
—— Cé, Annals of, lxxxii.
—— Dachaech, 135, *n.*[2]
—— Dachaech (Waterford), 54, 55.
—— Eathach (Lough Neagh), 33.
—— Erne, 85, *n.*[3]
—— Gabhor (Logore), 24, *n.*
—— Garman, 135, *n.*[2]
—— Gower, 24, *n.*
—— Oirbsen (Lough Corrib), 82, *n.*[1]
—— Re, 85 and *n.*[3], *ib.*
—— Tingwall, 161.
—— Uachtair, 85, *n.*[3]
Lochlanns, 40, *n.*, 50, 52, 63, *n.*, 115, 219.
Locusts, plague of, 49.
Lodbrog (see Regnar Lodbrog).
Lodge (John), lxxv., 93, *n.*[5], 151, *n.*[1]
Lodin, 97.
Loftus, Nicholas, lxxvii.
Logbergit, or Law Mount, 161.
Logore (see Loch Gabhor).
London Bridge, fear of the Dutch fleet coming to, 229.
—— built of wood, A.D. 993–1016, 216, *n.*; burnt, A.D. 1136, *ib.*; rebuilt of stone, A.D. 1203, *ib.*
—— stone, the, 179, 180, 182.
Long Stone, the, lxxii., lxxvi. cxviii., 150, 151, 152.
—— of the Stein, the, 179, 180.
Lorcan, s. of Cathal, 21, *n.*
—— son of King Muircadhach, 64.
Lords of the Isles, 120.
—— entrance to Parliament House, 239, 240, *n.*
Lothra (Lorra), 34, 35.

Loughbrickland, 17, *n.*
Lough Corrib, 83, *n.*, and see Loch Oirbsen.
—— Cuan, or Logh Cone (Strangford Lough), 44.
—— Derg (in Shannon), 34, 36.
—— Erne, 63, 69.
—— Neagh, 33, 34.
—— Owel (see Lough Uair).
—— Ree, 33, 34, 35, 63, 69.
Loch-ri, see Lough Ree.
Lough Shinney, cxvi.
—— Uair (Lough Owel), 31, 34, 36.
Louth (Lughmadh), 16.
Lucas, Thomas, lxxvii.
Lucan, inhabitants of the Cross of, 205.
Lucy, Sir Antony, 139.
Ludgate-hill, xciii.
Ludlow, Edmund, 213.
—— General Edmund, xiv.
Lughmadh (Louth), 16.
Luimneach, Limerick, foreigners of, 66.
Lundbhadh, J. F., 169, *n.*[2]
Lusk, 142, 16.
—— the Cross of, 205.


Mabbot's mill, 235, cxix.
Mac Aralt, 90.
Mac Cuileannan, Cormac, K. and bishop, 13, *n.*
MacCullagh, 162, *n.*[1]
Maccus (and see Amaccus) son of Aulaf Cuaran, 75.
—— son of Harald of Limerick, K. of Man, 87, 88.
—— or Magnus, K. of Man, 86, 87.
Maccusius Archipirata, 86, *n.*[1]
Mac Donogh, Gilpatrick, 97, *n.*[1]
M'Donnell, John, xli.
—— Sir Edward, *ib.*
Mac Elchi, The, 32, 62, 63, 64, 67.

M'Firbis Dudley, 21.
Mac Gilmoholmoc, Donuough, 142.
M'Gilmore Gerald, lxix., n.
—— Ivor, John, s. of, lxix., n.
Mac Guthmund, Philip, lxx., lxxi.
M'Murrough, lxv.
—— Dermot, K. of Leinster, 4, n., 145, n.³, 178, 185, 193, 221.
—— Dochad, 4, n.
Mac Otere, Maurice, lxx., lxxi., lxxii.
Mac Torkil, Hasculf, 149, n.¹
Mactus, 87.
Madden, Dr. R. R., xvii.
—— Thos. M. Madden, M.D., xxxvi., n.
Mael, 133.
Maebrighde, s. of Methlachlen, 31, 133, n.
—— s. of Cathasach, 132, n.²
—— bishop of Kildare, 132, n.²
Maelgarbh Tuathal, 132, n.
Maelgula Mac Dungall, K. of Cashel, 126.
Maelmadhog, archbishop, 13, n., 56.
Maelmary, 91.
Maelmithigh, 78.
Maelmor, 132, n.²
Maelmordha, brothers of Cearbhall, 56, 220.
Maelmhuire, daughter of Aulaf Cuaran, 78.
—— daughter of Kenneth, King of Scots, 77, 118, 119.
Maelnur, 47, n.
Maelnambo, 92, 128, 142, n.²
Maelphadraig, 133.
Maelseachlainn, King of Ireland, 23, 24, 31, 34, 45, 47, n., 77, 78, 89, 127.
—— King of Teamhair, 91, 119.
—— King of Meath, 132, n.²
—— s. of Domhnal, K. of Ireland, 221; besieges and takes Dublin from the Ostmen, 80; his famous proclamation of freedom for the Ui Neill, A.D. 980, ib.
—— Murchadh Ua, 214, n.
Magh Breagh (in East Meath), 17.
Maghera (Co. Derry), 16, n.

Magheralin, on the Lagan river, 64.
—— co. Down, 19, n.
Magh Liphthe (plain of the Liffey), 17.
Magh Nuadhat, 221.
Magnus Barefoot, King, lxiv., lxc., 96, 132.
Magni Regis Leges Gula Thingenses, 199, n.
Magnus (see Maccus), 86.
Maidstone (Mede Stane), xc., xci., 182.
Maines, the Seven, 226, n.
Malachy (see Maelsachlain).
—— K., 221.
Maladhun, son of Aedh, 67.
Malcolm, K. of Cumberland, 87.
Man, Isle of, liii., and see Monada, Monabia, Menavia, Eubonia, 82, 84, 85, 89, 90, 92, 93; held by Ptolemy for an Irish island, 82; and by the Romans while in Britain, 84; Manx and Irish legends concerning, 82, n.¹; the Monada of Ptolemy, Monabia of Pliny, Menavia of Orosius and Bede, Eubonia of Gildas, 84, n.⁶; its connexion with Ulster before the Danish invasion, 82; the Cruithne or Ulster Picts driven thither, A.D. 254, 83; expelled from Man, A.D. 580, by Baedan, K. of Ulidh, 84; thenceforth belonged to Ulster, ib.; Latin names of, ib., n.⁶.
—— Maccus or Magnus, K. of, 86.
—— son of Reginald, K. of Northumberland, King of, 87.
—— Tingwall in, 161.
Manannans, the Four, 82, n¹.; s. of Alloid, s. of Athgus, s. of Lir, ib.
Manannan MacLir, legislator of Isle of Man, 82, n.
Map, Sir Bernard de Gomme's, A.D. 1673, of river and harbour, 228.
—— of Dublin by Jean Rocque, 170, n.
—— of the North Lotts (1717), 248, n.

INDEX.    287

Map, Captain John Perry's rare map, with ship canal along Sutton shore toward the Bar, 1728, 249 and *n.*, *ib.*
Marche, Count de, 195, *n.*
Margad, 96.
Margate, xc.
Marstan, King, 29.
Martin, Thomas, lxxxiv., lxxxvi.
—— John, xli.
Mathghamhain, Ua Riagain, 91.
Mauritani, 115.
Mayo, ravaged (A.D. 807), 15.
Meath, 22, 34, 35, 74, 87, 134, 214, *n.*, 221.
—— southern part of, 204.
—— bishopric of, its long pre-eminence, 136, *n.*[1]
—— Earl of, 164, *n.*[2]
Medina-Sidonia, territory of, 117.
Mediterranean Sea, 115, 117.
Medway, the river, 182.
—— chain across mouth of, against the Dutch, A.D. 1667, 229.
Meersburg, castle of, xxviii.
Melbricus, K. of Ireland, 28, 29, *n.*[1] 31.
Mellitus, Abbot, 171.
Melkorka-haugr. 195, *n.*
—— daughter of Miarkartan, 108, 109, 110, 112,
Melrose, chronicle of, 8, *n.*
Memoranda rolls, calendars of, by Js. Fc. Ferguson, xxx.
Menevia, 84, *n.*[6], 89, 90.
Mensions (Mynchens) fields, 193, *n.*
—— (Mynchens) mantle, 193, *n.*
Merchants'-quay, 203, 204.
Mercia, 38, 39, 44, *n.*, 50, 51, 52, 57, 58.
Mercer's Dock, cxviii.
Meredith, Sir Robert, 212, *n.*
Merrion, lands of, 228, *n.* 2.
Merrion-square, cxxi., 242.
—— fort for defence of Liffey to be built at, 230.
—— sea flowed to foot of, A.D. 1673, 231.

Mesgedhra, King, 213.
Miarkartan, K. of Ireland (for Muircheartagh), lxv.
Midland Great Western Railway, 212, *n.*
Mills, the King's, near Dublin, xxx.
Milo de Cogan, lxvi.
Minchin's mantle, 193, *n.* (see Mynchens).
Mirgeal, Icelandic for Muirghael, 104, *n.*[4]
Mona, 84, *n.*[6], 85, *n.*[1], 87, 89.
—— Roman Anglesea, 84, *n.*[6].
Monada, Man of the Romans, 84, *n.*[2]
'Moon, the,' King's sloop, 241, *n.*
Moors of Spain, the, 114.
Moran, Patrick, Bishop of Ossory, 136, *n.*[1]
Morgan, Francis, solicitor, printed rental of estates of Corporation of Dublin by, 238, *n.*
—— Richard (1623), 232, *n.*[1]
Morland, Mr., to draw map of channel of Liffey from Essex-bridge to the bar, 234, *n.*[2]
Morney, Mr., 235, *n.*
Moshemhog, church of, 59, *n.*
Mote, the, near Pennenden Heath, 182.
Mountmellick, ci.
Mountmorres, Lord (1792), 240, *n.*
Mount Murray, 156.
Mount-street, 170, 242.
Mowena (Modwena), 224, and *n. ib.*
Moyle Isa, 71, *n.*[3]
Moylemoney, s. of Cassawara, 71, *n.*[3]
Muircheartagh, son of Niall Glundubh, 61, 64, 67.
—— of the leather cloaks, 71, 72, 142.
Muirghael, 104, *n.*[4]
Muireadhach, King of Leinster, 64.
Muiren, 129, *n.*
Muglins, the, pirates gibbeted at, cxxii., *n.*
Mullaghmast, hill of, 72, *n.*[1]
Mullarky, John, and John Pigeon, 231, *n.* 3.
Mulvany (1846), 240, *n.*

Mumha-ster (Munster), 135.
Mungairid (Mungret, co. Limerick), 17, $n^6$.
Munster, lxvii., 19, $n$., 31, 39, 34, 54, 55, 63, $n$.
Munster men, 55.
Murchad, 17.
Murchadh, 96.
—— son of Diarmid, 92.
—— son of Finn, 78.
—— s. of Finn, K. of Leinster, 91.
Murphy, Dr., R. C. Bishop of Cork, xvii.
Mynchens fields, lxxv.
—— mantle, $ib$. 193 (see Mensions).
Mynnthak, 100.

Naass, 3, $n$.
Naddad, 98, $n$.
Nanny river, 24, $n$.
Nannie water, 140, 141.
Nanny water and Arclo, limits of Admiralty jurisdiction of Dublin, 246, $n$.
North Strand, 247.
Nassau-street, or St. Patrick's well lane.
Naul, the, xxvii.
Navan (An Emain), 2, $n$.
Neale, son of Godfrey, King of Dublin, 48.
Neave, Mr. Serjeant, 246, $n$.
Neville, Parke, 208, 212, $n$.
New channel for Liffey, cxi.
—— kishing of, cxviii.
Newcomen, Beverly, commander R.N. (1614), son and heir of Sir Robert N., 241, $n$.
Newgate (old), 208.
—— prison, cxxii., $n$.
New Grange, tumulus at, 99, $n^9$.
Newman, Jacob, 196, $n$.
—— James, 203, $n$.
Niall, 48, $n$.
—— Brother of King Sitric, 60.
—— Glundubh, King of Ireland, 57, $n$., 54, 56, 58, 59, 77, 78, 119.
Nidarosia (Drontheim), lxv., $n$.
Nidbyorga, 53, $n^2$.

Nile, the, xlix., $n^2$. l. $n$.
Nineveh, researches in, 215.
Nordlendinga fiordung, 134, $n^2$.
Norfolk, circular churches in, 174.
Normans, 8, $n$.
Normandy, 42, 52.
—— Le Hogges in, 195, 196.
North Bull, cvii.
—— Lots, cxix., 248.
—— strand, cx.
—— wall, 237, cx., cxix.
Northmen or Danes, 5, 8, 10, 14.
—— Conquest of England by, 220.
Northumbria, 15, 24, $n$., 25, 26, 27, 33, 39, 40, 41, 43, 44, 45, 51, 52, 57, 60, 61, 64, 65, 66, 68, 69, 70, 71, 79.
—— bounds of, 24; story of Regnar Ladbrog's defeat and death in, proved false, 25-27.
—— Ivar, King of Dublin, becomes King of, 37; makes Egbert, viceroy of, 39; Ivar's brothers, Halfdan and Bœgsec, become Kings of, 41; Bœgsec slain, $ib$.; Halfdan apportions it amongst his followers, 44; Godfrey, s. of Ivar, becomes K. of, 48; dies A.D. 896, $ib$.; his sons received in Northumbria, 51.
—— Earldom of, 91.
Northumberland, 11, 24, 25, 26, 27, 33, 48, 73, 125.
—— Aulaf of Dublin, K. of, 220.
—— Norway, lv., lix., lxxvi., 11, 15, 25.
Norwegians, 15, 19, $n$.
Norwich, 194, $n.^3$
Notes and queries, C. Haliday's query in (A.D., 1854), for Captain John Perry's map of 1728, 248, $n$., 249, $n$.
Nottingham, William, 218, $n$.
Nuadhat, Mogh, 221.

Oakpiles for foundation of Dublin houses, 208.
Oates, Dr. Titus, lxvii., $n$.
O'Brien [K. Murrough], 221, $n$.

## INDEX.

O'Brien, Murchard, 93.
—— Murtogh, s. of Turlough, K. of Dublin, 93.
—— Turlough, K. of Ireland, 76, 93.
O'Byrnes, The, 164, *n.*
—— Gilla Mocholmog, chief of the, 132.
"O'C. E." (W. Haliday, junior), lxxxi.
O'Callaghan, John Cornelius, 128, *n*⁶.
O'Connell, Daniel, xlii.
—— his duel with D'Esterre, vii., *n.*
—— anecdote of, concerning the secret service money book, xviii.
O'Connor, K. of Connaught, 188.
—— General Arthur Condorcet, vi, *n.*, xc.
—— Cathal, K. of Connaught, 221.
—— Charles, 172, *n.*
—— Owen, *ib.*
—— Ruaidhir, 214, *n.*
—— Turlough, *ib.*
O'Curry, Eugene, xcvii, 227, *n.*
Odin, 126, 154, *n.*², 171, 176, 197.
Odin-ism, 125, 173, 175.
O'Donnell escapes across the Shannon by a hurdle bridge, (A.D. 1483), 215.
O'Donovan, John, LL.D., li, lxxxi, 224.
Offyns, The, lxxi, *n.*
'Ogh,' Virgin, 191, 196.
O'Hara, Colonel Robert, xcv.
Oirbsen Lough (Lough Corrib), 82, *n.*
Oisle, son of Sitric Gale, 71, *n.*
Oisili, brother of Aulaf, 21.
Oisin and St. Patrick, lxii, *n.*
O'Kelly, Teige, xlvii., 219.
—— Colonel Charles, 128, *n.*⁶
Olaf, Feilan, lviii, 103.
Olaf Pa, 108, 109, 110, 111, 112.
—— The Saint, King, 155, *n.*
—— Trygvesson, lxv, *n.*, 71, *n.*, 80, 89, 111, 124, 125, 127.
Olaf, s. of Gudrand, 20, *n.*
Olave, s. of Godred, K. of Dublin and of Man, 93.

'Old Shore,' The, near Peers' Entrance on map of ground plan of Chichester house (1734), 240, *n.*
O'Loghlen, Donald, 93, *n.*⁵
Ollchovar, King of Munster, 31.
O'Mahony, John, lxxxi.
Omar, s. of K. of Denmark, 71, *n.*³
O'Neill, see Ui Niall.
Onund, 101.
—— Trefotr, 95.
Orc, Islands of, 82, *n.*, and see Orkneys.
O'Reilly's English-Irish Dictionary, lxxxiii.
Orkney isles, liv, lv, lxix, xcix, 15, 102.
—— or Northern isles, 113, 114, *n.*, 156, 157.
—— John of The, 149, *n.*¹
Ormond, territory of, 17, 214, *n.*
—— James Bottiler, Earl of, 146.
—— Thomas, Earl of, 146, *n.*
—— Marquis of, 165, *n.*
—— Marchioness of, 152.
—— Duke of, xxxvii, lxvii, *n.*, lxxvii, *n.*
Ormond Market, on site of the Pill, 212, *n.*
Osas, 105.
Osbright, 26, 30, *n.*, 37.
Oscytel (or Osketell), 42, 43.
Oska, 104.
Oslin, s. of Aulaf the White, 121.
Ossraighe, 47, *n.*, 65, *n.*
Ossory, 23, 66.
—— 119.
—— Bishop of, cviii., *n.*
Osten, Mac Aulaf, (see Eystein), 43.
Ostmen (or Danes), 232.
—— Godfrey, King of the, of Dublin, 61, *n.*
—— (and see Dublin, Ostmen of), 4, 10, *n.*
Ostmantown, 138, 218, 222, *n.*, 332.
—— of Dublin, lxix, and *n.*, *ib.*
—— of Waterford, lxix, *n.*
Ostmen's grants of land, 186.

U

Ostmen, the Bridge of the, xlvii, lii, 218.
—— gate of the, *ib.*
—— old quarry of the, *ib.*
—— juries of, lxxii.
—— mints of, 186.
—— towns, 186, 188.
—— cantred of the, at Limerick, 138.
—— cantred of, at Cork, *ib.*
—— cantred of, at Waterford, *ib.*
Osulf, Count, 75.
—— Cracaban, 53.
Ota, wife of Turgesius, 36.
Other, earl, 52,
O'Toole, Alice (of kin to Archbishop Laurence O'Toole), 192.
—— Gilla Chomgail, chief of the, 132.
—— Laurence, Bishop of Dublin, the first consecrated at Armagh, all others (in Ostmen days) at Canterbury, 177.
Ottar, 53, 57.
O'Tuathail, see O'Toole.
Oxmantown Green, 163, *n.*, 223, *n.*, (and see Ostmantown), 232.
—— enclosed (1664), 248 *n.*
—— lotted for, *ib.*
Oxney isle (Kent), 182.

Pale, the English, 211.
Palls, the four, 135, 141.
—— (or palliums) from the Pope, 177.
Palmerston, the Lord, xv, xcvii.
Pamphlets by C. Haliday, xxxii–xxxv.
Parker, Alex., xli.
Papa Westra, 99, *n.*
—— Stronsa, 99, *n.*[1]
Pape, 99.
—— of Iceland, liii.
Pap-ey, 99, *n.*[1]
Paparo, Cardinal, 136, 141, 177.
Parry, Rev. John, cviii, *n.*
—— Rev. Edward, D.D., cviii, *n.*
Parliament House, 239, and *n. ib.*

Parliament House, Lords' entrance to, *ib.* (see Chichester House).
"Patterns," (for patron's days) 172, *n.*[3]
Pearsall, R. L., xxvii, xxviii.
Peel, Isle of Man, 11, *n.*
Pembroke-quay, xxi.
Penmon, 87.
Pennenden Heath, 182.
Perry, Captain John, cxiv, cvi, cvii.
—— "proposals for rendering harbour of Dublin commodious," (1720), 249, *n.*
—— his rare map of the harbour, with ship canal along Sutton shore to avoid the bar (1728), 249, and *n. ib.*
"Peter pence," 189.
Petty, Dr. William, lxxvi, cvi, cvii, 151, *n.*
Petrie, G., LL.D., li, lxxxiii, 224.
Pharaohs, the, l. *n.*
Philips, Thomas, his plans and elevations of the forts of Ireland, (1685), 243.
—— his ground plan of Belfast, *n. ib.*
Phœnix park, xxi.
Philip and Mary, K. and Q., 190.
Picts, 37, 38, 43, 53.
—— Irish, 16, 36, 83, 98, *n.*², 120.
—— driven from Ulster to Man and the Hebrides, (A.D. 254), 33; their Ulster lands occupied by Cairbre Riada, 84; hence called Dal Riada.
—— the Scottish, 16, 36, 120, 121.
Pictavia, capital of, 36, 48, 121.
Pictland, 121, 122.
Pightland firth, 157, *n.*[1]
Pigeon House, cxiii–cxvii, cxxii, *n.*, 238, and see Block-house, 231.
—— history of, 231, *n.*[3]
—— hotel and dock at, leased to government (1790), fort and magazine, *ib.*, sold (1814), *ib.*
Pigeon-house fort, xxix, xcviii, cxviii.
—— road, cxv; formed (A.D. 1735), 237.

Pigeon, John, cxvi, 231, *n.*³
Piling of the channel of the Liffey, 235, *n.*, 238, *n.*
Piles, the, pirates gibbeted at, cxxii, *n.*, 238, *n.*
—— men flogged for stealing, *ib.*
—— two murderers fall from their gibbets at, *ib.*
—— their bodies tossed by the waves amongst, *ib.*
Pill, the, 211, 212.
Pill-lane, 211.
Pincerna (or Butler), Theobald Walter, 145.
Pirates gibbeted at south wall, cxxii, *n.*, 238, *n.*
—— removed to the Muglins, beside Dalkey Island.
Pitt, Right Hon. William, lxxxix.
"Plan for advancing the trade of Dublin," (1800), 249, *n.*, with scheme for ship canal from Dalkey or Kingstown to Dublin, 249, *n.*
Place names, Danish in England, lxvi.
—— in Ireland, lxvi., lxvii.
—— in Hebrides.
Plunket, Gerald, (1566), 250, *n.*⁴
Poddle river, the, 23, 207, *n.*⁴
Pol gate, 194.
Pontifices, or company of stone bridge builders, 220.
Poolbeg, cxii., cxiii., 233, 245, *n.*
—— lighthouse, 234, 338.
Pope Adrian, 184, 187.
—— Adrian IV., 190, 191.
—— Alexander III., 184, 187, 188, 189, *n.*
—— Eugenius III., 135, 136.
—— Gregory, 171, 172, 175.
—— Innocent III., 141, 148.
—— Nicholas Breakspeare, 136.
—— Paul IV., 190.
—— Urban III., 217.
Porter, Lord Chancellor, i.
Ports of England and Ireland, defenceless (1673), 229.
Port Erin, 156.

Port and harbour of Dublin, history of, xlv.
—— Lairge (Waterford), 65, *n.*⁴
Portland, 89.
Portrane, 142.
Portsmouth, 230.
Portugal, 117.
Prince George of Denmark, 247.
Priscian, xlix, *n.*
"Provo' prison," the, lxxix.
Powerscourt, li.
—— in Fercullen, 225.
Puddle, see Poddle river.
Pue's Occurrences, 238.
Pyramids, the, 1, *n.*

Radnaldt, 78.
Rafarta, 101, 120.
Rafer, 26, *n.*², 29, *n.*²
Ragnall, son of Aulaf, 80.
—— grandson of Ivar, 54, 55, 56, 57, *n.*¹
—— h-Imair, 85, *n.*¹
—— Mac-h Ua Imair, 85.
Ragenoldus, princeps Nordmannorum, 60.
Ragnhild, son of King Eric, 75, *n.*
Rallis, the, xcvi.
Ramsgate harbour dues, xxxix, xl.
Ranelagh, the lord, xiv, cxvi.
Rangfred, son of King Eric, 75, *n.*⁶
Rath, the (near Dublin), 145.
—— Breasil, synod of, 140, 177, *n.*²
Rathdown, barony of, cviii, *n.*
—— half barony of, 151, *n.*²
Ratheny, 132, *n.*²
Rathfarnam, 59, *n.*
Rafernam, 232, *n.* (see Rathfarnam).
Rathfarnam water (the Dodder), 232, *n.*¹
Rathlin, Isle of, 11, *n.*²
Rath Luirigh (Maghera, co. Derry), 16.
Rathmines, lxxv., xcv.
Ratoath, 225.
Raughill, 77.
Raude, s. of Cellach, 101.
Rechru (Lambay), 11.

Red Sea, xlix, n., 1, n.
Reeves, Rev. W., D.D., lxvii., ciii., 11, n.$^2$, 19, n.$^1$, 84, n.$^2$, 113, n., 121, n.$^1$, 137, n.$^2$, 142, n.$^2$, 189, n.
Regan, Maurice, 184, n.
Reginald, 68.
—— sons of, 62.
—— O'Hivar, 85, n.
—— King of the Black and White Gentiles, 61.
—— King of the Dubhgalls and Finngalls, ib., n.$^1$
—— King of the Ostmen of Dublin, ib., n.
—— son of Godfrey, King of Dublin, 48, 54, 57, 60, 61.
—— settles and rules at Waterford, 55; spoils all Munster south of the river Lee, ib.; reprizals of the Munster men, ib.; the Irish, under Niall Glundubh, fight the battle of Tobar Glethrach, 56; Irish defeated, ib.; Reginald and Ottar, from Waterford, invade Scotland, 57; they are defeated, and Ottar is slain, ib.; Reginald attempts Mercia, ib.; had secretly engaged Alfwyn, daughter of Ethelflœd, lady of the Mercians, ib.; K. Edward, son of K. Alfred, hinders a marriage, ib.; adds Mercia to his kingdom, 58; his death, 60, 61.
—— son of Sitric, 65, 125, n.$^1$
—— brother of Sitric, 85.
—— son of King Eric, 75, n.$^6$
—— King of Northumbria, 53.
—— son of K. of Man, 86.
—— of Waterford, lxix., n.
Reginald's tower at Waterford, lxvi, lxxii.
Reghnall, s. of Halfdan, 115.
Regnar Lodbrog (Turgesius), 20, 22, 24, 25, 26, 27, 28, 29, 30, 31, 32, 33, 36, 37, 41, 45, 68, 121, 154.

Regnar Lodbrog, legend of his capture and death, by Ella, King of Northumberland, 24, 25; shown false, 26, 27; story of his taking Dublin, and being put to death by an Irish prince, 28, 29; captured by Maelseachlain, and (under name of Turgesius), drowned in Lough Owel, 31. Turgesius is Turgils Latinized, ib.
Rennie, Sir John, 250.
Repton, 42, 43.
Reynolds, Thomas Nugent, lxxxvii.
Riada, 84.
Ridgway, Sir Thomas, cvii., n.
Rin or Reen's End, 239.
Rin, rinn, meaning of, 211.
Rincurran, estimate for fort at, 230.
Ring, sacrificial, 171, n.
Ringagonal, 211.
Ringhaddy, 211.
Ringsend, cix., cxi., cxii. cxiii., cxiv., cxv., cxviii., cxxi., cxxii., n., 145, n., 147, 233.
—— cars (1699), 232, n.$^1$
—— coaches (1674), 242, n.
—— fort of, 228, n.$^2$
—— harbour projected at (1674), 242, n.
—— mistake as to origin and meaning of the name, 211, 228, n.$^2$, 231, and n. ib.
—— point, 234, n.$^2$, 235, n.$^1$, 239, 241, 242, 245, 248, n.$^1$
Roads, ancient Irish,—form of, 226, n.
Robinson, William, cix., n.
—— Sir William, knt., 239, n.
Rocque Jean, cxv, 170, n.
Rock-lane, 170.
'Rockers' (wreckers qu ?), at Pigeon House, 231, n.$^3$
Rogers, Samuel, iii.
Rogerson, Sir John's wall, cx, cxviii.
—— Sir John, 147, 235.
—— Recorder of Dublin, 238, n.
—— quay ground, 237.
—— his quay, 238.

Rogerson, Sir John, lease to (1713), 238, n.
—— death (1741), ib.
—— sale of his quay ground, ib.
Rognvalldr, 75.
Roilt (Harald), 64.
Rollo, King of Normandy, 42, 52, n.[4], 53.
Rome, 2, n., 91, 123, 128, n.
—— Church of, 76, 177, 186.
—— See of, 189.
Romans introduce walled towns in Europe, 2.
Roman bridges in Britain, xlviii.
—— wooden, 220.
Romona Isle, 157.
Roscrea, xv.
Ros Meilor, battle of, 50.
Round towers in Orkney Isles, 174.
Route, the, 84, n.[2]
Ruaidhri, son of Mormund, 43.
—— K. of the Britons, 19, n.
—— Ua Cananain, 74.
Runes, lx.
Runymede, 181.
Rupert, Prince, Sir Bd. de Gomme his engineer at Bristol, 230, n.
Russian hat, 108.
Ruta, see Route, the.

St. Andrew's Church, lxxiii., 208.
—— Andrew Thengmotha, Church of, 178, 179, 183, 191, 193, 198.
—— Andrew Thengmote, parish of, 162.
—— Audoen's Church, 208.
—— Augustin, 171.
—— Benedict and Company of stone bridge builders, 220.
—— Brendan, 35.
—— Brigit, 66, 134, n.
—— (Church of), 176.
—— no churches to, by the Scandinavians, 176.
—— but to the Virgin Mary, ib.
—— no churches to the B. V. M., in Ireland, until the example set by the Scandinavians, ib.

St. Bridget, "the Mary of the Gaedhill," 176.
Sancta Brigitha or Brigetta de Suetia, 134, n[1].
St. Cianan, 47, n.
—— Clair sur Epte, treaty of, 52.
—— Columba, 113.
—— Edmund, 41.
—— Edmondsbury Church, 198.
—— Ethelred's Church, Norwich, 174, n.[3]
—— James of Compostella, 148.
—— John, 172.
—— Joseph, granaries of, 1.
—— Gille, 130.
—— Lawrence Nicholas, 186, n.
—— Malachy, 135.
—— Magnus, 172.
—— Mary's Abbey, lxxii, 132, n.[2], 146, n.[3], 244, n.; ford near, 205, 212, 221.
—— Mary del dam, Church of, 193, 194.
—— del Hogges, 178, 196.
—— nunnery of, 191, 194.
—— del Ostmanby, 194.
—— le Hogges, nunnery of, xxx, lxxiii, lxxv.
—— les Dames, 194.
—— Ostmanby (St. Mary's Abbey, Dublin), 177.
—— —— of the Hogges or Mount, 195.
—— Church, Bangor, N. Wales, 176, n.[2]
—— Michael, 172.
—— Church of, 176.
—— del Pol, Church of, 193.
—— Michan's Church, 232.
—— Mullin's 55, n.
—— Olaf, 97.
—— Olave, 172.
—— Patrick, 34, 38, 172, 224.
—— Patrick's Island (near Isle of Man), 11, 12.
—— Well-lane, 166.
—— Paul's Cathedral, xciii.
—— Peter's del Hulle, Church of, 193.
—— Quintin, Richard, cxxii., n.

St. Ruadan (Rodan), 35.
—— Saviour's, Friars Preachers of, 2 2, *n.*
—— Senanus, 38.
—— Stephen's Church, 149.
—— Thomas, Abbey of, 164, *n.*, 186. *n.*
—— register of, xxx.
—— chartulary of, 217.
—— Abbot of, 164, *n.*²
Sabbath, two accounts of, in Deuteronomy, xx.
Sagas, Iceland, i., lviii., lix., lx., lxiii.
Saggard (co. Dublin), 4, *n.*
Sakkara, Pyramids of, l., *n.*
Salt, barony of, co. Kildare, 55, *n.*
Saltus Salmonis, 55, *n.*
Salmon Leap the, 55, *n.*
—— at Leixlip, 138, 141.
—— Pool, cxii., 235, 237, 245, *n.*
Saintes, School of, 216, *n.*
'Sainus,' the Irish sheep dog, 111.
Sandafels, 104.
'Sandwith,' The Ship, cxxii., *n.*
Sankey, Mrs., cviii., *n.*
Santry, James Barry, The Lord, 212, *n.*
Saxons, 6, 7, 8, 9, 11.
—— Aulaf, s. of Sitric, slain by, 128, *n.*³
—— Charlemagne's enforced conversion of, 6 ; fills Saxony with priests, *ib.* ; revolts of the Saxons, *ib* ; Witikind leads bands of them to Denmark, *ib.* and 7 ; Charlemagne beheads 4,500 in one day, *ib.* ; his war a crusade, 8 ; clergy crowd to his standards, *ib.* ; the fugitive Saxons forced by him out of Denmark, *ib.* and 9 ; the Saxons and Danes retaliate by raids on France, 9.
Scandinavian kings polygamists, 119.
Scots, King of the, 60.
Scottish isles, 113, 120.
Scotland, William, King of, 187.

Scuffle, The Dublin (by Jno. Dunton, 1699), 232, *n.*¹
Secret Service Money Book, xvii.
Senchus-Mor, 199.
Settlement, Act of, 228, *n.*²
Severn River, 53.
Seville, in Spain, 206.
Shannon, The, 17, *n.*, 24, 69, 85, 87, 213.
Shapinshay, Isle of, 159, *n.*
Sheehy, Father, xvii.
—— depositions concerning, *ib.*
Sheep dog, K. Aulaf and the Irish, lxiv., 111.
Sheerness and Tilbury Fort, 230.
—— and Chatham, alarm at, by Dutch raid, A.D., 1667, 229.
Shelburne-place, 193, *n.*
Shetland isles, liv., lv., 11.
Ship-street, 193.
Ship Canal to Ringsend, by Sutton shore, projected by Capt. John Perry (1728), 249.
—— map of, 249, *n.*
—— from Dalkey or Kingstown to Dublin, projected (A.D., 1800), to avoid the bar, 349, 350.
Sigefroi, 6, 9, 10.
Sigefrid, Sigefrith (Sitric), 46 *n.*, 47.
Sigurd, lxv.
—— s. of Regnar Lodbrog, 20, *n.*, 41, *n.*
—— Anguioculus, s. of Regnar Lodbrog, 32, *n.*
—— K. son of Magnus Barefoot, 96.
—— Sleve, son of King Eric, 75, *n.*
Sigrid, Queen, 127.
Simmonscourt, 232, *n.*¹ (*alias* Smoothescourt).
Sir Patrick Dun's Hospital, collier wrecked at, 248.
Sitric, son of Aulaf Cuaran, 78, 79, 91.
—— son of Godfrey, King of Dublin, 48, 54, 55, *n.*, 57, 58, 60, 61, 64, 65 ; recovers Dublin, 54 (lost on his father's death, to Cearbhall, son of Muiregan, K.

INDEX. 295

Sitric—*con.*
of Leinster, 49), wins the battle of Confey, co. Kildare, A.D., 918, 56; invades Mercia, 58; in his absence Niall Glundubh advances against the fortress of Ath Cliath, *ib.*; defended by the sons of Sitric and Reginald, *ib.*; named Imhar and Sitric Gale, 59; the battle is fought at Kilmashogue, near Rathfarnham (17th Oct., 919), *ib.*; the Irish defeated and Niall Glundubh slain, *ib.*; called by the Irish the battle of Ath Cliath or of Cillmosamhog, *ib.*; goes to Northumbria, 60; submits to Edmund, *ib.*; divides Northumbria with his brother Reginald, *ib.*; allies himself with Athelstan, illegitimate son of Edward, K. of Anglo-Saxons, 64; marries Athelstan's sister at Tamworth, A.D. 925, 65; is baptized, *ib.*; but relapses, *ib.*; dies, A.D. 926, *ib.*; leaves three sons, Reginald, Godfrey, and Aulaf, *ib.*; K. Athelstan ousts them from Northumbria, *ib.*

—— son of Ivar, 45; with his brother Godfrey ravages France, 46; slain by Godfrey, A.D. 885, *ib.*; marches to Boulogne, *ib.*; proceeds to Dublin, *ib.*; becomes king at Dublin, *ib.*; throne vacant there by Cearbhall's death in A.D. 855, *ib.*; Flann, Cearbhall's nephew, claims it, 47; is defeated, *ib.*; Sitric twice ravages Northumberland, 48; returns to Ireland, A.D. 894, *ib.*; is slain in fight with other Norsemen, *ib.*; his two sons, Aulaf and Godfrey, *ib.*; Aulaf slain in his father's lifetime, *ib.*; at Sitric's death Cearbhall, son of Muiregan, K. of Leinster, drives the foreigners from Dublin, A.D. 897, 49.

—— son of Ivar, 44, *n.*, 45, 46, 21.
—— Mac Ivar, 48.

Sitric grandson of Ivar, 47.
—— O'Himar, prince of the new and old Danes, 65.
—— of Limerick, 20, 21, 22.
—— Gale, 58, 71, *n.*
Sithfric, son of Sitrick Gale, 71, *n.*[3]
Sitric, founder of Christ Church, Dublin, 92.
—— sons of, 62, 67.
—— K. of Dublin, 85, 87, 124, 128.
Skelig, Michel, xcix., liv.
—— isle, 12.
Skerries, lxvii., 138, 139.
—— Lighthouse dues, xxxvii.
—— rock near Holyhead, xxxvii.
—— near Balbriggan, *ib.*, *n.*
Skiardbiörn, 99, *n.*[3]
Slane, 17, *n.*
Slaine (Slane), 17.
Slighes (or roads), the Five, to Tara, 225.
Slighe Cualann, li., 225; crossed the Liffey near Dublin, *ib.*
Slope of the Chariots (Fan-na-g-carbad) at Tara, 225.
Smith, Horace and James, vi.
Smithfield, 232.
—— part of Oxmantown-green, 248, *n.*
—— enclosed, 1664, *ib.*
—— lots for, *ib.*
Smoothescourt (*alias* Symons-court), 232, *n.*[1]
Smyth, Sir Samuel, cvii., *n.*
Snœbiorn, 100.
Snamh Eidneach (Carlingford), 19, 135, *n.*[2]
Snorri, lviii, 106.
Soarbes, 9.
Soder (Sudreyar), and Man, 114, *n.*[s]
See Sudreyar.
Somerville, Sir William, bart., xliv., *n.*
South Bull, cxiv., 234, 236.
—— lots, 231, *n.*, 248.
—— strand, sale of Sir J. Rogerson's lease of, 1744, 238, *n.*

South wall, cxxii, n. (*alias* Ballast Office-wall, Pigeon House wall, Lighthouse-wall, mall, or jettie), 238, n.
—— completed, 1790, *ib.*, 233.
—— breach in, A.D. 1792, 231, n.
—— Duke of Leinster shoots breach, in his yacht, and lands at Merrion-square, *ib.*
Southwell glen, 59, n.¹
Southwell, Sir Robert, iii.
Spain, the Moors of, 114, 115, 116, 117.
Spanish ship captured by French privateer near bar of Dublin bay, 243.
Speed, 240, n., 248, n.
—— map of Dublin (1610), 240, n.
—— shows a "pill" from Liffey running up to peers' entrance, *ib.*
Stadr, 135, n.¹
Stamford bridge, 90.
Standing stones by Odin's order for brave men, 154, n.²
Standish, James (1657), 240.
Stane or Stanes in Kent, in Hants, in Essex, in Herts, in Hereford, in Bucks, in Worcester, in Northampton, enumerated, 182.
Staneford (Northamptonshire), 182.
Stanhogia, 195.
Stayn, 145; and see Stein.
Steyne, the, lxxiii., lxxiv., lxxvi.
—— of Dublin, 143, 144, 145, 146, 148, 149, 151, 159, 160, 163, 164, 176, 178, 181, 183.
—— the Long Stone of the, 150, 179; and see Long Stone.
—— the river of the, 149.
—— bridge of, 150.
—— mill of, 150.
—— the port of, lxxvi.
—— Great Steyne, 146, n.¹
—— the Little Steyne, 146, n.
Steinsnessi, 157, n., 157, 158, 159, 164, 167, 170, 174, 176, 178.
Steinraud, s. of Maelpatrick, 101.
Steinraud stad, 101, n.⁴
Ster (in Mun-ster,&c.), for stadr, 135.

Stephen's-green, cxxii., n., 149, 163, n.², 161, 168, 170, n.
—— enclosed (1663), 248, n.
—— built upon, *ib.*
—— lotted for, *ib.*
Stokes, Gabriel (1734), 246, n.
—— William, lxxxiii.
Stone, the Long, 150, 179.
—— the black, of Odin, 159.
Stonybatter, 222, 225, n. 226.
Story, "War of Ireland," 241, n.
Strand, see North Strand.
—— of the Liffey, 147.
Strangfiord, lxvii.
Strangford Lough (see Lough Cuan), 94, 64, 137.
Strath Clyde, Britons of, 38, 43, 60.
—— Cluaide or Strathclyde (Dumbarton), 39, n.
Strongbow, 93, 132, n.², 145, 184, 185, 188, 221.
Sturla Thordson, lvii, n.
Sturleson Snorro, 155, n.¹
Sturlunga saga, lvii., n.
Suabia, xxviii.
Sudreyar (Southern Isles or Hebrides), 114, n.²
Suez (Clysma), l., n.
Suffolk, circular churches in, 174.
—— street, 162, 155.
Suibhne, abbot, xlix., n.
Suunlendinga fiordung, 134, n.²
Sutherland, liii.
Sutton creek, cvii.
—— shore, the, ship canal to Ringsend along, projected by Captain John Perry (1728), 249, and note *ib.*; to avoid the bar, *ib.*; map of, *ib.*
Swanscomla (Swine's or Sweine's camp), 182.
Swedes, 15.
Sweden, xxvi.
Swen, son of Knut, 41, n.
Swein, 181, 182.
Switzerland, 8, 1.
Swords, town of, 142.
—— Scandinavian, 155, n.¹
—— inhabitants of the cross of, 205.

## INDEX. 297

Taaffe, William, 146.
Talbot, Lord, xcvii.
Tara, 1, li., lxii., 2, 3, *n.*
—— history of, 224, 227.
—— hill of, map of monuments of restored, 225, *n.*[2]
—— The Five Slighes or roads to in the first century, 225.
Taylor, Philip Meadows, xli.
Teamhair, 17.
Teigmote, 162, 175.
Templetown, parish of, cxxii., *n.*
Terryglass (see Tir-da-glas).
Thame river (Bucks), 182.
Thames, 227.
—— works for defence of, A.D. 1667, 230.
Thebaïd, li., *n.*, liv.
Thebaud, John, lxxi., *n.*
Theodosius, Emperor, xlix., *n.*
Thetford, 41.
Things or Tings (and see Court-Thing, House-Thing, Althing), 159, 160.
Thinghoge, hundred of, 198.
Thinghow, 198.
Thingmote of Dublin, 162, 164, 170, 185, 186, 187.
Thingmotha, in parish of St. Andrew Thingmote, 162, 166.
—— church of Saint Andrew, 178, 198.
Thingmount of Dublin, lxxii., lxxiii., lxxiv., 164, 168, 169, 170, 171, 190, 156, 158, 159, 161, 163, 176, 178, 191, 197.
—— at Upsala, 176.
Thing-place, 175.
Thing vollr, 161, 176.
Thingwall, 156.
—— Mount, 158, 175.
Tholsel, The, 179, *n.*
Thomas Court Dublin, 217, *n.*, see Saint Thomas's Abbey.
—— Captain F. W., R.N., lxvi., *n.*, 174, *n.*
—— Court Abbey, Register of, xlvii.
Thor, 67, 123, 125, 126, 127, 128, 129, 131, 157, 158, 172, 175, 176, 178.

Thorsman, 31, 32, 62.
Thor's hammer sign, 125, *n.*[6]
Thors Rolf, 31, *n.*
Thora, 103, 132.
—— d. of Sigurd, 20, *n.*
Thorar, 106.
Thorbiorn, 105, 106.
Thordus Geller, 103.
—— married to Fridgerda, 102.
—— married to Theoldhilda, 102.
Thordis, 105.
Thorer, 98.
Thorgerda, 104, 108, *n.*[3]
Thorgils, 96.
—— (Turgils), 31, 96, 130.
Thorgil for Thorketil, 130, *n.*[4]
Thorgrim, 104, 101.
Thorkell, 130.
Thorkelin, Grimr. Johnson, 107, *n.*, 111, *n.*[4]
Thorketil by contraction Thorgil, 130, *n.*
Thormodr, 31.
—— Gamli, 104.
—— Keltie, 104.
Thorncastle, 228, *n.*[2]
Thorodd, 106.
Thorolf, Morstrarskegg, lviii., 103, 104.
Thorstein, The Red, lvii., lviii., 102, 104, 108, 120, 49.
Thor-stein, or Thor's stone, 126, *n.*, 159.
Thorskabitr, lviii.
Thorstein, Thorskabitr, 103.
Thorwald, Eric son, 107, *n.*[3]
Thrandus, Mioksiglandi, 102.
Thule (Iceland), 98, *n.*[2]
Thurgot, Simon, lxviii.
—— Johannes, 162, *n.*[3]
Thurida, 105, 106, 107, 120.
Thurles, Viscount, xxxvii., *n.*
Thyra, Danebot, daughter of King Edward, 51, *n.*, 62, 65, *n.*
Tib and Tom, 169.
Tidal Harbours Commissioners, xliii., 237.
—— report, 231, *n.*[3]

x

Tidal Harbour Commissioners Second Report of, with account of Captain John Perry and his projects, 249, n.
Tigh-Moling, 55, n.[1]
Tilbury fort, 230.
Timolin, see Tigh-Moling.
Ting, Law Ting, 161.
Tinghoges, 197.
Tingoho, 198.
Tingoha, 198.
Tingwall, in Isle of Man, 161, 166, 169.
Tipperary, 35.
Tir-da-glas (Terry glass), 34, 65.
Tochars, or causeways over rivers, 214, 221, 223.
Todd, Rev. Dr. J. Henthorn, 4, n., 19, n., 20, n., 34, 59, n., 82, n., 152, n., 219, n.
Tolka, the river, 232, n.[1]
Tomar, or Thorsman, for Turgesius, or Regnar Lodbrog, 31, 32.
—— chieftain of, 32.
—— race of, 32.
—— ring of, 32, 126, 128.
—— people of, 32.
—— wood of, 32.
Tomhrair, 31.
Tomar, Mac Elcli, 32, 62, 63, 67.
Tone, Theobald Wolfe, lxxix.
Tostig, Earl, 90.
Tooke, Horne, vi.
Topographical antiquities of Great Britain and Ireland, 249, n.
Topsham, xxviii.
Tor Einar, 75.
Toro, 67, n.
Torolbh, Earl, 67.
Tormentors, two, of iron, for dredging (1708), 234, n.[2]
Torsager (Tor's field), or Jutland, 175.
Townsend-street, 146, 147, 146, 151, 239, 242, 247.
Trench, William, xxxvii.
Trian Corcaigh, abbot of, 13, n.
Trinity, Holy, Church of (see Christ Church), 92, n., 221, n., 222.

Trinity College, 145, n., 147, 150, 165, n., 219.
—— tide flowed up to, in a storm (1670), 248.
Trinity House Brethren, Corporation of, xxxviii.
Trinity-street, xciv., 196, n.
Trondhjem. See Drontheim.
Trousseau, Dr., x.
Tryggve, Olafson K., 96.
Tuam, Archbishop of, 188.
—— Archbishopric of, 135, n.
Tuatha de Danann, 82, n.
Tuatal, s. of Fearadhac, 16.
Tubbar-Brighde, 172, n.[3]
—— Muire, 172, n.[3]
Tunstal, Francis, cxvii., 231, n.[3]
—— Mrs., ib.
Tunstal's hotel, cxvii.
Turgesius, lxvi., 18, 22, 23, 30, 31, 33, 34, 35, 134.
Turgeis, 32, 34, 134.
Turgesius (and see Regnar Lodbrog), a Norwegian, 18, the first conquering settler, ib.; the Irish for Thorgils, 31; supposed to be Regnar Lodbrog, ib.; his capture and drowning in Lough Owel, ib.; meaning of Thorgils discussed, ib.; his descendants called in Irish 'the race of Tomar,' 32. Rev. Dr. Todd's account of the aims of Turgesius, 33, 36.
Turvey, Barnewalls of, Viscounts Kingsland. See Kingsland.
Tyrone, Marcus Beresford, Earl of, xciv., n.
Tyrone House, xciv.

Ui Maine, 66, n., 214, n.
Uathinharan, 63, n., 85, and n., ib.
Ubi, brother of King Ivar, 37, n.
Ugaire, King of Leinster, 56.
Uaill Caille, 17.
Unilsi (see Oisile), 21, n.
Ui Ceinnsealaigh (O'Kinshelas), 16.
—— Fidhgeinte, 17.
—— Niall, 18, 23, 24, 56, 80, n.
Uisnech, the children of, 80, n.

## INDEX.                                299

Uladh-ster (Ulster), 134, 135.
Ulf, 37, n., 52.
—— Skialgi, 102, 105, n.
Ulfrick's fiord (Larne Lough), lxvii., 115, 137, n.
Ulidia, the King of, 59.
Ulidians (Ulster men), 16, 67.
Ulster, 82, n., 86.
—— creaghting in, 210, n.
—— De Courcy, Earl of, 93, n.[5]
—— K. of, celebrated bridge builder, A.D. 739, 223.
—— navy of, 54.
—— Scandinavians of, 54.
Umhall, in Mayo, 15.
—— Upper, barony of Murrisk, ib., n.
—— Lower, barony of Borrishool, ib. n.
Unst, island of, 161.
Upsala, 171, 176, 197.
Urr, isle of, mount at, 162.
Usher, Archbishop, 84, n.[2].
Usher's Island, 222, n.
Usher, John, drowned in crossing the Dodder ford, 232, n[1].
—— Sir Wm., cxxi.
—— son of Mr. John, 232, n,[1]

Vallancey, 207.
Valland, people of, 95, n.
Valscra, 95, n.
Van Homrigh, Mr. 234, n.; his house, 235, n.
Vartry Waterworks, xcviii.
Vatnsfiord, 100.
Vaughan, Edward, xv.
Vavasour, Counsellor (1792), 242, n.
Vekell (Holy Kettle), 130, n.
Vereker, Henry, xliv., xlv.
Vernon, Mr. (of Clontarf), 237.
Verstegan, Richard, lxxiii.
Vestfirdinga fiordung, 134, n.
Vidalin, Paul, 144, n.
'Vig,' the Irish Sheep Dog, 111.
Vigfusson and Cleasby, 129, n., 130, n., 134, n., 135, n., 155, n., 157, n., 160, n.
Vik, a bay, 135, n.
Vikia, 33, n.

Vilbald, 101.
Vivian, Cardinal, 93, n., 188.

Wales, Grufudd, K. of, 123.
—— Howel Dhu, K. of, 69.
—— 89, 96, 3, n. 28, 29.
—— North, 165, n.
—— South, 53.
—— West, 58.
Walls of Dublin, 204, and n. ib.
Walling-in of Liffey, cxvii.
Walsh, Robert, lxix., n.
—— Sir Robert, lxviii., n.
—— Sir James, ib.
Walstan, Archbishop, 73.
Walter, s. of Edric, lxviii.
—— Theobald, 144, 145.
Warburton, Elliot, 230, n.
Ware, Sir James, xxiv., xxx., n., xci., 21, n., 76, n., 92, n., 124, n., 125, n., 154, n., 206, 226.
—— Robert, 178, n.
—— Colonel, xci.
Wartenau, Chateau de, xxvii.
Washington, Captain, R.N., xliii., xliv., xlv., cxvi.
—— Report, Tidal Harbours Commissioners, 237.
Waterfiord, lxvii.
Waterford, lxv., lxvi., lxix., lxx.
—— city of (and see Loch Daechaech), 3, n., 4, n., 20, 21, 53, 55, 65, n., 87, 137, 177, n., 186.
—— Danes build a stronghold at, A.D. 912, 53.
—— river, cxxii., n.
—— Synod of, 187.
Watson, Mr., Mayor of Dublin (A.D. 1637), 232, n.[1].
Weald Hall, Essex, Patent of 27th Elizabeth dated at, 246, n.
Wednesday, or Wodin (i.e., Odin's) Day, 174.
Welsh, of Brittany, 53.
—— of Cornwall, 28.
—— of Wales, 28.
—— of the North, 53.
Wells, Holy, 172.
Welch, Richard, xcvi., ciii.

Wenix, the picture by, xciv.
Werburgh-street, xcii.
Weremouth, 11.
Wessex, 42, 47, 57.
Western Isles (see Hebrides), 15.
Westmanni, 100, *n.*
Westmanna-Eyar, 100, *n.*
Westmen, 95.
Westmen's Isles, lvii., *n.*
Westmorland, 24, *n.*
Westmoreland-street, lxxiv., xciii., 240, *n.*
West Saxons, 52.
West Welch, of Brittany and Cornwall, 95, *n.*
Wexfiord, lxvii.
Wexford, 137.
—— town of, 3, 64, *n.*$^1$, 222, *n.*
Wharton, Earl (1709), lands at Ringsend, 241, *n.*
White Book of City of Dublin, xxv.
Whitworth-bridge, 226, *n.*
Wicklow, 138.
—— co., Fercullen in, 225.
Wigfert, 13, *n.*
Wiking, William, lxviii.
Wikinglo (Wicklow), 138.
William, s. of Godwin, lxviii.
—— s. of Gudmund, *ib.*
—— s. of Ketill, *ib.*
Willis, Dr., of Ormond-quay, xix.

Windsor, Staines near, 180.
—— Treaty of (A.D. 1173), 188.
Wimburn, 51.
Winetavern-street, xlvi., 203, 208.
—— gate, 223, *n.*
Witikind, 6, 7, 9, *n.*, 10, 14.
Wodin, or Odin, 174.
Wood-quay, 203, and *n.*, *ib.*, 204.
Woodward, Humphry Aldridge, lxxvii.
Woolwich, nine ships sunk at, to bar the Dutch, 1667, 229.
Worthing (co. Norfolk), 174, *n.*
Writing, introduction of, into Iceland, lix., lx., lxi.
—— into Ireland, *ib.*
Wykinlo, lxvii.

Yarranton, Andrew (1677), 242, 243.
Yellow-batter, 222, *n.*
Yioletide, 173.
Yuletide, 183.
Yiolner, feast of, 173.
York, 24, 37, 38, 48, 60, 68, 76.
—— capture of, by the Danes, A.D. 869, 115, *n.*$^2$
—— the Danish capital of Northumbria,

Zekerman, Andrea, cxxii., *n.*
Zetland, 157, *n.*

www.ingramcontent.com/pod-product-compliance
Lightning Source LLC
Chambersburg PA
CBHW051723300426
44115CB00007B/434